Letters to the Little Ones

The Three-Century Story of a Pioneer Family
and Their Descendants Living in Baltimore Hundred,
Sussex County, Delaware
1675-2017

Second Edition

Letters to My Grandchildren
Early Evans, Hall, Dazey and Green Genealogy

A Local History

Gordon Evans Wood Sr.

Published 2002. Second Edition 2017
Second Edition: ISBN 978-1-62806-134-5

Author's Note: This Second Edition incorporates updated research,
corrects typos and errors and most importantly adds a Letter to Sarah,
a granddaughter who arrived after the First Edition.

Please direct all correspondence and book orders to:
Gordon E. Wood Sr.
58 Daisey Avenue
Ocean View, DE 19970

Library of Congress Catalog Card Numbers
First Edition 2002092635
Second Edition 2017951684

Second Edition by
Salt Water Media
29 Broad Street, Suite 104
Berlin, MD 21811
www.saltwatermedia.com

Printed in the United States of America

Farm drawing on cover by Richard Carter, with his permission.

This Book is Dedicated to

Catherine Wharton Evans (c. 1720-1797)
Elizabeth Breasure Hall Evans (1870-1909)
Sarah Eleanor "Nellie" Daisey Evans (1889-1967)
Hilda Elizabeth Evans Wood (1914-2004)

For the reasons herein[1]

---

1   See chapter 3, Letter to Caroline — Family

The Little Ones

Caroline	September 5, 1989	Richard and Betsy Wood
Brian	January 6, 1991	Rob and Claire Wood
Catherine	October 30, 1991	Richard and Betsy Wood
Richard (Chip)	December 14, 1993	Richard and Betsy Wood
Laura	February 15, 1994	Rob and Claire Wood
Annmarie	June 8, 1994	Gordon Jr. and Lauren Wood
Elizabeth	September 12, 1996	Gordon Jr. and Lauren Wood
Sam	June 16, 1998	Adam and Jill Hill
Neal	March 14, 1999	David and Karen Wood
Allison	March 30, 1999	Gordon Jr. and Lauren Wood
Sydney	May 2, 2001	Adam and Jill Hill
Christopher	May 5, 2001	David and Karen Wood
Sarah	August 2, 2004	Gordon Jr. and Lauren Wood

Caveat Emptor

A Welsh genealogist named J. Gwenogvryn Evans, after quoting a pedigree that began with "Adam son of God," said, "It does seem as if reason took its leave of every genealogist, sooner or later."

Table of Contents

Acknowledgments

In a stroke of genius, I asked cousin Gloria Evans Ingram's husband, Bill Ingram, if he would read and edit this effort. My first draft of the First Edition needed an objective editor like Bill with his extensive and most professional writing, editing and counseling skills! He brought so much to enhancing the readability of this often detailed effort. Then, as the manuscript was almost complete, he read and edited it a second time. His editing skills and tactful suggestions were perfection. I am deeply indebted to him for his immense help. Bill and Gloria also provided the tape of the interview of France Evans in Appendix A. It relates first-person accounts on the early life of Alonzo and Elizabeth Evans' children after their mother died, as well as his life on the tugboats. It is a wonderful addition to this chronicle.

My son, Rob, has developed a good understanding of the history and genealogy in this work. This, combined with writing skills I have always admired, equipped him also to read and edit both editions of this work. His recommendations and comments were uniformly excellent. A talented, perceptive son.

Dr. Ray Thompson of Salisbury University and a co-founder of the Edward H. Nabb Research Center for Delmarva History and Culture read the first manuscript and deemed the history sections to be "correct." His comments eased the mind of a novice historian. His most helpful edits and suggestions improved the finished product.

The wonderful resources and staff at the Edward H. Nabb Research Center were so valuable and contributed so much and are so appreciated. The director, Rebecca Miller, and staff, including Corrine Les Callette, Pat Taylor, Polly Batchelder and others, willingly and ably helped this genealogy neophyte tap the Center's extensive resources. The Nabb Center is commended to anyone wishing to learn more about Delmarva families and history.

About 1982, Dick Carter, then the Sussex County Historian, introduced me to Sussex County Courthouse records. His demonstration of the ease in going back five generations in ten minutes got me hooked, and I proceeded innocently with no idea future efforts might require as much as two days of research to complete a simple thought. Little did I know then that the required research would consume so much time—or that I would become hooked on the challenge. Years later, Dick read the first manuscript and liberally applied a red pen for edits. Each was on-point and improved on my prose and history. Dick, an accomplished artist, also did the pen and ink copy of the Phil Short Jr. map of early land patents in Baltimore Hundred and the outstanding, detailed drawing of a late 1700s Baltimore Hundred farm. I have enjoyed establishing a friendship with Dick, and this work has benefitted immensely from his contributions.

Brian Page, Sussex County's Historic Preservation Planner, read the first manuscript and provided many on-point recommendations which contributed to historical accuracy and readability.

Uncle Maurice Daisey, who had researched the Dazey/Daisey family, left records and a 1782 Dazey family Bible, printed in Philadelphia, which was given to me by his widow, Fran. His efforts provided the needed head start on this family line. Great-Aunt Gertie Evans Phillips gave me the pages from a nineteenth century Evans Family Bible which helped so much in developing the Evans family genealogy. These two invaluable gifts encouraged my early efforts when the task was so daunting.

There are many others who granted access to their research notes. Foremost is Dorothy Pepper of Selbyville who provided early assistance on Evans family genealogy and history. Cousins Phyllis Hudson Meyer and Olive Ann Dukes Milutin, shared their notations on Dazey/Daisey family genealogy, and Sam McLaughlin let me use a letter from his great-great-grandfather containing significant early Evans family history. Steve Dougherty provided information on the Green and Sockrider families which helped fill in necessary details. Without these contributions, links in the chain of connection would otherwise have remained unknown.

Gerald and David Wilgus generously allowed me to read and extract important information from Ocean View's Captain John W. James' household and schooner logs. They add so much detail and insight on everyday life in Baltimore Hundred in the mid-nineteenth century.

Family and friends, including Mom, my sister Susan, Bill Evans, Aunt Daisey Furman, Eleanor Breasure, and Steve Dougherty provided many of the photographs which enrich this story and our memory and understanding of our family. Each is most appreciated.

George and Betty Jane (Evans) Keen allowed me to transcribe and incorporate their taped interview of my Great Aunts Mary, Dorothy and Maria in Appendix B, adding further insight into the life and times of Great-Grampop Alonzo Evans and his children.

The Delaware Public Archives and its excellent staff, including Russell McCabe, Cliff Parker and Heather Jones, made my many visits to Dover so productive. They were always patient. The archivists were all a great help in allowing me to review original documents over two centuries old in order to verify original signatures.

Then there are those wonderful stories provided by Cousin Lon Evans III in the "Boys Will Be Boys" section in Appendix C. They add so much—bringing the

Evans boys to life. Something would be missing without these decades old, real-life episodes of brothers so close.

Before bringing the second edition to a publisher a complete edit was necessary. My good fortune was to meet Fran Feighery at an Ocean View Historical Society meeting where discussion of an editing need resulted in a capable volunteer, Fran. Her edits on almost every page resulted in needed correction of syntax, typos, spelling errors and an erratic use of commas, semicolons and colons. Fran was a perfect answer for a real need!

The final manuscript, almost ready for publishing by Salt Water Media, was then thoroughly edited by Ida Crist, a professional editor, whose excellent edits and suggestions helped make the manuscript ready for publication.

Then, serendipity stepped in. Never having been satisfied with the Henry Dazey/Daisey mystery in Chapter 15, I asked Barbara Slavin, a local historian, to check on Henry's history. She did and found that the missing Henry Dazey/Daisey was resting in Mariner's Bethel Cemetery under a tombstone for Samuel Henry Dasey. The Samuel first name was new, and the Dasey spelling had confounded my research and reporting in the First Edition. Thanks to Barbara, the mystery of Henry's history has been resolved in this Second Edition.

Stephanie Fowler of Salt Water Media took my manuscript in an old Word Perfect format and successfully converted it to a useable, current word processing program, relieving a great personal concern. I picked the right publisher for this Second Edition.

Last and so appreciated was my wife Pat who left me to work alone on both editions when there were many things to do which would have been more fun for both. Thank you.

Word processing was simplified, especially footnotes, by Word Perfect 8 and 12. The descendants' charts in the four chapters on the Evans, Hall, Dazey/Daisey and Green families were made using Family Tree Maker, Version 5.0.

Article by Gordon Evans Wood Sr. from Vol. 9, No. 3, of the March 2002 issue of *Shorelines*, the monthly publication of the Edward H. Nabb Research Center for Delmarva History and Culture at Salisbury University

Letters to the Little Ones
BY GORDON EVANS WOOD SR.

You too can get hooked and it happens before you know it. *Letters to the Little Ones* started out simply as an attempt to learn a little about Great Grampop Alonzo Evans' forebears. It ended up as an over 300-page book for my grandchildren and others.

How did it happen? It was quick, easy and almost terminal. Sussex County Will Books in Georgetown quickly brought me from Alonzo to John A. to Clemeth to Zadoc to Daniel (died in 1800) to–a dead end. Off-and-on for almost two decades, the search was fruitless. Making a very long story short, I realized I had compiled a lot of information and no answers. But, the answer was there and I did not realize it until I compiled everything I knew about a Daniel Evans, including a very obscure and fairly recently found (by accident) notation in an inventory of another Sussex Countian which addressed a John Evans "(brother to Daniel)."

Simple, identify the John Evans referred to in the notation. Well, there were more contemporary, local John Evanses than one could imagine. Compiling everything I could about these Johns, I hoped, would quickly identify the John and, hence, Daniel. Wrong again! And that is part of the charm–and frustration–of family history quests.

After a thorough review of a small mountain of information on the various Johns, I believe I identified the right John and, therefore, Daniel. But I could not prove it. Daniel and his brother John were the son of John and Catherine Wharton Evans of **North Petherton**, today's Bethany Beach. My conclusion relied on the "preponderance of the evidence" and absence of conflicting evidence. With the right John and his father identified, it was a simple matter to take the line back three more generations to the Walter Evans who married Mary Powell, (the daughter of the Walter Powell of **Greenfields**, at the mouth of the Pocomoke River).

Having done so much work, it seemed the only responsible thing was to write a report on my search and conclusions. If my conclusion were correct, a report would help others. If incorrect, it would serve as a head start for others. I also wanted a growing roster of grandchildren to have easy access if they someday want to know more about their family, so I wrote a letter to my grandchildren to accompany the report. Then came more letters to individual grandchildren on what ancestors' lives were or might have been like. And these required more research! And this led to more letters and more curiosities to be researched and more unexpected sources. Where to stop? I had no discipline, and subjects ranged from "clothing from the ground up" through growth in Baltimore Hundred, schooners on the Indian River, family involvement in the Civil War, my memories of recent generations, and on and on.

I really realized I had the makings of a real book for my grandchildren late in the game. *Letters to the Little Ones* became a compendium of Evans, Hall, Dazey/Daisey and Green family history, a local history (Baltimore Hundred in Sussex County, DE), and the letters with wide-ranging subjects to the special little ones, my grandchildren. Over 300 pages and over 400 footnotes later, *Letters* . . . is almost ready to be printed.

It was fun; I met so many helpful and very nice people. It kept me busy, and I wondered how I ever had time to work and have a career. I became familiar with wonderful resources–the Nabb Center being the best. I ended up being on the board– and chairman.

Little did I know when I visited the Sussex County Courthouse so long ago that I would so enjoy a new avocation and end up writing a book for my grandchildren–and others who in some way attach to the families or the Eastern Shore.

Foreword

This is a Second Edition (with edits and additions to the First) of a story of a Baltimore Hundred[2] family spanning more than three centuries. It begins in 1675 when Walter Evans, my eighth great-grandfather, left Wales for Maryland. He and his wife, Mary Powell Evans, who was born near Pocomoke, Maryland, eventually settled on a tract they purchased in 1702 named <u>South Petherton</u> that included most of today's South Bethany. This account chronicles Walter's and nine succeeding generations up to my own. It is about enduring, if not always thriving, in the South Bethany, Bethany Beach, Ocean View, Clarksville and Roxana areas of Baltimore Hundred in present-day Sussex County, Delaware.

This account of the ancestors of my mother, Hilda Elizabeth Evans Wood, and the origins of my father, Richard Kenneth Wood, and his family was written primarily for the precious little ones of the latest generation, my grandchildren, to whom the letters in this volume are addressed. The genealogical and historic delineations are evocative of and pertinent to this extended family, and in a larger sense to Baltimore Hundred and the entire Eastern Shore for over three centuries. The Evans family are stalwarts of Delmarva civilization. They stuck around and set down everlasting cultural roots.

This story concentrates on the ancestors of my maternal grandfather, John Linwood Evans, and my grandmother, Sarah Eleanor "Nellie" Daisey Evans, whose parents were from the Evans, Hall, Dazey/Daisey and Green families. Through the generations dating back over 340 years, these families and their stories were enriched by brides with maiden names Breasure, Vaughn, Inloes, Prettyman, Jones, Kenney, Sockrider, Hopkins, Quillen, Hart, Leatherbury, Lynch (likely), Johnson, Jefferson, Barns (possibly), Wharton, Powell, White, Berry, Keyser, West, Hill (possibly), Burton, and others unknown, from families inhabiting early Eastern Shore Delaware, Virginia, and Maryland

The families were typical of their times, yet extraordinary in their close-up view, and dear to me. They stake no claims to fame save for a most pronounced attribute, the focus on family, which persists today, I can proudly proclaim, in my children and their families.

---

2   For origins of Baltimore Hundred and the very meaning of the term "Hundred" see Chapter 1. Baltimore Hundred in Delaware's Sussex County originated as a part of Somerset County, Maryland, becoming a part of Worcester County, Maryland, when it was established in 1742. It has been conjoined with Sussex County, Delaware, since 1775.

This book has four main components spread over the six time-based parts:

- First, a portrayal of the Evans ancestors of Linwood's father, my great-grandfather, Alonzo Evans, who lived in Bethany Beach. An extensive inquiry, Who Was the Daniel Evans Who Died in Baltimore Hundred in 1800?, constitutes Chapter 7. Until now, my fifth great-grandfather's ancestry was a mystery confounding me and others of his many thousands of direct descendants all over America who inquired. This section of the book contains the elusive documentary details. The footnotes are intended to help other researchers review my research and analyses. The conclusions are based upon extensive circumstantial evidence vis-a-vis the absence of contradictory evidence. It amounts to a case study peering into what would otherwise be a genealogical dead end.

- Second, parallel studies of the genealogy of the Daisey, Hall, Green and related families of Baltimore Hundred.

- Third, generational succession in Baltimore Hundred, with a chapter centering on each male-line Evans ancestor. The level of detail in each chapter on an Evans male ancestor and his bride results in duplication of details in preceding and subsequent chapters on their parents and children. This is the price for the necessary level of detail in each chapter.

  Enter the party of the first part, Walter, who arrived in Somerset County, Maryland, in 1675 and bought a piece of Baltimore Hundred in 1702. Then, in order, William, John Sr., Daniel, Zadoc, Clemeth, John A., Alonzo and Linwood. Throughout, the exposition consists of documented facts on the principals, highlighted by wills, climaxing chapters on Walter and Mary Evans, William and Catherine White Evans, John Sr. and Catherine Wharton Evans, Daniel and Sarah Evans, Zadoc and Nancy Evans, and Clemeth and Elizabeth Hopkins Evans. The principals are placed in historical and cultural context by archival information on daily life spanning more than three centuries. Prime examples: Walter Evans' exodus from Wales and his ocean voyage to Maryland in 1675; the trans-peninsula family move to the shores of Chincoteague Bay and then Bethany Beach; life in 1760 on John Sr. and Catherine's large farm that embraced parts of South Bethany, Bethany Beach, Ocean View and Cedar Neck; the saga of Alonzo and Elizabeth and their eleven surviving children after her untimely death in 1909 and, finally, Linwood's and Nellie's family moves from Bethany Beach to Brooklyn, New York, and back again. These accounts offer an often understated but deeper and truer understanding of what our ancestors faced and endured. Real and unvarnished, hardly conventional "close up and personal" materials multiply with each generation. Walter's story is mostly archival. Linwood's is based upon personal living memories and interviews with his children. The chapters on Zadoc and Clemeth between 1800 and 1850 are abbreviated because Baltimore Hundred was frozen in time and space until roads were improved and the railroad was laid down in 1874 when times began to change.

- Fourth and last, those letters to my grandchildren, symbolically to each and to all at the same time, plus, without apology, a eulogy of sorts.

Chronologies of significant, contemporaneous historical events are included at the beginning of the chapters on each successive generation to provide a political, cultural and technical frame of reference. For example, Daniel and Sarah Evans were married circa 1771-1774, concurrent with events leading up to the Declaration of Independence in Philadelphia in 1776. In matters large, birth of a Nation, in matters small, birth of another Evans, the various generations and events are oriented in the greater context of their particular time.

An added element is Chapter 27 elaborating on the life of my father, Richard Kenneth Wood. It is in the form of a letter to his namesake, my grandson, Richard Kenneth "Chip" Wood III. It characterizes his great-grandfather, a "Bay Stater" from Massachusetts, and arguably not a "Sussex Countian." His forebears were from Prince Edward Island, Canada, and earlier, Colchester, England (Wood) and Scotland (Ramsey). Until recently in Sussex County, being a "furriner" was an obstacle to early acceptance. Not for Dad. Being married into a "right proper" family helped, but simply and accurately said, he fit in probably from the first day. He was like that.

Letters to the Little Ones is written for the universal child, somewhere between four and twelve—or perhaps seventy. The archival materials are for teenagers and above, which my grandchildren will be all too soon (as said in the First Edition and are now at the completion of this Second Edition over fourteen years later).

The evolution of our family fosters an understanding of each generation's contributions, responsibilities and place in the world, hence the unforgettable stories. We can review but can't relive. Earlier generations faced a different set of opportunities and constraints—a different culture. We might suffer real cultural shock if we tried to walk in their shoes. But understanding them and revering them and trying to emulate them in our own way can be elevating.

Again and again, I learned research is time-intensive; you have to stop somewhere, so the level of detail varies from section to section. "The Daniel Evans Puzzle," (Chapter 7) is extremely detailed because identifying the parents of the Daniel Evans who died in 1800 and who is my Fifth great-grandfather is the basis for carrying my Evans family male-line back to Walter Evans, progenitor, who came from Wales in 1675. The balance of the genealogical materials is sufficiently detailed to carry the Green families back to an early Somerset County, Maryland, ancestor and the Hall and Daisey families back at least to their first ancestors in Baltimore Hundred. Most, though not all, of the genealogical materials are based upon original sources; though, in some cases secondary sources are used. Both are duly footnoted.

Close family ties and sentimentality aside, this book may have fewer details than some readers would like, but footnotes and references are a good starting point for further inquiry. In a real sense, a work like this can never be completed; there is always more to research, more to learn, and so much "imaginary" history we can conjure. The wonder to this writer is the volume of materials available. Yet, there are gaps we could have filled but never did. What great stories we could tell, had we simply asked our elders when we had the opportunities. Don't procrastinate. Ask yours now! It is a continuing saga with no end in sight; new generations add so much. Having entered a new millennium, a vivid reminder of the passage of time, we have an opportunity, with absolute time constraints, to memorialize the family—who they were and how they lived. They deserve to be honored; their gifts cannot be lost or forgotten.

Our Baltimore Hundred forebears were part of the mold that cast us as we are, and they should not be unknowns. Yet, who will remember them when we who do are but a memory? The task deserves a chronicler who can gather the necessary information and convey a true feeling of who his kin were, what they gave, and how it was then. The little ones should know them as people who were both ordinary in the context of their times and extraordinary in their legacy to us. Further, the surnames of the men in the family lines, so hallowed to me, should never obscure the personae of the women—mothers and grandmothers, mentors and examples to emulate; hence the dedication to four of these special women.

Reader's note: Some items reported herein occurred between the publication of the first edition (2002) and this second edition (2017). In these cases a date is included to indicate something either not included in the first edition or updated since.

Finally! Engineers can't write, they say. Lawyers' writings are painful to read. Managers learn to be brief, clear and concise, but overly so. With these handicaps, my effort proceeds, with the hope I am up to my history and story-telling aspirations about people we knew or wish we could have known—our family. It's a story worth telling. May this setting forth of their story and the attendant letters and materials be worthy of them.

PART I

FROM WALES TO BALTIMORE HUNDRED

Chapter 1   Baltimore Hundred in Sussex County

Baltimore Hundred, the locus of this family story, encompasses that area of southeastern Sussex County, Delaware, south of the Indian River, east of Dagsboro, Frankford and Gumboro, and north of the Maryland line. It covers a continuous stretch of Atlantic beach between the Indian River Inlet and the Maryland line in Fenwick Island. First settled in the seventeenth century, it changed with the times, but in many ways, especially population diversity and growth, change was relatively recent. For most of its history Baltimore Hundred has been rural and agricultural. It remained geographically isolated and insular until the 1950s, even though the arrival of the railroad in 1874 and the Du Pont Highway in 1924 opened the county for commerce and efficient shipping of crops and wood products.

First, to answer the inevitable, what is a "hundred" as in Baltimore Hundred? According to historian Dick Carter, hundreds are "quaint geographical subdivisions largely unknown outside of Delaware . . . roughly established as assessment districts during the brief rule of the Duke of York between 1674 and 1682."[3] At that time the English custom was to divide "land among ten families—assuming each family with its servants was ten in number—making one hundred . . ."[4] As Carter notes, "they were later confirmed by William Penn upon his assumption in 1682 of the proprietorship of the Three Lower Counties upon [the] Delaware [River]" which became today's Delaware.

Maryland, with roots in England, also had hundreds as early as 1636, designated as the first civil divisions of the Province. Baltimore Hundred was established as a subdivision of Somerset County, Maryland, under the proceedings of Somerset Court in November 1697.[5] It became a part of Worcester County when it was created in 1742, and a part of Delaware's Sussex County in 1775 when boundary disputes were settled. Each hundred had an appointed constable who was the chief officer and, before the establishment of county courts, an appointed justice of the peace. After counties were established, hundreds were the lowest political subdivision of counties.[6]

---

3   Dick Carter, *The History of Sussex County*, (Millsboro, DE: Community Newspapers, 1976).
4   J. Thomas Scharf, *History of Delaware 1609-1888*, Vol. II (Philadelphia: L. J. Richards & Co., 1888), p. 1203.
5   Clayton Torrence, *Old Somerset on the Eastern Shore of Maryland*, (Baltimore: Reprinted by Regional Publishing Company, 1973), p. 491.
6   Newton D. Mereness, *Maryland as a Proprietary Province*, Doctor of Philosophy Dissertation, Columbia University, 1901, (Bowie, Md.: Reprinted by Heritage Books, Inc., 1997), p. 232.

Map of Baltimore Hundred in Sussex County, Delaware

Wilmington

New Castle

Dover

Kent

Ocean View

Bethany Beach

South Bethany

Frankford

Fenwick Island

Selbyville

Baltimore Hundred

Sussex

Residents of a particular hundred in Delaware "considered themselves first as residents of a particular hundred and then as Sussex Countians and Delawareans."[7] The first U. S. Census of Delaware and those which followed were compiled by hundreds. While hundreds have no contemporary government subdivision role, they survive in deed descriptions and planning and zoning documents and notices.

The first European visitor to Worcester shores was Giovanni Da Verrazano, the Florentine navigator in service to the King of France, who sailed the *Dauphine* into Sinepuxent Bay, the bay west of Ocean City, in 1524 and anchored.[8] Next was Captain John Smith of Jamestown and his companions, who visited the area in the summer of 1608. The first English settlement on the Eastern Shore of Maryland was at Kent Island in 1642. Somerset and the Sea Side were settled about 20 years later by settlers from Northampton and Accomack Counties on Virginia's Eastern Shore, the first of whom were Quakers.[9]

The first explorers and settlers on Delmarva encountered Indians, but little has been done to address Indians in this history. There is a reason. As happened so often to Indians in North America, white settlers came and took land either directly, by fraud, or in the form of purchases paid for with insignificant trinkets or tools. Not surprisingly, there was constant friction between settlers in Maryland and the indigenous Nanticoke Indians. While there were Indian tribes in Baltimore Hundred, there is little recorded interaction until the time settlement was encouraged early in the eighteenth century. By 1678, when Baltimore Hundred was just beginning to be settled, the Nanticokes had left the area and were principally located at the head of the Indian River near present-day Millsboro, in the western parts of Sussex County, and in the vicinity of today's Vienna, Maryland, near the mouth of the Nanticoke River. In 1742, the Nanticokes planned an uprising with the Pocomoke, Assateague, Choptank, and affiliated tribes, but stopped before it really started. The leaders were arrested. Most of these Native Americans eventually moved north, some as far away as Canada.

Readers interested in Indians on Delmarva are referred to Clark's *The Eastern Shore of Maryland and Virginia*.[10]

---

7   Carter, op. cit.
8   Torrence, op. cit., p. 429.
9   Charles B. Clark, *The Eastern Shore of Maryland and Virginia, Vol. I*, (New York: Lewis Historical Publishing Co., Inc., 1950), pp. 7 & 48.
10   Ibid.

William Penn's Three Lower Counties on Delaware, which became Delaware, did not include the southern tier of today's Sussex County, including Baltimore Hundred, until 1775. Penn and his heirs disputed Maryland's claim, and the location of the border was contested over the years between the original Lord Baltimore and his successors and members of the Penn family.

Lord Baltimore's land grant from the King in 1632 included not only Maryland, but also all of present-day Delaware and a part of Pennsylvania and Virginia. William Penn's 1681 charter was supplemented by two deeds from the Duke of York that included all that tract of land extending southward from New Castle along the Delaware River to Cape Henlopen.[11] The boundary issues were joined by these actions. While we know where Cape Henlopen is today, that boundary was not so obvious in the late seventeenth century.

The boundary controversy is a complicated story, often embittered with bouts of bloodshed and filled with court intrigue. Decisions supporting different favorites were made by rulers of England that changed with revolutions. And, amazingly, the most important decision was based upon an erroneous map. While the story of the boundary disputes actually started with the Dutch and Swedes and continued through the establishment of Lord Baltimore's Maryland and Penn's Pennsylvania which included the Three Lower Counties, this commentary is confined to the establishment of Baltimore Hundred's and Delaware's southern border with Maryland.

The disputes continued with numerous pleas to London and many delays until 1723 when the then Lord Baltimore and Penn's widow agreed-to-agree and develop a settlement. More delays ensued, and border skirmishes continued, causing the parties to become fed up and petition the King for a decision. It was not until May 1750, after the establishment of a commission, due deliberations and surveys, including the Trans-Peninsular Survey of 1750-1751, which first established the southern boundary of Penn's lands, that the Crown issued a decree establishing the boundary as beginning at the ocean at "Cape Inlopen," (a false cape at today's Fenwick Island). The basis for this decision was the original Dutch map by Nicholas Visscher, over a hundred years earlier which referred to today's Cape Henlopen as Cape Cornelius, and named the false Cape at today's Fenwick Island, "Cape Inlopen." Unfortunately for Lord Baltimore, even though the early map may have been incorrect or misconstrued, the Court of Chancery in England described the boundary as being on an east-west line through the location of the false cape at today's Fenwick Island.

---

11   Scharf, Vol. I, op. cit., p. 114. Readers wanting more information on the boundary disputes are referred to Chapter XI of Scharf's excellent history, which includes a thorough discussion.

After unsuccessful attempts to change the decision, Frederick Lord Baltimore finally tired of the fight and entered into an agreement on July 4, 1760, accepting the boundary set forth in the 1750 decree.[12] (Incidentally, shouldn't July 4 celebrations in Baltimore Hundred also recognize the important 1760 agreement? Otherwise, Bethany Beach, with all its charm, would be a part of Ocean City.) Time apparently was not of the essence, and it wasn't until 1763, three years later, that Charles Mason and Jeremiah Dixon of England were retained to survey and mark the boundary. They finished in 1767, establishing the Mason-Dixon Line, the north-south line dividing Delaware and Maryland, and submitted their report in 1768. Time apparently was still not a concern and the final proclamation by the Governor of Pennsylvania was not issued until April 8, 1775. Prompt action followed in the Assembly of the Three Lower Counties on Delaware which declared the boundaries and decreed that affected residents were citizens of the Three Lower Counties on Delaware.[13] Baltimore Hundred was now officially a part of Delaware. As noted above, if not for the map error depicting "Cape Inlopen" at Fenwick Island and not at the current Cape Henlopen, Baltimore Hundred, a part of Sussex County, Delaware, would now be in Maryland.

Seventeenth and eighteenth century population growth in Baltimore Hundred was fostered by incentives. As early as 1666 Maryland offered land patents to new settlers or those who sponsored new settlers. By 1672 numerous such warrants were issued.[14] But after the surge of newcomers in Somerset County, Maryland, in the late 1600s and early to mid-1700s, the influx slowed. The boundary dispute and security issues impacted growth in Baltimore Hundred. Not only did it impede immigration, it also restricted homebuilding. The reduced population growth and threat to land titles constrained the few, large resident landowners. They avoided constructing the types of substantial eighteenth and nineteenth century homes seen elsewhere on the peninsula. Brick buildings were rare here because the clay was too sandy for making bricks.

Baltimore Hundred's isolated location, the farthest northeast part of the area Maryland could reasonably claim and the farthest south claimed in Penn's grant, contributed to the low rate of settlement. This "northern frontier" was tucked below the Indian River, above the Assawoman Bay, east of the Great Cypress Swamp and along the Atlantic Ocean. The resultant isolation slowed population growth for over one-and-a-half centuries. Real growth didn't come until the rush to the ocean beginning in the 1950's, from Pennsylvania, Washington and Baltimore,

---

12   Ibid., p. 121.

13   *Act of the Territorial Assembly of the Three Lower Counties on Delaware*, September 2, 1775.

14   Torrance, op. cit., p. 472.

the wartime buildup of the poultry industry, and the opening of the Seaford nylon plant in 1939.

Many residents of the Baltimore Hundred of my school days had a local and wonderful speech dialect that is rapidly disappearing. It is not unlike that of Smith Island in the Chesapeake Bay, where residents also came from Wales and stayed for centuries with a minimum influx of new citizens. Baltimore Hundred and adjacent areas of Maryland were similarly influenced, retaining remnants of the old dialect of the original immigrant's accent and expressions. Such treasures are lost to time.

Nonetheless, the early settlers' footprint was long, deep and lasting. Compare the list of family names in the 1800 Census for Baltimore Hundred with those of my twenty-nine classmates in the Lord Baltimore High School Class of 1953. With only five or fewer exceptions, my classmates and I bore names attesting to the fact that our families had been indigenous in Baltimore Hundred for over 150 years.

Lord Baltimore High School Class of 1953

Evans (2)	Hudson	Wood (Evans)
McCabe (2)	Layton	Savage (Cobb)
Megee / McGee (2)	Long	Card
Murray (2)	Lynch	Fordham
Powell (2)	Melson	Iannascolio
Banks	Rickards	Munoz
Bennett	Shockley	Quigley
Calhoun	Steele	
Hill	Turner	

Except for the seven surnames in the third column, each family surname was recorded in the 1800 census. At least two of the seven (Wood and Savage) had roots on their maternal side, and some of the others may have. Now, in the twenty-first century, over sixty years later, the elementary school roster reflects a sea-change of names. Baltimore Hundred originals have become a diminishing minority. Thus passes something special in Baltimore Hundred.

Chapter 2   The First of Our Family in America

Our earliest known Evans, Hall, Daisey and Green family ancestors in America include Walter Evans (documented), William Hall (a possibility), Thomas Dayse/Dazey (documented), and Ezekiel Green Sr. (documented). William Hall as well as Walter Evans came to America from the British Isles in or about 1675. Thomas Dazey's grandfather probably came to Accomack County, Virginia, or Dorchester County, Maryland, from the British Isles late in the seventeenth century. Ezekiel Green Sr. came to Baltimore Hundred, probably from Accomack County, before 1726.

We have excellent information concerning the first settlers on the Eastern Shore of Maryland, not only from the early records in the Archives of Maryland, but also from such books as Clayton Torrance's *Old Somerset on the Eastern Shore of Maryland*,[15] and Pauline Batchelder's *A Somerset Sampler*.[16] Excellent detail on early life on Virginia's Eastern Shore and the Bay area is provided by Reginald Truitt and Millard Les Callette's *Worcester County - Maryland's Arcadia*,[17] Nora Miller Turman's *The Eastern Shore of Virginia 1603-1964*[18] and David Freeman Hawke's *Everyday Life in Early America*.[19]

Chapter 7 concludes that the Daniel Evans of Baltimore Hundred who died in 1800, a proven ancestor, was the son of John Evans Sr. This link made it an easy matter to carry the Evans line to Walter Evans. Pauline Batchelder, in *A Somerset Sampler*, provided information on Walter Evans, a tailor, who came to America from Wales in 1675, his wife, Mary Powell, and their descendants including their son, William, and grandson, John Evans Sr.[20]

The first known Hall family ancestor in America was the William Hall of Somerset County who died in 1740.[21] He may have been descended from the William

---

15   Torrence, op. cit.
16   Pauline Batchelder, *A Somerset Sampler* (Baltimore, MD: Gateway Press, 1994).
17   Reginald V. Truitt and Millard G. Les Callette, *Worcester County, Maryland's Arcadia* (Snow Hill, MD: The Worcester County Historical Society, 1997).
18   Nora Miller Turman, *The Eastern Shore of Virginia 1603-1964* (Bowie, MD: Heritage Books, 1988 reprint).
19   David Freeman Hawke, *Everyday Life in Early America*, First Permanent Edition, (New York: Harper and Roe, 1989).
20   Batchelder, op. cit., pp. 103-104.
21   Probate of Will of William Hall, Maryland Hall of Records, Wills, Vol. 22, p. 207.

Hall of Somerset County, who came from England between 1666 and 1700.[22]

The first proven Daisey ancestor was Thomas Dazey Sr. who had land holdings on Assawoman Sound and died in Baltimore Hundred in 1777.[23] Thomas's first ancestor in America probably was one of the following:

- The James Dawsye, who was transported to Accomack County from England in 1671[24] (Possible).

- The Thomas Dayse/Daisey, who was a runaway servant in Accomack County in 1683 and a tithable in 1691[25] (Speculative and unproven, but again possible).

- The Ralph Dasey who was transported to Maryland in 1660[26] (Also possible).

While we do not know for sure where the first Hall and Dazey came from, or when, we know they were contemporaries of Walter Evans and most likely were from somewhere in the British Isles. The Dazeys possibly came from Scotland[27] and the Halls probably came from England.[28] This is discussed at length in Chapters 9 and 15. Their stories are intertwined with the Evanses through more than two centuries by way of numerous intermarriages which are discussed throughout this book.

The first proven Green ancestor in America, Ezekiel Green Sr., settled in Worcester County in the early 1700's and obtained patents for land near present-day Millsboro.

Each of these early ancestors left the British Isles for his own reasons. Economic opportunity and freedom of religion were certainly not the least of their motivations.[29] These are powerful rousers; they are the story of America.

---

22   Torrence, op. cit., p. 465.
23   Will of Thomas Dazey Sr., Sussex County Wills, Liber C, pp. 129-132.
24   Jo-Ann Riley McKey, Accomack County, Virginia, Court Order Abstracts, Vol. 3, (Bowie, MD: Heritage Books, 1998), p. 50.
25   McKey, op. cit., Vol. 7, p. 41.
26   Gust Skoras, Editor, *The Early Settlers of Maryland* (Baltimore: Genealogical Publishing Co., 1979), p. 122, and Maryland Hall of Records, Patent Series, Vol. 7, Liber 5, Folio 535.
27   The original home of the Dazeys is discussed in Chapter 15.
28   The Hall family history is discussed in Chapter 9.
29   We have no record of any being transported by court action, a common occurrence.

Chapter 3   Letter to Caroline – Family

March 1999

Dear Caroline,

My first grandchild! Was I proud for me and your daddy when he called in the middle of the night heralding your arrival. Your daddy has been special in many ways to me and his brothers, just as he is to you. I knew you would be special too, and you are.

While we have had the good fortune to be together on many family occasions, we have one most wonderful memory of a very perfect day together. I was so proud at Pat's and my wedding on October 4, 1997, in the Old Blackwater Presbyterian Church, to have you as my groom's attendant. No groom ever had such a pretty, attentive and precious attendant.

The significance of the Old Blackwater Presbyterian Church that was built in 1767 and was the church home to many of our ancestors somehow ties together the generations of our family over the last two hundred and thirty-plus years. Thank you for having been an important part of our wedding in this beautiful church.

Caroline, this book is about our family and is dedicated to four special women. I want to share important stories about them and their positive impact on generations of our very close family. Being a part of a close family is a real joy, but close families don't just happen; there are reasons, and these special women demonstrated it takes unending love and hard work.

I had two families while growing up – the Evans family and the Wood family. Mom's family was close by in Delaware, ever present, always welcome. The other was seemingly far away in Massachusetts and New Hampshire. I have always regretted that I had few opportunities to spend time with them, especially my grandmother, Sarah Ramsey Johnston. The Evanses were a family to be envied, rich in the important things – close, huge, there when needed, loved, seen often – a family whose members sought each other out and, in sum, thrived on their company. The Woods were far away, divided by a divorce many years ago, smaller, loving and loved still, but simply not the same. Why?

The answer lies, I believe, in the qualities demonstrated by the four special women in our family to whom this book is dedicated. The most obvious to you is your Great-Mom-Mom Hilda. How she loves her nine grandchildren and great-grandchildren (soon to be seventeen in 2017). Think about the many many hours of work and love that have gone into the dozens of beautiful sweaters she has knitted for everyone. The obvious care and love that has gone into their knitting shows in their beauty. This is just one way in which she has shown her love for her family.

There was much more; ask your daddy about the wonderful holiday dinners and picnics at Mom-Mom and Pop-Pop's house in Millville. Just like her mother, my Mom-Mom Nellie, she made Thanksgiving and Christmas dinners a special opportunity for her family to be together. She did this because she loved us and because she wanted her family to want to be together. It worked! She also did it because of the example set by Mom-Mom Nellie, and for her it was even more hard work. She and Pop-Pop Linwood had eight children and twenty-one grandchildren. To me, Thanksgiving with her family dinner, the large crowd and story-telling may have been an even better day than Christmas.

My Mom once asked her mother why she worked so hard to hold these dinners every year. Her response was so like her – "This is my gift to my family to get and keep them together as a family." Remember this and take advantage of opportunities for your present and future family to be together as a family. Families are the greatest source of love and we reap much more than we give.

The third woman to whom this book is dedicated is my great-grandmother, Elizabeth Breasure Hall Evans. Elizabeth was known to some as Lib and at least for awhile as Lizzie to her husband Alonzo whom she married in 1887 at the age of seventeen. Lib had eleven surviving children when she died in 1909 at the age of 39, three weeks after the birth of her daughter, Delena Louise.

Imagine Lib's leaving eleven children between the ages of the infant, Delena, and the twenty-year-old Linwood, my grandfather. Her husband, my Great-Grampop Alonzo, was in the Life Saving Service and away from home six days a week on his job at the Indian River Life Saving Station where he became Boatswain's Mate and second in command. It was not possible for him to keep the children together. The infant, Delena, was adopted by another family, and the six next youngest children went to live with others in the community willing to provide shelter and sustenance and/or needing help on their farms. Their new homes varied from good to very much less than good.

Lib always reminded her children of the need to help everyone, according to her son, Uncle France. This lesson was important because, notwithstanding their loss and necessary separation, they were determined always to help each other and not lose their family ties. The thought of the loss of their mother and of what she would want them to do had a great impact. The children's being together and helping each other when needed had to have been Lib's fondest, heaven-sent wish. Their deserved love for her and her inspiration had to have influenced her children's determination to support each other and maintain family ties.

It made a great impression on me as a child that they carried out their determination. I saw them as adults, vacationing together, visiting, making it clear for all to behold that their family ties were important. Their mutual support, love, affection and pleasure at being together was impressive, the impact lasting. It would have been impossible for me as a child and young adult not to be influenced by seeing the pleasure they gained from being together.

As a boy, family gatherings, especially with my Pop-Pop Linwood and his brothers, Bill, Lon, France, Louis and Neal, including listening to their tales from "on the boats," and the family fishing trips with the "men" were memorable and fun. I also saw most of my great aunts often.

While Lib departed this life early, she left a wonderful legacy to her family. She gave much and was loved and respected for it. Her immediate family's example has lasted with far-reaching impacts.

The last special woman lived over two hundred years ago—Catherine Wharton Evans, your sixth great-grandmother. Her will demonstrates how much her family meant to her. She was the wife of John Evans Sr., one of the early Evanses in Sussex County, Delaware. She died in Cedar Neck in 1797, two years after her husband.

She had at least six grandchildren and a number of sisters. Her will is fascinating to read because she was thoughtful and took care to leave an important personal possession to her sisters and a number of her grandchildren:

• Sister Nanny Melson – Her worsted (wool) gown and coat as well as a cow and ewe.

• Sister Mares Wharton – Her riding gown and one bed and two sheets.

• Grandson John Cord Evans – A yearling.

16

- Granddaughters Elizabeth and Mary – A gold ring to each.

- Granddaughter Sarah Cord Evans – Silver shoe buckles and sleeve buttons.

- Granddaughter Ann – Best calico gown.

- Granddaughter Martha – "My stripe linning gown."

- Sarah Evans [Granddaughter or daughter-in-law?] – New silk bonnet, best fine apron and fine shift and side saddle.

Catherine was a widow who lived in Cedar Neck on a large farm. Hard work was the routine of every day but the Sabbath. Even though her farm was large, she would not be considered to be wealthy by today's standards; yet, Catherine made sure her sisters and granddaughters each received something obviously special to her. She showed her love and caring for her family – initiating over two hundred years ago what is now a tradition. Just like Lib, Nellie and Hilda, Catherine loved her family and was an example worthy of imitation.

Caroline, I urge you, Chip, Catherine and your cousins to remember what we received from these four women and the importance of the love and sharing in families. What fine examples to follow.

Much love,

Pop-Pop

Chapter 4   The Evans Family

This chapter summarizes the genealogy of Evans family ancestors starting with my grandfather, John Linwood Evans, who was the son of Alonzo Harrison and Elizabeth Breasure Hall Evans of Bethany Beach. Hall family genealogy is reviewed in Chapter 9. The story of Alonzo and Elizabeth from 1887 to 1955 in Baltimore Hundred is in Chapter 24.

Alonzo's father was John A. Evans who was born near Roxana on December 24, 1833, and died in Clarksville, Delaware, on May 6, 1899. His mother, also an Evans, Harriet Jefferson Evans, was born November 18, 1837, and died February 22, 1875, at age 37. This is but one example of the numerous times an Evans ancestor married an Evans, as we will see later. (Readers are referred to the Chart of the Descendants of Walter Evans at the end of this chapter.) John A. and Harriet were married on January 3, 1855. He was 21 and she was 17. The story of John A. and Harriet and life in Baltimore Hundred from 1855 to 1900 is in Chapter 23.

John A., a house carpenter, was the son of Clemeth and Elizabeth R. Hopkins Evans who lived on a farm west of Roxana. Elizabeth and Clemeth were married on September 19, 1832. More research may positively identify Elizabeth Hopkins' parents. The story of Clemeth and Elizabeth in Roxana from 1832 to 1865 is in Chapter 21.

Harriet was the daughter of Stephen Riley Evans and Sarah Elizabeth Jefferson Evans who were married on October 7, 1835. Sarah Elizabeth Jefferson was born May 19, 1819, probably near Jefferson's Bridge in Muddy Neck on the back road from Ocean View to Bethany Beach. She died January 27, 1897. Stephen was the son of Enoch Evans, a grandson of John Sr. and Catherine Wharton Evans of Cedar Neck, who were also Clemeth Evans' great-grandparents. Enoch was born in 1768 and died in 1842. He also married an Evans relative, Elizabeth Evans, the daughter of William Riley Evans and Keziah Evans. She was born in 1772 and died February 3, 1865.

Clemeth was the son of Zadoc and Nancy Evans (maiden name possibly Lynch), who lived on a tract called <u>Sandy Ridge</u> near Johnson's Corner on the road from Roxana. He was born in 1808 and died in 1868. Nancy was born in 1813 and died in 1875. Alonzo had told Paul McCabe, a local historian, around 1950 that "Clemma" was from near Johnson's Corner or Williamsville.

Zadoc was the son of Daniel and Sarah Evans (maiden name unknown, possibly Barns) and was born about 1772 and died in 1852. Zadoc's wife Nancy predeceased Zadoc, probably about 1848-50. The farm Zadoc inherited from Daniel was on a tract of land called Partnership that was located in an area along the Ocean in either what is today's Bethany Beach or South Bethany. They subsequently bought and lived on the tract Sandy Ridge near the Roxana Fire House, on the road from Roxana to Johnson's Corner.

Daniel was the son of John Sr. and Catherine Wharton Evans of Cedar Neck. The connection of Daniel to John Sr. and Catherine Wharton Evans is the subject of an extensive analysis set forth in Chapter 7, The Daniel Evans Puzzle. Daniel was born about 1740 and died in 1800, probably on the oft-mentioned tract, Partnership. The story of Daniel and Sarah in Bethany Beach from about 1775 to 1800 is in Chapter 14.

John Sr., the son of a William and Catherine White Evans, married Catherine Wharton, the daughter of Daniel Wharton, and lived in Cedar Neck near Ocean View. The story of John Sr. and life in Cedar Neck in the late 1700s is in Chapter 12.

William was the son of Walter and Mary Powell Evans. William and his wife, Catherine White, lived in or near what is now Bethany Beach on a tract called South Petherton, part of which he inherited from his father. The pioneering Walter Evans, who was transported to Somerset County, Maryland, in 1675,[30] is by now readily identifiable as my earliest-known, direct male-line Evans ancestor. He came directly from Wales.[31] He married Mary Powell (c. 1688), the second daughter of Walter Powell and Margaret Berry Powell. Walter Powell arrived in Somerset County from Accomack, in Virginia, in 1669,[32] and Mary was born January 30, 1669, near present-day Pocomoke, Maryland.[33]

The story of William Evans and Catherine White Evans and early life in Bethany Beach is in Chapter 10, and the story of Walter Evans and Mary Powell is in Chapter 5.

---

30   Archives of Maryland, Liber 18, Folio 313, and Batchelder, op. cit. p. 103.
31   Clarice Neal, *The Dales of Eastern Shore Maryland and Tennessee* (Privately Published: Austin, Texas, May 1986), p. 229. A June 5, 1787, letter from a John Dale noted that Walter Evans emigrated from Wales "about 150 years ago."
32   Torrence, op. cit., p. 107.
33   Batchelder, op. cit. p. 215.

The following five pages depict a chart of the descendants of Walter Evans and Mary Powell down to my mother, Hilda Elizabeth Evans. The chart includes the spouses and children of each generation before my mother's.

In at least seven instances, Evans cousins married, and we became relatives of each other in multiple ways. My mother is also related to cousins in a number of other ways because of instances of intermarriage of Evanses with Daiseys and Halls and between Daiseys and Halls. If the full Hall and Daisey families were included, the descendants chart would be even more extensive and complicated.

Descendants of Walter Evans

```
1  Walter Evans  1660 - 1721
..  +Mary Powell  1668/69 - 1731/32
.........  2  Mary Evans  1691/92 -
.........  2  John Evans  1693 -
............  +Margaery
.........  2  Marjery Evans
.........  2  William Evans  1697 - 1766
............  +Catherine White  1698 -
...................  3  John Evans, Sr.  1716 - 1795
......................  +Catherine Wharton
...........................  4  Daniel Evans  1738 - 1800
............................  +Sarah Barns  - 1812
..............................  5  Daniel Evans
..............................  5  Zadock Evans  - 1852
..............................  +Nancy
.................................  6  Clemeth Evans  1808 - 1868
..................................  +Elizabeth R. Hopkins  1813 - 1875
.....................................  7  Rhoday Elizabeth Evans  1830 - 1865
.....................................  7  [2] John A. Evans  1833 - 1899
....................................  +[1] Harriet Jefferson Evans  1837 - 1875
.......................................  8  [3] Joshua B. Evans  1857 -
.......................................  8  [4] Stephen H. Evans  1859 -
.......................................  8  [5] Sara Arabil Evans  1861 - 1864
.......................................  8  [6] Louise Kate Evans  1863 -
.......................................  8  [7] Josephine Evans  1865 -
.......................................  8  [8] Archibald A. Evans  1873 -
.......................................  8  [9] Alonzo Harrison Evans I  1868 - 1955
.........................................  +[10] Elizabeth Breasure Hall  1870 - 1909
...........................................  9  [11] John Linwood. Evans, Sr.  1889 - 1966
............................................  +[12] Nellie  1889 - 1967
...........................................  9  [13] Sarah Gertrude Evans  1891 - 1984
............................................  +[14] George E. Phillips  1885 - 1944
...........................................  9  [15] Linda Myrtle Evans  1892 - 1978
............................................  +[16] Harry Knox  1870 - 1940
...........................................  9  [17] William David Evans  1894 - 1971
............................................  +[18] Mildred Spache  1896 - 1984
...........................................  9  [19] Edith Elizabeth Evans  1898 - 1955
............................................  +[20] Walter B. Carey  1893 - 1971
...........................................  9  [21] Alonzo Harrison Evans II  1900 - 1974
............................................  +[22] Sophie Peterson  1901 - 1930
...........................................  *2nd Wife of [21] Alonzo Harrison Evans II:
............................................  +[23] Edna Quinn  1910 - 1995
...........................................  9  [24] DeWitt France Evans  1901 - 1973
............................................  +[25] Ray Antoinette  1897 - 1962
...........................................  9  [26] Stephen Cornealius Evans  1903 - 1958
............................................  +[27] Maria Carolina Doderer  1908 - 2001
...........................................  9  [28] Mary Elizabeth Evans  1905 - 1997
............................................  +[29] Otto Beck  1893 - 1973
...........................................  9  [30] Louis Baxter Evans  1907 - 1990
............................................  +[31] Dorothy Viola Doderer  1912 - 2003
...........................................  9  [32] Delena Louise Evans  1909 - 1990
............................................  +[33] Alton Rogers  1909 - 1993
.........................................  *2nd Wife of [9] Alonzo Harrison Evans I:
..........................................  +[34] Emma West  1873 - 1947
......................................  *2nd Wife of [2] John A. Evans:
.........................................  +Angeline T. Daisey
............................................  8  Elena Harriet Evans  1876 -
............................................  8  Lizzie Elender Evans  1877 - 1880
............................................  8  Artemis Edgar Evans  1878 -
```

.... 8 Merty May Evans 1880 - 1880
.... 8 Calvin Aydelotte Evans 1883 -
.... 8 Charles Warren Evans 1887 -
.... 7 William J. Evans 1839 - 1873
.... +Jane
.... 7 Unnamed Infant Evans 1841 -
.... 7 Mary A. C. Evans 1842 -
.... 7 Sara G. Evans 1845 -
.... 7 Margaret Caroline Evans 1847 -
.... 7 Harriet M Evans 1850 -
.... 7 Hetty M. Evans 1852 -
.... + Ebe Godwin
.... + 2nd Husband of Hettie M. Evans:
.... +Edward W. B. Murray
.... 7 George M. Evans 1855 -
.... 6 John W. Evans
.... 7 Zadoc Aydelotte Evans
.... 6 William l. Evans
.... 6 Henry Evans
.... 6 Jacob Evans
.... 6 Rhoda Evans
.... 6 Nancy Evans Bennett
.... 6 Elizabeth Evans Linch
.... 5 Martha Evans Taylor
.... 4 John Evans, Jr. 1740/41 -
.... +Catherine Wharton
.... 5 Eli Evans 1767 -
.... 5 Elijah Evans 1763 -
.... 5 Elizabeth Evans 1765 -
.... 5 [56] Enoch Evans 1768 - 1842
.... +[55] Elizabeth Evans 1772 - 1865
.... 6 [57] Stephen Riley Evans 1809 - 1893
.... +[58] Sarah Elizabeth Jefferson 1819 - 1897
.... 7 [1] Harriet Jefferson Evans 1837 - 1875
.... +[2] John A. Evans 1833 - 1899
.... 8 [3] Joshua B. Evans 1857 -
.... 8 [4] Stephen H. Evans 1859 -
.... 8 [5] Sara Arabil Evans 1861 - 1864
.... 8 [6] Louise Kate Evans 1863 -
.... 8 [7] Josephine Evans 1865 -
.... 8 [8] Archibald A. Evans 1873 -
.... 8 [9] Alonzo Harrison Evans I 1868 - 1955
.... +[10] Elizabeth Breasure Hall 1870 - 1909
.... 9 [11] John Linwood. Evans, Sr. 1889 - 1966
.... +[12] Nellie 1889 - 1967
.... 9 [13] Sarah Gertrude Evans 1891 - 1984
.... +[14] George E. Phillips 1885 - 1944
.... 9 [15] Linda Myrtle Evans 1892 - 1978
.... +[16] Harry Knox 1870 - 1940
.... 9 [17] William David Evans 1894 - 1971
.... +[18] Mildred Spache 1896 - 1984
.... 9 [19] Edith Elizabeth Evans 1898 - 1955
.... +[20] Walter B. Carey 1893 - 1971
.... 9 [21] Alonzo Harrison Evans II 1900 - 1974
.... +[22] Sophie Peterson 1901 - 1930
.... *2nd Wife of [21] Alonzo Harrison Evans II:
.... +[23] Edna Quinn 1910 - 1995
.... 9 [24] DeWitt France Evans 1901 - 1973
.... +[25] Ray Antoinette 1897 - 1962
.... 9 [26] Stephen Cornealius Evans 1903 - 1958
.... +[27] Maria Carolina Doderer 1908 - 2001
.... 9 [28] Mary Elizabeth Evans 1905 - 1997

```
.............................................................  +[29] Otto Beck  1893 - 1973
.............................................................  9 [30] Louis Baxter Evans  1907 - 1990
.............................................................  +[31] Dorothy Viola Doderer  1912 - 2003
.............................................................  9 [32] Delena Louise Evans  1909 - 1990
.............................................................  +[33] Alton Rogers  1909 - 1993
.............................................................  *2nd Wife of [9] Alonzo Harrison Evans I:
.............................................................  +[34] Emma West  1873 - 1947
.............................................................  7 [59] William Evans  1840 - 1866
.............................................................  7 [60] Louisa Evans  1844 - 1928
.............................................................  7 [61] Silas Evans  1847 - 1931
.............................................................  7 [62] Mary Evans  1850 - 1884
.............................................................  7 [63] Margaret Evans  1850 - 1920
.............................................................  7 [64] Edmund Evans  1852 -
.............................................................  7 [65] Stephen Evans  1854 - 1877
.............................................................  5 [35] Mary Evans  1748 - 1839
.............................................................  +[36] William Hall  1745/46 - 1798
.............................................................  6 [37] John Hall
.............................................................  6 [38] William Spence Hall
.............................................................  6 [39] David Hall  1784 - 1868
.............................................................  +[40] Sally F
.............................................................  7 [41] William R. Hall  1809 - 1874
.............................................................  +[42] Catherine Vaughn  1808 - 1878
.............................................................  8 [43] Sarah J. Hall  1825 -
.............................................................  8 [44] John C. Hall  1839 - 1924
.............................................................  +[45] Sarah Jane Breasure  1842 - 1883
.............................................................  9 [46] Catherine Hall
.............................................................  9 [47] David Cornelius Hall
.............................................................  9 [48] Mariah Hall
.............................................................  9 [49] William A. Hall
.............................................................  9 [10] Elizabeth Breasure Hall  1870 - 1909
.............................................................  +[9] Alonzo Harrison Evans I  1868 - 1955
.............................................................  7 [50] Mary J. Bennett
.............................................................  7 [51] Charles W Hall
.............................................................  6 [52] Sarah Hall
.............................................................  6 [53] Nancy Hall
.............................................................  6 [54] Hannah Hall
.............................................................  5 Tabitha Evans  1775 -
.............................................................  5 Elisha Evans  1777 -
.............................................................  5 Catherine Evans  1779 -
.............................................................  5 John Evans  1782 -
.............................................................  4 William Evans
.............................................................  4 Rebecca Evans
.............................................................  4 [35] Mary Evans  1748 - 1839
.............................................................  +[36] William Hall  1745/46 - 1798
.............................................................  5 [37] John Hall
.............................................................  5 [38] William Spence Hall
.............................................................  5 [39] David Hall  1784 - 1868
.............................................................  +[40] Sally F
.............................................................  6 [41] William R. Hall  1809 - 1874
.............................................................  +[42] Catherine Vaughn  1808 - 1878
.............................................................  7 [43] Sarah J. Hall  1825 -
.............................................................  7 [44] John C. Hall  1839 - 1924
.............................................................  +[45] Sarah Jane Breasure  1842 - 1883
.............................................................  8 [46] Catherine Hall
.............................................................  8 [47] David Cornelius Hall
.............................................................  8 [48] Mariah Hall
.............................................................  8 [49] William A. Hall
.............................................................  8 [10] Elizabeth Breasure Hall  1870 - 1909
.............................................................  +[9] Alonzo Harrison Evans I  1868 - 1955
.............................................................  9 [11] John Linwood. Evans, Sr.  1889 - 1966
```

```
........................................................................ +[12] Nellie  1889 - 1967
........................................................................ 9  [13] Sarah Gertrude Evans  1891 - 1984
........................................................................ +[14] George E. Phillips  1885 - 1944
........................................................................ 9  [15] Linda Myrtle Evans  1892 - 1978
........................................................................ +[16] Harry Knox  1870 - 1940
........................................................................ 9  [17] William David Evans  1894 - 1971
........................................................................ +[18] Mildred Spache  1896 - 1984
........................................................................ 9  [19] Edith Elizabeth Evans  1898 - 1955
........................................................................ +[20] Walter B. Carey  1893 - 1971
........................................................................ 9  [21] Alonzo Harrison Evans II  1900 - 1974
........................................................................ +[22] Sophie Peterson  1901 - 1930
........................................................................ *2nd Wife of [21] Alonzo Harrison Evans II:
........................................................................ +[23] Edna Quinn  1910 - 1995
........................................................................ 9  [24] DeWitt France Evans  1901 - 1973
........................................................................ +[25] Ray Antoinette  1897 - 1962
........................................................................ 9  [26] Stephen Cornealius Evans  1903 - 1958
........................................................................ +[27] Maria Carolina Doderer  1908 - 2001
........................................................................ 9  [28] Mary Elizabeth Evans  1905 - 1997
........................................................................ +[29] Otto Beck  1893 - 1973
........................................................................ 9  [30] Louis Baxter Evans  1907 - 1990
........................................................................ +[31] Dorothy Viola Doderer  1912 - 2003
........................................................................ 9  [32] Delena Louise Evans  1909 - 1990
........................................................................ +[33] Alton Rogers  1909 - 1993
................................................ 6  [50] Mary J. Bennett
................................................ 6  [51] Charles W Hall
........................................ 5  [52] Sarah Hall
........................................ 5  [53] Nancy Hall
........................................ 5  [54] Hannah Hall
.................... 3  Walter Evans  1720 - 1796
........................ 4  William Evans  1749 -
................................ 5  Lemuel Evans  1772 -
........................................ 6  William Riley Evans  1794 - 1822
........................................ +Keziah Truitt
................................................ 7  [55] Elizabeth Evans  1772 - 1865
................................................ +[56] Enoch Evans  1768 - 1842
........................................................ 8  [57] Stephen Riley Evans  1809 - 1893
................................................................ +[58] Sarah Elizabeth Jefferson  1819 - 1897
........................................................................ 9  [1] Harriet Jefferson Evans  1837 - 1875
........................................................................ +[2] John A. Evans  1833 - 1899
........................................................................ 9  [59] William Evans  1840 - 1866
........................................................................ 9  [60] Louisa Evans  1844 - 1928
........................................................................ 9  [61] Silas Evans  1847 - 1931
........................................................................ 9  [62] Mary Evans  1850 - 1884
........................................................................ 9  [63] Margaret Evans  1850 - 1920
........................................................................ 9  [64] Edmund Evans  1852 -
........................................................................ 9  [65] Stephen Evans  1854 - 1877
................................................ 7  Samuel Evans
................................................ 7  Lemuel Evans
........................................ 5  Polly Evans Evans
........................ 4  Leah Evans  1752 -
........................ ⁴4  Ann Evans  1754 -
........................ 4  Rodah Evans  1756 -
........................ 4  Rachel Evans  1760 -
.................... 3  Joshua Evans
.................... 3  Solomon Evans  1793 - 1808
.................... +Agnes West
........................ 4  Jacob Evans
........................................ +Comfort Johnson  1755 - 1831
........................................ 5  Leah Evans  1790 - 1865
........................................ +Prettyman Marvel Dazey 1798 - 1868
```

24

```
....................................................  6  Thomas Dazey  1820 -
....................................................  +Eliza Ann
....................................................  6  William Jacob Dazey  1822 -
....................................................  6  Betsy M. Dazey  1827 -
....................................................  +Holt
....................................................  6  Abigail M. Daisey  1830 - 1904
....................................................  +Furman
....................................................  6  Samuel Henry Dasey  1824-1887
....................................................  +Sarah A. Quillen  1831 - 1914
.............................................  7  Thomas Frank Daisey  1868 - 1943
.............................................  +Anna Fernetta Green  1868 - 1935
.........................................  8  Ebe Royal Daisey  1887 - 1945
.........................................  8  [12] Nellie Daisey  1889 - 1967
.........................................  +[11] John Linwood. Evans, Sr.  1889 - 1966
.........................................  9  Daisey Emma Evans  1913 - 2004
.........................................  9  Hilda Elizabeth Evans  1914 - 2004
.........................................  +Richard Kenneth Wood  1910 - 1986
.........................................  9  Linwood Harrison Evans  1918 - 1970
.........................................  9  Irene Myrtle Evans  1921 - 1994
.........................................  9  Lorne William Evans  1922 - 2006
.........................................  9  Royal Louis Evans  1926 - 1986
.........................................  9  Ralph Frank Evans  1927 - 2015
.........................................  9  Eleanor Evans  1934 -
.........................................  8  David Henry Daisey  1891 - 1967
.........................................  8  William Martin Daisey  1893 - 1951
.........................................  8  Archie Frank Daisey  1896 - 1969
.........................................  8  Lora Birch Daisey  1898 - 1979
.........................................  8  Axie  1901 - 1979
.........................................  +Rollin Hudson
.........................................  8  Bertha Ann Daisey  1905 - 1971
.........................................  8  George Vaughn Daisey  1905 - 2000
.........................................  8  Olive Daisey  1908 - 1919
.........................................  8  Maurice Daisey  1910 - 1991
.........................................  8  Frances Elnora Daisey  1913 - 1994
.............................................  7  William Jacob Daisey
.............................................  7  Ebenezer Daisey
.........................................  8  Harry Daisey
.........................................  8  Robert Daisey
.............................................  7  Lucy Daisey
.............................................  +Barnett
....................................  4  Isaac Evans
....................................  4  Nancy Taylor
....................................  4  Tabitha Cord
....................................  4  Thomas Evans
....................................  4  Solomon Evans
....................................  4  Nathaniel Evans
............................  3  Joseph Evans
............................  3  Martha Evans
............................  3  Rachel Johnson
............................  3  Comfort Justice
............................  3  Mary Hudson
............................  3  Elisha Evans
....................  2  Gamage Evans
....................  2  Powell Evans
....................  2  Margaret Evans  1691/92 -
```

Chapter 5   Walter (1657?-1721) and Mary Powell Evans (1669-1732)

Contemporaneous Happenings

1620   The *Mayflower* leaves England for America

1633   The *Ark* and the *Dove* leave England for the Chesapeake

1687   Sir Isaac Newton publishes his *Philosophiae Naturalis Principia Mathematica*

1705   Edmund Halley correctly predicts return of comet in 1758

1729   Johann Sebastian Bach composes "Saint Matthew Passion"

The earliest ancestors of the Evans, Hall and Dazey families of Baltimore Hundred in Sussex County, Delaware, probably came first to the Chesapeake Bay, landing either in Accomack County, Virginia, or Somerset County, Maryland. Walter Evans, who was probably born in Rhydwillan, Caernarvonshire, Wales, was transported to Somerset County in 1675.[34] Mary's father, Walter Powell, landed somewhere in Accomack County but moved to Somerset County, Maryland, near Pocomoke, possibly because life became increasingly difficult for Quakers in Virginia.

Separation of Church and State is a pillar of our Constitution, for the good reason of avoiding the mischief and tragedies through the ages brought about by state religions. Imagine for the moment what a Quaker or Presbyterian faced in Accomack County in the 1660s. As a family head and tithable,[35] Walter Powell was restricted from disposing of his tobacco until the Church of England minister was satisfied (salary paid) with the first and the best tobacco and corn, ten pounds of tobacco and one bushel of corn.[36] The law set a minister's salary at 80 pounds sterling—the equivalent of 16,000 pounds of tobacco.[37] It was not unusual for ministers to complain to the courts that their tobacco and corn had not been levied.

---

34   Batchelder, op. cit., p. 103, also Skoras, op. cit., p. 154, and Maryland Hall of Records, Patent Series, Vol. 21, Liber 18, Folio 313.

35   Tithables were those who were subject to taxation "per poll."

36   Susie M. Ames, *Studies of the Virginia Eastern Shore in the Seventeenth Century* (Richmond: The Dietz Press, 1940), p. 220.

37   Ibid, p. 221.

In 1662, tithables included all male persons, Negroes male or female, and Indian servants male or female sixteen years old.[38] (Note the difference in the law between a "person" and a "negro" at this early date, a difference persisting in many ways for over two centuries.)

Quaker life in Accomack County became increasingly difficult. Failure to pay the proper corn and tobacco tithe was thought of as undermining the Church. Their protests and militant tactics brought about a bill passed by the Assembly to suppress the Quakers, "a turbulent sort of people. . ."[39] The combination of religious persecution and entreaties by Maryland, offering both religious freedom and free land, made moving hard to resist.

Walter and Mary Powell left Accomack County for greener pastures and a more peaceable life. Maryland's encouragement of the Quakers to move was not a totally altruistic act. The boundary on the peninsula between Maryland and Virginia was contested, and Maryland was anxious to encourage settlers to come to that part claimed by Maryland.

<u>Wales and Why They Left</u>

The Evans family history, the primary focus of this book, is rooted in Wales. Why did they leave Wales for the Eastern Shore? Again, the Evans story is the story of America. Like most, they came either for religious freedom or economic opportunity, or both, doubtless leavened in some cases with a sense of adventure. To avoid the confusion of reconstructing a whole series of individual histories, let us characterize the typical immigrant from Wales. We start with what life was like in Wales for the young Walter Evans and his future father-in-law, Walter Powell.

Mid-seventeenth century Wales experienced religious turmoil and diminishing economic opportunity. Primogeniture, the exclusionary right of inheritance of the oldest son, also restricted the opportunities of other sons. Land was scarce and labor plentiful. Of necessity, they often looked either to the military, the trades or opportunities across the ocean.

From Luther's nailing his theses to the door of the Schlosskirche in Wittenberg in 1517 to Henry VIII's break with the Pope in 1536 with the publication of the Ten Articles of the Faith, anti-Catholic religious turmoil troubled Wales for hundreds of years. In 1662, the Anglicans published the *Book of Common Prayer*

---

38   Ibid, p. 108, n3.
39   Ibid, p. 232.

and passed the Act of Uniformity. Refusal to take communion in the Church of England deprived Nonconformists of any role in public life. While basically an anti-Puritan Act, the Presbyterian, Baptist and Independent traditions also suffered.

Compounding the religious persecution of Nonconformists was the economic plight of the small farmers and tradesmen. While the basic economic focus of the small farmers was subsistence farming, the small cities and communities their farms surrounded had a more broadly based economy subject to cycles of prosperity and penury. Increasingly, the growth of farms to achieve economies of scale and the concomitant centralizing of wealth to the hands of the few squeezed smaller farmers. Compounding this squeeze was the enclosure of previously public grazing lands and commons into large manors and estates. The small farmer who depended on public lands was further restricted. Hardship alone caused many to migrate to America.

Opportunity in America was an attractive prospect. Especially attractive was the opportunity to be a landowner. Walter Powell was or became a Quaker and probably was a farmer, and Walter Evans was a young tailor. The opportunity to realize their economic and social potential was most limited in Wales. Lacking money and land meant that they were marginal breadwinners and being poor was to be their lot. They were, however, rich in their sense of freedom, imagination and, above all, guts. That is, willingness to take great risks and venture into the unknown to seek a future with promise.

The Delmarva Peninsula was not blessed with the riches of gold and silver mines like the Spanish Main or the wealth of spices in the Indies which might enrich the Crown or the appointed Lord Proprietor. Land, natural resources and water were plentiful, but they could only create income if there were renters, sufficient crops, purchasers and employees. Settlers were necessary if the Lord Proprietor were to have income from his lands and the New World enterprise were to pay its way.

The major lure was patent incentives—e.g., fifty acres of land by or for every person transported to Virginia. Few had the money to pay for their own ocean transit. Those with resources, however, could pay for the transit of a number of immigrants and obtain a patent for 50 acres of land for each and thereby develop significant land holdings. The lure had a catch, however: with sufficient settlers, the Lord Proprietor was actually running what could be a lucrative business because the land patents were not in fee. The land actually was rented as if from the Crown. An annual quit-rent was required of those who had such "freeholds" or private land. Alienation fees were also required for transfer of patents to another "owner," usually a year's rent. Income grew with the number of settlers.

The head right system in Virginia was replaced with a new land patent policy in 1666, according to which an individual could patent a tract and obtain possession of it by building a house and fencing in and tending a garden on the land for one year.[40] The rent for such a tract was two shillings per fifty acres per year. Only men who could make the land yield a profit could pay the King's rent. Large tracts for cattle grazing were patented by individuals with sufficient money.

The Lord Proprietor had the added incentive to help justify border claims by encouraging settlers to move into border areas. This happened in Maryland along the Virginia border and along the border with the Penn tract to the north and east. The encouragement to settle what is now Baltimore Hundred in Sussex County, Delaware, was based mainly on Maryland's desire to justify and protect the disputed boundary with Penn's Three Lower Counties which became Delaware.

Individuals transported by another person "owed" him and often paid dearly. They were required to repay the cost of ocean passage either by binding themselves over by contract to serve as an indentured servant for a period of years, generally four to seven, or signing over their head right to fifty acres to their sponsor, or both. Upon the completion of faithful service for the period of indenture, the debt was considered paid and transported persons were free to pursue their future. The owner's need for settlers and the settler's desire for transport and possible land coincided fortuitously to the benefit of each. The term of indentured service was limited by law in Maryland in 1715. Still, prospects for those completing their service, often with cruel treatment, were bleak for those without land or a trade.

Convicts constituted still another class of settlers, transported in lieu of prison time or worse by a sponsor who had the right to their service for a specified period of time, often with cruel treatment.

The Journey to America

It took bold men and women to seek to overcome economic hardship and religious persecution and leave home only to encounter a voyage of many weeks under severe conditions to unknown shores. Walter Powell (c. 1669) and Walter Evans in 1675 clearly were such bold men. Walter Powell, like most settlers of the Eastern Shore of Maryland, came first to Accomack County in Virginia and moved

---

40   Nora Miller Turman, *The Eastern Shore of Virginia 1603-1964* (Bowie, MD: Heritage Books, Reprint 1968), p. 69.

with his wife and daughter to Maryland. Walter Evans was originally transported to Maryland.

Bear in mind that the land incentive was overwhelming. Even if the two Walters did not come of their own charge and were indentured via prior agreement or an agreement struck upon landing and were not eligible to receive free land immediately, upon the completion of their required service they would normally be eligible for 50 acres of land. This was an enormous attraction even though not everyone received land. Some bargained it away and others were simply cheated.

Presumably, Walter Powell also came to Somerset County, Maryland, to escape religious persecution. Absent a diary or biography, we can only speculate about an individual's motivation. Reasons that are relevant generally to the Welsh who emigrated to America may or may not apply specifically to Walter Powell and Walter Evans.

We know Walter Evans came to Maryland from Wales via Bristol, England, a city second only to London in size and influence late in the seventeenth century. Bristol was a large seaport, possibly the largest in England at the time. Over 10,000 sailed from Bristol between 1654 and 1685,[41] most like Walter Powell (possibly) to Virginia and many like Walter Evans to Maryland.

Since Walter Evans' history is a blank prior to his leaving Bristol, we will assume his leaving home, the trip to Bristol, the trip across the seas, and his arrival and early experiences in Maryland were typical. Instead, we have an imaginary composite of his journey using facts that apply to Walter where available, supplemented with general information on the locale and times. Factual information is generally footnoted. Novelistic parts draw from history of the times. Passages on persons not clearly supported by original sources pertinent to that individual are in *italics*. By so doing, it is possible to tell Walter Evans' story and to provide an understanding of what it was like then. This incorporates a sense of reality in the narrative. We begin with Walter leaving for Bristol.

* * * * * * * * *

Walter Evans was a bright, hardworking young man of twenty, about five feet four inches tall with a solid build, red face, freckles, and a thin but shaggy beard.

---

41   R. Hargreaves Mawdsly, *Bristol and America 1654-1685* (Baltimore: Genealogical Publishing Co., Inc., 1978), p. 152. A Walter Evans did leave from Bristol for Virginia in the period 1663-1679, but there is no way of knowing whether this was our Walter. Walter Evans was a popular name so it is possible but not likely.

He was a journeyman tailor[42] in Rhydwillan, Caernarvonshire, Wales, *in January 1675, having just completed his apprenticeship to John Davis, a local tailor and friend of his father.[43]*

Apprenticeships were not always easy to obtain via the local constable, and it was a great favor to Walter's father that he supported an apprenticeship for his son and that Davis agreed to take in the disciplined and determined young Walter. His parents, John and Mary, had been very strict with Walter and his siblings. The burden of primogeniture fell particularly hard on Walter, considering his deep desire to be a landed farmer and his clear unhappiness over the realization that because he was not the oldest son he would not inherit his father's small house or have any right to rent the farm plot his father had tilled for many years. That was the gist of primogeniture, the oldest generally inherited everything.

Walter lived away from home during his apprenticeship with Davis. That hardship was compounded by his love of the land and his family, granted that life at home had not been easy. Without land, however, his choices were limited to a career in the military, service with the East India or Virginia or like Companies, being a tradesman, or enduring a lifetime of work on a local estate. The apprenticeship offered the opportunity to acquire a trade.

Walter's parents farmed a small plot near the tiny house they owned in a small town in northern Wales. The land had been leased for many years from a local estate owner. They had minimal financial resources and no political influence, so Walter could not be an officer in the military or the Companies and there was no opportunity for any real education. Like most contemporaries, he could not read or write. An apprenticeship to a tailor, however unexciting with hard work, offered the means to support an eventual family.

Exacerbating Walter's situation was John's and Mary's dissatisfaction with the required tithes and taxes to support the Church in Wales, the State Church. At great peril they had met in the home of friends where they could worship God according to the dictates of their conscience. They had not committed to the Nonconformist or separatist views publicly, but their concerns and the risks of following their conscience were obvious to young Walter.

At this very same time, Walter was increasingly drawn toward America. The

---

42   Batchelder, op. cit., p. 103. We know Walter was a tailor because he described him-self as a "taylor" in his will.

43   We have no other information about when, where or how Walter became a tailor. In the absence of this information, this account is based upon a story typical of the times.

promise of opportunities to obtain land and experience religious freedom exerted a strong pull on a young man dissatisfied with future prospects. It was more than a dream. Numerous friends and neighbors had taken the lead. Yet, discussion with parents John and Mary brought no support. Instead, it produced outright opposition. To John, the assured prospects of an industrious tailor were more, perhaps, than Walter had a right to expect. In John's eyes, Walter was throwing away an assured future with no real downside. John and Mary, who had lived a life of unremitting labor and sacrifice, thought Walter was rejecting a trade he had worked for long and hard. Their opposition increased with Walter's growing determination.

Walter sought more information on opportunities in America, his primary interest. Then he learned of a flyer from Bristol extolling those opportunities as well as offering free passage for anyone willing to be indentured for up to seven years upon arrival in Virginia. He was galvanized when the local parson read it aloud. Having a trade could smooth the way for Walter; tradesmen were needed in Virginia. One in seven immigrants was a textile worker, a category which included tailors and fabric makers.[44] *Wanting to know more, Walter, emboldened by his apprenticeship, traveled to Bristol, a city with a monopoly on the Virginia trade, telling his parents he was going to seek a job in a big city. Traveled is an euphemism; slogging is more like it. Walter walked the whole way, almost 140 miles, in the dead of winter. He did odd jobs along the way, including tailoring, to obtain food and a place in the barn or a shop loft in which to sleep. It was a slow, harsh trek but Walter made it in three weeks, arriving late in January.*

The city was overwhelming with its commercial activity and seeming opportunity for a young man with a trade. Any lingering thoughts of remaining in Bristol and plying his trade died, however, with the realization that living conditions were deplorable and opportunities were unexpectedly limited for one with no immediate resources. There were many others like Walter looking for work. Most made their decision to emigrate not when they left the home village but after arriving in the city and realizing work was scarce.[45]

He soon found himself in the harbor area and spotted a crowd huddling around a billboard at the head of a quay. It described an immediate opportunity to leave for Maryland before the end of the month. At this time, most ships carried

---

44   Thad W. Tate and David L. Ammerman, Editors, *The Chesapeake in the Seventeenth Century* (New York: W. W. Norton & Co., 1979), p. 59.
45   Ibid, p. 65.

passengers to Virginia. Probably fewer than ten percent of passengers to the Chesapeake were destined to disembark in Maryland, and most of those headed to the Western Shore.

All but a small handful were laborers, farmers or tradesmen, and most came from Wales and England's west. Those unable to pay their passage to America, about six English pounds, could sign an indenture with a local sponsor or a ship captain who agreed to take them over the ocean for whatever compensation he could get when he sold the indenture contract in the New World.[46] Alternatively, or additionally, right to the new immigrant's head right to 50 acres in Maryland upon arrival might be given to the sponsor. Whatever the land disposition, Walter would still have to put in four to seven years of labor without remuneration, only food, shelter and clothing. That was the price of whoever paid Walter's passage. But he could wind up as a free man in Maryland with a trade when the terms of the indenture expired.

That did it—the opportunity to be a free man and perchance even a landholder offered more than John and Mary had achieved after a lifetime of work. Walter was overwhelmed and signed up for the unknown, notwithstanding his close ties to his parents and his two brothers and two sisters. His love and respect for them knew no bounds, but he was determined to make it on his own. The future was now. Walter's sponsor was John Saunders, a Bristol merchant, who sponsored nine other young emigrants on the ship.[47] *Having served his apprenticeship as a tailor, Walter had a trade and was deemed a promising prospect for Saunders to make a handsome profit.*

How his conscience tormented him. There was no time to return to the farm, make his goodbyes, and explain his reasons. A letter would be an answer, but Walter always worked on the farm before being apprenticed to a tailor, and his lack of any formal education and his resulting inability to write made written communication impossible. Ever resourceful, however, Walter traded a few days of work with a parson for a letter setting forth his plans. As much as Walter wanted to share his dreams with his parents, his letter was short and to the point, not expressing his emotions and love for his family. These feelings were just too difficult to relate through another. Walter could not write, and presumably could not read, until his dying day. His will was signed with "his X mark."[48]

---

46   John A. Munroe, *Colonial Delaware – A History* (Millwood, New York: KTO Press, 1978).

47   Maryland Hall of Records, Land Patents, Vol. 21, Liber 18, Folio 313.

48   Will of Walter Evans, Jan 6, 1720, Maryland Hall of Records, Prerogative Court (Wills) Liber 16, Folio 509.

Later, in Maryland, Walter's pastor wrote a letter for him to his parents in Wales, but receiving no answer, Walter never knew if it was received. His love for his parents was reflected a number of years later when he named his first son John and his first daughter Mary,[49] a tradition which carried through subsequent generations.

By the time John and Mary received his letter from Bristol, Walter was at sea with William Nickles, Mariner of Bristol, along with at least 26 other passengers.[50] *They knew they would never see him again. His contract* with John Saunders, a Bristol merchant,[51] *for passage to America required Walter to serve as an indentured servant for four years to a person willing to purchase the indenture.*[52] Other passengers, in addition to those sponsored by Saunders, included eight sponsored by Captain Nickles, a John Pickering and his family of four plus a servant, and four others.[53] The passengers were probably typical of emigrants of the times. Their average age generally was 15-24 with three men for every woman, most of whom were generally at or below marriage age.[54] *Like Walter, most immigrants came voluntarily.* They were generally people with the spirit, energy and courage to make a new life.[55]

Frederick Robinson James[56] described Thomas Fenwick, who came to Maryland in 1669, as one of those restless, adventurous men who emigrated from England to Maryland during the latter part of the seventeenth century, but not in order to worship according to the dictates of their conscience. "His object was the betterment of his very much impaired fortunes. He had the fibre of a man, but not the making of a martyr. He was one of those practical, close-grained pioneers who

---

49   Batchelder, op. cit., p. 103.
50   Maryland Hall of Records, Patent Series, op. cit. Vol. 21, Liber 18, Folio 313.
51   Ibid.
52   The "four-year" indenture contract was set arbitrarily. Part of the agreement regarding being an indentured servant for four years is assumed since this was a typical arrangement of the times. We know from Saunders' land patent that Walter did agree to relinquish his head right to Saunders, so the added indenture conceivably could have been a voluntary act to allow him to have a job and home.
53   Ibid.
54   Tate, op. cit., pp. 61 & 65.
55   Hawke, op. cit., p. 1.
56   Frederick Robinson James, *The Colonization of the Middle States and Maryland,* (Bowie, MD: Heritage Books, Inc., A Reprint of 1904 Edition, 2000) op. cit., p. 436.

made possible a successful struggle with the forests and savages of the New World. Both kinds of men were necessary for the successful establishment of the colony—men who would sacrifice their lives for the sake of conscience, and men who were not afraid to lose their lives in pursuit of their fortunes. Colonial Maryland developed men of both types."

Walter considered himself lucky to be indentured for only four years. The other sponsored passengers had no trade or ability to pay for their passage and had to agree to serve for seven years. At this time the cost of passage averaged seventy shillings[57] per head to Penn's settlement on the Delaware and, presumably, was about the same to Maryland.[58] *It seemed a small price to pay for the promise of future advantage, including the chance to squeeze in after-hours tailoring and save a small amount of money for the purchase or lease of land.*

Nickles' ship was provisioned. Her cargo included trade goods such as Spanish wine, spirits, sugar, cheese, other foodstuffs, clothing, shoes, candles, and nails. In addition to the twenty-six other passengers and a crew of thirty-five, there were numerous bullocks, pigs and fowl in the hold.[59] Nickles was ready to sail on the last day of January 1675.

Walter had never been on a boat of any kind before and the ten-week trip in the overcrowded ship was dreadful for a landlubber. Sleeping space was cramped in the small cabin he shared with eleven others. Food consisted generally of salt beef or cured pork of dubious quality, dried salt codfish almost too salty to eat because it was cooked in the water used to soak out the salt, cooked dried peas and beans and dried ship biscuits containing weevils, all washed down with his ration of less than a quart of fresh water that tasted awful and stale beer or cider beyond its time and "turning." While he forced himself to eat a necessary minimum, it was almost impossible much of the time with his "mal de mer," an around-the-clock condition of varying intensity. Any thoughts of possibly returning to visit Wales in the future were suppressed by Walter's determination never again to venture on the sea.

Captain Nickles and the crew worked to keep a reasonably clean ship, but the

---

57   There are 12 pence to a shilling and 20 shillings to the pound. To give a comparison, at the outside, the cost of land for a new family might be between six and ten pounds.

58   Scharf, Vol. I, op. cit, p. 162.

59   Hester Dorsey Richardson, *Side-Lights on Maryland History* (Baltimore: Williams and Wilkins Company, 1913), pp. 16-24. Includes an excellent account of the about thirty years earlier trip of the *Arc* and the *Dove* to the Potomac shores (now St. Mary's County) in 1638.

minimal sanitary facilities at the "head" compounded the seasickness and intestinal maladies. The ever present rats and their filth contributed to the general discomfort. The daily airing of bedding in the shrouds during fair weather helped as did the periodic wash-down with vinegar, but general discomfort persisted.

Even though he was sick much of the time, Walter became a favorite of Nickles because of his ability with a needle and shears. He was somewhat gainfully employed at his trade for most of the voyage and escaped the assigned common chores associated with accommodating many passengers on such a small ship.[60] He even occasionally got to share a small bunk with another passenger, a smelly, ill-tempered and significantly older seaman from Bristol who seemed to be running from something. This little luxury was better than sharing a poorly ventilated cabin with almost a dozen others sleeping in cramped hammocks. Everything upset his turbulent stomach which would defy even modern medications.

Leaving at the end of January with a planned arrival in late March via the shorter and quicker northern route avoided the dreadful storms that often battered the Atlantic Coast of America in the late summer and early fall. There was also a reduced risk of sickness and disease aboard the ship and less risk of the high mortality accompanying the ague (malaria) among those who arrived in Virginia and Maryland during the summer and early fall.[61] One in three new arrivals did not survive beyond the first few years in these new climes.

Unfortunately, the winds were unfavorable, and progress was slow; daily runs were shorter than expected and the voyage went on and on. A week becalmed in mid-Atlantic doldrums reduced the ship's pitch and roll and offered some respite for Walter's stomach, but the length of the voyage and exposure to the cold and dampness below seemed interminable. This combined with a necessary reduction in the almost putrid rations and water and an increasing sick list contributed to the extreme irritability of the captain, crew and passengers to the point where severe disciplinary measures were required. One miscreant sailor was whipped before passengers and crew for stealing rum from the spirits locker, another for stealing food.

---

60   Readers with interest in the ship and conditions are referred to the *Kalmar Nykel* a recently constructed true replica of the ship that brought settlers in 1638 from Sweden to the Christiana River near Wilmington. Materials are available describing this magnificent ship which is often berthed in Lewes during the summer.

61   Arthur Pierce Middleton, *Tobacco Coast* (Baltimore and London: Johns Hopkins University Press, 1984), p. 14. Includes an excellent account of ocean voyages in the seventeenth century (pp. 3-37).

Good Lord! The poor winds extended the trip by over three weeks. Life became ghastly: the continuing dampness and cold and the terrible conditions below, the dreadful and limited rations, and seasickness around-the-clock resulted in irritability and a sinking of both body and spirit. Two passengers died of the flux (dysentery). This was not unusual, and death lists at sea were often significantly higher.

"Could anything be worse?" Walter asked. He soon got his answer. The glass plummeted and the obvious looks of concern on the faces of the Captain and the Master caused great apprehension among passengers and crew. Their fears were realized when a storm followed ominous clouds with winds shrieking like banshees, drenching rain soaking everything below, and waves pouring over the bow further inundating everything. Fortunately, the Captain was experienced and the small ship survived more than three days of battering by a spring northeaster which pushed them many miles to the south.

"How foolhardy I have been in leaving home for such a journey," Walter lamented. Finally, after three agonizing, sleepless days, it ended quickly with a bright sky and an April rainbow of a sort he had never seen before with three obvious, intense arches over the ocean. It was the most beautiful and inspiring phenomenon he had ever seen. Bible lessons and long sermons back home had taught Walter the promise of the rainbow. "God obviously cares and will protect —it is a good omen!"

Crossing the Gulf Stream produced an unending panoply of seabirds, some who seemed always to be following the ship, and the occasional pod of porpoise riding together on the bow wave when there was good wind. Tasty fish caught from the fantail during the beautiful nights after the storm offered some sense of order to one sick of the ship and the sea. As pleasant as these interludes were, they didn't sufficiently counterbalance the continuing general misery. The passengers were passengers in name only. They were required to work, and most were expected to do daily chores, including housekeeping and assistance with meals. Most were sick and now four had died, unable to survive fevers and fluxes brought on by the awful conditions. "Never again!"

In the eighth week of the trip the color of the ocean seemed to change and bits of land matter, leaves, branches and plants appeared on the surface. Shore birds appeared regularly. The Captain supplemented his dead reckoning longitude determination by making soundings with the lead line, a tallow-tipped lead weight on a long line, which could determine both the depth and the nature of the bottom when the continental shelf was reached. Experienced captains knew the sea-bed at the mouth of the Bay contained mud, sand and small oyster shells, while there was a hard sand bottom to the north and south. Bottom normally was found on the continental shelf at eighty to ninety fathoms (about 500 feet) and forty or fifty leagues (over 100 miles) off-shore.[62]

Other standard navigation tools of the times included simple devices to measure the elevation of the sun and stars. The maximum elevation of the sun varied with the seasons, and it was necessary to consult a solar declination table for the given date. When it was possible to sight the north star at night, its elevation at any time was also the latitude in degrees. Latitude, thus, was relatively easy to determine accurately, but longitude depended on dead reckoning based upon a chart of daily courses and speeds. Clearly this was less accurate, but skilled captains could be surprisingly precise. Chronometers, which could determine longitude based upon elapsed time and noon sightings of the maximum elevation of the sun, came later.

Like most of the passengers, Walter spent most of his time below decks, required to be out of the way. Being a somewhat favored passenger because of his tailoring chores for the captain and crew, Walter, who was fascinated by navigation in the endless ocean expanse, was tolerated more than others by Nickles. Even though he had no schooling in mathematics or the sciences, by the end of the trip he had a surprisingly good grasp of the process and was even allowed to hold the astrolabe for the Master when he made his sightings to determine latitude.

After eleven endless weeks the lead line found bottom—a muddy bottom. Three days later land was sighted shortly after sunrise! It surpassed the rainbows; never had anything looked so beautiful to Walter. "Land, and I have survived!" What a splendid sight: white sandy beaches with gentle ocean waves, tall pines gently waving in the breeze, beautiful plump cedars, green holly with the shiny bright leaves glistening in the sun, serene inlets, rivers and bays along the coast. Walter had an overwhelming sense that all would be well. The New World beckoned; a truly miserable trip was almost over.

However, upon landing on the western shore of the Chesapeake Bay at St. Mary's near the mouth of the Potomac River, Walter was apprehensive about his future. The misery of the ocean voyage immediately became a fleeting memory because of a stark new uncertainty; Walter was about to meet his new master.

---

62   Ibid, p. 34.

His willing work on the ship paid dividends and upon Captain Nickles'
recommendation, Walter was taken on by a landowner from across the Bay near the
mouth of the Pocomoke River. The services of a hand who also was a willing tailor
would be an asset on his farm. Walter was quickly signed on and became a part of
the abrupt and businesslike master's estate. He was now at the master's mercy for
four years.

A relatively brief and surprisingly pleasant sail in a small shallop with the
new master, an overseer, and a boy who tacked the shallop across and down the
Bay like a seasoned veteran, brought them to a small bay and then a small river
surrounded by a broad expanse of marsh with grass waving in the pleasant breeze.
Two other new servants for the estate had also signed an indenture agreement with
John Saunders of Bristol and had crossed the ocean on Nickles' ship.[63]

While Walter had been too sick and busy to spend much social time with others
on board, the cramped quarters and resulting crush of humanity ensured regular
contact with these two future servants—Moses Jones, a landsman, and Joyce
Rogers, who was destined to be a housekeeper on the estate. At this point they had
become his best and only close friends. The trio's destinies inextricably joined.
Moses and Joyce, having no specific trade, were bound for seven years.

As they approached the shore, the master's estate, consisting of a large wooden
house with at least a dozen out-buildings, appeared beyond the marsh. It seemed
stark and alone in the great expanse of pine and cedar woods and tobacco fields. It
was to be Walter's home, where he would labor and progress for the next four years.

* * * * * * * * *

An Indentured Servant in Somerset County

The narrative of Walter Evans' life in Somerset County continues. Remember,
documented facts ascribed to Walter and his acquaintances typify hundreds of
immigrants to Maryland's Eastern Shore.

* * * * * * * * *

---

63   A Moses Jones and a Joyce Rogers entered into an agreement with John Saunders of
Bristol and crossed on Nickles' ship. Maryland Hall of Records, Patent Series, Vol. 21, Liber
18, Folio 313.

39

Our Walter, Moses and Joyce settled in at the master's estate known as <u>Contentment</u>. *The estate's master, Thomas Jones, was a successful planter who had come from a family of means in England. With a family stake of over two hundred English pounds and favorable political connections, he had obtained over 5,000 acres of land on the Bay side. A number of years of hard work and great care resulted in a flourishing tobacco crop, many head of cattle, sheep and pigs, and an ever expanding manor house with furniture, both hand-built on the manor and imported from England. Jones had become a man of wealth and influence and was a major exporter of tobacco to England.*

For Walter, life settled into a regular and demanding routine. Walter was worked as hard as any household slave on the estate. Walter knew his term was of limited duration, but so did the master who, in some respects, had a greater incentive to look out for the long-term welfare of the slaves who were bound to him for life. Walter was comparatively fortunate, however. Servants of some masters were beaten, overworked and underfed. Clothing the family along with the other servants and hands on the estate meant hard work six days a week, not just during planting and harvest seasons. A good part of the Sabbath was always required to be spent attending services at the established church.

The combination of his tailoring skills, willingness to work and generally agreeable attitude rendered Walter invaluable to the family, and he was allowed to take in tailoring work from neighbors. The days were long because the master's work came first and the added two or three hours each day doing work for others left him exhausted every evening. Conditions were reasonably good, however, and after the first year Walter was able to earn as much as two shillings a week from his after-hours work. The master provided food and shelter so Walter's expenses were minimal.

The second and third year, Walter, saving an average of a shilling a week, had accumulated five pounds. This whetted his appetite for income, and by dint of hard work he saved an additional three pounds in his last year.

Walter had served the master well and worked hard, but he chafed at having to attend regular services at the Anglican Church. The vestries were still required to collect taxes for the poor and look after the moral well-being of the people according to church standards. Like his father and mother, Walter was becoming a dissenter, but not wishing to antagonize the master and his family, his protests were very low key. The New World, Somerset County, and the bay shores were wonderful— teeming with life, and Walter loved it, but his religious views nonetheless caused him to think of leaving the Jones Estate. The Proprietor, Lord Baltimore, was offering incentives to settle and generally allowed settlers the freedom to worship as they chose. It wasn't total altruism on the Proprietor's part. The best way to protect his border with Virginia was to encourage settlement in this corner of Maryland. *The combination of new population growth and attendant economic opportunity with religious freedom was a bright beacon. Walter kept his eyes open for opportunities.*

He had attended a number of meetings of the Friends and admired the personal convictions and qualities of the Quakers. He wasn't a member and didn't then intend to be, but he was irritated by his inability to make an open and personal decision regarding church. Hence, moving from the Jones estate when his term was completed offered an attractive prospect.

Walter was also lonesome; Moses and Joyce were his best friends in the world, but at the end of their third year on the estate, their growing mutual affection led to the servants' social event of the year. Marriage between servants was normally not permitted by their masters.[64] But when Moses and Joyce agreed to extend their term of indenture by two years, their wedding was blessed by the Jones family. Like many brides of the times, Joyce was a pregnant bride.[65] Everyone on the farm and some neighbors celebrated their wedding, and the Jones family gave them the use of a one-room cabin as their home. Shortly before Walter's term of service expired, Moses and Joyce had a fine son. The combination of their happiness with each other and little Moses Jr. reminded Walter of the emptiness in his own life. His sense of loneliness increased.

Walter's term was to expire during the summer of 1679, and he had decisions to make. Difficult as it was, he turned down an offer from the Jones family to stay on the estate as a hired hand and tailor with the opportunity to take in outside work and earn extra income. Walter decided to strike out on his own that summer, and he did, as a freedman with some savings and no land.

---

64   Tate and Ammerman, op. cit., p. 127.
65   Ibid., p. 132.

A Freedman in Somerset County

There are no records of where Walter settled and what he did between 1675 and 1687, the year he probably married Mary Powell, the daughter of the Walter Powell, who was transported to Somerset County, Maryland, from Accomack County, Virginia, in 1661. Mary was born January 30, 1669, probably on her father's tract, Greenfields, located on the north side of the Pocomoke River in Somerset County just west of present-day Pocomoke City, on today's Route 667, about 2.4 miles from Route 113. Mary's mother died in November 1679, a year-and-a-half after the birth of her last child, when Mary was ten.

Walter was probably one of those numerous men who, having survived servitude, joined free society at the intermediate stage between servant and independent planter as a tenant, agricultural worker, craftsman or overseer for a wealthy planter. The early years as a freedman were probably difficult, and the following limited, circa 1708, inventory of a John Williams, who may have been similarly situated, was probably a good reflection of Walter's possessions which also included his tailoring tools.

Inventory of John Williams - c. 1708[66] (spelling as in original)

One horse

One cow and yearling

One steare of five years old

One small feather bed

A small pot and pan

Three old blankets and one old shirt

One bedsted and cord and one piller

One old chist and one small trunk

One peare of pistells and holsters

Old saddle and bridle

Three chears frames and one old ??

A dozen and nine puter spoones and one puter ??

A parcel of old lumber

Walter Evans does not appear on either Somerset County rent rolls[67] or land records, and he apparently owned no land before he married Mary Powell. He presumably rented a small tract on a short-term lease (six or seven years) as a step toward establishing himself on his own land. He also probably took in tailoring on the side.

* * * * * * * * *

---

66   Worcester County Inventories JW15, Folio 38.
67   *Calvert's Papers, Rent Rolls of Somerset County, 1553-1723,* Transcribed by Ruth T. Dryden, 1985.

Our narrative resumes seven years after Walter became a freedman and before he met his wife-to-be, Mary Powell.

This continued to be a difficult and lonely time for Walter. The distance to other settlers' homes in some places averaged five miles. While the leased land was partially cleared, many stumps and the hulks of dead, girdled trees remained standing. There were no cash crops in the early years. Planting and harvesting barely provided for daily needs. His hardscrabble life was typical of the times and was probably little better than those of the destitute in Wales. The one-room house on the plot had a dirt floor and a barely adequate wood and clay fireplace and chimney. Improving the leasehold provided no real long-term economic benefits.

Even so, by 1686, the still-single Walter Evans was making headway as a farmer and tradesman (tailor) in or near Pocomoke. Utilizing a hired hand, he was able to more than double his tobacco crop, at the same time continuing to clear land, put up fencing, build outbuildings, and stock the larder for winter. The population of the area was growing, and the lonesome Walter's willingness to put in long hours in his small shop and on the farm was paying off.

The shortage of women caused many men to marry late in life.[68] Opportunities to meet young women were limited. But the single Walter did attend occasional meetings at the homes of local Quakers, notably that of Walter Powell. He also attended meetings at the home of George Trewett (Truitt) which was approved and sanctioned as a meeting house by the Somerset County Court.[69]

As time went by, Walter attended more and more meetings at Walter Powell's home on Greenfields. *In fact, he realized he was regularly looking forward to the next meeting. Being honest, he asked himself whether the attraction was the message of and association with the Quakers or the comely Mary, Powell's 17-year-old eligible daughter. He had to confess to himself that it was Mary, who was delightful to be around, an outstanding seamstress, and the possible heiress of considerable land holdings to boot. His interest grew and grew and Mary certainly did nothing to discourage his bashful attempts at the niceties of conversation. After a few months of visits, Walter knew. He now saw Mary regularly on Saturday evenings as well as at the Sabbath Services.*

---

68   Tate and Ammerman, op. cit., p. 209.
69   Torrence, op. cit., p. 108.

Even though he was over thirty years old and almost twice as old as Mary, their relationship was not unusual in these times. Walter approached her father to ask for permission to court her. He could barely restrain his emotions when Walter Powell indicated his intentions would meet with approval–provided that Mary agreed and that they would be married by a Friend (Quaker).

Marriage to Mary Powell

Relief from loneliness at last. Mary agreed to marry Walter. After the proper notices and banns (the public announcement of a planned marriage), they were married by George Johnson, a Quaker and Justice of the Peace.[70] *In the restrained manner of the Quakers, the wedding and celebration were most modest. Walter's privation was no more. He knew he was again a part of a loving, giving family.* Mary's mother, Margaret, had died in 1679 from complications resulting from childbirth a year and a half earlier and was buried on their plantation, <u>Greenfields</u>. Three of Walter and Margaret's five children, William, John, Margaret, Catherine and Sarah, still lived with their father[71] who remained on <u>Greenfields</u> until he died in 1695.[72] Another daughter, Elizabeth, had married Hugh Tingle four years earlier.[73]

* * * * * * * * *

Mary moved to Walter's rented farm and combined house and tailor shop in Pocomoke only a few miles from Mary's father. Life with Mary was wonderful, and their shop prospered. Their first child, Mary, was born in 1689. *While the market for tobacco had suffered a decline in recent years, Walter had worked hard before he and Mary were married. He had saved a sum equal to a year's work as a laborer and had tobacco credits amounting to well over 20 English pounds.*

On July 1, 1690, Walter purchased 100 acres of a 630-acre tract, <u>Teuxberry</u>, from William and Ann Woolhave.[74] *The tobacco credits provided most of the 5,000 pounds of tobacco paid by Walter for <u>Teuxberry</u>.* The annual quit rent on this tract

---

70   There was a contemporary George Johnson who was a Quaker and a Justice of the Peace at this time. Ref. Batchelder, op. cit. p. 70.
71   Hester Dorsey Richardson, *Side-Lights on Maryland History, Vol. 2*, (Baltimore: Williams and Wilkens Co., 1913), p. 403-404.
72   Will of Walter Powell, Maryland Hall of Records, Prerogative Court, Wills, Liber K, No. 7, p. 151.
73   Batchelder, op. cit., p. 215.
74   Maryland Hall of Records, Deeds, Liber 1, pp. 110-113.

was 12 shillings.[75] *Clearly, Walter and Mary were diligent and provident workers.*

Teuxberry was located just southeast of today's Berlin, Maryland, at the head of a branch or creek that entered into Mobjack Bay—the northwest extreme of today's Chincoteague Bay. The Creek was known as Holly Branch when they purchased the land and as Porters Creek in the early 1800s—the exact location could not be readily identified. Their new home, small and rustic, was approximately 25 miles from Walter Powell's Greenfields.

On moving day, their few possessions were carried on one small wagon along the old Indian trail that tracked close to the Pocomoke River from below Snow Hill to near its head.

The 5,000 pounds of tobacco which paid for Teuxberry constituted a significant price because one man could only raise 2,000 to 2,500 pounds of tobacco in a year.[76] If a price of one-and-a-half pence per pound is assumed (240 pence per English pound), a farmer's annual income from tobacco, before costs, was about 15 pounds. Tobacco was a labor-intensive crop requiring a large part of a settler's time for nine months of the year. One man could tend about 10,000 plants on perhaps three acres of cleared land, which generally still contained the stumps of the original trees.

The annual crop started in March or April with the planting of seeds in prepared flats. They sprouted within a month and were sturdy enough by June to be planted in rows of hillocks.[77] Because tobacco cultivation exhausted the unfertilized soil, new land had to be cleared every few years, adding to the labors of tobacco farming. The rest of the summer was spent weeding, removing worms, topping each plant after the desired number of leaves appeared, and removing unwanted suckers (new leaf sprouts) and lower leaves. After six weeks or so the plants were from four to more than six feet tall and ready for cutting and hanging in sheds to dry, a process that took four to six weeks. The leaves were then removed from the stems and packed in large hogsheads, wooden barrels about four feet high and two-and-a-half feet in diameter, which weighed almost a half a ton when filled. One farmer's crop might fill around ten such containers. The packed hogsheads were rolled by hand to a creek landing where they were picked up by the tobacco boat.

---

75   Maryland Hall of Records, Rent Rolls of Somerset County Maryland 1663-1723, Liber 1, p. 118.

76   Tate and Ammerman, op. cit., p. 213.

77   Middleton, op. cit., pp. 111-112.

Walter and Mary ultimately prospered on their new lands as farmers. Tailoring continued to bring in some extra money. Teuxberry was somewhat remote—their nearest neighbor was almost a half a mile away. "Prospered" was a relative term in these times. Their typical one-room house with a loft on Teuxberry was very small, about 15 feet by 20 feet, and sparsely furnished. The first floor served as their parlor, bedroom and kitchen as well as the tailor shop.

Extra income from tailoring elevated their existence to the upper end of the lower class. Their life was good for the times in Somerset County but probably did not exceed that of the poorer class in Wales. Through their backbreaking labors, augmented at times by hired hands, the perpetual clearing of additional land continued. Only a small part of their 100-acre farm was cultivated.

They were able to raise vegetables such as squash, beans and corn in their small but productive kitchen garden in the summer and early fall, but they had to depend on tailoring and crop income to buy other necessities. They slaughtered one or more hogs each fall and stored smoked and salted pork for the winter. Fish and game were plentiful, and deer, rabbits, ducks and geese and other birds and salted fish supplemented their diet. Each year, Walter netted and salted down a large quantity of shad and other river and bay fish for the winter. Staples such as wheat flour and corn meal were ground by the women as required from vermin-assaulted, stored grain.

Four more children were born in their Teuxberry house—Margaret in 1692, John about 1694, Marjery about 1695, and William on December 29, 1697.[78] *The first two births were attended by a neighbor woman with many children. Mary was a sturdy and strong woman, but labor for her was long, difficult and perilous. Death of both mother and child at or shortly after childbirth was always a significant risk; mortality rates were very high. The later births were aided with a midwife, an added expense willingly paid by Walter.*

With all of the births, the family outgrew the house at Teuxberry. A lean-to was attached for more sleeping space. They eventually added two rooms on the first floor and a finished room on the second floor, replacing the loft. The house now had wood floors, a luxury at the time, and a rustic corner cupboard. Walter did most of the building work, trading clothes he made and farm produce for the necessary timbers, planks and sheathing. The children slept in the two sleeping rooms and Walter and Mary slept in the upstairs room with the infants. A large fireplace made

---

78   Batchelder, op. cit., p. 109.

of logs and clay provided heat and a place to cook in winter. Their house was adequate, barely.

Mary's father, Walter Powell, died in 1696/7.[79] Walter directed in his will that he "be buried in the Quaker burying ground." In accordance with Walter's wishes, his surviving children probably arranged for his burial in the Bogerternorton Meeting burial ground, believed to be located about five miles north of today's Snow Hill on the Snow Hill-Berlin road.[80]

The death of Mary's father, Walter Powell, brought about significant changes in Walter and Mary's lives. He left his extensive land holdings to his children, and Mary was the beneficiary of one-half of the 256-acre Powell's Inclusion and the 150-acre Hilliard's Discovery tracts, both near Berlin, Maryland,[81] probably just southwest of the intersection of today's Routes 113 and 50. Walter and Mary Evans were upward movers—now significant landowners on the seaboard side of Maryland's Eastern Shore. The Walter Powell land holdings had transformed them, in all probability, to people regarded as having considerable means. Whether rented or sharecropped, the two tracts boosted family income so Walter and Mary were now known as "people of substance." They may have moved from Teuxberry to either Powell's Inclusion or Hilliard's Discovery, but there is no record of it.

They probably continued to take in tailoring. Over twenty years later in his will, Walter called himself a tailor. Whether it was because this trade was a source of pride or that he had continued in the trade is not known.

The combination of the labor-intensiveness of tobacco farming, a drop in tobacco prices, and the poor tobacco productivity of seaboard-side lands had a cumulative effect. Walter stopped raising tobacco except for a very small plot for personal use. His main crops now were corn, wheat, barley, and rye.

Early Settlers in South Bethany

In 1702, Walter and Mary purchased South Petherton, a 430-acre tract including essentially all of today's South Bethany, from Matthew and Hannah

---

79   The 1696/7 date means he died between January and March of 1697. The Church in Rome had changed the calendar. Under the old calendar system the year began on March 1. Thus, after the change the period between Jan. 1 and March 1 of a new year was written as 1696/7 until people got used to it.

80   Torrence, op. cit., p. 108.

81   Will of Walter Powell, op. cit.

Scarborough.[82] We know that Walter and Mary lived on South Petherton because in his will of January 6, 1720, Walter left to . . . "my well-beloved sons William and John all the tract of land called S. Petherton containing 430 acres equally to be divided. William, the part where he now liveth, John the part where I live."[83] Further, Walter was witness to the 1708 will of a neighbor, William Hall, who owned Hall's Lott across a "small branch dividing it from Walter Evan's land."[84] The family continued to increase with the births of Gamage, Elizabeth and Powell.

South Petherton was originally patented in 1688 by Matthew Scarborough of Somerset County. Its 430 acres approximated today's South Bethany. The tract was bounded on the south more or less by a line representing the northern boundary of the State beach lands, on the west by today's Assawoman Canal, and on the north by the northern limits of South Bethany. It included most of today's dredged lagoons in South Bethany and approximately three-quarters of a mile of beachfront.[85] Much of the tract was poorly drained wetlands, as indicated by a provision in the 1766 will of Walter's son, William,[86] granting his wife Catherine a privilege in all his marsh and pasture lands, directing they be available for Catherine's use.

Walter and Mary probably moved to South Petherton reasonably soon after the 1702 purchase, and certainly before 1708, when Walter witnessed William Hall's will. *They built a reasonably substantial house, typical of the times, with one-and-a-half levels, including two rooms on the first floor and a sleeping loft. It had plank flooring on the lower level and a large clay and wood fireplace. They also had a number of small outhouses, including a kitchen and small barn.* Their home was probably similar in construction to the original first stage of the somewhat later Spring Banke House which still stands in Clarksville on a plot at the northeast corner of Routes 26 and 348. Neighbors—other than the William Hall family across the branch—were from half-a-mile to a mile away.[87]

---

82   Maryland Hall of Records, Deeds, Liber L #2, pp. 702-704.

83   Will of Walter Powell, op. cit.

84   Will of William Hall, September 10, 1708, Maryland Hall of Records, Wills EB #5, Folio 181.

85   Phillip Short Jr. Map of Baltimore Hundred delineating Maryland patents before 1700. Prepared by Mr. Short of Bethany Beach and donated by his family to the Delaware Public Archives. Used with permission of the Delaware Public Archives. The copy on page 53 was redrawn by Dick Carter.

86   Will of William Evans, Maryland Hall of Records, Prerogative Court, Wills, pp. 271-275.

87   Harold B. Hancock, *Liberty and Independence, The Delaware State During the American Revolution* (Wilmington, Delaware: The Delaware American Revolution Bicentennial Commission, 1976), p. 6.

Walter and Mary's family continued to grow and Gamage, Elizabeth and Powell were born after the purchase of <u>South Petherton</u>. Gamage and Powell were minors in 1728 when Mary signed her will with "her X mark."[88] She provided that Gamage and Powell should "be of age after my decease."

There is no record that Walter and Mary were slave-holders, so any required land clearing was probably done by their own sons and hired hands. This was a back-breaking task because only under favorable conditions could an able-bodied man convert two acres of virgin forest to tillable land in a year's time. Walter's will mentioned two homes on <u>South Petherton</u>, probably also built by hired hands.[89]

The weather and temperatures in Walter's time were essentially the same as today's, although the winters were harsher. Northeast storms and hurricanes were a regular threat to Walter and Mary's farmland. Crops could be flattened or flooded and lost, roads could be blocked, and in extremes, homes and farm buildings would be flooded or severely damaged. While free-ranging cattle and sheep moved inland to higher ground, other farm animals were lost. Walter and Catherine probably often incurred heavy losses and damage during their residency of approximately a quarter of a century on <u>South Petherton</u>.

Notwithstanding the periodic storm threats, Walter and Mary's life together on <u>South Petherton</u> probably was reasonably comfortable for the times. We have no information on their life in Baltimore Hundred, but they had large land holdings and were substantial persons in this sparsely settled area. But, while life could be pleasant, it was also a struggle in sometimes harsh surroundings. Close neighbors, most probably a mile away, struggled too. Walter and Mary had considerable livestock and many acres of grazing land, including considerable hay marsh. We know Walter left to daughter Margaret "a cow, a calf and her choice of all my mares," and to daughter Marjery "a heifer" and to daughter Eliza "a cow and two-year-old mare."

Their land holdings and numbers of livestock meant they probably had few needs. Their house was probably reasonably well-furnished but Spartan with furniture made on the farm, including bedsteads, a corner cabinet, chests and a large plank kitchen table with simple chairs. Vegetables from the kitchen plot, wheat and corn, beef, pork and seafood amply filled the family table.

---

88   Will of Mary Evans, Maryland Hall of Records, Prerogative Court (Wills) 20, pp. 591-593.

89   Will of Walter Evans, op. cit.

For the bulk of this period, cash crops were probably corn and tobacco, although farmers in this area were unable to duplicate the success of those along the Chesapeake in raising tobacco, and they eventually turned to the cultivation of wheat, rye, barley and corn.[90] Before about 1735, planters had raised tobacco almost exclusively, but by now wheat and corn had replaced much of the tobacco crop.[91]

Many of Walter's debts, however, were paid with tons of tobacco as the medium of payment, at least a portion of it possibly home-grown. Reasonably convenient access to the Indian River and Delaware Bay may have meant some degree of water-borne trade, but it is likely Walter's products were sold locally or to agents who handled transport of commercial-sized lots. Tools and farm equipment necessary for any farm were made by local blacksmiths or imported from England by merchants on the Chesapeake Bay shore.

There was little civil unrest during this period. To be sure, there were the occasional skirmishes with Marylanders supporting Lord Baltimore's claims against the Penns, and pirate raids along the shore were not uncommon. But life was generally quiet, and these threats probably had minimal impact on Walter and Mary.

Frederick Robinson James wrote that Thomas Fenwick's son-in-law, William Fassett (Fassitt), was captured by the pirates that thickly infested the coast during the late seventeenth and the early eighteenth centuries. "These pirates made coastwise traffic dangerous and frequently made raids upon the coast, as several chain balls discovered on Fenwick's Island early in the last century (19th) testify." According to James, this Fasset misadventure ended when he was thrown overboard and saved by swimming ashore.[92]

Walter Evans died in 1721. The inventory of Walter's assets during probate of his will is missing, but it is not unreasonable to assume the inventory of William Wouldhave/Woolhave in 1704 (below) is somewhat representative of his and Mary's possessions a few years after they moved to South Petherton.[93] Walter and Mary had earlier purchased Teuxberry from the Wouldhaves. Wouldhave's inventory is

90   Hoffecker, Carol E., Delaware, *A Bicentennial History* (New York: W. W. Norton and Co., 1979), p. 23.

91   Ibid.

92   James, op cit, p. 439.

93   Worcester County Inventories, JW15, Folio 20, as copied by students at the Nabb Center at Salisbury University. Spelling as close as possible to original, but includes some editing and explanations (in brackets).

instructive in determining the value of typical possessions at the beginning of the 1700s. Walter and Mary, however, probably had a larger inventory of possessions when Walter died in 1721.

In 1719, Walter and Mary's son William purchased 250 acres of the 500-acre tract North Petherton from Robert and Elizabeth Johnson for 5,000 pounds of tobacco. William had married Catherine White about two years earlier when both were about seventeen. William and Catherine probably received assistance from their parents.

With this purchase, Walter and William together owned the much of today's Bethany Beach, in addition to present-day Middlesex and South Bethany.

William Woolhave Inventory – 1704

An inventory of all the goods and chattels of William Woolhave - appraised by Charles Rackliff and Thomas Collins on May 31, 1704

	Pounds, Shillings & Pence		
9 cows and calves and four barren cows	18	19	
3 four year old stears and 2 of three years old	6	18	
one 5 year old bull and one of three years	1 16		
3 two year old stears and one two year old heffer	2	10	
5 yearlings but four of them bulls uncut	1	15	
11 barrows [castrated male hog] and 19 sows	9	3	
29 shoats: of sundry sorts	2	18	
12 tame geese		15	
1 bed, two old bolsters, one pillow, 1 old rugg and blanket and sheets and half a side of curtains and vallin [valance?]	2	15	
one new bed and bolster and one old quilt and blanket and half a side of curtains and vallin		3	
one old bed and pillow with bolster and pillow		15	
two potts and hooks and one pot rack		1	5
two old brass kittles and one frying pan and a pare of pot hooks			3
one good iron and one fire tongs and old bellow		1	6
1 table two chairs and 3 old chests	1		
2 old bedstead and cords old and seven old coolers [?]		7	6
1 handmill but small and one old gunne unfixed	1	10	
3 large chests but old 11 old cyder casks	2	3	
a sett of iron wedges and a parcell of iron		6	
5 pistols and one pare of holsters and one gunne unfixed	1	10	
1 froe [tool for splitting cask staves and shingles from a block], and one augger and a parcel of old wooden ware		2	
9 yards of new lining [linen] 2 hare sifters		10	
2 mares but one old	3	13	
two coats but one old and 2 pair of leather breeches	1	1	
one shirt and one white vest coate and one old hat	9	6	

Item	£	s	d
2 horn hooks [knitting or crocheting needles?] and a parcel of thread and one pound of wool	1		
2 looking glasses and 3 old riddles [coarse sieve]		8	
9 old brass trays and one narrow ax		1	6
45 shillings in money and one silver dram cup [measuring cup]	9	6	
1 old plow and irons worne out		2	6
1 old ?????? and one sadle and bridle		9	
3 small bollons of wooling yarn			5
107 pounds of backon and 38 pounds of beef		14	10
11 bushels of wheat and one of corn	1	4	
2 pounds of tallow and a small matter of canvas		4	
2 yearling skins and one undressed hide		4	6
a parcell of indian corne and one hat brush	1	5	6
7 puter spoons and 2 puter candelsticks and one brass ditto		2	6
one puter chamber pott and one puter salt and 12 puter cups		2	6
1 box hafted [handled] knife and 1 quart pot			4
48 pounds of worn pewter and 111 pounds of nals [nails]		4	
1 bolle (bowl) and a brass simmer ? and a puter funnell		6	
a parcel of shot and one old cotah [coat?]		4	
One grindstone and two old matate but under beds?		6	
one night cap and an iron cittle [kettle]		9	
one small glass bottle and a primmers [gun primers?]		6	
1 earthen pot with hoggs lard and a mustard bottle		3	
orphen boy Sall [Saul?] three years and seven months to serve	4		
4 hogsheads of tobacco at a penny per pound [approx 270#/hogshead]	3	13	3
Total appraisal	79	5	5

Next page - Map of Maryland Patents in Baltimore Hundred Before 1700 by Phillip Short Jr. (Redrawn in 2002 by Dick Carter for Gordon Wood)

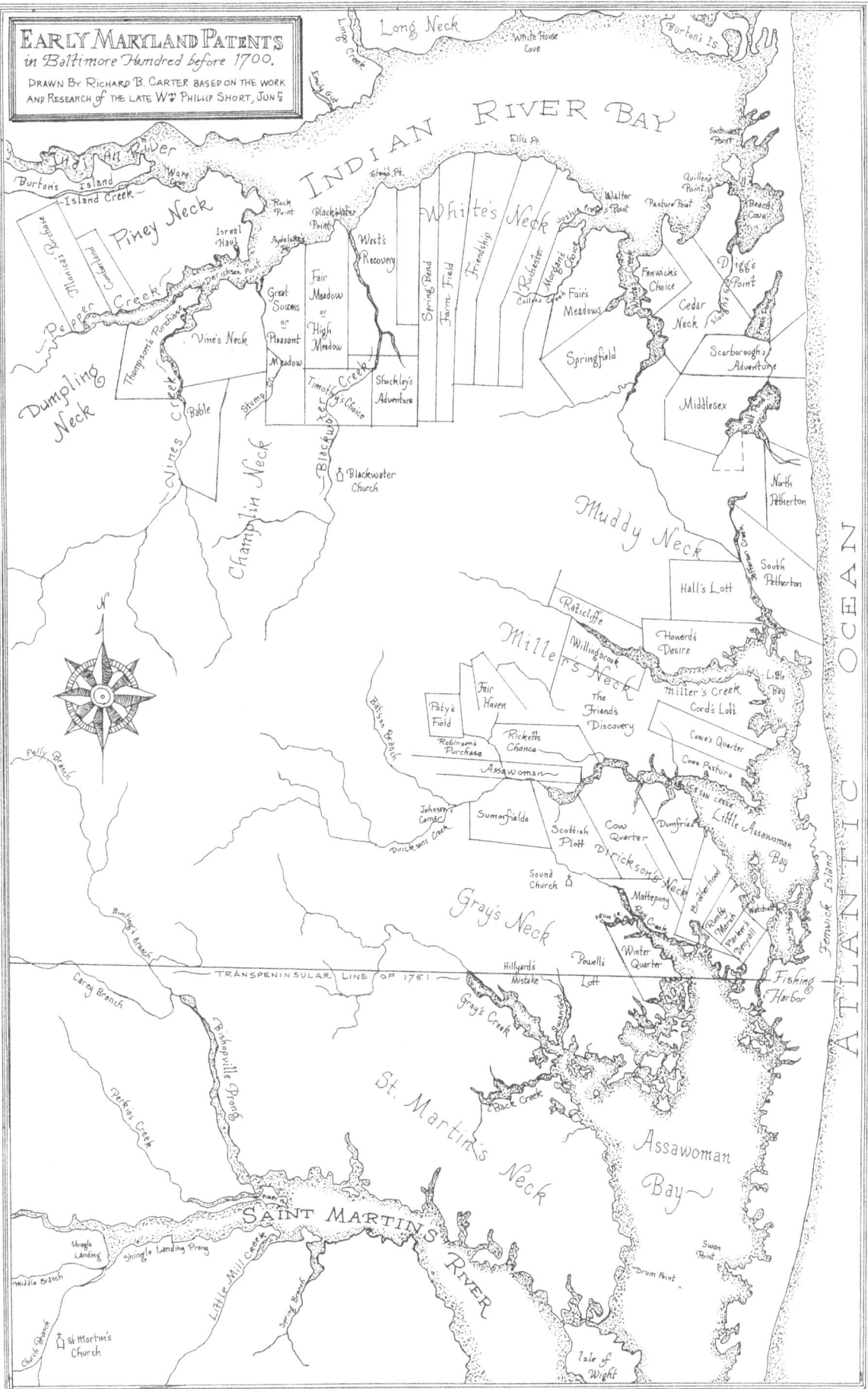

EARLY MARYLAND PATENTS
in Baltimore Hundred before 1700.

DRAWN BY RICHARD B. CARTER BASED ON THE WORK
AND RESEARCH OF THE LATE WM. PHILLIP SHORT, JUN.R

INDIAN RIVER BAY

Long Neck

Lingo Creek

White House Cove

Burton's Is.

Southwest Point

Ellis Pt.

Gray's Pt.

Walter Point

Quillens Point

Beach Cove

Pasture Point

Josiah Prong

Piney Neck

Burton's Island

Ware

Island Creek

Little An River

Rock Point

Blackwater Point

Israel Haul

Ayde loates

Derrickson Point

White's Neck

Rochester

Morgans

Colly's Creek

Fairs Meadows

Fenwick's Choice

Diggs Point

Cedar Neck

West's Recovery

Fair Meadow or High Meadow

Morgan's Choice

Scarborough's Adventure

Pepper Creek

Thomas's Purchase

Cumberland

Great Success or Pleasant Meadow

Spring Bend

Farm Field

Friendship

Springfield

Middlesex

Thompson's Purchase

Vine's Neck

Babte

Stumy

Timothy's Choice

Shockley's Adventure

North Petherton

Dumpling Neck

Vines Creek

Champlin Neck

Blackwater Creek

Blackwater Church

Muddy Neck

South Petherton

ATLANTIC OCEAN

Fenwick Island

Hall's Lott

Ratcliffe

Howard's Desire

Willingbrook

Miller's Neck

Miller's Creek

Little Bay

Cord's Lott

Batson Branch

Fair Haven

The Friend's Discovery

Cowe's Quarter

Poty's Field

Ricketts Chance

Cowe Pasture

Robinson's Purchase

Polly Branch

Assawoman

Johnson's Corner

Dirrickson's Creek

Sumerfielda

Scottish Plott

Cow Quarter

Dumfries

Little Assawoman Bay

Dickson Creek

Dirickson's Neck

Mattepong

Sound Church

Gray's Neck

Bay Creek

Brotherton

Handy March

Parkers

Marryall

Watchall

Powell's Lott

Winter Quarter

Buntings Branch

Hillyards Mistake

TRANSPENINSULAR LINE OF 1751

Fishing Harbor

Carey Branch

Gray's Creek

Perkins Creek

Bishopville Prong

Assawoman Bay

St. Martin's Neck

Black Creek

Shingle Landing

Shingle Landing Prong

Little Mill Creek

Middle Branch

Spring Branch

SAINT MARTINS RIVER

Swan Point

Drum Point

Church Branch

St. Martin's Church

Isle of Wight

(Page Intentionally Left Blank)

(See previous side for map of Early Maryland Patents)

On August 16, 1720, seven months after he wrote his will and five months before he died, Walter (and Mary) sold Teuxberry to a William Simpson for 5,000 pounds of tobacco, the same price Walter paid for these same 100 acres thirty years earlier.[94] The lengthy and detailed deed is fascinating to read. It attests that Walter was a planter (a land-owning farmer). The deed also notes that the sale included "houses" (plural), probably referring to the family house and quarters for hired hands or even renters.

As one would expect, Walter provided sizable bequests for each of his children. He left all lands to his and Mary's sons, and, as was common for the times, did not make any specific provision for Mary. He did name ". . my well-beloved wife Mary Evans my whole and sole executor of my last will and testament . . ." Mary, who had originally inherited Hilliard's Discovery and Powell's Inclusion from her father, and likely being an independent person not wanting to be dependent on her sons, renounced the will and claimed her dower rights or legal widow's share. Probably through an agreement with her adult sons, her share included Hilliard's Discovery and Powell's Inclusion which Walter would have left to the minor sons, Gamage and Powell, except for Mary's claim.

Curiously, he left but one shilling to his married daughter, Mary "Simson." A nominal bequest of one shilling often indicated either displeasure with an heir or signaled earlier gifts were made in lieu of a bequest. Assuming, without having researched it, Mary was the wife of the William "Simpson" discussed above, she and her husband received a bargain sale of Teuxberrry from her father for the thirty-years-ago price. This would explain the lack of a specific bequest.

Where the 63-year-old Mary lived after Walter's death is not recorded, but she probably remained on South Petherton. Her will left Gamage ". . . my best bed and furniture" and Powell ". . . my other bed and furniture." Her possessions might seem to be limited, but it is likely Mary remained in the South Petherton home and lived comfortably with her son John who inherited that part of South Petherton where she and Walter had lived.

Upon her death in 1732, Mary ultimately left the inherited tracts, Hilliard's Discovery and Powell's Inclusion, to her last-born sons, Gamage and Powell, in accordance with her 1728 will.[95] She also provided that the minors, Gamage and

---

94   Maryland Hall of Records, Somerset County Land Records, Liber JK, p. 77.
95   Will of Mary Evans, op cit.

Powell, ". . . shall be at age and liberty after my decease," so they clearly were minors when she wrote her will in 1728. Ever the concerned mother, Mary also provided in her will that "my son Gamage Evans should help truly and diligently my son Powell Evans to clear five thousand corn hills [and] also to help fence it with good sufisient fences and further to help to build a house for my son Powell Evans being fiveteen or sixteen foott squair."

Mary's "five thousand corn hills and fencing" is a good indication that corn had replaced much of the tobacco cultivation on the "seaside" of the peninsula. In these times, corn was planted in the Indian manner, in hills about four feet apart, so about 2,500 hills could be planted on each cleared acre and fewer where the stumps or hulks of girdled trees remained.

Livestock foraged freely, and fences were a necessity. Cutting down trees, splitting rails, and erecting zig-zag fences was time-consuming work, and two men were expected to take a week to fence in an acre.[96] Mary had imposed a significant burden on her son, Gamage, by requiring him to help his brother. This probably tended to provide equality in her bequests to her sons.

Planting season was a time of heavy labor, mostly with a hoe, and the whole family usually participated. As described by Scharf,[97] the corn-hills were either hoed into shape by hand or with the assistance of a wooden plow pulled by an ox (a castrated bull). Furrows were thrown up by plowing rows in one direction for one side and then reversing for the other side. A harrow broke up the tops of the furrows, and little hills were stepped off and hoed out about every four feet. Several grains of corn were planted in each hill in holes scooped out and then covered with hoed soil.

When the corn was a few feet high, pumpkins and beans were planted around the corn, the stalks serving as bean poles. After the corn had tasseled and the silking process was completed and the corn was fully developed, all the blades and tops were removed by hand and hauled from the field for winter fodder. When dried, the corn was shucked and the stalks knocked down. The ground could be roughly plowed and sowed in wheat. One field provided annual crops of corn, wheat, pumpkins and beans.

96   Hawke, op. cit., p. 34.
97   Scharf, op. cit., Vol I, pp. 155-156.

Corn as developed by the Indians was truly the settlers' manna from heaven, notwithstanding the ever-present threats of insects and disease and raccoons and deer who had a special fondness for the fresh ears. Beyond that, storms could knock down the stalks. One laborer could produce—grow and shell—between 17 and 25 bushels of shelled corn a year,[98] enough to feed a family of five persons as part of the regular diet—wheat, pork, game, vegetables and fish.

Walter and Mary Evans do not have a known gravesite. They may be buried in an unmarked grave in the old Cat Hill Cemetery on Black Gum Drive in South Bethany which is sited on their South Petherton farm. If not there, they probably are buried somewhere in today's South Bethany or the Sea Colony development, west of Route 1. Others in their generation and at least the two following may also be buried in the Cat Hill Cemetery.

When it resumes (Chapter 10), the Evans Family Story devolves to Walter and Mary's son William and his wife, Catherine White Evans. Walter and Mary return in Chapter 10 as the parents of young William.

Will of Walter Evans, June 6, 1720 Maryland Hall of Records, Prerogative Court, Wills, Liber 16, Folios 509-511

In the name of God Amen the Sixth Day of June in the year of our Lord 1720 I Walter Evans of Somerset County in the Province of Maryland Taylor being very sick and weak of body but of perfect mind & memory thanks be to God therefore Calling to mind the Mortality of my body and Knowing that it is appointed for all men once to Dye Do make and Ordain this my –
Last will and Testament that is to say first of all I give and Recommend my Soul into the hand of God that gave it and my body to be buried in a Christian Like Manner at the Discretion of my –
Executors and as Touching Such worldly Estate – which it has pleased God to bless me with, I give and Bestow in the manner and form as followeth
Item I give and Bequeath to my well beloved Sons William and John Evans all
    that Tract of Land Called South Petherton containing four hundred and thirty
    acres of land Equally to be divided between them Beginning at a place called
    Snaps Gutt I mean that my son William afsd. Should Enjoy half of the land
    afsd. Is on which part he now Liveth him and his heirs and assigns and that
    my son John Evans Should Enjoy and Inheritt the Other half of this tract of

---

98   James Horn, *Adapting to a New World* (Chapel Hill, NC: The University of North Carolina Press, 1994), p. 279.

Land on which I now Liv myself with all the appurtenances thereto belonging to him his heirs and assignes -------

Item   I give and Bequeath to my well beloved Sons Gamage and Powell Evans all that tract of land called Hilliards Discovery and Powells Concution [Conclusion] being part of the two tracts of Land and Containing Two hundred and three acres Lying and being in the County of Somerset in the province of Maryland – Equally to be Divided between both for Quantity and Quality to them their heirs and Assigns but I will if either Gamage or Powell Should Die without Issue that then the Other Should Injoy his part of Land above mentioned ------

Item   I give and Bequeath to my Daughter Mary Simson one Shilling in Cash to be Delivered by my Ex'or.

Item   I give and Bequeath to my Daughter Margrett one Cow and Calf and also her Choice of all my Mares and one five gallon pott --------

Item   I give and Bequeath to my Daughter Mariorey one two year Old heifer to be Delivered in the Spring first Coming

Item   I give and Bequeath to my Daughter Eliza one Cow and one two year Old Mare --------

And I Doe Constitute make and Ordain my well beloved wife Mary Evans my whole and Sole Ex:or of this my last will and Testament willed and Bequeathed Ratifying and Confirming this and no other to be my last will and Testament in witness whereof I have hereunto set my hand and Seale the day and year above written------

                                                                    his
                                                        Walter X Evans
          SEAL his   his mark
Testes George GH Howard
          mark
          her
     Sarah S Howard
          mark
Somerset County
     Mem:d That this day the 2d of June 1721 came before the Administration Committee Mary Evans Ex:r of the a:d Will did renounce the a:d Will as to her own part and Fly to her thirds according to law.
                                                  Testis Sam'l Hopkins

                          * * * * * * * * * *

Having claimed her thirds (widow's share), Mary Evans possessed one third of Walter's Estate. Apparently Mary received the lands Walter left to their sons, Gamage and Powell, that had been willed to Mary by her father, Walter Powell. The following excerpts from her will bequeath these lands and her two beds and furniture:

Will of Mary Evans, Seamsteris [Seamstress]

Imprimis – I Desire that my Two Sons Gamage and Powell Should be at Age &
    Liberty after my decease ------

Gift   I give and Bequeath unto my Son Gamage Evans my Best bed and
    furniture
Gift   I Give and Bequeath unto my Son Powell Evans the other bed and
    furniture
Gift   I Give and Bequeath unto my two Sons Gamage and Powell Evans all
    that Land called hilliards Discovery & Powells Conclusion being parts of a
    Tract of Land Containing two hundred & three Acres Lying in and being in
    the County of Somerset Equally to be Divided between boath for quantity
    and Quality To them their heirs & Assigns But I will that if Either Gamage
    and Powell Should Die without Heirs that then the other should Injoy his
    part of land above Mentioned I Will that my Son Gamage Evans Should
    help truely and Dilligently my Son Powell Evans to Clear five Thousand
    Corn hills also to help to fence it with Good Sufisient fences and further
    to help to build a house for my Son Powell Evans being fifteen or sixteen
    footts Squair. . . . .
her
 Mary M Evans
mark

Chapter 6   Letter to Brian – Special Roots

April 1995

Dear Brian,

Just being my first grandson makes you precious to me. But you are special and fun too in your own right. You have your Daddy's inquisitiveness, guile, spirit, and love of the beach. And, oh yes, critters.

It will be hard to forget a three-year-old wanting to show one of those guys, rolling over a large rock to catch a newt or a worm or something. Seeing you be as excited as you were with your catch as you showed it to your pop-pop. Hearing you say the critter should "return to his mommy." Watching you place him back in the hole, and then – seeing you roll the rock back into the hole so he "would be home." Sweet, but, as your dad said, "Oh well . . . ."

Brian, what a rich family background you have. Imagine, a family that combines your Nanny, Jean Barkan's, family in Australia and your Papa, Bill Barkan's, Latvian roots and the Wood and Evans ancestors. What a wonderful combination! Learn everything you can about the Stewart and Hooley families in Australia and the Barkan Eastern Europe roots and when and how they came to America, including your Great Grandfather Barkan's trip to America with his sewing machine on his back. There must be many interesting, important, and wonderful things to know. Learn about and be proud of the fascinating heritage of the Australians in Botany Bay and the wonders and richness of Bill Barkan's Jewish heritage. The Barkan heritage is special, a source of justifiable pride, a treasure of wonderful traditions and devotions. Don't lose any of it; learn more and cherish the knowledge.

I have another assignment for you. Your Dad is named after your great-grandfather, Robert Kimmel. Work with your Ohio and Virginia cousins to learn more about your Nana Sue's family, including your dad's namesake, Robert Kimmel. Your dad has information on his family which will lead you to other great American names – Adams, Eastman, and Lane.

60

The Kimmel name comes from Germany. So does Sockrider, the name of my Mom-Mom Nellie's grandfather. I only recently became aware of the Sockrider roots.

Germany is a country rich in music, technology, philosophy, and literature; great food too. Germany has had a great role in history and many proud accomplishments, along with the notorious dark side. While we can and should be proud of our German forebears and their accomplishments, we must remember that some of history's grimmest days were imposed on Europe, indeed the world, by Germany.

History demonstrates over and over again that people often follow the wrong leaders in many countries, not just Germany. We have seen it again in Bosnia and Kosovo. This potential exists in white and non-white races, Christian and other religions, and different cultures. It is not always someone else in far-away places. White, Anglo-Saxon Christians are not immune. We, you and I, are not immune.

You will learn these lessons of recorded events as you advance in school. Listen, study and learn. History's mistakes are repeated unless we understand the lessons and are vigilant and participate in government. Ask yourself why and think about how we can encourage contributions to education and knowledge and discourage jealousy and malice over possessions, culture or race.

A good start is to be conscious always of the Golden Rule: Do unto others as you would have them do unto you. Think about others positively. Look for the good side in everyone. Assess people by how they treat you and why, not by who or what they are.

With much love to a great little guy,

Pop-Pop

PART II

ESTABLISHING EVANS AND HALL FAMILY ROOTS

Chapter 7   The Daniel Evans Puzzle

This chapter is a stand-alone, extensive study on my fifth-great-grandfather, Daniel Evans, who died in Baltimore Hundred in 1800. Based upon this study supported by wide-ranging research reported herein, I concluded that Daniel was the brother of John Evans Jr. and the son of John and Catherine Wharton Evans of <u>North Petherton</u>, a tract located in today's Bethany Beach. This conclusion is based upon extensive circumstantial evidence and the lack of any contrary evidence, but I was not able to prove the conclusion.

My conclusion completes the link from Daniel and his descendants down five generations to Zadock, Clemeth, John A., Alonzo and my grandfather Linwood Evans and up another three generations to John Sr., William and Walter Evans of Baltimore Hundred.

"The Daniel Evans Puzzle" is inserted at this point to provide an anchor for the Evans Family Genealogy in Chapter 4 and subsequent chapters on Daniel's ancestors and descendants. A word of advice: This chapter is very detailed and will be boring to all but dedicated family history researchers. That said, some may wish to skip to Chapter 8.

This chapter has its own table of contents (pp. v-vi), alphabetized sections and appendices. Footnotes, however, are numbered consecutively with footnotes in preceding and subsequent chapters of this book.

****

THE DANIEL EVANS PUZZLE:

WHO WAS THE DANIEL EVANS

WHO DIED IN BALTIMORE HUNDRED

IN 1800?

Note: Sections H, N, O and P develop this paper's conclusions by identifying the various John Evanses in Baltimore Hundred, identifying Our Daniel's brother named John, analyzing the possible John Evanses who could be Our Daniel's father, and analyzing and justifying the paper's conclusion. Of necessity, information developed in earlier sections is required for each of these purposes. Each section, therefore, contains many of the same facts and analyses. This duplication is somewhat burdensome to readers, and I apologize, but it is necessary to maintain continuity in developing the facts, surmises, analyses and conclusions herein.

A.   PROBLEM

The ancestry of the Daniel Evans who lived with his family in Baltimore Hundred[99] and who died in 1800 has defied genealogical researchers and remained a mystery notwithstanding the wealth of information supporting his existence. While studied fairly extensively, no study known to this author has correctly resolved Daniel's ancestry. The research and analysis described herein were intended to identify Daniel's parents, if possible, and uncover a vital commodity—evidence.

Daniel's thousands of direct descendants deserve an answer to his ambiguous ancestry. A part of our heritage is in limbo. Ignorance of our origins beyond Daniel disowns us—makes each of us an orphan of a generation past.

B.   INTRODUCTION

The Daniel Evans, known herein as "Our Daniel," my great-great-great-great, great-grandfather (fifth great), until now had been the earliest generational, certain, direct, male-line, Evans ancestor of my great-grandfather, Alonzo H. Evans, who lived on Kent Avenue in Bethany Beach and died in 1955. Daniel lived on a tract known as Partnership or an adjacent tract near the ocean in what was known as Muddy Neck and is now known as South Bethany. We know the ancestry from the line of wills and Bible information[100] carrying his line through Our Daniel's son, Zadoc, who died in 1852 at or about age 72; and on through to Clemeth, who died in 1868 at age 60; John A., who died in 1899 at age 65;W and the venerable Alonzo, whom I knew well.

Tracing Alonzo's line back to Our Daniel was disarmingly simple. In a matter of a few minutes in 1982, Dick Carter, a Sussex County historian, helped this neophyte work through the Will Books at the Sussex County, Delaware Courthouse. From then until now, the formidable task has been extending this Evans line back beyond Our Daniel.

---

99   As previously stated, an Administration subdivision of a county, similar to a township in other states, encompassing that area of Southeastern Sussex County, Delaware, generally bounded on the north by the Indian River and Bay, on the east by the ocean, on the south by the Maryland line, and on the west by Dagsboro Hundred and the Great Cypress Swamp.

100   Evans Family Bible (Original pages containing family entries only—separated from missing Bible). Original pages in possession of Gordon Wood—copy in Archives of Delaware, Bible Records, Evans 1.2.

My research was a 16-years off-and-on effort with little success until recently (2001). The details of resolving the puzzle offer commentary on genealogical research by an amateur, a recognition of its propensity to become an obsession, and the requisite luck—finding important facts in unlikely places. The whole process of approaching and, it is believed, resolving this puzzle demonstrates the need for many days and hours of research fully catalyzed (thank Heaven) by strokes of luck.

I now claim with reasonable confidence to have solved the puzzle based upon the preponderance of the combination of circumstantial evidence and available data, the analyses posited herein, and the absence of conflicting evidence. As is often the case in quandaries like this, however, short of stumbling on proof via land transaction records or other data not known to me, absolute confirmation of this determination may not be possible.

Is this an approximate story told by an optimist? Wishful thinking by a dreamer? Simple guesses buttressed by a modicum of facts? While there are still many unknowns, and the complete reconstruction of this history may forever elude our grasp, it is hoped readers will realize the significant investment of time and energy to pursue facts and be accurate. More could be done; some answers are assuredly still out there—unfound. But eventually, it becomes unproductive to wish for what could not be found. I am satisfied.

C.   THE RESEARCH AND ANALYSIS PROCESS

This amateur's early approach to trying to identify Our Daniel's past first included an unorganized review of everything found in published compilations of will and probate and land records as well as basic public records in the Sussex County Courthouse in Georgetown, Delaware, the Worcester County Courthouse in Snow Hill, Maryland, the Somerset County Courthouse in Princess Anne, Maryland, and the Delaware and Maryland State Archives. All of this resulted in a lot of poorly organized notes, no solution to the puzzle, and the identification of as many as five, suspected, contemporary Daniels who lived in the last half of the 1700s, one in Kent County in Delaware, as many as three in Sussex County (earlier Worcester or Somerset Counties in Maryland), and one in Baltimore County, Maryland.

Upon retiring, I returned to the task with more time, greater determination and a somewhat more systematic effort. The initial renewed efforts focused first on what we know about Our Daniel, a surprising amount. This was followed by a more systematic review of the literature on the Evans family published by others and information from all sources about the other Daniels who could be Our Daniel. The renewed investigative sweep covered census and tax assessment records, land transaction records, church records, court records, military records, and probate and administration records. Analysis led to obvious as well as obscure research targets and intermediate surmises which further focused the effort. It added up to a systematic-as-possible review of the research and analysis leading to my conclusion.

The weight or preponderance of all the evidence and analyses resulted in a supportable conclusion, though not absolute proof.

D. <u>THE DANIELS IN SUSSEX AND KENT COUNTIES IN DELAWARE AND WORCESTER, SOMERSET AND BALTIMORE COUNTIES IN MARYLAND</u>

Of the five suspected Daniels, the most promising who might have been Our Daniel and one who, incidentally, could be traced back a few more well-researched generations, turned out, instead, to be a **DAVID** Evans, the son of Major John Evans from the West Berlin, Maryland, area.

Relying at my peril on an entry in *Land Records of Worcester County, Maryland, 1666-1810* by Ruth T. Dryden,[101] which reports that in 1768 a John Evans willed a tract of land, <u>Grays Endeavor</u>, to his son, "Daniel" Evans, I thought the puzzle was solved. Unfortunately, scrutiny of the microfilm of this John Evans' will[102] by Rebecca Miller, then of the Edward H. Nabb Research Center for Delmarva History and Culture at Salisbury State University, clearly showed he had a son, David, but there is no known-to-me record of his having a son Daniel. Try writing the words Daniel and David quickly; the difference between the written "Daniel" and "David" can be discerned only where the penmanship is careful and clear. This Daniel, much to my disappointment, was not Our Daniel.

The Dryden mistake on Daniel has been replicated by experienced genealogists. This is not to criticize the excellent work of Ruth Dryden and others, but, rather, to emphasize an important warning: do not rely solely on the handy and generally excellent secondary-source compilations or abstracts of land and inheritance documents. The numerous secondary-source publications of materials focusing on Sussex County, Delaware, and Worcester County, Maryland, are a most excellent starting point, but when information from such sources is used as the

---

101   Ruth T. Dryden, *Land Records of Worcester County, Maryland, 1666-1810* (Westminster, Md: Family Line Publications, 1992), p. 271.

102   Will of John Evans, April 15, 1768, Worcester County Wills, Liber 36, p. 506.

foundation of important conclusions, it must be confirmed by review of original sources such as the original wills, deeds, patents, etc., or of quality microfilms. Other unexpected information may also be found in these pertinent originals, because the harder you research, the luckier you get.

The second Daniel, from near Smyrna in Duck Creek Hundred in Kent County, Delaware, was the son of a David Evans who died in 1750 and Elizabeth Evans.[103] He had two married sisters in 1750, and he witnessed the will of William Jacobs on November 27, 1750,[104] presumably as an adult, so he was at least twenty-one years old when his father died. This Daniel, therefore, was born before 1730, likely making him a little too old to be Our Daniel who, as we will see below, was probably born about 10 years later. Further, a careful review of the signatures of the Duck Creek Daniel on the Executor's Bond from the probate of his father's estate with Our Daniel's signature on his will and on other wills as a witness demonstrates they were not the same person. The signatures are sufficiently different, beyond even what could be expected with the passage of thirty years. Finally, as analyzed in Section F, below, Our Daniel had a brother, John, and there is no record of a brother, John, in the Kent County Daniel's family.

A possible third Daniel enlisted on May 28, 1758, in Captain French Battell's Company of Lower Delaware Provincials during the French and Indian Wars.[105] Battell's Company was organized in Dover in Kent County, and names of others in the Company are not consistent with contemporaries of Lower Sussex County. This Daniel may also be the Duck Creek Daniel; although, enlistment at the age of 28 or older probably was not the norm. He could be Our Daniel, but it is not likely because Baltimore Hundred was a part of Maryland in 1758. I know of no way to check further.

The fourth Daniel, the son of a Job Evans in Baltimore County,[106] is discussed in Appendix 3 of this chapter. He is not Our Daniel.

---

103   Administration of Estate of David Evans, May 9, 1750, Kent County Reg. of Wills, Liber K, folio 26.
104   Will of Jacob Evans, November 27, 1750, Kent County Reg. of Wills, Liber K. Folio 67.
105   *Delaware Archives, Military, Volume I* (Wilmington, DE: Mercantile Printing Company, 1911), p. 16.
106   Will of Job Evans, June 9, 1774, *Maryland Calendar of Wills*, Volume 16 (Westminster, MD: Family Line Publications) p. 112.

The fifth Daniel was our now known Daniel whose ancestry is the subject of this paper.

Having gotten this far and being somewhat stymied, the track and clues to identify Our Daniel and his father were limited. The only obvious next step was to review in detail the extensive information known about Our Daniel and the other Daniels who might be Our Daniel.

E. WHAT WE KNOW FOR SURE ABOUT OUR DANIEL

Our Daniel's will[107] dated September 1, 1798, and admitted to probate on December 10, 1800, identifies his wife, Sarah, who was named Executor; his sons, Daniel and Zadoc; a daughter, Elizabeth; a legatee, Martha Taylor, most likely a daughter, who is to receive certain property "after her mother's death," and two other beneficiaries, Rhoday Barns and Sarah Barns. Since they have the same surname, one can speculate that they could be the sister and mother of Our Daniel's wife, Sarah, whose maiden name may have been Sarah Barns. We know very little about Sarah, and this is a subject worthy of further study. A Sarah Barns was the wife of a George Barns of Dagsboro Hundred who died in March 1789,[108] —the right time frame. The probate file on George Barns offers no further information. Sarah survived Our Daniel and carried out her role as Executor. Sarah (with her mark "X") and a Thomas Evans signed the Executor's Bond. Tax Assessment Lists include Sarah through 1812, so she lived at least 12 years after Daniel died in 1800. There are no known will or probate records to confirm this date.

The 1800 U.S. Census of Baltimore Hundred landowners lists a Daniel whose family includes two males aged 16/26, two females aged 10/16, and one female over 45, his wife, Sarah. This must be Our Daniel because the recorded family is consistent with Our Daniel's will, but there is some confusion. Daniel's sons are consistent with the two males aged 16/26. His married daughter, Martha Taylor, likely would not be included. The females aged 10/16 are possibly his daughter Elizabeth, and Rhoday Barnes. The female over 45 could be Daniel's wife, Sarah, or Sarah Barns. As noted above, this is worthy of further research.

Our Daniel's will left a tract of land known as <u>Partnership</u> to be divided equally between his two sons, Daniel and Zadoc, and "all the remainder of my Land and Plantation where I now live..." to Zadoc. We know from the list of bequests

---

107   Will of Daniel Evans, September 1, 1798, Sussex County Wills, Liber F, p. 17
108   Will of Diana Leatherbury, October 8, 1790, Sussex County Wills, Liber B, pp. 506-509.

in Our Daniel's will and the probate inventory that he had two tracts of land and very limited personal property.

We know that Our Daniel witnessed a will by Charles Whaley in Sussex County on April 10, 1790,[109] which was also witnessed by John Evans (School Master's signature) and a Robert Evans and probated in 1791. The original of this will was reviewed side-by-side with Our Daniel's will to compare the Daniel Evans signatures, and they are truly identical. The Daniel Evans signature on the Whaley Testamentary Bond is also identical. This will, in a stroke of good luck, describes land left to Charles Whaley Jr. and states it adjoins lands of Daniel Evans, assuredly Our Daniel. The John Evans who witnessed the will along with Daniel and Robert was John Evans, School Master, as determined by comparison of signatures of the numerous John Evanses in Baltimore Hundred at that time.[110]

A Thomas Evans signed the Executor's Bond during the probate of Our Daniel's will.[111] This, plus Robert's leaving part of his estate to James, the son of a Thomas,[112] raises intriguing questions. Were Daniel, Robert and Thomas related? To John, School Master? If so, which Thomas? This was worthy of further study, but no original records were found of a Thomas Evans supporting this possibility.[113]

No known probate record of any Evans from either Worcester County or Sussex County includes a bequest to any Daniel.

Our Daniel signed the Executor's Bond for the probate of the 1791 will of John Evans, School Master—probated in 1794.[114] Daniel's signature on the bond is identical to both his signature on his will and his signature as a witness on the Charles Whaley will. This raises again the question whether Our Daniel was a brother of John, School Master. It is believed, however, that their being neighbors in Muddy Neck and John's being School Master, connoting an educated man who witnessed many local wills, had more to do with his role as witness than family ties.

---

109   Will of Charles Whaley, April 10, 1790, Sussex County Wills, Liber D, pp. 324-325.
110   See Section M.
111   Will of Daniel Evans (original copy), Sussex County Probate Records, Delaware Public Archives, 1798-1800.
112   Will of Robert Evans, July 24, 1833, Sussex County Wills, Liber D, p. 210.
113   See Appendix 3.
114   Will of John Evans (School Master), op. cit.

This is analyzed further in Sections M and N.

Our Daniel witnessed the will of Elizabeth McDaniel[115] on September 22, 1793, (clearly Our Daniel's signature). This will was also witnessed by John Dazey and a John Evans whose signature appears to be that of John Evans, School Master—more evidence that John Evans, School Master, John Dazey and Our Daniel were neighbors.

F. <u>WHAT WE KNOW ABOUT A DANIEL WHO COULD BE OUR DANIEL</u>

The Inventory of Assets during the probate of the Will of Thomas Dazey Sr.[116] <u>of Sussex County, dated January 30, 1778, included a "debt due from John Evans **brother to Daniel**, of 15 shillings." **This indicates that a Daniel had a brother John in 1778. It defines the problem addressed in this chapter: Which John, and who is the father of this John and Daniel?**</u> Is the brother the John who was the son of the John Evans of West Berlin whose will included a David and a John but not a Daniel,[117] or is this one of a list of John Evanses in Baltimore Hundred which included John Evans, School Master, and John Evans Jr., among others? One would definitely think the latter because of land locations, but as noted above, there is no record of either the John Evans of West Berlin or any John Evans of Baltimore Hundred having a son, Daniel. Section M discusses the possible John Evanses who could be Our Daniel's brother, and Section O addresses John Evans Sr. who could be Our Daniel's father.

Baltimore Hundred Tax Assessment Records[118] list a Daniel Evans for the years 1775 and 1778 and 1789 thru 1800, when Our Daniel died. Absent any other known Daniel in Baltimore Hundred, this must be Our Daniel. Unfortunately, there are no Worcester County Tax Assessment Records for the period prior to 1775, and the available Debt Lists[119] for the period before 1775 do not include a Daniel and, therefore, provide no information about Daniel's whereabouts before 1775. The

115   Will of Elizabeth McDaniel, September 22, 1793, Archives of Delaware, Vol. A87, p. 146.

116   True Inventory of the Goods, Chattles [sic] Rights and Credits of the Late Deceased Thomas Dazey, January 30, 1778, Delaware Public Archives, Sussex County Probate, Thomas Dazey Sr., 1778.

117   Will of John Evans (Worcester County), op. cit.

118   Sussex County Levy Court Tax Assessment Records (microfilm), Public Archives of Delaware, 1775-1800.

119   Debt Books of Worcester County, Liber 53, Maryland Hall of Records, Annapolis, MD.

1775 and 1778 listings (1776 is missing) raise the question; why was Daniel not a landowner from 1779 to 1789, the missing years? Some time before or during 1789, Our Daniel somehow acquired at least one of the two parcels of land he left to his sons. One is discussed in the analysis of the will of John Dazey[120] regarding Partnership, below, and in Section G. The second possibility is discussed in Section H in connection with the lands of Daniel Wharton Sr. No land acquisition records were found for Our Daniel in either the Sussex or Worcester County Grantee or Grantor indices.

The will of John Dazey Sr., the son of Thomas Dazey Jr., dated September 23, 1795, includes the following provisions (grammar and spelling given as close as decipherable to the original document):

"I give and bequeath to Danneal Evans sixty acres of land that he has a conveyance bond [emphasis added] for that is not yet made over to him to be taken of the southwest corner of old tract called Partnership [Note: Original land patent was dated September 1760] beginning where Joseph [may be John] Dazey line crosses home lane of the old tract running East to peach ___ ___ tree before mentioned as upon thence East as far as a South Lott two degrees. It shall contain sixty acres west of the southwest corner of said tract to him and his heirs and assigns for ever."

This same will leaves land to Dazey's son George which apparently is next to the Danneal Evans land—"part of an old tract of land called Partnership part of a Resurvey beginning where the said Evans line turns of two degrees East thence running East till it comes to the run of the branch being a division between him and George Dazey then down and with the said run until it comes to the outgoin line of the Resurvay then with the several lines of the resurvay till it comes to a marked maple staning close to a path that leads from Danneal Evans to Robbart Wilgoos [*now known as Wilgus*] thence with the lines of the Resurvay twenty poles further towards Dannel Evans thence north till it strikes Dannel Evans line that I will to Dannel then running the lines that I will to Dannel till it comes to George Dazey first beginning . . ." Witnessed by Moses Dazey, Jessey Dazey, and William Evans.

---

120   Will of John Dazey, September 23, 1795, Sussex County Wills, Liber F, p. 449.

There is no record known to me of this "conveyance bond"[121] ever being executed even though we know from Our Daniel's will[122] that he left that part of Partnership that he owned to his sons, Daniel and Zadoc. The original records on Partnership are discussed fully in Section H.

There are no references to any Daniel in the three compilations of a part of Sussex County land records; (1) Land Records of Sussex County, Delaware, 1769-1782 from, Deed Book L, No.11, and M, No. 12, as compiled by F. Edward Wright; (2) Land Records of Sussex County, Delaware 1782-1789 from Deed Book N, No 13, compiled by Elaine Hastings Mason & F. Edward Wright; and (3) Land Records of Sussex County, Various Dates, compiled by Mary Marshall Brewer, all three published by Family Line Publications of Westminster, Md. Unfortunately, these compilations are not complete for the years 1789-1800, the most likely time of Daniel's receiving the lands he left to his sons; although, as we will see below, Daniel already owned or at least lived on some part of this or adjacent lands. More importantly, an extensive search of Grantor and Grantee indices for Worcester and Sussex Counties for the period 1769-1800 found no mention of any Daniel Evans.

The April 30, 1759, Probate Account of the Estate of William Robinson[123] (will dated March 1757), late of Worcester County, includes under payments and disbursements: "Of money paid Daniel Evans ____ Proved account and rec't appears, 0 Pounds, 2 Schillings and 6 Pence." While we do not know what this debt was for, two Schillings and 6 Pence is the worth of about one day's labor in 1759. Daniel, presumably, was an adult (at least 16) in 1759 and his birth date, therefore, was before 1744. This William Robinson was the son of the Michael Robinson who left to his son, William, "the Plantation he now lives on with 130 acres of land and marsh."[124] This William Robinson lived on Ricketts Chance, 80 acres of which his father Michael had purchased from Joshua Robinson and the balance of which he received when Joshua died.[125] This tract was located on Assawoman Bay. Our Daniel, therefore, was in this area in 1757.

---

121   A bond is a certificate or evidence of a debt. A conveyance bond or agreement of sale of land is a certificate or evidence of a debt, or a debt to be assumed, to be settled by the unexecuted ("made over to him") conveyance of a tract of land.
122   Will of Daniel Evans, op. cit.
123   Probate Account of William Robinson, June 5, 1759, Maryland Hall of Records, Prerogative Court Records of Maryland, Folio P, 43:206.
124   Will of Michael Robinson, October 27, 1753, Maryland Hall of Records, Wills, Liber 29, Folio 151.
125   Dryden, op. cit., p. 521.

The True Inventory of the Goods Chattels Rights and Credits of the late deceased Daniel Barns[126] dated April 13, 1778, includes "To a debt due from Daniel Evans of 5 Shillings." We know from this and Tax Assessment Records, below, that Daniel was in Baltimore Hundred in 1778. Was Sarah the daughter of Daniel Barns?

The Inventory of Assets of Travour Taylor[127] whose December 13, 1783, will was witnessed by John Evans, School Master, includes "to a disporate [difficult to read in original—may be "separate" or "disparate"] debt due from Daniel Evans – 2 schillings." Another difficult entry to decipher indicates Daniel also apparently owed some items to Taylor which may have included bowls and tack (horse harnesses?), so they likely were neighbors. Taylor's son-in-law was Robert Wilgoos, who lived adjacent to the tract of land, <u>Partnership</u>, which was a subject of the John Dazey will.

A Daniel Evans is listed in a February 21, 1765, inventory of James Smyly, merchant, of Snow Hill, Maryland, as owing Smyly 4 pounds, 1 shilling and 11½ pence, a significant debt equal, for example, to the cost of two cows in these times.[128] The inventory was entered in probate of Smyly's estate in 1766. James and his brother, Samuel, had commenced a partnership on February 21, 1765.[129] Smyly clearly was a merchant; the inventory of assets included a long list of stock of a typical store of the times. Samuel was listed as a merchant when he sold part of Lot #13 in Snow Hill Town in 1773.[130] This is a good indication that a Daniel Evans visited or was in Snow Hill in 1765 or before. No other information was found about Daniel Evans in Snow Hill. In the absence of any other references, it is unlikely this was another Daniel.

These two sections and Sections J and K below, which deal with census, tax assessment records, and land records, include the sum and substance of documented facts known to me about any and all Daniels. Unless and until abstracts of Administration and Inventory Accounts and complete compilations of land records with the names of involved parties are published for Baltimore Hundred for the 1750-1800 period, it is not likely further information on Our Daniel will turn up

---

126   True Inventory of the late Daniel Barns, April 13, 1778, Public Archives of Delaware, Sussex County Probate, Daniel Barns, 1778.

127   True Inventory of the late Trevour Taylor, December 13, 1783, Public Archives of Delaware, Sussex County Probate, Trevour Taylor, 1783.

128   Inventory of the Debts Due to James Smyly, Deceased, Maryland Hall of Records, Liber 90, Folios 3211-336.

129   Ibid.

130   Dryden, op. cit., p. 586.

except for those lucky situations where references unexpectedly turn up on other documents reviewed for other purposes. When more abstracts are published of land, will, final inventories, court and other records, more significant information will assuredly shed further light on Daniel and Sarah. Until then, comprehensive research of original files beyond the grantor and grantee indices would be too time-consuming.

G.   ANALYSIS OF THE JOHN DAZEY WILL

The knowledge of the information in the September 23, 1795, John Dazey Sr. will[131] was derived from a note in my Uncle Maurice Daisey's materials on Dazey Family genealogy. This was another stroke of luck, because, without it, there may have been no initial reason to research Dazey Family information for this effort. It would have turned up eventually because John Dazey was the brother of Moses Dazey, a direct, male-line ancestor of my grandmother, Sarah "Nellie" Daisey Evans.

Unfortunately for Daniel/Danneal, this John Dazey did not die until 1811, eleven years after Daniel died and sixteen years after the will was signed. The True Inventory of John Dazey's assets during probate[132] was dated April 27, 1811. Careful review of the original document in the Delaware Public Archives in Dover confirmed the accuracy of the dates. A John Dazey Sr. is included in Tax Assessment Lists, without break, through 1814, presumably when the probate actions were completed. The will was witnessed by the William Evans, the son of John Evans Sr. (as shown by signature comparisons), and by Moses and Jessey Dazey. It was proved by Moses and Jessey in March 1811, William having died earlier in 1811.[133] It can be asked why this 1795 will was drafted long before John Dazey's death. This was certainly not the normal situation in this period when the timing of wills seemed to anticipate dying. Perhaps he suffered from a serious illness in 1795 and recovered.

While Our Daniel may have been an equitable owner of sixty acres of Partnership, he may not have been the seized or recorded owner in 1795, five years before his death. He obviously owned (or believed he did) this or another part in 1798, when he wrote his will, leaving each of his sons one half of Partnership.[134]

---

131   Will of John Dazey, op. cit.
132   True Inventory of the Assets of the late John Dazey, April 27, 1811, Delaware Public Archives, Sussex County Probate, John Dazey, 1795-1811.
133   Will of William Evans (of John Sr.), op. cit.
134   Will of Daniel Evans, op. cit.

Remember, Our Daniel was included in the 1778 Tax Assessment List, so he was a landowner then. He is not listed again until 1789. There are two significant possibilities. We know Our Daniel owned or lived on a tract of land in 1790[135] adjacent to Charles Whaley and in the immediate area of Partnership. The extensive review of land records discussed in Section H suggests Our Daniel may have received a tract of land adjacent to Partnership, which might have been a part of a lot owned by Daniel Wharton Sr., the father of Catherine Wharton Evans. It is also possible that the Partnership provision in the Dazey will was executed in some other unrecorded manner to transfer the land to Daniel in 1795 or even earlier. As discussed in Section H, below, John Dazey did not receive his approved Resurvey of Partnership and Addition until April 10, 1795.[136] This possibly operated as a constraint on recording the conveyance for all these intervening years. Perhaps Daniel was living on this land pursuant to some associated agreement as early as 1778 or 1779.

H.   IMPORTANT LAND RECORDS

The Thomas Dazey, Rhodes Clark and John Evans Sr. Land Transactions:

As discussed in Section F, above, we know from the Inventory of Assets of the Estate of Thomas Dazey Jr. that a Daniel Evans was the brother of a John Evans. We also know from the following land records from that part of Baltimore Hundred in Worcester County, Maryland, that became a part of Sussex County, Delaware, in 1775, that there was a close financial and possibly family or neighbor connection between this Daniel, his brother John, the Dazey family and a Rhodes Clark which requires analysis.

From *Land Records of Worcester County, 1666-1819*[137] (with analysis):

Hazzards Agreement & Evans Venture:

- John Evans of Indian River patented Hazzards Agreement in 1742.
- John Evans of Indian River patented Evans Venture for 100 acres on July 20, 1754, a resurvey of Hazzards Agreement.
- John Evans Sr. sold 100 acres of Evans Venture to Rhodes Clark on Nov. 7, 1757.

---

135   Will of Charles Whaley, op. cit.
136   Sussex County Land Records, Vol. X, #22, p. 447.
137   Dryden, op. cit.

- Resurveyed to <u>Clarks Venture</u> on September 10, 1760.
- Rhodes Clark mortgaged to Thomas Dazey 100 acres on January 9, 1764 (Copy in Appendix 1 of this chapter).
- Rhodes Clark and Thomas Dazey Jr. sold 52½ acres of <u>Evans Venture</u> and <u>Clarks Venture</u> to Joshua Hill in October 1764.

The above <u>Hazzards Agreement</u> and <u>Evans Venture</u> information indicates that John Evans of Indian River was also known as John Evans Sr. This is a key and most useful conclusion when referring to Census records to look for our Daniel's father. John Sr. died in 1795.[138]

While there are information voids on land records, and no original record of a transaction has been found, as noted above, it is not unreasonable to assume the John Dazey bequest to "Danneal Evans," not a known relative, was to satisfy some part of the debt created by the Clark/Dazey mortgage of land sold by John Evans Sr.[139] Did Rhodes Clark not fully pay John Evans Sr.? Did Clark mortgage <u>Evans Venture</u> to Thomas Dazey to pay John Evans' part of the cost of his land? Was there some other obligation remaining? It is also not unreasonable at this point to surmise some relationship between Our Daniel and John Sr.

<u>Partnership, a Bethany Beach Area Land Grant:</u>

This is the tract of land, a part of which was willed to Our Daniel by John Dazey Sr.[140] It was originally patented in Maryland and then resurveyed in Delaware on May 21, 1776, by John Dazey. Additions were made periodically by John Dazey and his son John Dazey Jr.

The original <u>Partnership</u>, before additions, included 215 acres in Baltimore Hundred in Worcester County, 21 acres of which were granted to William Holland on April 22, 1760, by a Special Warrant. Holland assigned this warrant over to a "certain John Dazey Jr." and John Dazey received a Worcester County Patent for 215 acres on September 16, 1760.[141] The land was described as "all that tract of Land called <u>Partnership</u> situate lying and being in the county afsd. Back in the woods from Indian River bounded as follows: beginning at a marked white oak standing on the west end of a ridge on or near the head of a branch called Michaels Mill Branch and

---

138   Probate of the Will of John Evans Sr., Archives of Delaware, Vol. A70, p. 131.
139   See Appendix A of this chapter.
140   Will of John Dazey, op. cit.
141   Worcester County Land Records, Sept. 16, 1760, BC&GS Vol. 13, pp. 570-572.

on the south side of Caesar Godwin's Plantation thence running east 126 poles (*Note: pole, rod = 16.5 feet*) thence southwest for sixty six poles thence west 130 poles thence with a right line to the first bounder containing and was laid out for 215 acres of land more or less." On the back of the certificate was the following. "I have received the sum of Nine Pounds fourteen Shillings for the within vacancy and seven shillings and 5 pence for Improvements Patent. May they issue with his Exce'ys approbation. Approved, Sept. 16, 1760".

John Dazey's Maryland Warrant was accepted by Delaware on May 21, 1776, pursuant to a 1775 proclamation by Governor John Penn of a new Delaware law recognizing the newly defined southern border of Delaware with Maryland which added Baltimore Hundred and its residents and landowners to Sussex County, Delaware.[142] This law also authorized and **required** a resurvey of all tracts, including any adjacent vacant lands authorized to be added to Partnership. Pursuant to this authority, Partnership was resurveyed with an addition of 196½ acres of vacant lands, and the approved Resurvey for 411½ acres was issued on April 10, 1795.[143] Both this Partnership and another Dazey tract, Salt Meadow, are described as being near or adjacent to lands of Andrew Gibbs, Elisha Rickards and John Evans. The Salt Meadow Patent is described as being "on a beach ridge on the east side of a gum swamp" and on the "east side of the head of the sound road between Elisha Rickards and John Evans."[144] This land clearly is north of the head of Assawoman Sound and on or near the ocean beach.

John Dazey Jr. added ninety-nine acres to Partnership via a February 22, 1814, Delaware Patent.[145] This land was originally granted to Thomas Hazzard in 1794 but was now vacant. The lands are described as being adjacent to Halls Lott and Pasture Lott, 77 acres of which was purchased by Daniel Wharton Jr. from Ebenezer and Sophia Evans on June 7, 1758,[146] and owned by him when he died in 1792. A map included in the Partnership Patent shows the addition as being a significant strand of ocean beach. This John Dazey was the son of John Sr., who died in 1811 and whose September 23, 1795, will[147] included the provision leaving 60 acres of Partnership to Our Daniel that is discussed in detail in Section F.

---

142   Scharf, Vol. I, op. cit. p. 123
143   Sussex County Land Records, Vol. X, p. 447.
144   Ibid., Vol. T, p. 74.
145   Ibid., Vol. U, p. 331.
146   Dryden, op. cit., p. 464.
147   Will of John Dazey, op. cit.

The land willed to Our Daniel is described in the will as being part of Partnership, specifically, sixty acres in the southwest corner. Parts of Partnership including the Resurvey were also left to Dazey's sons, George and Joseph Dazey, and is partially described as starting at the home line of Joseph Dazey and (Quoted as close as possible to original) "on a line to a marked maple Staning Close to a path that leads from Dannel Evans to Robbert Wilgoos thence with the lines of the Resurvay twenty poles furter towards Dannel Evans thence north till it strikes Dannel Evans line that I will to him thence running the line that I will to Dannel till it comes to George Dazey first beginning . . ."

While it has not been possible to locate exactly Our Daniel's lands, we know from the above discussion that it is part of a large gum swamp on the east side of the head of the Sound (Assawoman Bay's headwaters) and along a beach ridge (sand dune) along the ocean. It probably includes a part of the original 430-acre, South Petherton land grant in 1688 to a Matthew Scarborough, parts of which were owned in later years by Dazeys, Whartons and Evanses.

Our Daniel's home probably was on land back from the ocean in what is now the south end of Bethany Beach and the North end of South Bethany that he owned or occupied before the Dazey will and the Partnership Resurvey as discussed in the preceding section. This location, adjacent to Daniel Wharton's Pasture Lott and close to lands of John and Catherine Evans, lends weight to the surmise that Our Daniel was the son of John and Catherine and the grandson of Daniel Wharton. Our Daniel probably received his home lands either from Daniel Wharton or John and Catherine Wharton Evans.

Our Daniel left one half of his part of Partnership to each of his sons, Daniel and Zadoc, pursuant to his will of September 3, 1798.[148] Unfortunately, for some reason, this Partnership is not included in *Dryden's Land Records of Worcester County, Maryland, 1666-1810* under either the William Holland or Dazey names. Dryden does include a Partnership patented by Thomas Wildgoose on October 7, 1761, for 504 acres, a resurvey of Pearson's Choice.[149] This same Thomas Wildgoose, who was the father of Robert Wilgoos,[150] also patented Sandy Ridge in 1760, part of which was owned by Our Daniel's son, Zadoc, and left by Zadoc in 1849 to his son, Clemeth Evans, and grandson, Zadoc Aydelotte.[151] (Note: both

---

148   Will of Daniel Evans, op. cit.
149   Dryden, op. cit., p. 458.
150   Will of Robert Wildgoos, December 28, 1781, Sussex County Wills, Liber E, Folios 43-44.
151   Will of Zadoc Evans, February 5, 1848, Sussex County Wills, Liber K, Folio 43.

Wildgoose and Wilgoos are included in documents as variations of today's Wilgus).

There were many tracts named <u>Partnership</u> in Sussex and Worcester at this time and it was confusing initially and thought that the Wildgoos <u>Partnership</u> near Roxana was the tract later owned by John Dazey and was the <u>Partnership</u> left to Our Daniel. This clearly is not the case as discussed above, but it demonstrates pitfalls in land records research. Information from research on <u>Sandy Ridge</u> is given below; it may be useful to other researchers. It is also included below in Chapter 4 on Our Daniel's son, Zadoc.

<u>Daniel Wharton's Lands Adjacent to Partnership:</u>

Daniel Wharton Jr./Sr. (son of Daniel Sr.) left a tract adjacent to his son, Daniel Jr.,[152] that probably was a part of <u>Pasture Lott</u>. Another of Daniel Wharton's sons, Isiah, had land adjacent to the 1814 <u>Addition to Partnership</u>. This raises the question whether Catherine Wharton Evans, an heir of Daniel Wharton Sr., or her husband, John Sr. might have given land to Our Daniel. One could speculate that this might have happened because if Our Daniel is the son of John Sr. and Catherine, he is the grandson of Daniel Wharton Sr. This is circumstantial evidence and not proof, but it has considerable weight.

<u>Sandy Ridge, a Roxana Area Land Grant:</u>

Our Daniel's son, Zadoc, in his 1848 will,[153] bequeathed equal parts of <u>Sandy Ridge</u> to his son, Clemeth, and his grandson, Zadoc Aydelotte Evans. It was initially thought this was an important clue to the location of Our Daniel's home, because the widow of the William Robinson who purchased 106 acres of <u>Sandy Ridge</u> in 1761[154] married William Evans, the son of John Sr., in 1783.[155] It was not unreasonable to surmise that Our Daniel had somehow obtained <u>Sandy Ridge</u> from him. This was not the case at all, however. A check of land records determined that Zadoc had purchased approximately fifty acres of <u>Sandy Ridge</u> on February 9, 1829, from a John Lynch[156] who had purchased the land on February 3, 1829, from Thomas

---

152   Will of Daniel Wharton Sr., June 22, 1785 (Admitted to probate August 8, 1792), Sussex County Wills, Liber D, pp. 371-372.
153   Will of Zadoc Evans, op. cit.
154   Maryland Land Records, Microfilm 13-73, p. 206.
155   Probate of Will of William Robinson, December 15, 1783, Public Archives of Delawares, Vol. A96, p. 192.
156   Sussex County Deeds, Georgetown, DE, Book 40, Folio 70.

Robinson, a son of William Robinson. This tract has been positively identified as being located on the Roxana-Johnson's Corner Road.[157]

I.   ANALYSIS OF OTHER WILL AND PROBATE RECORDS

The Will of Thomas Dazey - The Inventory and Accounts records of the administration of the 1777[158] will of Thomas Dazey Jr. included the paying of a debt of 10 pounds and 5 shillings to Rhodes Clark and 5 shillings and 6 pence to a John Evans, possibly John Sr. This could be further evidence of relationships, adding some weight to the surmised Daniel Evans - John Evans Sr. relationship. As discussed above, there are no concomitant land conveyance records that might explain the relationship.

Catherine's Granddaughters - The September 22, 1797, will of Catherine Evans,[159] the wife of John Evans Sr., included as heirs her granddaughters, **Elizabeth, Mary, Sarah Cord, Ann and Martha Evans**; a Sarah whose relationship is not listed even though she is included in the will in the middle of a series of the named granddaughters; her grandson, John Cord Evans; and her son-in-law, William Evans. Our Daniel provided for his daughters, Elizabeth Evans and Martha Taylor, in his 1800 will. **Are they the granddaughters, Elizabeth and Martha?**

Our Daniel's daughter, Martha, is identified in his September 1, 1798, will as Martha Taylor. The granddaughter, Martha, in Catherine's September 22, 1797, will is identified as Martha Evans. This leaves three possible conclusions: (1) They are a different Martha, (2) Martha married after Catherine's 1797 will and before our Daniel's 1798 will, and (3) Catherine did not include Martha's married name in her will. There was another Martha Taylor who was married to a Tandy Taylor. They both witnessed the will of a Parthena Tingle in 1791. If she is Our Daniel's daughter, this would mean she was Our Daniel's oldest child and was born in 1773 or earlier. Without extensive further research which it is not believed would bear fruit, there are no answers. It is quite possible to believe there was more than one Martha. The

---

157   A comparison of current tax maps with a map of Sandy Ridge included in Sussex County Chancery Court proceedings of a suit for division of Sandy Ridge by Clemeth Evans was conclusive. The bounds of present day tracts matched exactly with a map in the Chancery Court documents.

158   True Inventory of the Assets of Thomas Dazey, op. cit.

159   Will of Catherine Evans, September 27, 1797, Sussex County Wills, Liber E. Folio 135.

discussion below on John Cord Evans tends to confirm there was more than one Martha.

The paragraph on John Evans Sr. in *A Somerset Sampler*[160] lists John and Catherine Evans' sons as Ebenezer, John, and William. Notwithstanding this listing of Ebenezer as their son, the time line in Appendix 2 of this chapter demonstrates that Ebenezer is not the son of John Sr. and Catherine, so Ebenezer and Sophia's daughter, Sarah, is not Catherine's granddaughter.

Catherine's son, John Jr., in his October 30, 1786, will,[161] provided for his daughters, **Elizabeth** (age 21 in 1786), **Mary** (age 14 in 1786), Tabitha (age 11 in 1786), and Catherine (age 7 in 1786). The daughters' ages are from birth dates in *A Somerset Sampler*.[162]

An extensive review of the wills of the numerous contemporary, local William Evanses provided no clue to the names of William's daughters. The 1800 United States Census lists two persons of the name William Evans Sr. One had two daughters and the other had three. John Sr. and Catherine's son, William, married Sarah Cord who was the daughter of John and Rhoda Cord. Rhoda Cord's will[163] names her daughter, Sarah Evans, and a son-in-law, William Evans. The will of Catherine Evans provides for a granddaughter, **Sarah Cord Evans**, and a grandson, John Cord Evans. Further, the will of Catherine's grandson, John Cord Evans,[164] made on September 15, 1809, left everything to his father, William, who was the son of John Sr. and Catherine Evans. John Cord Evans and Sarah Cord Evans clearly are two of the children of Sarah and William Evans and the grandchildren of John Sr. and Catherine Wharton Evans.

Even though John Cord's 1809 will does not name heirs other than his father, two of the witnesses are **Ann** and **Martha Evans**. Unfortunately, this could mean that Ann and Martha Evans are also the sisters of John Cord Evans and Sarah Cord Evans, the daughters of William and the granddaughters of Catherine. Such an implication possibly negates a level of proof of a tie of Our Daniel to Catherine via his daughter, Martha Taylor, who might otherwise have been the Martha mentioned

---

160   Batchelder, op. cit., p. 104.
161   Will of John Evans Jr. (M.N.), October 30, 1786, Sussex County Wills, Liber D, Folios 195-196.
162   Ibid.
163   Will of Rhoda Cord, December 30, 1784, Sussex County Wills, Liber D, p. 187-188.
164   Will of John Cord Evans, September 15, 1809, Sussex County Wills, Liber F, p. 440.

in Catherine's will. While Daniel still might be Catherine's son, a tie via his daughter Martha remains unproven; wishful thinking doesn't make it so. Further, no other Ann Evans has surfaced.

While Catherine's granddaughters may be identified and possibly included, Our Daniel's daughters, Martha Taylor and Elizabeth, a question remains: Who was the Sarah in Catherine's will?[165] No granddaughter, Sarah (no last name), has been identified and it raises the question whether this Sarah might be the wife of Our Daniel; although, she could also be the Sarah who was the wife of Catherine's son, William, and the daughter of John and Rhoda Cord. This analysis of Catherine's will leaves us with very indefinite and, therefore, weak, additional circumstantial evidence of a relationship between Catherine and Our Daniel.

J.   CENSUS, TAX ASSESSMENT AND DEBT BOOK RECORDS

The 1782 Reconstructed Census for Baltimore Hundred[166] lists five persons named John Evans (children are not included):

	Assessment	Notes
John	12	M. N. (Muddy Neck)
John	2	Constable
John	4	Of Ebe
John	4	Miller
John Sr.	10	–

The 1785 Baltimore Hundred Tax Assessment list from Scharf's *History of Delaware*[167] includes the following John Evans landowners:

Evans, John Sr.
Evans, John Jr.
Evans, John
Evans, John (miller)
Evans, John in Dagsboro Hundred

---

165   Will of Catherine Evans, op. cit.
166   Ralph D. Nelson, et. al., *Delaware – 1782, Tax Assessment and Census Lists* (Wilmington, DE: Delaware Genealogical Society 1994).
167   Scharf, *Vol. II*, op. cit. p. 1341.

The 1790 Reconstructed Census of Baltimore Hundred[168] includes the following relevant Evanses:

> Catherine
> Daniel
> John, Constble
> John of Ebe
> John Sr.

This Census was reconstructed from Tax Assessment lists because the first U. S. Census of Delaware either was lost when the British burned Washington during the War of 1812 or it never reached Washington. Only the taxable heads of families are included; non-property owners are not recorded.

The 1800 U. S. Census of Baltimore Hundred under Evans includes:

> Daniel with two males (16-26), two females (10-16) and a female over 45
> Catherine with a male 10/16 and a female over 45.
> No John Evans

The U. S. Census registered not only heads of families and family members but also registered all other free persons and slaves.

In addition to the above lists that have been included in other publications, the Tax Assessment lists for Baltimore Hundred are available for most years from 1775 through 1816, when checking ceased, and thereafter. They include a wealth of information, some of which is included in the following table which goes through 1802:

Sussex County Levy Court Tax Assessment Lists for Baltimore Hundred

Year	Relevant **Evans** Listings (Notes are as close as possible to originals)
1775	**Daniel**, John, John Jr., John (Sea Side), William Evans (Son of John), John (Head of Sound, probably John, Const.)

---

168   Leon DeValinger Jr., *Reconstructed Census of Delaware* (Genealogical Publication of the National Genealogical Society, No. 10, January, 1954, Washington, D. C.).

84

1776	The Volume is missing.
1777	John (Muddy Neck), John (Son of Ebe), John (Cedar Neck), John (?) (**Note: No Daniel – probably an oversight, but maybe not**)
1778	**Daniel**, John (Const.), John (Cedar Neck.), John (Muddy Neck), John (Son of Ebe.)
1779	John (Cedar Neck) – List is very short and obvious names from 1778 and 1780 are missing.
1780	John (of Ebe.), John (Muddy Neck), John (Cedar Neck), John (Con.), John (Jr. of Maj. – difficult to read). John Jr., son of Maj. Evans of West Berlin Evans, apparently briefly owned land in Baltimore Hundred – this was not researched further.
1781	John (C.N.) – List is abbreviated
1782	John (M.N.), John Sr., John (Con.), John of Ebe, John (Miller)
1784, 1786-7	John (M.N.), John Sr., John (Const.) John (Miller) disappeared from list after 1785.
1788	John, Catherine, John Evans (Const.), John (of Ebe.) Note that John (M.N.) is not included; however, his wife Catherine (also a Catherine Wharton Evans, the daughter of Hinman Wharton[169]) is included in lieu of him. John Jr. who was also known as John (M.N.) died in 1788. The John that is included is John Sr. who is also known as John of Cedar Neck.
1789	**Daniel**, John Sr., Catherine , John (Const.), John (of Ebe.)
1790-1791	**Daniel**, John Sr.,Catherine, John (Const.), John (of Ebe)
1794	**Daniel**, John (Cedar Neck), Catherine, John (of Ebe). Note that John (Const.) disappears from the list. The John Evans known as School Master died in 1794. John, Constable, and John, School Master, must be the same person.
1795	**Daniel**, John (C.N.), Catherine. Note that John of Ebe is not on this list. His father, Ebenezer, died in 1793, and John of Ebe reappears in 1796 as John M.
1796	**Daniel Sr., Daniel (farmer)**, Catherine (C.N.), Catherine (M.N.), John M. Note that John Sr. died in 1795.
1797	**Daniel Sr., Daniel (farmer)**, Catherine (M.N.), John M. Note that Catherine of Cedar Neck died in 1797.

---

169   Batchelder, op. cit., p. 104.

1799	**Daniel Sr., Daniel Jr.**, John M., Catherine (M.N.), Margaret (who is wife of John, Constable/School Master).
1800	**Daniel Jr.**, John M., Catherine (M.N.), Margaret. Note that Our Daniel died in 1800.
1801	**Daniel, Zadoc of Daniel** (Note: There is also a Zadoc of William), John M. (heirs), Daniel Sr. (Must be heirs who are taxed until estate is settled. Daniel Sr.'s estate was not settled for a few years), Margaret.
1802	Daniel, Zadoc of Daniel, **Daniel Sr.** (heirs?), Margaret.

In each case in the above table where it is noted that an individual has died, the basis is the confirmed date of acceptance of the relevant will into probate.

Worcester County Debt Books for 1762, 1768, 1769, 1773, 1774[170]

Knowing Our Daniel was listed in the Sussex County Levy Court Tax Assessment Lists for 1775 and 1778, The Worcester Debt Books were carefully reviewed for the preceding years with no success. No Daniel was listed for any of the above years. Further, no other Baltimore Hundred Evans was listed in the Debt Books except for the following who owned lands in Worcester County, but not that part of Baltimore Hundred which became part of Sussex County in 1775:

| 1768-9 | John Evans of Muddy Creek – New Addition and Teagues Contentment, William Riley Evans – Showell Addition, Cropton, Temple Hall, Little |
| 1794 | John Evans (Ceder Neck, sic) – Chance William Riley Evans – Same as 1768-9 |

The John Evans of Muddy Creek is John Evans Jr. who lived in Muddy Neck. The lands, New Addition and Teagues Contentment, were in St. Martins District and were sold by John Jr. and his wife, Catherine, to John Holloway in 1772.

This John Evans of Cedar Neck patented the tract, Chance, in St. Martins District in 1768. In 1785, now a resident of Sussex County, he sold Chance, which

---

170   Debt Books are the record of the rents due by the present owner of a patent to the Lord Proprietor who granted patents. They include rent payers in alphabetical order with a list of each payer's patent. Available Debt Books are maintained in the Maryland Hall of Records as the Debt Book Series. The Worcester County Debt Books for the period given herein are in Folio 53, except for 1773 which is bound with the Somerset County Debt Book for 1755.

was improved with grist and saw mills, to Henry Bell. Apparently, when he moved to Sussex County he settled in Cedar Neck. This John Evans was known as John Evans (Miller) in contrast to John Sr., who also lived in Cedar Neck.

William Riley Evans also had lands in St. Martins District.

These John Evanses are discussed in more detail in <u>Section M, Sorting Out the Many John Evanses of Baltimore Hundred</u>.

Nothing in the Debt Books contradicted any other record or conclusion. It is most perplexing that there are no listings in the Debt Books of owners of lands in that part of Baltimore Hundred which became part of Sussex County in 1775. Why? The only reasons which can be offered are: (1) remoteness from the County Seat in Snow Hill and (2) the ongoing issue between Maryland and the Penns over where the Delaware-Maryland boundary was located. It is disappointing this information is not available.

K.   <u>ANALYSIS OF CENSUS AND TAX ASSESSMENT RECORDS:</u>

• Our Daniel was included in Tax Assessment Records in 1775 and 1778; he was a taxable landowner. The 1776 Volume is missing, and his not being listed in 1777 may be an error. He does not reappear in the Records until 1789. What was he doing and where was he?
• Our Daniel was included in both the 1789-1799 Tax Assessment Records and the 1800 Census. He became a taxable or full land owner again in 1789 and probably also became an equitable but not taxable owner of <u>Partnership</u> in 1795 or earlier, <u>perhaps even as early as 1778</u>.
• We know from our Daniel's will and its probate that he died in 1800.
• We know from the 1850 U. S. Census of Baltimore Hundred that our Daniel's youngest son, Zadoc, was 72 years old, and was, therefore, born in 1778. He was 22 when our Daniel died.
• Assuming Our Daniel's son, Daniel Jr., the oldest son, was born two years before Zadoc, he was born in 1776. Zadoc appears in the Tax Assessment records five years after Daniel, so Daniel may be four or five years older than Zadoc, and he may have been born as early as 1772, but there is nothing else to confirm this possibility.
• Assuming Daniel Sr. and Sarah were married as much as two years before the birth of their first child, Daniel, they were likely married in 1774 or 1775, and possibly as early as 1771 or before.
• Assuming Our Daniel was over 21 when he married Sarah, he was born before 1754 and was at least 46 when he died.

- We know from the 1800 Census that a female in Daniel's household was over 45 in 1800, the year of Daniel's death. If this were Daniel's wife, Sarah, and if Daniel were not much older than his wife, he would have been just over 45 when he died in 1800. This is one possibility, but it is also possible that Daniel could have married late, 30 or over, and been significantly older than his wife. We know from the Prerogative Court records discussed in Section L that a Daniel Evans received a cash payment from the settlement of the Estate of William Robinson in 1758. If this is Our Daniel, he was clearly at least a teenager in 1758, and he was born before 1745. This is consistent with his marrying late and being over 60 when he died. Either possibility is consistent with 52 years elapsing between the deaths of Our Daniel and his son, Zadoc.

The two possibilities from the above are that Daniel was born before 1745 or around 1754. The 1754 date of birth is inconsistent with the William Robinson payment in 1758. The 1754 date of birth would mean there was a second Daniel, and there is no evidence to support this possibility. If Our Daniel were born before 1745 and his father lived to be around 70, he probably died before 1796. The date of the death of Our Daniel's father could possibly be circumstantial evidence to help confirm his identity.

L.   WHAT WE KNOW ABOUT THE MANY EVANSES NAMED JOHN

We know that a Daniel Evans had a brother John Evans, so he may also have been the son of a John; it seems all Johns named a son John. From all the preceding, including the John Dazey will and Our Daniel's land adjacent to Partnership, it is reasonable to suspect strongly this was John Evans Sr. The next step then was to review everything known about each contemporary John Evans. All information found is included because, while some entries may not help identify the brother, John, or confirm John Sr. as Our Daniel's father, it might help exclude other Johns. The full information may also assist other researchers on this or other puzzles.

From <u>Census Records</u>:

We know that there were at least five different land-owning John Evanses in Baltimore Hundred during the relevant period. These are discussed in detail in Section M, Sorting Out the Many John Evanses of Baltimore Hundred. While there may have been others who were not land owners, they do not show up in the records.

From <u>Land Records of Worcester, County, Maryland, 1666-1818</u>[171]

Note: See also the information in <u>Section H, Important Land Records</u>, which addresses <u>Hazzards Agreement</u> and <u>Evans Venture</u> and the John Evans-Rhodes Clark-Thomas Dazey transactions, including the mortgage or indenture.

- John Evans (son of Walter) and wife Priscilla sold 70 acres of <u>South Petherton</u> to William Evans on June 10, 1735, that Walter Evans willed to sons John and William.

- William Holland of Indian River sold 287 acres of <u>Hollands Discovery</u> to John Evans (of West Berlin) on March 16, 1759. John willed 300 acres to daughter Elizabeth Tunnel.

- Daniel Wharton with wife Esther; John Evans with wife Catherine; and William Melson with wife Ann in 1761 sold to Matthew Wise 42 acres of <u>Hog Quarter</u> that Daniel Wharton Sr. had patented in 1742 and willed to his children in 1752. John Evans' wife Catherine was the daughter of Daniel Wharton.

- Joshua Holloway sold 120 acres of <u>New Addition</u> to John Evans on October 30, 1761.

- Joshua Evans patented <u>Timber Land</u> for 50 acres in 1748 and Joshua Evans with wife Betty sold 50 acres to John Evans **in** Muddy Neck on March 11, 1765. <u>Timber Land</u>, now called <u>Beauty</u> in Sussex County Land Warrants, was owned by John Evans on July 9, 1776.

- Joshua Holloway sold 30 acres of <u>New Addition</u> to John Evans **of** Muddy Neck on May 8, 1764.

- William Evans in 1764 willed part of 250 acres of <u>North Petherton</u> that he had purchased in 1719 from Robert and Elizabeth Johnson to his son John Evans, 100 acres to son Solomon Evans, and 100 acres to son Elisha Evans in 1764. John Evans resurveyed to Sussex County land warrants 102 acres on February 27, 1776.

- John Onions and his wife Susanna sold 20 acres of <u>Adkins Lot</u> in Muddy Neck to John Evans in 1765.

- John Evans, son of "Jumping John" in 1769 patented 49 acres called <u>Stevens Island</u> in St. Martins District #5.

---

171   Dryden, op. cit. (The tract names in this work are listed in alphabetical order. The particular John Evans in each bulleted paragraph is not always identified; although spouse or family names may provide important clues.)

• John Evans (of Muddy Neck) with wife Catherine sold 120 acres of <u>New Addition</u> to John Holloway on September 17, 1772.

• John Evans of Muddy Neck with his wife Catherine sold his part of <u>Teagues Content</u> (St. Martins District), which was purchased from Joshua Holloway in 1761, to John Holloway on September 22, 1772.

• John Evans patented <u>Chance</u> for 60 acres in St. Martins Neck on October 11, 1768, and John Evans, now of Sussex County, Delaware, sold these to Henry Bell on August 15, 1785. Land was improved with grist and sawmills.

• John Evans sold 60 acres of <u>South Petherton</u> to Solomon Evans, his brother, on February 18, 1761.

From *Calendar of Sussex County Delaware Probate Records 1680-1800*[172] (With author's commentary)

• John Evans and William Evans witnessed the November 12, 1777, will of Thomas Dazey Sr. The signature of this John Evans in 1777 clearly is the same as that of John Evans Sr. on his 1791 will, even though the 1791 signature is that of a wobbly and possibly infirm man. The signature of the William Evans, who witnessed the John Dazey will in September 1795, is identical to the signature of the William Evans on the Inventory of the assets of John Evans Sr. who died in 1795 and was the husband of Catherine Wharton Evans. The John Sr. and William Evans signatures as witnesses further demonstrate a relationship between the Evans and Dazey families.

• John Evans (signature appears to be School Master), Moses Dazey and Eliphaz Dazey were witnesses to the will of Thomas dated May 12, 1778.

• John Evans (signature appears to be School Master) was witness to December 13, 1784, will of Travour Taylor. Heirs included Taylor's son-in-law Robert Wilgoos.

• John Evans, School Master, was witness to the August 1, 1783, will of Mary Lockwood.

• John Evans, School Master, was witness to the May 3, 1785, will of Joshua Evans who had a son, William. John's wife Margaret was also a witness.

• John Evans, School Master (named in will as "School Master"), was named executor in the September 9, 1787, will of Elisabeth Callaway.

• John Evans, D.B.N. granted as Administrator of will of William Callaway in lieu of Elizabeth Callaway, granted before May 9, 1788.

---

172   Leon De Valinger Jr., *Calendar of Sussex County Delaware Probate Records 1680-1800* (Public Archives Commission of the State of Delaware, 1964). (Entries in chronological order.).

- The will of John Evans Jr., made October 30, 1786, and entered into probate on November 4, 1788, listed as heirs: sons John, Job, Enoch, Elijah and Eli Evans and daughters Elizabeth, Mary, Tabitha and Catherine Evans. The original of this will is not available in the Delaware Public Archives.

- John Evans, Daniel Evans and Robert Evans witnessed the April 10, 1790, will of Charles Whaley.

- John Evans (appears from signature that it was School Master) was witness to the March 18, 1790, will of Robert Barnes. This John Evans is the same John Evans who witnessed the Charles Whaley will along with Daniel and Robert Evans. The signatures are identical and they were signed within weeks of each other.

- John Evans was a witness to the October 3, 1788, will of William Rickards.

- John M. Evans was an heir in the March 1, 1793, will of Ebenezer Evans Sr.

- John Evans, School Master, Our Daniel and John Dazey were witnesses to the September 22, 1793, will of Elizabeth McDaniel. The John Dazey was the one who left land to Daniel Evans.

- The will of John Evans, School Master, was made June 6, 1791, listing as heirs wife, Margret (sic), and children Joney, Azarian, Thomas, Edey, Charlotte and Barsheba. (Was Joney a John?)

- The will of John Evans Sr. was made on February 15, 1791, and entered into probate on May 27, 1794, listing as heirs: wife Catherine, sons John and William and daughters Rebecca Mumford, Elizabeth Dale and Mary Hall. Witnesses included James Wharton, who probably was a close relative of Catherine Wharton Evans.

From <u>Maryland Calendar of Wills</u>

- The will of Daniel Wharton Sr. made on December 18, 1762,[173] left land to daughters Catherine (wife of John Evans Sr.) and Nannie, and son Daniel (<u>Hog Quarter</u> and "tract I now live on"),[174] and sons, Himmom (<u>Water Melon Hammock</u>, thence to sea), Baker (<u>Buck's Delight</u>), George (<u>Daniel's Luck</u>).

- A Joshua Evans of Worcester County in his July 1, 1773,[175] will left to a son John after the "death of my wife [Betty] [the] plantation, [a] desk and a hand

---

173   Will of Daniel Wharton, <u>Maryland Calendar of Wills</u>, Volume 10, p. 281.
174   The "tract I now live on" is part of the 265 acres of an old patent, <u>Cedar Neck</u>, which Daniel Wharton purchased in 1727 from the heirs of William Whittington. This tract extended from Whites Creek to the Fresh Pond in present day Cedar Neck.
175   Will of Joshua Evans, July 1, 1773, <u>Maryland Calendar of Wills</u> 1772-1774, Vol. 15, p. 62.

mill." This Joshua had a son Joshua who was also named as an heir. Possibly this was the tract Summerfields.[176]

• William Evans Jr., the brother of John Sr. and the son of William Sr., left "clothing" to sons Caleb and John.[177] Caleb and John were probably teenagers or young men in 1763. This John is a nephew of John Sr. and Catherine Wharton Evans.[178] No other records of this John were found.

From Prerogative Court Records of Maryland[179]

• A Daniel Evans received payment of 2 shillings, 6 pence from estate of William Robinson on April 30, 1759.

• A Daniel Evans was a debtor to the estate of James Smyly of Snow Hill in 1765.

From *A Somerset Sampler*[180]

• The John Evans who was determined, above, to be known also as John Evans of Indian River, John Evans of Cedar Neck and John Evans Sr., married Catherine Wharton, the daughter of Daniel Wharton c. 1738. They are reported in *A Somerset Sampler* to have had children (1) Ebenezer who died in 1793, (2) John who was born in March 1740/1741, (3) William, (4) Rebecca, (5) Elizabeth who was born in April 1746 and (6) Mary. The son, John Evans, married another Catherine Wharton, the daughter of Hinman Wharton c. 1760. John Evans Sr. was the son of William and Catherine White Evans. As discussed earlier and in Appendix 2, notwithstanding the inclusion of an Ebenezer in the list of their sons, we know that John Sr. and Catherine did not have a son, Ebenezer. The will of John Sr. includes sons,

---

176   Dryden, op. cit., p. 618.
177   Will of William Evans, October 24, 1763, Maryland Calendar of Wills 1764-1767, Vol. 13, p. 2.
178   This relationship is established via land records of the tracts Morris Purchase and Evans Addition (Dryden, op. cit. pp. 211 and 411) which establish that William Jr. is the son of the William Sr. who was also the father of John Sr. (Batchelder, op. cit., p. 103).
179   Estate of William Robinson, Prerogative Court Records of Maryland, op. cit.
180   Batchelder, op. cit., p. 104.

John and William, but no Ebenezer.[181] The will of Catherine Evans[182] does not include a son Ebenezer.

From Church Records in Baltimore and Dagsboro Hundreds

- Blackwater Church: Built in 1767. Ebenezer and a John Evans were elders, and a John and William Evans were financial supporters.[183]
- Prince George's Chapel (Dagsboro): Land was purchased in June 1755, from Walter Evans, a brother of John Sr.[184]

From *They Lived in Somerset, 1725-50*[185]

Includes a reference to a Daniel Evans in 1728. This Daniel died in 1728; the Inventory and Account of his estate was dated May 20, 1728. No other information was found about this Daniel.

M. SORTING OUT THE MANY JOHN EVANSES OF BALTIMORE HUNDRED

Six John Evanses in Baltimore Hundred are reviewed: John Sr., John (Miller), John (of Ebe), John (M.N.), John, Constable/School Master, and John, the son of William Jr. and grandson of William Sr.

From land records and the discussion in Section H, we know that John Sr. is also John Evans of Indian River, and from Tax Assessment Records we know he is also known as John Evans of Cedar Neck. He married Catherine Wharton Evans whose family included a son, John, Jr.

---

181   Will of John Evans Sr., February 15, 1791, Sussex County Wills, Liber E, Folios 48-49.
182   Will of Catherine Evans, op. cit.
183   F. Edward Wright, *Vital Records of Kent and Sussex Counties Delaware, 1686-1800* (Westminster, Md: Family Line Publications, 1987, 1994), p. 154.
184   Dryden, op. cit., p. 162.
185   Wilmer O. Lankford, *They Lived in Somerset, 1726-50* (Princess Anne, Md: Manokin Press, 1992) pp. 24 & 43.

John (Miller) appears to be the John Evans from St. Martins Neck who had a saw and grist mill. According to Dryden,[186] this John patented Chance in St. Martins District on October 11, 1768. Further, this John, now of Cedar Neck in Sussex County in 1785,[187] sold Chance, including a grist and saw mill, to Henry Bell. He disappeared from the Tax Assessment lists in 1784. The 1783 and the 1785 Lists are missing. Did he live with a Cedar Neck Evans such as Ebenezer and Sophia or John Sr. and Catherine? Land records were not searched to attempt to answer the question, and relevance is doubtful.

John (of Ebe) is John M. Evans who was the son of Ebenezer and Sophia Evans. Ebenezer's will[188] includes his wife Sophia and sons, John and Samuel, as heirs. Sophia's will[189] lists son, John M. Evans, as an heir.

John (M.N.) is John Evans Jr., the son of John Evans Sr. and Catherine Wharton Evans. M.N. stands for Muddy Neck which includes a lot of what is now Bethany Beach and the current Muddy Neck, the area between today's Bethany Beach and Ocean View and the Assawoman Bay. This John was born March 11, 1740/1, and died in 1788. He married another Catherine Wharton, the daughter of Hinman Wharton, c. 1760.[190] John Jr. and Catherine had sons, John, Job, Enoch, Elijah and Eli.[191] John of Muddy Neck and Catherine sold New Addition, land in West Berlin, to John Holloway on Sept. 17, 1772, that John had purchased in 1764 (at approximate age 24) from Joshua Holloway.[192] John and Catherine of Muddy Neck also sold Teagues Content in St. Martins Neck District to John Holloway on September 29, 1772.

John, Constable or School Master, was first included in Sussex County Tax Assessment Lists in 1778 and possibly in 1775 as John, Head of Sound (northern end of Big Assawoman Bay). The listings may have meant he was a landholder in Baltimore Hundred in Worcester County before it became a part of Sussex County,

186   Dryden, op. cit., p. 109.
187   Debt Books of Worcester County, op. cit., 1774.
188   Will of Ebenezer Evans, March 1, 1793, Sussex County Wills, Liber D, Folios 390-391.
189   Will of Sophia Evans, April 13, 1799, Sussex County Wills, Liber E, Folios 239-240.
190   Batchelder, op. cit., p. 104.
191   Will of John Evans Jr. (M.N.), op. cit.
192   Dryden, op. cit., p. 426-427.

but it was not possible to confirm this by reviewing Worcester County Debt Books; because, as discussed in Section J, they do not exist for these years.

John, School Master, was married to Margaret,[193] and he died in 1794. Margaret appears in the Tax Assessment Lists from 1799 through 1802, and "Margaret, heirs" then appears through 1815. This can only be because one or more of their children was a minor when he died, and the designation was retained in the lists, over twenty years after John's death. His and Margaret's youngest child apparently reached adulthood (21) in 1815 and was, therefore, born in about 1794. They had other very young children when he died in 1794, and it is likely that he died as a fairly young man, possibly at about age 35. Our Daniel was about 50 years old when John, School Master, died. While John, School Master, could be Our Daniel's brother, it is unlikely because of their age difference. It can't be fully discounted, however, because Our Daniel signed School Master's Executor's Bond during probate of his will.

The sixth John is the son of William Jr., grandson of William Sr. and nephew of John Sr. His father, William Jr., died in 1763, before his grandfather, William Sr. The reference to this John in William Jr.'s. will is discussed briefly in Section L. A simple time line would indicate he was probably born between 1740 (43 years after his grandfather was born) and about 1760 (before his father died). If this John and his brother Caleb were teenagers or young men in 1763 (the date of their father's will which left them "clothing,") they were possibly about the same age as Our Daniel. There are no other known records of this John. The absence of a Daniel in William Jr.'s will would seem to negate the possibility that this John is Our Daniel's brother.

N.   OUR DANIEL, BROTHER TO A JOHN EVANS

As discussed earlier, the most important fact found in the extensive research of probate records to help identify Our Daniel is the **"brother to Daniel"** entry in the 1778 True Inventory and Accounts from the administration records of the Estate of Thomas Dazey Sr.[194] first discussed in Section F. The appraiser who included the "brother to Daniel" entry wanted to identify clearly which John was in debt to Thomas Dazey. As noted in Section F, the entry defines the problem of this chapter: Which Baltimore Hundred John Evans was Our Daniel's brother, and who was his father?

---

193   Will of John Evans (School Master), op. cit.
194   True Inventory of the Goods Chattles [sic] Rights and Credits of the Late Deceased Thomas Dazey, op. cit.

There were four reported John Evanses in Baltimore Hundred in 1778:[195]

- John (Cedar Neck), who was John Sr.
- John (Const.), also known as School Master
- John M.N., who was John Jr., the son of John Sr.
- John, Son of Ebe(nezer),who was named John M.

Why did he write, "brother to Daniel," in 1778? It would seem that if he were John, School Master, the appraiser would have so stated since he was well known by this designation. However, the first public acknowledgment of "School Master" known to me was in the 1787 will of Elisabeth Calloway.[196] If he were John M. of Ebenezer, the appraiser would likely have written "of Ebe." On the other hand, if Our Daniel is the son of John Sr., he could have stated, "of John Sr." or "brother to Daniel." The possible answer is that "brother to Daniel" was the easiest way to make it obvious, because there were numerous other Johns and only one Daniel. It is useful to note that other debtors in the True Inventory were Eliphas Dazey, Benjamin Taylor, William Robinson, William Clark, and Jonathan Dazey, individually; and Peter Waples, Jonathan Dazey and William Powders, collectively, all of whom likely lived in close proximity.

As analyzed in Appendix 2 of this chapter, Our Daniel was not the son of an Ebenezer who was the son of John Sr. and Catherine because the time lines demonstrate that it was not possible. If Ebenezer is not the son of John Sr. and Catherine, Our Daniel is not then precluded from being the brother of John M. Evans, Ebenezer and Sophia's son. The absence of any supporting evidence suggests this possibility is not likely, but it cannot be rejected out of hand.

Our Daniel was neither the brother of John Sr. nor the son of William Sr., because John was about 62 years old in 1778, and Our Daniel was in his thirties.

John, Constable/School Master, could be Our Daniel's brother, but no evidence has surfaced in land, probate, census, tax or other records suggesting this is the case other than one salient fact: Our Daniel signed an Executor's Bond during probate of School Master's will. He died in 1794 as a relatively young man at about the time the youngest of his six children was born. School Master was born around 1755 and probably married Margaret around 1780. By this reckoning he was considerably younger than Our Daniel and it is unlikely they were brothers.

---

195   Sussex County Levy Court Tax Assessments, op. cit., 1778.
196   Will of Elisabeth Calloway, September 9, 1787, Sussex County Wills, Liber D, p. 156.

John, School Master, witnessed many wills in the area. He and Margaret both witnessed Joshua Evans' June 6, 1791,[197] will which was admitted to probate on May 27, 1794. This Joshua, whose will does not include a son, John, was the son of William Evans and the brother of John Sr. John School Master's signature on wills exhibited beautiful penmanship, a mark of education and training. Limited local education opportunities may mean he was not an original local. Further, his children's names such as Azarian, Barsheba and Charlotte are not typically local names, another indication he may be from elsewhere.

A John and Margaret Evans witnessed the May 3, 1785, will of a Joshua Evans.[198] It is confusing because this was a different Joshua. He was the son of William Evans, the brother of John Sr. This Joshua Evans' wife was named Elizabeth, not Betty, so he was not the Joshua who sold land to John Evans Sr. in Muddy Neck. He likely was the same Joshua Evans who witnessed the September 15, 1777,[199] will of Benjamin Dirickson with Jonathan Dazey who lived in the Muddy Neck area of Baltimore Hundred.

In 1797, Betty Evans, the widow of a Joshua Evans, willed a tract of land to her son, Joshua Evans, until her grandson, John Evans, reached the age of 21.[200] This is an interesting set of facts because John, School Master, died in 1794, and his son, John, was a baby when he died. This appears to be no mere coincidence because Betty and Joshua Evans had owned land in Muddy Neck and John, School Master, lived in Muddy Neck. This combination of facts regarding a Joshua and Betty Evans and John, School Master, is confusing in that the Joshua who, with his wife Betty Evans, sold land to John Evans Sr. in Muddy Neck was not the Joshua Evans whose will was witnessed by John Evans, School Master. It does mean, however, that John, School Master, likely was the son of the Joshua and Betty Evans who sold the land in Muddy Neck.

The absence of any information in his family background connecting John, School Master, with Our Daniel and their apparent age difference leads to the conclusion that John Evans, School Master, was a neighbor and associate but not a close relative of Our Daniel. A close relationship is possible, however.

197   Will of Joshua Evans, June 6, 1791, Sussex County Wills, Liber D, Folio 419.
198   Will of Joshua Evans, May 3, 1785, op. cit.
199   Will of Benjamin Dirickson, September 15, 1777, Sussex County Wills, Liber C, p. 8.
200   Dryden, op. cit., p. 618.

John, M. N. (Muddy Neck), is John Jr., the son of John Sr. The possibility that Our Daniel is the brother of John Jr. and the son of John Sr. is discussed in detail in the next section, which addresses the relationship of Our Daniel to John Sr.

The John Evans who was the son of William Jr., the grandson of William Sr. and the nephew of John Sr., could possibly be the "brother to Daniel," but nothing has been found confirming this possibility. This John Evans' father, William Jr., had land in Baltimore Hundred, Evans Addition, which he inherited from his father, and this John Evans possibly is Our Daniel's brother. The lack of any confirming information makes this unlikely. If Our Daniel is this John's brother, however, the line from Our Daniel still goes through William and Catherine Evans and Walter and Mary Powell Evans—not John Sr. and Catherine Wharton Evans. There is no proof one way or the other.

All of the above information and discussion on possible brothers to Our Daniel leaves two remaining possibilities as Our Daniel's brother, John Jr., the son of John Sr. and Catherine, and John M., the son of Ebenezer and Sophia. The total absence of supporting evidence for Our Daniel's brother being John M. Evans suggests Our Daniel's most likely brother is John Jr.

O.   OUR DANIEL, THE SON OF JOHN EVANS SR.?

The question at this point: Was Our Daniel another son of John Evans Sr. and Catherine Wharton Evans, the daughter of Daniel Wharton, and the brother of John Jr.? There is no direct evidence to say he was, but the following circumstantial evidence is compelling. **This evidence, together with the absence of contradictory evidence, justifies a conclusion that Our Daniel is the son of John Sr. and Catherine.**

A Daniel received a payment from the settlement of the Estate of a William Robinson in 1758.[201] This Daniel could have been born in 1740 or earlier if he were an adult in 1758 and as late as 1746 if he were a teenager. Teenagers were employed by others if not needed on the home farm, and this Daniel could have been as young as 12 in 1758.

Our Daniel was born before 1754, as shown in Section K from analysis of census records, and, more likely, as early as before 1740, based upon the known payment a Daniel received from William Robinson in 1758. This latter birth date is

---

201   Estate of William Robinson, op. cit.

consistent with the birth dates of the other children of John Evans Sr., 1740-1748.[202] If Our Daniel is the son of John Evans Sr., he was born during this period. This is circumstantial evidence, however weak.

Was Our Daniel both the grandson and nephew of a Daniel Wharton (Daniel Sr. and Daniel Jr.) and named after them? This is more circumstantial evidence of little weight when considered alone, but of greater weight when considered with the other information and analyses available and inferences drawn.

We know that the Administrator of the Estate of Thomas Dazey Sr. in 1778 recognized a debt to a "John Evans **brother to Daniel**,"[203] and we can find no Sussex or Worcester County record of a John with a brother Daniel in 1778. The absence of another proved John/Daniel relationship is circumstantial evidence and weak, but it adds weight.

As discussed in the previous section, the only possible Johns who could be Our Daniel's brother are John Jr. (probable), John M., (possible) and John, School Master (unlikely). Thus, the only possible fathers to our Daniel are John Sr., Ebenezer, or the father of John, School Master—with the probabilities indicated.

Hazzards Agreement was patented in 1742 and it had been resurveyed in 1754 to Evans Adventure for 100 acres. John Evans Sr. sold this 100 acres to Rhodes Clark in 1757, and Rhodes Clark mortgaged the 100 acres to Thomas Dazey in 1764.[204] We know that John Dazey Sr., the son of Thomas Dazey, not a known relative of Our Daniel, included a provision in his 1795 will to give and bequeath to Our Daniel sixty acres of land, part of Partnership[205] that Daniel subsequently bequeathed to his sons, Daniel Jr. and Zadoc. When considered along with the Clark/Dazey mortgage, this is more circumstantial evidence, but considerably stronger than the Wharton connections.

We know from the discussion in Section N of the "brother to Daniel" entry in the True Inventory from the Estate of Thomas Dazey[206] that Our Daniel was a neighbor of the Clark, Dazey and Robinson families that are closely associated with

---

202   Batchelder, op. cit., p. 104.
203   Will of Thomas Dazey Sr., op. cit.
204   See Appendix A, in this chapter.
205   Will of John Dazey, op. cit.
206   True Inventory of the Goods Chattles [sic] Rights and Credits of the Late Deceased Thomas Dazey, op. cit.

John Evans Sr. and his family. This is more circumstantial evidence of moderate weight.

We know that Our Daniel, a witness to the April 10, 1790, will of Charles Whaley, was living on land adjacent to land described in the will and left to Charles Jr.[207] We know further that Daniel was included in the 1789 Tax Assessment Records, an indication of land ownership. We don't know how Daniel actually got a tract of land in or before 1789. Was it <u>Partnership</u> in satisfaction of a debt to John Evans Sr., and did he have a conveyance bond for the balance; or was it originally Daniel Wharton's land obtained either from Daniel Wharton Sr., or John Sr. and Catherine Wharton Evans? It probably was the Dazey land because the Wharton land probably was further north.

We know that when he died Our Daniel left two tracts of land to his sons, Daniel and Zadoc, but there is no evidence concerning his acquisition of these lands in either the Worcester County, Maryland, or Sussex County, Delaware, Grantor or Grantee Indices for 1769-1800 or in any known will. The most likely possibilities, therefore, are the John Evans/Dazey and Wharton connections discussed in the previous paragraph.

The lack of evidence on land transfers is perplexing and may be explained by Evelyn Hastings Mason, in her introduction to *Land Records of Sussex County Delaware, 1782-1789*,[208] where she notes that there are voids in the Sussex County records for the period 1769 to 1782 because of the confusion created by the Revolution, loyalties to Maryland that persisted for a number of years, and the lack of a centralized County Seat in Georgetown until 1791.

Sussex County land records include early warrants and patents of significant additions to the original <u>Partnership</u> patent lands. While the Dazeys retained some of <u>Partnership</u>, sufficient land was clearly available to provide for that sixty acres of <u>Partnership</u> which Our Daniel obtained in some fashion.

Did Catherine Wharton Evans' will provide for Daniel's wife, Sarah? We know the provision regarding Sarah may also refer to her daughter-in-law, Sarah, William's wife. While this could be evidence of Daniel's relationship to Catherine, it is not convincing.

---

207   Will of Charles Whaley, op. cit.
208   Evelyn Hastings, *Land Records of Sussex County Delaware, 1782-1789* (Westminster, Md: Family Line Publications, 1990), p. iv.

Since many years passed between the deaths of Our Daniel in 1800 and his son, Zadoc, at age 72 in 1850, Our Daniel must have died at a relatively young age, or he married later in life than normal, or both. His son, Zadoc, was born in 1778, and Daniel Jr. likely was born in 1776 or earlier, and Our Daniel and Sarah were married in 1774 or 1775 and possibly as early as 1771 or before. From earlier discussions regarding the payment to a Daniel from the Estate of William Robinson, Our Daniel was probably born between 1740 and 1746. Our Daniel was, therefore, between 54 and 60 when he died. He married Sarah before 1776, at between the ages of 30 and 35. Our Daniel predeceased Sarah by 12 years.

As discussed in Section F, Our Daniel's father may have died in 1796 or before. John Evans Sr. died in 1795. This is a further indication, however weak, that he might be Daniel's father.

No Daniel was mentioned in either John Sr.'s or Catherine's wills. Possible reasons:

- If he were the oldest son of John Sr., it would not have been unusual for him to have received his share of the estate from his father before his death. Land usually was the most valuable of possessions, and sometimes fathers made over their lands to unmarried sons during their lifetime. Similarly, parents of betrothed couples often granted land to the new husband either before or after the marriage or upon the birth of an heir. Very often in such cases the eldest son was not mentioned in the will.[209] Is this how Our Daniel received land from Daniel Wharton or John Evans Sr.?

- He was the beneficiary of either or both (1) the Clark/Dazey debt discussed earlier or, in another fashion on the same issue, the beneficiary of the Dazey will of 1795[210] and (2) the Daniel Wharton relationship.

- As remote as it might sound, Our Daniel may be the Daniel who joined French Battell's Company of Lower Delaware Provincials in 1758 during the French and Indian Wars. If so, this might not have endeared Daniel to his parents. Perhaps he wasn't around much between 1758 and 1775 or possibly even between 1758 and 1789, further alienating his parents.

---

209   Stratton Nottingham, *Wills and Administrations of Accomack County, Virginia 1663-1800* (Bowie, Maryland: Heritage Books, 1990), p. vii.
210   Will of John Dazey, op. cit.

- Finally, could Our Daniel have predeceased his father, and, therefore, not have been a beneficiary of his father's will? A thorough search disclosed no pre-1800 will or probate record to support this marginal possibility.

There are no other even marginally sustainable answers.

From all of the above and the discussions in preceding sections, and as noted earlier, there are only three possible fathers of Daniel, each with attendant supporting actual and circumstantial evidence: Our Daniel could be the son of either John Sr.; Ebenezer; or John, School Master's father (unlikely).

P.   CONCLUSIONS

The weight of the whole body of evidence, analyses and reasonable inferences, it is believed, answers the question at hand. The extensive chain of circumstantial evidence carries great weight, and it is most unlikely that this combination of evidence vis-a-vis the lack of contradictory evidence, could be shown to lead to any conclusion other than that Our Daniel is the son of John Evans Sr. and Catherine Wharton Evans and the grandson of Daniel Wharton, for whom he was possibly named. As such, he was the brother of John Jr.

Our Daniel was born between 1740 and 1746 to John Sr. and Catherine Evans. He could have, but probably did not, serve in the French and Indian War in 1758. He received a payment from William Robinson's estate in 1759; had sons born about 1776; and in 1778 was mentioned in the 1778 Daniel Barns and Thomas Dazey Jr. estate settlements. He was listed in the 1775-1778 and 1789-1800 Sussex County Tax Assessment Records and received land around 1795 from John Dazey and possibly earlier from his father or mother. He died in 1800.

All this means that Our Daniel was the missing man in Worcester and Sussex County records from 1758 when he possibly joined the Army and 1759 when he received the payment from the Robinson estate until he showed up in records over fifteen years later. Daniel is recorded in the 1775 and 1778 and 1789-1799 Tax Assessment Records, in the 1778 settlement records of the estates of Thomas Dazey and Daniel Barns, and in the 1784 probate records of Trevour Taylor. Our Daniel possibly lived on the Dazey property during the missing Tax Assessment years. During this period (before 1776) he married Sarah (possibly Sarah Barns) and started raising a family.

A Daniel Evans was in Snow Hill, Maryland, in or before 1765, as indicated by a Daniel's debt in 1765 to James Smiley, the Snow Hill Merchant (set forth in

Section F). It is possible that this was Our Daniel inasmuch as there is no other information on Our Daniel from 1759 to 1774. This may explain the absence of Our Daniel from Baltimore Hundred. We have no information on what this Daniel was doing in the Snow Hill area. This is a good area for further research. Did Smyly's commercial territory extend fifty miles north to Baltimore Hundred?

With these conjectures, it is now possible to extend the family line from Daniel to John Sr. to William Evans, and to Walter Evans who, according to *A Somerset Sampler*,[211] emigrated from Wales to Accomack County, Virginia, in 1675 and married Mary Powell.

There are remaining possibilities and questions. Notwithstanding the supportable conclusion that Our Daniel is the son of John Sr. and Catherine Wharton Evans, there remains the slight possibility that Our Daniel could be the brother of John, School Master, or the son of Ebenezer; because, the conclusion is based upon a preponderance of evidence rather than absolute proof. Questions remaining include:

- What did Our Daniel do, and where did he live between 1758/9 and 1778? This is another puzzle with only the 1765 Smyly debt in Snow Hill to fill in the blanks!

- If John Sr. and Catherine are his parents, why was he not included in their wills? Was it because he was the eldest son and had already received Partnership via the Clark/Dazey/Evans sale and mortgage and adjacent land from his parents?

- Were they displeased with Daniel and why?

- Why were Daniel's daughters Martha Taylor and Elizabeth possibly not the Martha and Elizabeth included in Catherine's will when she carefully provided mementos for most of her granddaughters?[212]

- It would be nice to be able to fill in the blanks and have a more complete history, but as noted in the Introduction, it becomes unproductive to wish for what could not be found, and I am satisfied with the efforts. More research may provide

211   Batchelder, op. cit., pp 103-104.
212   Will of Catherine Evans, op. cit.

additional answers or refute my conclusions. This is a task for a resourceful and energetic relative or descendant. Pending new data, I stand on my conclusions.

Q. EPILOGUE – WE ARE RELATED TO JOHN EVANS SR. IN MORE WAYS THAN ONE

It should be noted for descendants of John A. Evans and Harriet Jefferson Evans, the parents of my Great-Grandfather Alonzo, that even if my conclusion that Our Daniel was the son of John Sr. and Catherine Wharton Evans is not correct, we are still John Sr. and Catherine's direct descendants. Harriet Jefferson Evans was the daughter of Stephen Riley Evans[213] and Sarah Elizabeth Jefferson Evans and the granddaughter of Stephen's father, Enoch Evans.[214] Enoch was the son of John Jr.,[215] and the grandson of John Sr. and Catherine. Harriet was the third great-granddaughter of John Sr. and Catherine. Alonzo's mother and father were both third great-grandchildren of John Sr. and Catherine and were, therefore, fourth cousins.

It is still more complicated. Enoch's wife, Elizabeth Evans, is a direct descendant of John Evans Sr.'s father, William Evans. She was the daughter of Keziah Truitt Evans[216] and William Riley Evans;[217] the granddaughter of Lemuel and Tabitha Evans;[218] the great-granddaughter of the William Evans who was the son of John Sr.'s brother, Walter; the great-great-granddaughter of this Walter Evans;[219] and, thereby, the third great-granddaughter of the first William Evans. Enoch was the son of John Jr., a grandson of John Sr., and a great-grandson of William Evans. These are just two of the lines whereby we are direct descendants of William Evans.

We are also descended from John Sr. and Catherine via their daughter, Mary, who married the William Hall who was the son of Adam Hall, Elizabeth Breasure Hall Evans' great-great-grandfather.

---

213   Edmund J. Evans, Memorandum, Genealogy of the Evans Family, March 22, 1932. (Copy given to this author by Sam McLaughlin, a direct descendant of Edmund).
214   Will of Enoch Evans, March 27, 1848, Sussex County Wills, Liber K, p. 251.
215   Will of John Evans Jr., October 30, 1786, Sussex County Wills, Liber D, pp. 195-196.
216   Will of Keziah Evans, September 30, 1812, Sussex County Wills, Liber G, p. 22.
217   Dryden, op. cit., p. 439.
218   F. Edward Wright, op. cit., p. 157.
219   Will of Walter Evans, February 18, 1796, Sussex County Wills, Liber E, pp. 74-75.

Believe it, it gets even more complicated for descendants of Prettyman Dazey, an ancestor of my grandmother, Nellie Daisey Evans. Prettyman's wife Leah is a great-granddaughter of William Evans, John Evans Senior's father. It reaches the point of becoming almost nonsensical. Alonzo's grandchildren are each other's cousin at least four and as many as eight times over. As another author in another state once wrote fondly about our Evans family, "It is no wonder we are the way we are."[220]

APPENDIX 1.

THE RHODS CLARK, THOMAS DAZEY, JR., AND JOHN EVANS MORTGAGE OF JANUARY 9, 1764[221]

The following is a transcript with original spelling of the subject mortgage which seems to have such relevance to Our Daniel Evans (less than perfect and with undecipherable words indicated with underlined spaces):

"This Indenture made the ninth Day of January in the year of our Lord one thousand seven hundred sixty and four, Between Rhods Clark of Worcester County in the Province of Maryland Planter of the one part and Thomas Dazey Junr. of the County and Province afors. Planter of the other part. Witnesseth that whereas John Evans of the County and Province aforesaid was Seized and lawfully Possessed of one Tract or Parcel of land called and known by the name of Evans Venture lying and being in the County afores. on the Sea board side on the head of Cedar Creek Neck by virtue of a special warrant of Resurvey by his Lordships Agent Granted to the said Evans Containing one [sic] acre more or less recourse to Original Patent being had may more fully appear. Now this Indenture further Witnesseth that the said John Evans for and in consideration of the sum of Twenty Pounds current money of Maryland to him in hand paid by the above named Roads Clark did alienate convey and Release and Confirm to the said Rhods Clark all that parcell of land afores. Called Evans Venture to him his Heirs and Assigns forever. Recourse to the said Deed now in the Records of Worcester County Court being had may more fully appear. Now this indenture further Witnesseth that the said Roads Clark for diverse good cause and considerations him thereunto mo__ing but more Especially for the consideration of forty Pounds current money of Maryland to him in hand by the afores. Thomas Dazey Jun'. the receipt whereof I hereby Acknowledge hath promises releases and forever Quit claimed and by these presents for himself his heirs doth

---

220   Edythe Whitley, *Evans Family, Maryland and Tennessee* (Published by the author. 1971).
221   Indenture, October 16, 1764, Rhods Clark and Thomas Dazey to John Evans, Worcester County Land Records, Liber F, microfilm.

fully clearly and absolutely promise release and forever quit claim unto the aforesaid Thomas Dazey in his full and peaceable possession thereof now being and to his heirs and assigns forever such Right Estate Titel and which the said Roads Clark has or ought to have of in or to the Afores. Tract or Parcel of land called Evans Venture containing one hundred acres more or less as afores. together with all the Benefits Privileges and Appurtenances thereunto belonging to or any ways appertaining. To have and to hold all the said hundred acres of land unto the said Thomas Dazey his heirs and assigns to the only use and behoof of the said Thomas Dazey his heirs assigns forever to be _____ of the chief _____ or ____ of fee of the promises for the rents and services for the _____ due and of right accustomed so that he the said Rhods Clark nor his heirs nor any other person or persons for him or them or in his or their names Right or S___ of any of them shall or will by any ways or means hereafter have claim challenge or demand any Estate Right Title or Interest of in or to the Premises or any part or parcell thereof but for all and every Action Right Estate Title Interest or Demand of in or to the premises or any part thereof they and every of them shall be utterly excluded and denied forever by those present and allow the said Roads Clark and his heirs and said land with all benefits and appurtenances there made belonging to the said Thomas Dazey Junr. his heirs and assigns and every of them and against all persons whatsoever shall and will warrant and forever defend by these Presents. In Witness whereof the said Rhods Clark both hereunto Interchangeably with his hand and offers his seal the Day and year forth above written.

Signed by Roads Clark with his Mark"

Continues with October 16, 1764, sale of land by Clark and Dazey to John Hill. NOTE: Witnessed by a John Evans.

APPENDIX 2.

TIME LINES ON EBENEZER AND JOHN AND CATHERINE

The book, *A Somerset Sampler*, relates under the subheading, John Evans (Sr.), that his eldest son was Ebenezer who died in 1793.[222] It notes that Ebenezer married Sophia _____. I believe, instead, based upon the will of Isaac Marshall, that he married Sophia Marshall, Isaac's daughter.[223] I suggested at this point, to myself only, that Ebenezer might be the father of Daniel, remembering that Daniel

---

222   Batchelder, op. cit., p. 104.
223   Will of Isaac Marshall, March 8, 1750, *Maryland Calendar of Wills, Volume 10*, op. cit., p. 137.

had a brother John and that Ebenezer and Sophia had a son, John M. Evans. The following time line analysis indicates that this is not a possibility.

Ebenezer's reported father, John Sr., and Catherine married circa 1738. A brother, John, was born March 11, 1740/1, so Ebenezer likely was born one to two years earlier, in 1738/9. If so, and if Ebenezer married at age 21, he married in 1762/3. If Daniel were his oldest son, he might have been born no earlier than 1763/4. If born in 1763/4, and if Daniel married at age 21, his first child would have been born in 1785/6. We know, however, that Daniel's oldest son Daniel was born in about 1776 according to an analysis of the 1850 Census (Sec. XIII).

Even if John Sr. and Catherine married in 1736 (two years earlier than reported), and if Ebenezer were born in 1737, married at age 20, and had his first son, Daniel, at age 21, Daniel would have been born not earlier than 1758. Then, even if Our Daniel married at age 20, and had his first son, Daniel Jr., a year later, Daniel would have been born in 1779 at the earliest. All this combination of rushed marriages and early births is unlikely. The net result of this time line is that it is most unlikely that Ebenezer was the son of John Sr. and Catherine Wharton Evans. The information in *A Somerset Sampler* must be incorrect. This same analysis applies to John Sr's. other sons.

While Our Daniel could not be the son of an Ebenezer who was erroneously reported to be the son of John Sr., Our Daniel still could have been the son of another Ebenezer who was not the son of John Sr. The Will of Isaac Marshall of March 8, 1750, indicates he had a daughter Sophia Evans, so Ebenezer and Sophia married in 1750 or earlier. The Tax Lists of Somerset County, 1730-1740, include an Ebenezer of Bogerternorton Hundred who, therefore, had reached the age of at least sixteen (the age at which one was included on the list) during or before 1730. This Ebenezer had established his own household in 1735 in Bogerternorton Hundred and showed up in Baltimore Hundred in 1736, where he bought 100 acres of land called Dispute in Jan. 1738. Further, we know that an Ebenezer and his wife Sophia sold a tract of land, Pasture Lot, to Daniel Wharton in June 1758.[224] Clearly, Our Daniel could have been born to Ebenezer and Sophia in 1751 or earlier. If so, the time line now works to the extent that Our Daniel could have married and had a child by 1778 without straining credibility.

---

224   Dryden, op. cit., p. 464.

In Section F there is a discussion of the payment in 1759 to a Daniel Evans from the Estate of William Robinson[225] and the conclusion that this Daniel's birth date was before 1744. This is consistent with the possibility of Our Daniel's being the son of Ebenezer and Sophia who had a son, John M. Evans, who could be the requisite "brother to Daniel." The time lines are consistent with Our Daniel being the son of Ebenezer and Sophia. But that possibility notwithstanding, it is unlikely because there is no other known nexus in land, probate, or church records.

APPENDIX 3.

THE DANIEL, ROBERT, AND JOHN EVANS OF BALTIMORE COUNTY AND THE ROBERT EVANS OF SUSSEX COUNTY

A Daniel, Robert and John Evans witnessed the will of Charles Whaley on April 10, 1790.[226] It was initially thought this Robert Evans might be the Robert Evans of Baltimore County (today's Baltimore City) who had brothers, Daniel and John. The coincidence of there being contemporary brothers, Daniel, Robert and John Evans in Baltimore County required checking their history. Result: This is not the case. The Robert Evans in question died in Sussex County in 1833, 33 years after the death of Daniel.[227] Notwithstanding the passage of many years, the signatures of this Robert on the original of his will[228] and the original Whaley will are truly identical. It can be said for sure that the Baltimore County Daniel and Robert have no relevance to the Baltimore Hundred Daniel and Robert. Census records placing them in Baltimore County at relevant times, signature checks on wills witnessed by the Baltimore County Daniel, and property ownership records all support a firm conclusion of no relevance. This information is included here simply to help other researchers avoid a blind alley.

Robert Evans of Sussex County left a life estate in his over 90 acres of land to his wife, Sally, and after her death to James Evans, son of a Thomas Evans. Remembering that a Thomas Evans had signed the Executor's Bond during the probate of Our Daniel's will, I sought to identify this Thomas by attempting to compare signatures on the wills of the numerous, contemporary Thomas Evanses.

---

225   Estate of William Robinson, op. cit.
226   Will of Charles Whaley, op. cit.
227   See Section N, this chapter.
228   Will of Robert Evans, July 24, 1833, Sussex County Wills, Liber H, p. 210.

This was not successful because no Thomas who was living in 1800 had a will. John M. (son of Ebenezer and Sophia), had a son, Thomas,[229] as did William,[230] and John, School Master.[231] Is this an indication that Robert and Daniel were related to John M., William or John, School Master? Robert died in 1833, and John M., William and John, School Master, died around thirty years earlier. Hence, they are probably from different generations. While Robert could have been the son of John M., there is no other evidence purporting that this is the case. Robert's will mentions no children and the beneficiary of the remainder from his wife's life estate appears to be his nephew, James. This Robert left Baltimore Hundred and eventually had land in Broadkill Hundred and George Town (now Georgetown).

POST SCRIPT – DNA TESTING

Another thought: DNA testing. Everything known to me in this area came from reading about a 1998 DNA study of Thomas Jefferson's children with Sally Hemings, so, absent further study by me, this new thought may be quite wrong. Dr. Ray Thompson of Salisbury University reported that there are scholarly attempts to do such DNA tests on people which go back centuries.

It would seem that if we could find living "untainted" descendants of John Sr., both through Our Daniel and through either of his other sons, John Jr., or William, it would be possible to utilize Jefferson-like DNA tests to confirm the common ancestry of Our Daniel and one of his brothers.

Being "untainted" means that there must be very clear genealogical proof that each of the currently living Evans subjects had no intermarriages in his ancestry which would have also introduced John Sr.'s genes into their DNA. Such living subjects might be very difficult if not impossible to find.

Starting with Our Daniel, it would be necessary to go back at least to John A. Evans' father, Clemeth, and start tracing both his wife and his son's families to make sure they are not "tainted." In the case of John Jr., Our Daniel's brother, who had more sons than the other brother, William, it would be necessary to track descendants of his sons, Eli, Elijah, Jobe, Elisha, or John. With this many lines to track, it might be possible to find a candidate. The odds of finding such a living descendent from both Our Daniel and one of his brothers may be low. The odds of having sufficient

---

229   Will of John M. Evans, November 11, 1799, Sussex County Wills, Liber E, p. 256.

230   Will of William Evans (Of John Sr.), October 20, 1810, Sussex county Wills, Liber F, p. 438.

231   Will of John Evans (School Master) June 6, 1791, Sussex County Wills, Liber D, p. 419.

confidence in the supporting genealogy to justify the expense may also be too low. A large investment in genealogical research time would be required to develop the required level of confidence.

At this time (First Edition), the cost of such a test is unknown. Considering the large investment of time in this project to date, it might be an economical approach. The number of intermarriages within these families, however, probably make such verification and testing impossible.

Chapter 8   Letter to Catherine—Relatives

May 1997

Dear Catherine,

Your mother and dad gave you a beautiful name, Catherine MacGregor Wood. While they may not have known this at the time, Catherine is an old family name. Catherine White Evans and Catherine Wharton Evans are your lots-of-greats grandmothers from the eighteenth century. Catherine Wharton Evans is one of the ladies to whom this book is dedicated. Check them out.

Catherine, always remember how important your family is. I always told your dad and his brothers that their brothers would always be valued friends. Even though they had other good and dear friends, I knew their brothers would always be there ready to provide good company with their families and support or comfort in times of need. Blood is thicker than anything else. Now, as they are older and with families of their own, I find it gratifying to see them and their families seek out each other—and enjoy it.

Your immediate family numbers five people: you, Caroline, Chip, Mommy and Daddy. How lucky you are to have both a brother and sister. I never had a brother to get into my things and pester me. Even so, as much as my sisters, Lois and Susan, mean to me, I believe I would have liked a brother like Chip. Caroline and Chip will be your lifetime friends.

You have more relatives than most people. Capt. Alonzo Evans, your third great-grandfather, had 359 living descendants as of the August 5, 1995, reunion of his family which many attended. These reunions are in keeping with the spirits of Lib, Nellie and Hilda; they reflect the importance of family to us. Right now, I suppose, the younger family members see them as a chore, something their parents want them to go to. As we get older, reunions mean more and are special times. We share experiences, tales and recollections, and good company—our family.

How many other relatives do you have? The answer is a lot! If Capt. Alonzo and Lib were only two of your thirty-two great-great-great-grandparents and they had 359 surviving descendants in 1995, think about how many relatives you have. While the Evans family is much larger than most, and few of our forebears had as many children as the eleven Alonzo and Lib had, you probably have over two thousand aunts, uncles, or cousins descending from your third great-grandparents. But that's not all. Think about going back even two generations beyond that of Alonzo and Lib—the numbers grow and grow to maybe as many as ten thousand.

This story goes back to Daniel, Alonzo's great-great-grandfather, your seventh great-grandfather. There may be thirty thousand or more relatives, not counting the double relationships. An example is your cousin Annmarie who is related to you two ways. Read Annmarie's letter in Chapter 13 to understand this. That's more people than there are in some small cities. It is amazing to think about.

Tell your friends that you may have as many as thirty thousand aunts, uncles or cousins. They won't believe you, but it could be true.

The family trees will give you an idea of how the family size increases with each generation. Think about it. We are each just a bit of each other. I think it is important for you, Caroline, Chip, and your cousins to get a feel for who our forebears were and where and how they lived. That's why I wanted you and your cousins to have this story.

I couldn't close this letter without relating a wonderful memory of a very sweet little girl. I hope you remember a number of springs ago when you rode with me to the aquarium in Virginia Beach. That ride was such a delight. I couldn't imagine a three-year-old would have so many really good questions about things and surroundings. Having raised four boys, I was used to that, but I had forgotten they can come from someone so young. The best part of it was your response to each of my attempts at answers. "Oo-oh," you exclaimed. At least twenty or thirty times. I don't remember enjoying such an intelligent conversation with a little one quite as much as that. It was a truly charming ride. Thanks for joining me.

Love,

Pop-Pop

Note for Second Edition: It was reported at the August 6, 2016, Family Reunion that there were now 491 blood descendants of Alonzo H. Evans.

Chapter 9   The Hall Family

Elizabeth (Lib/Lizzie) Breasure Hall Evans – Her Family and Ancestors

Elizabeth Breasure Hall Evans was born January 31, 1870, and died April 1, 1909, at age 39. Elizabeth was baptized at Old Sound Church in 1870.[232] She was 17 when she married the 19-year-old Alonzo Evans in 1887. She was first buried in the Millville Cemetery and later moved to where she now rests next to Alonzo in the Mariner's Bethel Methodist Church Cemetery in Ocean View.

Elizabeth's mother, Sarah Jane Breasure, was born May 30, 1842, and died June 7, 1883, at age 40 years, 11 months, and 12 days. The bond for the marriage of Sarah Jane "Brashier" to John C. Hall was dated December 7, 1863.[233] John C. was serving at this time as the Assistant Keeper of the new Fenwick Island Lighthouse where his father, William R. Hall, was Keeper (See section on William R. Hall). Sarah Jane now rests in the Hall Family plot at the Ocean View Presbyterian Church with her husband, John C. Hall, one on each side of her husband's parents, William R. and Catherine Hall.

The 1850 U. S. Census lists her father, James Brasure, as being 32 and her mother, Elizabeth, as 34. Also listed are Elizabeth (8), her sisters, Mary (14) and Ann M. (12), and a brother, James L. (6). Ten years later, in 1860, her father, James, is listed as being 44 and her mother, Elizabeth, is listed as being 42 – the 1860 listing is likely correct. Three additional siblings are listed in the 1860 Census: Julia E. (9), Margaret H. (3), and Nancy (1). Elizabeth Brasure was the mother of at least seven and was another of the women in the family who died young. Remember, both Harriet Jefferson Evans, wife of John A. Evans and Alonzo's mother, and Elizabeth Breasure Hall Evans, Alonzo's wife, also died young. Giving birth to many children may have been inconsistent with longevity. Alonzo and Elizabeth's oldest daughter, Sarah Gertrude Evans Phillips, was named after Sarah Jane Breasure Hall.

Elizabeth's father, John Cornealius Hall, was the son of William R. Hall and Catherine Vaughn Hall. He was born September 7, 1839, and is listed in the 1850 Census as being 11 years old. He died on February 10, 1924, at age 84, and now rests with Sarah Jane in the Hall Family plot in the Ocean View Presbyterian Church Cemetery (N.E. corner). As discussed below in the section on his father,

---

232   Peggy Timmons, *Heritage of Old Sound Church* (1978).
233   Archives of Delaware, Marriage Records, Vol. 48, p. 61.

William R. Hall, John C. served two terms in the 1860s as Assistant Keeper of the Fenwick Island Lighthouse. The June 20, 1870, Census records William R. as a farmer and John C. as a mariner. John C. owned real estate assessed at $400. His family included his wife, Sarah (27), and three daughters, Elizabeth (4 mo.), Catherine (4), and Mariah (2). He and Sarah J. subsequently had two sons, William A. (8) and David Cornealius (1) who were recorded in the 1880 Census. John C. was recorded as a farmer in 1880.

John C. was married two times, first to Sarah Jane Breasure, Elizabeth's mother, and then to Henrietta J. Johnson.[234] John C. and Henrietta J. were married pursuant to their marriage bond dated March 26, 1887. Henrietta was born February 28, 1840, and died March 29, 1910. She is buried in the Old Sound Church Cemetery at Johnson's Corner,[235] the only known Hall in the cemetery. Since this

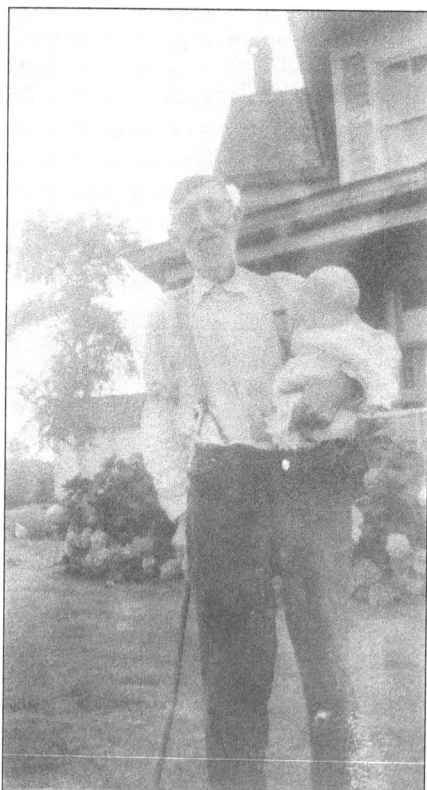

Captain John Cornealius Hall of Bethany Beach—1917
My great-great-grandfather

---

234   Ibid.
235   The cemetery is located about two miles from today's Sound Church.

cemetery is known as the Johnson's Cemetery, it is likely the middle initial, J., stands for Johnson. She was 47 when they married. I am not aware of her having children, so she may not have been previously married. After the death of Henrietta, John C. lived with Uncle Dave and Aunt Katie in a home where Bethany West is now located (behind John C. in the picture on the previous page). This home was deeded by John C. to Uncle Dave. John C. built and at one time lived in the house owned by Linwood and Nellie Evans which stood where the St. Ann Catholic Church classroom building is now located. I remember that house well—loved vacations and holiday dinners there. The old cedar tree in the front yard had a well-used swing 60 years ago. It was cut down in 2000 to accommodate widening Route 26.

Aunt Daisey remembered John C. as being over six feet tall, and very thin. She tells about how he used to walk across the road from Uncle Dave's to see Linwood and Nellie every morning and to sit on their side porch. Usually, he spent part of the morning rocking one of Linwood and Nellie's small children. His picture on the previous page certainly demonstrates his love for his little ones.

As recorded in the 1860 U. S. Census, John C. was known as Captain Hall and was a mariner. According to John W. Hall (his grandson), he sailed from Indian River loaded with grain and local produce. He was quarantined once in Philadelphia because of a smallpox epidemic. The schooner trade from the Indian River through the Indian River Inlet is discussed in greater detail in Chapter 23 on John A. Evans and Chapter 24 on Alonzo Evans.

According to my mother, Hilda Evans Wood, who as a child knew her Great-Grandfather John C., he was considered to be "a wonderful man and well off." He owned many acres in Bethany Beach as discussed below. John C. was devoted to his church and in his will he left $8 per year to the Ocean View Church of Christ until $100 had been donated.

In his will of August 11, 1885,[236] David Hall, John C.'s grandfather, left his four children numerous tracts of land, including hundreds of acres in Bethany Beach. Among his holdings was a stretch of ocean beach. His heirs included his four children, William R. Hall, Mary J. Bennett, Nancy F. Hall and Charles W. Hall, and his grandson, David M. Hall. Nancy and Charles who both died intestate, unmarried and without issue, sold their interest in their father's estate to John Cornealius and James D. Bennett (Mary's husband).

---

236   Sussex County Wills, Book 12, p. 478.

John C. and Henrietta Hall and Mary and James Bennett sold a 263-acre tract to Elisha Dukes in April 1897 for one thousand dollars—$3.80 per acre! Over the years, a number of other parcels of David Hall and John C. Hall's lands along today's Route 26 were sold. The following samples of land prices over the years prove again that land in Bethany Beach is a good investment.

Year	Seller, Tract Size, Buyer and Price
1820	David and Rose Hall sold 100 acres with buildings to Zadoc Waples at $13 per acre.
1884	J. C. Hall sold 8 acres to Elisha Evans at $10 per acre.
1905	Alonzo H. Evans bought 11 acres at $25 per acre.
1906	Alonzo H. Evans sold 7 acres to John Addy at $29 per acre.
1928	Alonzo H. Evans sold 20 acres to Harvey Collins at $100 per acre.

It is interesting to note in 2001 that land from these same tracts was priced at $50,000 or more for a building lot of one-quarter acre or less ($250,000 in 2016).

John C. and Henrietta and the Bennetts sold seven tracts of land totaling about 243 acres on Jan 6, 1903, to the Bethany Beach Improvement Company.[237] The deed describes the tracts as being on the "Ocean View-to-Hall's Beach" road. The name, "Hall's Beach," was also used to locate a one-acre-plus lot sold in 1900. Until this time, today's Bethany Beach was called Muddy Neck in all references to land or peoples' homes.

In 1885, the current Ocean View-to-Bethany Beach road was known as the "Ocean View-to-Salt Pond Inlet" road. This was described in a land deed from John C. Hall to Elisha Evans.[238] There are other references to the Salt Pond Inlet in a number of contemporary deeds, including the August 19, 1891, deed of land from a Melson to Benjamin W. T. Burton. This inlet is apparently the reason the Salt Pond was "salt," as compared to the nearby "Fresh Pond." A map prepared by John L. Amrhein Jr., Cartographer,[239] using old naval charts as his source shows the old inlet,

---

237   Sussex County Deeds, Book 142, p. 413.

238   Ibid, Book 102, p. 424.

239   Section of map: The Ancient Seacoast of Maryland, Including part of Delaware and Virginia, 1690, John L. Amrhein Jr. Cartographer (Salisbury, Md: Ryan and Black, Publishers, 1986). I apologize to Mr. Amrhein for this infringement on his excellent work.

probably a storm washover, located north of the present day Loop Canal in Bethany Beach. William S. Hall of Hall's Store (present day Ocean View) kept a diary, and numerous entries mention the opening or closing of the inlet which intermittently connected the Salt Pond with the ocean.

Notwithstanding the sale of these large tracts, John C. and Henrietta still owned hundreds of acres in Bethany Beach, including all of what is now Bethany West and most of the land on the other side of Route 26 back to the Bethany Beach Canal, from just west of Route 1 to well beyond St. Ann Catholic Church.

John C.'s will became a source of controversy. Because he had previously given land to his son, David Cornealius, Elizabeth's brother, he left no more land to him. The balance of his land holdings, except for one acre deeded to May Hearn, his daughter-in-law's (Aunt Katie Hall) sister, was to be sold with the proceeds of the sale to be split eleven ways, a share for each of Elizabeth's children when they were 21. The lands were not sold, however, and they somehow ended up being owned by Alonzo H. Evans and Uncle Dave Hall. We do not know how this happened, but Aunt Mary Beck, Pop-Pop Linwood's sister, said to me that Linwood, the oldest child, and Uncle Dave (Elizabeth's brother) went to Georgetown and "did something," such that the land was not sold and Elizabeth's children did not receive their share of the proceeds of a sale. This was clearly a source of consternation to her. A third of a century later, Alonzo left all he owned to his children, except for his last child, Delena, who had been adopted after her mother died.

Elizabeth's grandfather was William R. Hall and her grandmother was Catherine Vaughn Hall. The 1840 U. S. Census listed him as Captain William R. Hall – mariner. The 1850 Census, lists the 40-year-old William R. as a farmer. Apparently he gave up life on the water. Also listed are Catherine (40) and children, Sarah J. (15), John C. (11), William David (8), Henry F. (6), Isiah M. (5), and Maria C. (1).

William R. was the second keeper of the Fenwick Island Lighthouse which was first lighted on August 1, 1859. He served during and after the Civil War from July 17, 1861, to July 26, 1869, when he was removed."[240] Apparently these appointments were to some extent political. His annual salary was $660. His son, John C. Hall, served as his assistant keeper at an annual salary of $300 per year from August 15, 1861, to December 28, 1865, when he resigned. He was reappointed on

---

240   Register of Lighthouse Keepers 1845-1912, National Archives, Microfilm Roll M 1373 #2.

April 25, 1867, at an annual salary of $400 and served until August 10, 1869, when he was also "removed," probably because of election-based patronage changes.

William R. married Catherine Vaughn on June 20, 1832. There were Vaughns in Indian River Hundred on the other side of Indian River and in Southwest Sussex in 1782. Catherine possibly was the daughter of a Nathaniel Vaughn who lived in Indian River Hundred. William R.'s will was made September 1, 1874, as he lay on his deathbed, and was admitted to probate eight days later on September 9. His tombstone in the Ocean View Presbyterian Church cemetery lists his death on September 2, 1874, and notes he lived to the age of 64 years, 10 months and 15 days. He was born, therefore, on October 18, 1809. Catherine died December 24, 1878, at the age of 69 years, 9 months, and 5 days, so she was born on September 19, 1808.

Elizabeth's grandfather was James C. Breasure. The 1860 Census for Baltimore Hundred lists James as being 44, so he was born in about 1816. His wife, Elizabeth, is listed as being 42 in 1860 so she was born in about 1818. It is most likely this line of Breasures came originally from Bogerternorton Hundred in Somerset County (the area in Maryland south of Baltimore Hundred including Ocean City and Berlin). A James Mumford "Brozer" is included in the 1736 Tax Lists. James "Brazier" is listed in Bogerternorton in 1735. James and Ann "Brayser" are listed in Pocomoke Hundred in 1734. Ann, a widow, and James "Brasher" are listed in 1733. William and James "Braser" are listed in Pocomoke Hundred in 1731. Breasure, Brasure, Brashur, Brazier, Brayser, Brashier, Braser, and Brozer: all appear to be phonetic stabs at spelling the same family name. These folks sure had a hard time with the spelling of their name. There were no landowners in the 1782 Sussex County Census and Tax Assessment Lists with any of these names. A review of Sussex and Worcester County Tax lists would probably provide more definitive information.

Elizabeth's great-grandfather was David Hall. His will was made August 11, 1855, and admitted to probate thirteen years later on October 15, 1868. Heirs included his wife, Sally F., and children, William R., Mary J. Bennett, Charles W, and Nancy F. Hall, the last two of whom, as noted above, died intestate and unmarried without issue. This David was born to William and Mary Hall on January 13, 1784.[241] Deeds show that David lived south of the Salt Pond and north of the current Route 26, not far from the present-day St. Ann Catholic Church. He is listed in the 1850 U. S. Census as a farmer owning land valued at $2000, probably way over 200 acres. A deed actually includes a sketch locating the house on his lands which included Cedar Island, an apparent island in the Salt Pond. This same deed

---

241   Daughters of the American Revolution Bible Records, DAR II, p. 167.

also shows the Salt Pond Inlet. There is no known record of Sally's maiden name. Furman perhaps.

Elizabeth's great-great-grandparents were William Hall and Mary Evans Hall. William was born Nov. 1, 1746, and he died October 25, 1798, at age 58.[242] He was reportedly a blacksmith.[243] He married Mary Evans, the daughter of the same John Sr. and Catherine Wharton Evans who were Alonzo's third great-grandparents. Mary was born April 20, 1748, and died January 25, 1839, at age 90 years, 9 months and 5 days. William's will, dated January 29, 1795, was admitted to probate on March 29, 1799. Heirs were his wife, Mary; sons, David (not yet 21), Adam, John, and William Spence Hall (Called Spence in his will); and four daughters, Elizabeth, Sarah, Nancy and Hannah, who was born October 26, 1777. The will mentions buildings, including a schoolhouse, which he intended to remain as such. This William Hall was the only land-owning Hall in Baltimore Hundred for most of the 1790s. His wife, Mary, remained on lists until 1810. His son, William S. Hall, became a store owner in about 1820 on the east side of what is now Central Avenue, near the present landscaping shop. A post office was included in the store in 1822 that was known as Hall's Store Post Office. This post office designation gave the local town area its name, Halls Store, which lasted decades until the town became known as Ocean View. The Ocean View Council first met in 1889.

William's 1795 will included a number of bequests of slaves to children. The will also freed "a negro wench Candis and her son Mike." Another slave, James, was to be freed after four years "if he behaved himself" in service to William's wife, Mary. These bequests are a commentary on the nature of slaves as chattels, subject to their owner's whims.

Elizabeth's third great-grandfather, Adam Hall, was born in February 1714 and died January 21, 1780. He was a neighbor of John and Catherine Wharton Evans. As noted earlier, his son, William, married John and Catherine's daughter, Mary. Generations later, this first known marriage between our Evans and Hall ancestors made Alonzo and Elizabeth fourth cousins once removed. Daughters of the American Revolution records report that Adam was the son of a William and Margaret Hall.[244]

---

242   Ibid.
243   Sussex County Chancery Case W #31.
244   DAR Bible Collection, op. cit., p. 167.

A William and Adam Hall and two slaves are listed as a taxable family unit in Bogerternorton Hundred in 1731, 1733, and 1734. William, Adam, and Pheonix and two slaves were listed in 1735 and 1736. Adam was listed alone in 1737, 1738, 1739, and 1740. In 1737, William Hall willed 140 acres of <u>Head of St. Laurence Neck</u> to Adam Hall along with 40 acres to Phoenix Hall. This tract was on Assateague Bay (today's Chincoteague Bay) east of today's Berlin, Maryland, not far from Walter and Mary Evans' <u>Teuxberry</u>. In 1749, Adam and his wife, Mary, sold 103 acres of this land to a Solomon Collins.[245] William also willed 100 acres of <u>Folly</u> to Phoenix. In 1751, an Adam Hall and his brother Phoenix Hall were beneficiaries of the estate of their brother, John Hall. John also left a bequest to the Presbyterian Church in Snow Hill, an indication that the Hall family may have been from the Snow Hill area. In 1752, Adam lived adjacent to land owned by Daniel Wharton in Worcester County. Adam patented <u>Halls Chance</u> for 71 acres in 1756. Twenty years later this became a Delaware land warrant. Adam of Worcester County purchased 50 acres of <u>Haphazard</u> and 66 acres of <u>David's Lott</u> from William Hazzard on Jan. 17, 1771. These new lands were resurveyed for Adam to become part of <u>Halls Chance</u>. Adam apparently moved to Baltimore Hundred in 1771. He subscribed to Blackwater Church in 1779 a year before he died in 1780. His son, William, supported Blackwater in '78, '79, and '80, as did a William Jordan Hall. Adam's November 16, 1778, will was admitted to probate on March 6, 1780. His heirs included a son, William Hall, who was born on April 6, 1736, a daughter, Mary Hall, and grandsons John Buckley and Alexander and Adam Roberts.[246] Adam Hall must have also had at least two married daughters not named in his will (married to a Buckley and a Roberts). Adam's wife's maiden name is not known.

Elizabeth's fourth great-grandparents were William and Margaret Hall. William Hall of Somerset County in his Sept. 17, 1737, will (probate June 18, 1740) left part of <u>Saint Larance Neck</u> (sic) to sons Adam and Phenix, 200 acres on the Wicomico River to sons Joshua and Ezekiel and his dwelling plantation (home farm) to his son, William Jordan, who was born on April 6, 1736.[247] His wife Margaret was executrix with Phenix (Phoenix, Pheanix—spelled differently in different documents), probably his brother.

Possible earlier ancestors: There are a number of references to Halls in the book *Old Somerset on the Eastern Shore of Maryland*. I do not know how they tie in, but they are included for the benefit of other researchers.

---

245   Dryden, op. cit., p. 291.
246   DAR Bible Collection, #229.4.
247   Ibid.

A William Hall is included in a list made up of deed records and judicial records in Somerset County between 1666 and 1700.[248]

A William Hall and a Humphrey Hall are recorded on December 16, 1662, as each having a right to 50 acres of land for settling into Maryland, which rights were apparently assigned to a Randall Revell and Ann Toft.[249] Charles Hall is reported as one of the first settlers.[250] Seaboard Side rights were encouraged in July 1666, but, according to Torrence, "It was several years later before there was any movement towards the section comprehended by the proclamation."[251] This area is now southern Sussex County. By 1672, numerous warrants were issued.

A Charles Hall, who died in 1695, married Alice (Unknown) and had six children, among them a William.[252] One of Charles' daughters, Rachel, married Randall Revel Jr.

On May 18, 1689, a William Hall patented Halls Lott for 450 acres in Baltimore Hundred "at a creek out of Assawoman Bay."[253] On September 10, 1708, William willed this land to his son William Jr.[254] He died intestate and the land went to his brother, Joseph. He, in turn, left the land to his Stepfather George Howard who left it to his wife Sarah Howard. John Hall, possibly another brother or William's son, sold the 450 acres in 1744 to Joseph Miller, apparently the namesake of Millers Neck. It is not believed this Hall line has any relevance to Adam. This William died intestate and we know Adam's father, William, left a will.

It does not appear that the Halls were from Accomack County, Virginia. They likely were immigrants to Somerset County from England or Scotland around 1665.

A chart of the descendants of William Hall is on the following page:

---

248   Torrance, op. cit, p. 465.
249   Ibid., p. 474.
250   Ibid., p. 279.
251   Ibid., p. 473
252   Ibid., p. 445.
253   Dryden, op. cit., p. 278.
254   Will of William Hall, September 10, 1708, Maryland Calendar of Wills, Vol IV, p. 169.

Descendants of William Hall

```
1 William Hall  1746 - 1798
.. +Mary Evans
........ 2 John Hall
........ 2 William Spence Hall
........ 2 Elizabeth Hall
........ 2 Sarah Hall
........ 2 Hannah Hall
........ 2 Nancy Hall
........ 2 David Hall  1784 - 1868
............ +Sally F.
.................... 3 William R. Hall  1809 - 1874
...................... +Catherine Vaughn  1808 - 1878
............................ 4 Sarah J. Hall  1835 -
............................ 4 John C. Hall  1839 - 1924
................................ +Sarah Jane Breasure  1842 - 1883
...................................... 5 Catherine Hall
...................................... 5 David Cornelius Hall
...................................... 5 Mariah Hall
...................................... 5 William A. Hall
...................................... 5 Elizabeth Breasure Hall  1870 - 1909
.......................................... +Alonzo Harrison Evans  1868 - 1955
............................................... 6 John Linwood. Evans, Sr.  1889 - 1966
............................................... +Nellie Daisey 1889 - 1967
............................................... 6 Sarah Gertrude Evans  1891 - 1984
............................................... +George E. Phillips  1885 - 1944
............................................... 6 Linda Myrtle Evans  1892 - 1978
............................................... +Harry Knox  1870 - 1940
............................................... 6 William David Evans  1894 - 1971
............................................... +Mildred Spache  1896 - 1984
............................................... 6 Edith Elizabeth Evans  1898 - 1955
............................................... +Walter B. Carey  1893 - 1971
............................................... 6 Alonzo Harrison Evans II  1900 - 1974
............................................... +Sophie Peterson  1901 - 1930
............................................... *2nd Wife of Alonzo Harrison Evans II:
............................................... +Edna Quinn  1910 - 1995
............................................... 6 DeWitt France Evans  1901 - 1973
............................................... +Ray Antoinette Carpenter  1897 - 1962
............................................... 6 Stephen Cornealius Evans  1903 - 1958
............................................... +Maria Carolina Doderer  1908 - 2001
............................................... 6 Mary Elizabeth Evans  1905 - 1997
............................................... +Otto Beck  1893 - 1973
............................................... 6 Louis Baxter Evans  1907 - 1990
............................................... +Dorothy Viola Doderer  1912 - 2003
............................................... 6 Delena Louise Evans  1909 - 1990
............................................... +Alton Rogers  1909 - 1993
............................ 4 William David Hall
............................ 4 Henry F. Hall
............................ 4 Isiah M. Hall
............................ 4 Maria C. Hall
.................... 3 Mary J. Bennett
.................... 3 Charles W. Hall
.................... 3 Nancy F. Hall
```

PART III

EIGHTEENTH CENTURY BALTIMORE HUNDRED

Chapter 10   William (1698-1766) and Catherine White Evans
(c. 1698-17??)

<table>
<tr><td colspan="2" align="center">Contemporaneous Happenings</td></tr>
<tr><td>1740</td><td>Frederick the Great decrees freedom of the press and freedom of worship in Prussia</td></tr>
<tr><td>1758</td><td>Samuel Johnson publishes Dictionary of the English Language</td></tr>
<tr><td>1760</td><td>George II succeeded by his grandson, George III, as King of England</td></tr>
<tr><td>1763</td><td>The Treaty of Paris concludes the French and Indian War and ends role of France as a power in North America</td></tr>
<tr><td>1764</td><td>Mozart composes his first symphony at the age of eight.</td></tr>
</table>

William married his first cousin, Catherine White, the daughter of William White and Catherine Powell White. Her mother, Catherine Powell White, was the sister of William Evans' mother, Mary Powell Evans. William Evans and his wife, Catherine, therefore, were both grandchildren of Walter and Mary Powell and first cousins. This is the first of the numerous known marriages in the Evans family between close relatives.

William White was the son of John and Sarah Keyser White of Somerset County. John White, one of the early founders and leaders of Somerset County, served as Commissioner of the Peace in August 1666 when Somerset County was established.[255] His daughter, Catherine, was probably born around 1698. She married William about 1715 at around age 17, considering that her first child, John, was born about 1716/18.[256]

William moved with his parents and brothers and sisters to the tract, South Petherton, which included most of today's South Bethany, in or after 1702 and before 1708. While his early childhood may have been spent on Teuxberry on Chincoteague Bay, southeast of Berlin, Maryland, most of his childhood and all his teen years were spent in and around today's South Bethany.

In the same manner as in Chapter 5 concerning the lives of Walter and Mary Powell Evans, the story of William Evans and Catherine White Evans is based upon

---

255   Torrance, op. cit., p. 283.
256   Batchelder, op. cit., p. 103.

known facts as well as general knowledge about life in Baltimore Hundred. Information which strays from specific facts about William and Catherine is in *italics*.

While we know nothing of William's early life not specific to his parents, we do know that William lived at a time when diligence offered a more promising future than adventure. A perilous ocean voyage, treks as an adult across the Delmarva Peninsula to new frontiers, or major encounters with the unknown were not in the cards for William. He grew up on <u>South Petherton</u> in the South Bethany area and lived most, if not all, of his life on this tract. He was tied to the land. His was a time in which his economic prospects depended on his own unremitting labor and prudent decisions on land acquisitions. He bought or patented a number of tracts on his own in today's Bethany Beach, Ocean View and Cedar Neck areas.

Catherine's father, William White, had died in 1708 at about age thirty-five and left her an interest in the 500-acre tract, <u>Convenience</u>, near Berlin, Maryland.[257] Catherine was probably around ten years old at this time. With or without Catherine's interest, young Catherine's mother clearly had sufficient resources to provide a proper level of care.

We do not know the cause of William's death, but the closeness of the dates of his will (1706) and probate (1708) possibly mean he was not in good health when the will was signed. Premature death was commonplace in the early eighteenth century in the Chesapeake area. Malaria, while not usually considered the primary cause of death, was debilitating and increased the likelihood of early death from other devastating diseases, such as typhoid, pneumonia, influenza, typhus and dysentery. Losing one or both parents was a common childhood experience. One child in four lost a parent by age nine, one in four lost both parents by age thirteen, and only one in three had both parents at age eighteen. While the general health of Bay area residents had improved over the seventeenth century, the eighteenth century was still a time of significant infant mortality. One baby in ten and one woman in five died from causes tied to childbirth.[258]

William and Catherine's life was typical of small, mostly self-sustaining, family-run farms cut off from daily contact with the world. Developing a farm demanded total sticking-to-it. In these times, it took a half a century to carve a large

---

257   Dryden, op. cit., p. 134.
258   Hawke, op. cit., pp. 59 and 72.

farm with cleared fields out of the untamed trees and bushes.[259]

We pick up their story in about 1712, when William was about 14 years old, the second of four sons and the fifth of eight children.

A Boy on South Petherton in Baltimore Hundred

William's childhood was typical of the times and included a stern and repressive discipline which was conscientious and grounded in Biblical examples. His parents, Walter and Mary, like so many rural parents, aimed honestly and matter-of-factly to fear God and to respect family, property, neighbors and, perhaps at a lower level, government—in sum, a life of usefulness and honor.[260] There was a regular routine. The Sabbath was important and Saturday was tub night. All in the family were expected to work on the farm and around the house. Unfortunately for William, schools were not available and he never learned how to write his name;* his 1764 will (reproduced at the end of this chapter) was signed with his "X" mark.

One of William's early experiences was the trauma of moving from Teuxberry to Baltimore Hundred. The idyllic conditions for a five-year-old boy living on Mobjack Bay at the head of Assateague Bay (today's Chincoteague Bay) were difficult to leave. Even for a very young boy, the lure of fishing, crabbing, and collecting oysters along the shore and clams from the sandy bottom was very strong.

The thirty-mile trip lasted two days over the rudimentary roads and ox-cart trails through the woods. Even under the best of conditions, loaded wagons could not make more than thirty miles a day. They traveled together by horsecart and small wagon, his parents, three older sisters, Mary, Margaret, and Marjorie, and older brother John. Notwithstanding the trauma of moving from the only home he had known and the difficult trip, little William was impressed at his first sight of the small house on South Petherton with its wonderful surroundings and nearby seascape. He did not miss his former home for long.

Their two-room house with a loft, the three small outbuildings, a smoke house, a privy and a farm shed, had been rebuilt by his father, Walter, and his two older brothers with some help from neighbors. It was typical for the area, where homes did not change much for over a century. His parents had paid 9,000 pounds of tobacco for South Petherton and had also kept their previous home and 100-acre

---

259   Hawke, op. cit., p. 32.
260   James Shouler, *Americans of 1776* (Bowie, Maryland: Heritage Books, 1995), p. 41.

tract, Teuxberry, so the family had comparably ample assets for the times. They were able to pay for hired labor and materials for the new construction. Young William's parents now owned 430 acres of land between Assawoman Creek and the ocean. The new farm had marsh and pasture for their small but growing number of cattle, sheep and hogs, as well as the three farm and riding horses. The cattle roamed free and could be identified by owners' brands or ear notches, hundreds of which were registered with the Somerset County Clerk.

William's father and his older brothers immediately started to clear land for wheat and corn, a small orchard, family gardens, and a family tobacco plot. Some tobacco was sold, but William kept most for personal use. Methods had not changed, and the first step was girdling the trees to make them wither and start to dry. They became firewood and construction timber for future additions to their house and buildings. New crops were planted between the drying hulks before they were cut down and between the remaining stumps thereafter. Required sunshine filtered through the withering limbs. The stumps were too difficult to remove and were left to rot.

As the seasons and years passed, the family increased both the acreage tilled and the productivity of the land. Chores were unrelenting: cutting and hauling firewood, building and repairing fences, tending crops, feeding and overseeing stock, sweeping the cleared pommeled area around the house, and splitting timbers and sawing boards for new outbuildings.

Sawing large boards from trunks was a two-man job usually done over a large pit. The log was placed over the pit and the two-handled ripsaw was pulled by one man in the pit under the log and one man above. Imagine the conditions in the pit with a regular cascade of sawdust. Two sawyers could produce about a hundred board feet a day.[261]

The farm's proximity to the ocean brought not only needed rain and cooling breezes but also severe storms. In at least three of the early years, hurricanes wreaked havoc on the corn and wheat crops which were flattened by the high winds and torrential rains. While the wheat crops were lost, the corn, which was generally made in early September, was saved by immediate, sunrise-to-sunset, shucking of the ears from the fallen stalks which were then piled into corn stacks. That was to be the tactic for more than two centuries thereafter. The hard-pressed families relied on stored dried corn to subsist through the winter, hence little was available for sale.

---

261   Hawke, op. cit., p. 145.

Food for the kitchen remained the same for almost two centuries. Hogs were raised and butchered, a mainstay. Some of the meat was smoked and the rest was salted down in barrels for the winter. Four hogs were sufficient to carry the family through the winter. Seafood was abundant. A man could harvest as many as thirty bushels of oysters a day in the bay. Fish were netted in the Indian River and, in spawning season, in small streams. Most were salted down for the winter.

Unlike his father, William loved boating on the ocean, river and bay. He was adept at rowing the small flat-bottomed row boat, just as he was sailing the shallow-draft shallop, which was used for short social trips, fishing and shell-fishing ventures, and to deliver produce for sale to agents and neighbors. William was the first real waterman in the Evans family. He was to be emulated by many others in coming generations.

His parents worshiped regularly, and Sabbath meetings were held in their and neighbors' homes. Attendance was small, but families attended regularly. Yet, life was not all work and no play. It was communal. The Evans family visited regularly with friends and neighbors in the area. Indeed, that was their main recreation.

William was about fourteen years old in 1712 and one of the few teenagers in the immediate vicinity. *By now, he had become quite aware of girls, who were few and far between in this part of Baltimore Hundred. By the age of sixteen, William and his family had visited his mother's sister and family near Teuxberry south of Berlin, MD, and he got to know his White cousins, including the young Catherine. In fact, they and their widowed mother, Catherine White, visited South Petherton at least once a summer.*

The family visit in the summer of 1713 caused quite a stir in the White and Evans families. It was obvious to all that first cousins, Catherine and William, were quite taken with each other. Their parents sought to discourage them but to no avail. The young cousins fell in love. Determined, the 17-year-old William and the 16-year-old Catherine made known their intentions to marry. She was strong willed. Her childhood was impacted by the tragedy of her father's premature death in 1708 when she was about 10 years old.

Marriage of cousins was of some concern, but William and Catherine were determined. Their young age was not particularly objectionable because the average age of new brides at this time was sixteen-and-a-half. For young men, it was just over twenty. Romance was in vogue. One in five brides of the time was reckoned to be pregnant at their wedding.

The wedding took place in the spring of 1715 in the Presbyterian Meeting House located on <u>Buckingham</u>, a tract near Berlin patented by Catherine's grandfather, John White, in or about 1679.[262] *Catherine's father, William White, had subsequently owned the 400 acres of this tract where her widowed mother still lived.*

William's parents, Walter and Mary, made the overnight trip to <u>Buckingham</u>, thereby showing their approval of the wedding. The twenty-mile trip on horseback and in the family cart from <u>South Petherton</u> (today's South Bethany to Berlin) took all day, first to near today's Selbyville over the rudimentary roads, trails and crude ox-cart paths crisscrossing Sussex in the early 1700s, and then via the somewhat less rudimentary Seaside Road from what is now Selbyville to Berlin.

Newlyweds On South Petherton

Newlyweds William and Catherine immediately moved her belongings into a one-room house on his father's farm. Catherine had a nice bed, feather mattress, chest of drawers and the minimum kitchen utensils necessary to set up housekeeping. William and his brothers made simple benches, chairs and a table. It was a simple home with a log and clay fireplace, a small loft and a dirt floor which Catherine insisted be planked immediately. This plus a coat of whitewash and a woman's touch quickly made it cozy and livable, however small.

As the years passed, they enlarged and improved the house. The farm was reasonably productive and Walter and Mary and Catherine's mother were generous to the young couple. On February 6, 1719, William and Catherine purchased the north half of <u>North Petherton</u> for 5,000 pounds of tobacco. The purchase included about a half mile of ocean beach extending south from below today's Salt Pond almost to the south end of Bethany Beach and extending west to a north-south line at about today's Bethany West. William and Catherine now owned approximately the north half of the oceanfront in today's Bethany Beach. Upon the death of his father, Walter, in 1721, William inherited the half of <u>South Petherton</u> where he and Catherine lived, and his brother John inherited the part where his mother and father lived.[263] In 1735, William purchased 70 acres of brother John's part of <u>South Petherton</u>. William and John together owned essentially all of today's South Bethany and half of today's oceanfront in Bethany Beach.

William and Catherine soon started a family. John, the first of eleven, was

---

262   Torrance, op. cit., p. 258 – meeting house information, p. 259 – on William White's lands.

263   Will of Walter Evans, op. cit.

born in 1718 or earlier, and Walter, Joshua, Solomon, Joseph, Elisha, William, Martha, Rachel, Comfort and Mary soon followed.[264]

William and Catherine clearly prospered and continued to invest in land throughout their lives. This list of their land patents, purchases and sales is impressive.[265]

> Peppers Delight - Bought 100 acres in 1733 at head of Baltimore (Indian) River and sold the tract in 1753.
> Daniels First Choice - Bought 100 acres at head of Baltimore River in 1733.
> Buck Ridge - Patented in 1750 for 50 acres.
> Evans Part - Patented in 1751 for 175 acres (between North and South Petherton).
> Morris Purchase - Bought 150 acres in 1733 and patented in 1734 as Evans Addition.
> Timber Ridge - Acquisition date and size unknown. Left to son Joshua in William's will.

The original patent for North Petherton was taken out in 1688 by Matthew Scarborough for 500 acres and included the eastern half of today's town of Bethany Beach. Matthew Scarborough and his wife, Hannah, sold North Petherton to Robert Thomas in 1702. Thomas willed the tract in 1715 to John Shockley and William Hall (this Hall does not appear to be an Evans relative). Shockley gave his half to Robert Johnson, who with his wife sold their half of North Petherton, 250 acres, to William Evans. John Hall (of William) sold his 250 acres to John Massey.[266]

We know the Johnsons had a house on their land because in 1740 William gave to his son, John, "that part of a tract of land called North Petherton whereon he now liveth being the north part of that moiety I bought of Robert Johnson that is to say all that part northward of a line drawn east and west across this tract of land through the plantation by a single apple tree standing a little to the southward of the house where the said Robert Johnson lived. . ."[267] It is probable William and Catherine's first son, John, lived in the Johnson home which William and John had probably expanded and improved. It is interesting to note that early in his adult life,

---

264   Will of William Evans, May 26, 1764, Maryland Hall of Records, Prerogative Court, Wills Liber 34, pp. 272-275.
265   Dryden, op. cit.
266   Ibid, p. 439.
267   Somerset County Land Records, Deeds, Liber MF-O-20, p. 209-210.

John, who became known as John Sr., probably lived just south of the Salt Pond, possibly about where his fourth great-grandson and my great-grandfather Alonzo lived for many years.

At the same time in 1740 that William gave the north part of North Petherton to his son, John, he also gave the tracts Daniel's First Choice and Evans Enlarging to his son Walter,[268] and the tract, Morris Purchase, to son William Jr.[269] Fifteen years later, their son Walter sold a part of Daniel's First Choice to the vestrymen of Worcester Parish for the construction of Prince George's Chapel in Dagsboro, a structure still standing today.[270]

In his 1764 will, which was admitted to probate on November 5, 1766, William left part of North Petherton to son, John, and 100 acres each to sons, Elisha and Solomon. There is some duplication here because the gift to John in 1740 and the bequests in 1764 appear to total more than the 250 acres purchased in 1719. It is possible the gifts are duplicated in the 1764 bequest. More research would be required to clarify the land history, and that is beyond the purpose of this work. It is sufficient to know that John owned the north half of today's Bethany Beach where his father, William, had lived.

William and Catherine lived either on North Petherton or on Evans Part, a tract inland of North Petherton. William left their home to Catherine along with "a privilege in all my marshes and pastures during her life."[271]

William and Catherine ended up wealthy for their time and place. William's inventory of goods and chattels was appraised at almost 80 English pounds. He also left five pounds to two daughters. He and Catherine had invested wisely in land and had worked hard. They accumulated well over a square mile of land and at least two houses, outbuildings, and considerable livestock and household furnishings and farming equipment. While we have no information other than his will and inventory, it is reasonable to assume he and Catherine lived in a house with a colonnaded porch, at least four rooms, and an upstairs with dormers. One room probably had a gin and loom and a place to sew. There likely was a kitchen with a large fireplace, possibly connected to the house by a colonnade, a wash house or laundry where they made soap from rendered animal fat and wood ashes, a milk house and a smoke

---

268   Ibid, p. 205.
269   Ibid, p. 207.
270   Dryden, op. cit., p. 162.
271   Will of William Evans, op. cit.

house. The farmyard probably contained one or more barns, a pigsty, a corn crib, and a storage shed.

Daily life had not changed significantly from the time of William's parents, Walter and Mary. Income from the farm did allow them to purchase pewter plates for the kitchen, an occasional piece of silver, a variety of cooking utensils and metal farm tools. These could be purchased in the larger towns on the western side of the peninsula or ordered from England. There is no evidence that William and Catherine owned any slaves. William and his sons did the farm work with help from Catherine and their daughters during planting and harvesting seasons. Fishing, hunting and harvesting of abundant shellfish were pleasant and diversionary tasks that supplemented the dinner table. Some crops and livestock were sold locally or to agents, who made pickups at landings on the river and creeks. The state of general health and medical care was improving and infant mortality declining. Life was fairly routine, producing contentment. Baltimore Hundred remained a secluded if not isolated place where farm and family were the focus of everyday life. This order of things would not change for families like William and Catherine's in Baltimore Hundred for the next one hundred and fifty years.

There is no evidence that William participated in government. Being remote from Snow Hill, Worcester's county seat, there was little opportunity to participate. The acrimony over the location of the east-west boundary between Maryland and Penn's Three Lower Counties continued, but it probably meant little to William and Catherine.

Will of William Evans, May 26, 1764   Maryland Hall of Records,
Prerogative Court, Wills,
Liber 34, Folios. 271-275

In the name of God Amen the 26th day of May Anno Dom – I William Evans of Worcester County being in perfect sence of mind and memory Thanks be given to God and calling to mind the mortality of my body knowing that it is appointed for all men once to Dye I do Make and Ordain this to be my last Will and Testament & first I do recommend my Soul into the hands of Almighty God that gave it & my body to be buried in a desant and Christian like manner at the diserction of my Executors hereafter mentioned and as Touching such Worldly goods as it has been pleasing God to bless me with I do Will and bequeath them in the manner & form following

Item   I give and bequeath unto my well beloved wife Catherine Evans my Dwelling house and Plantation whereon I now live together with a previlage in all my Marshes and pastures during her natural life. Also I give her two feather beads & furniture my Riding horse and two Mairs two potts two putter dishes and three plates, Two Cows and Calves, Six head of Shep and two Spining Wheals to be holden of her & her Heirs forever --------

Item I give and bequeath unto my eldest son John Evans part of a Tract of Land called North Pertherton, Joyning to a former Deed I gave him to against two Marked Red Oaks Stand on each side of the Plantation to be holden of him & his Heirs forever -----

Item I give & bequeath unto my son Walter Evans Twenty Shillings in money to him & his Heirs forever.

Item I give and bequeath unto my son Joshua Evans the Plantation whereon he liveth called Buck Ridge containing of fifty Acres to him and his Heirs lawfully begotten of his body forever -------

Item I give and bequeath unto my Son Sollomon Evans the Land and Plantation whereon he now liveth Beginning at a marked Ceder post Standing near the Creek and from thence running North One hundred & Sixty pole to a marked live Oak standing near the path and near a Place called Conners Hole Thence North two degrees West thirty six pole Thence North twenty seven Degrees West forty Pole Thence North twenty four degrees West forty pole Thence North Eight degrees West to a marked white oak Standing near the head of the Land and from thence to the head of the Land so as to conclude one hundred Acres out of North Perthornton and thirty five Acres out of a Tract of Land called Evans part, To be holden of him & his Heirs forever.

Item I give and bequeath unto my Son Joseph Evans part of Two Tracts of Land called South Pertherton & Evans Part, Beginning at a Live Oak Standing near Conners Hole it being the Second Bounder of my Son Sollomons Land thence running to a marked Tree Standing near Black Snake Pond Thence running Northerly to a marked White Oak Standing near the fence on the Eastward side of the Plantation thence to a Walnut Tree standing on the South side of the Barn, thence Westerly to a White Oak marked in the Swamp, Thence with a line drawn to the head of the Land so as to Include one hundred and forty five Acres out of South Perthrenton and Sixty Acres out of Evans Part but all the Marsh part of South Perthrenton to be for an Equal privelage between by above said Son Joseph and my Son Elisha Evans and their Heirs forever, Never to be sold only from one to the other & and to be holden of them and there Heirs forever.

Item I give and bequeath unto my Son Elisha Evans all the remainder part of my lands (that is to Say) all the remaining part of North Perthernton from my son Johns Bounds (which is two marked Red Oaks standing on the East and West sides of the Plantation) and likewise all the remaining part of Evans part containing of eighty Acres and all the remaining part of South Perthernton containing of one hundred & twenty five Acres, and Sixty one Acres in the

Woods called Timber Ridge, to be holden by him & his heirs forever but if my Son Elisha should die without Issue then al his said Lands to fall to my Son Joseph & his heirs forever.

Item I give and bequeath unto my Grandson William Evans Son of Joshua Evans one gun to him and his Heirs forever.

Item I give and bequeath unto Comfort Justice five pounds in money to her and her Heirs forever.

Item I give and bequeath unto my Daughter Martha Evans one Bed and furniture two putter dishes & three plates two Chears one spinning Wheel one Iron Kittle and one Cow and Calf to be holden of her & her Heirs forever.

Item It is my will and desire that all the remainder part of my Estate not allredy given be equally divided between my wife Catherine Evans Elisha Evans Mary Hudson and Martha Evans to be holden of them & their Heirs forever

I do appoint my well beloved Wife Catherine Evans and Elisha Evans to be my Sole Executors of this my last Will and Testament. I do revoak & disanul all former Will or Wills heretofore by me made, and do acknowledge this to be my last Will and testament. In Witness where of I have set my Hand Seal the day and date first written

his
William E Evans
mark

Signed Sealed pronounced) Wm Tunnell
) her
and declared In the) Comfort X Tunnel
) mark
Presents of us) Ginnethon Harney

On November 5th 1766, Catherine waved her right of dower or thirds of the deceased's estate, real and personal, and elected to abide by William's will.

Note: This will was copied from the Maryland Hall of Records microfilm of the will book which contains a transcribed copy of the original. The form, grammar and spelling of this and all wills herein are as close as possible to the copies or originals. Note also the various spellings of Petherton.

Chapter 11   Letter to Laura —The Beach

July 1995

Dear Laura,

What an engaging little person you are. I saw you walking this past weekend - so proud, head erect, full of yourself. How I enjoyed your marathon crawl to the water on the beach over Memorial Day - you loving every minute, me loving it even more. Pop-Pops enjoy such things. Your Mom and Dad were so proud!

Speaking of your mom, she is a fine young woman. Your Dad did himself and his father proud in marrying Claire. It is comforting to know you and Brian are so loved and well cared for, just like your cousins.

Your brother Brian will remember well my phoning him – "Let's go to the beach!" That's a call that has been familiar to me for fifty years, to your Dad and uncles for thirty, and to our ancestors for almost three hundred. It's a place to enjoy, relax, refresh, see nature's seashore wonders, and be either alone or with friends and families, equally a pleasure. We do have fun at the Beach House.

Bethany Beach hasn't always been as it is now. When the first Evans and Hall families lived there, as early as 1702, the inland ponds were a place to make salt and the marshes were a place to cut hay. The beach was always a place to fish, I suppose. While the Evans and Hall families lived in Bethany Beach for almost three centuries, it didn't become a resort until almost a hundred years ago when land was sold along the ocean for a Christian Camp in 1901. Some of it was sold by Capt. Alonzo Evans, your great-great-great-grandfather.

When my Mom was a girl, the beach was generally deserted. She tells of being there on a summer's day with no more than ten other sunbathers. Imagine having the whole beach to yourselves. Now, with the large numbers of people all being there to enjoy the beach and being together, it is still nice, but different from what it was.

I like to call it Pop-Pop's beach, but it isn't; many preceded us to Bethany Beach. My grandfather, Linwood Evans, and his father lived in Bethany Beach for years. Linwood's mother, Elizabeth Breasure Hall Evans, was raised in Bethany Beach and the Evans and Hall Families lived there for most of three centuries. In fact, at the turn of the century (1900), the Beach was known as Halls Beach, its first known-to-me recorded name. We know this from deeds for land sales in Bethany Beach which described the land as being on the road from Ocean View to "Halls Beach." Before that, it was part of "Mud Neck" and "Muddy Neck," names on old road petitions and maps.

The beach has been a part of our family history since 1702, when Walter and Mary Evans of Somerset County, Maryland, bought a tract of land called South Petherton. Their son, William, also purchased a tract known as North Petherton, and together they encompassed all of South Bethany and almost one-half of today's Bethany Beach. At least three generations of Evanses lived on these tracts in the 1700s. Later, parts of these tracts were owned by Dazey/Daisey and Hall ancestors. In fact, Cornelius Hall owned most of today's Bethany Beach in the late nineteenth and early twentieth centuries, including both sides of Route 26 from Bethany West to the ocean.

While Bethany Beach has changed a lot, not always for the better, let's hope it doesn't change too much from what it is now. It's a place where families can vacation secure in the notion that it will be peaceful, quiet and wholesome. I think it would be best if it always stays a place where generations of families will want to visit to enjoy the qualities we experience—and value highly.

Let's hope area and state elected officials always understand Bethany's charm and always maintain its family atmosphere. I want you and all of your cousins to have Bethany Beach and the Beach House to enjoy. We should share it with visitors willingly, but not change it to accommodate those who don't see its real values.

Enough of that. We enjoy the beach. The most important part of what now makes the Beach House special is my grandchildren. Love it as I do and enjoy it with your cousins—often!

Love,

Pop-Pop

Chapter 12   John Sr. (c. 1716/18-1795) and Catherine Wharton Evans (c. 1720-1797)

John Evans, the first son of William and Catherine White Evans, was born circa 1716-1718 on South Petherton, his father's farm in today's South Bethany. He married a neighbor, Catherine Wharton, the daughter of Daniel and Catherine Wharton, in about 1738.[272] John died in 1795, and Catherine died two years later in 1797.

Both John and Catherine were the children of significant landholders, William Evans and Daniel Wharton. In 1740, they received an economic head start when his father, William Evans, gave John the north part of North Petherton (about 250 acres), a tract he purchased in 1719, which included the Robert Johnson home. This gift tract encompassed today's northeast quarter of Bethany Beach and the National Guard Base. This land was south of the Salt Pond and the Johnson house probably was located north of today's Route 26 and west of today's Route 1.

Daniel Wharton was probably the son of Francis Wharton of Accomack County, who died in 1700.[273] Daniel and his wife, Catherine, sold their lands in Accomack County in 1713 and moved to Baltimore Hundred, either to a tract, Daniel's Luck, which he patented in 1713, or Turtle Swamp on Herring Creek near Dagsboro which he patented in 1714.[274] In 1722, he patented a 100-acre tract,

---

272   Batchelder, op. cit., p. 104.
273   Ibid., p. 278.
274   Dryden, op. cit., pp. 162 & 652.

<u>Daniel's First Choice</u>, at the head of today's Pepper Creek in Dagsboro which includes the site of Prince George's Chapel. In 1727, Daniel purchased 265 acres of <u>Cedar Neck</u> which encompassed a large part of today's Cedar Neck east of the Cedar Neck Road. Daniel willed 150 acres of this tract to his daughter, Catherine Wharton Evans.[275] I believe John Sr. and Catherine lived on this tract in their last years.

Like others in Baltimore Hundred late in the eighteenth century, John and Catherine's goals were not much different from those prevailing today: ". . . (maintain) a comfortable home, earn decent livings, and provide opportunities for their children."[276] "For spiritual support they turned to churches" that were now available.[277]

Starting with their marriage and move onto <u>North Petherton</u>, the following is a review of life for John and Catherine and their family in "Bethany Beach" in the mid-to-late 1700s. This story of John and Catherine is based upon Daniel Evans being their first son.[278]

Available Historical Data

The only family-specific references to support this account of the story of the daily lives of John Sr. and Catherine Wharton Evans are the ages of their children, land records, the December 10, 1795, Inventory of the "Goods, Chattels and Credits" of John Evans' estate (next page), their wills and a number of church records and references which document their support for the Blackwater Presbyterian Church. Beyond these limited references, the description of the house and farm, their daily routine and important issues and events are based upon the numerous published accounts of life on the typical Mid-Atlantic farm during colonial times.

The inventory of John Sr.'s estate after his death in 1795 sets forth the contents of John's and Catherine's household and farm. The listing of John's possessions helps define the house and sheds light on their daily and seasonal household and farm activities. The 347 English pounds total appraised value is not a pittance; John and Catherine had prospered.

---

275   Will of Daniel Wharton, op. cit.
276   Quoted from Hancock, *Delaware Two Hundred years Ago: 1780-1800* (Wilmington, Del.: The Middle Atlantic Press, 1987), p. 41.
277   Ibid.
278   Pursuant to my conclusion in Chapter 7, "The Daniel Evans Puzzle," that Daniel Evans was the son of John and Catherine.

True Inventory of the Estate of John Evans Sr., December 10, 1795[279]

One Large Bible	Small skillet	3 Old barrels
A Child's Bible	Pair iron tongs	2 Cow hides
Cupboard	Box of iron heaters	Fishing line
Square large table	Pair of sheep shears	Small trunk
Small table	4 Ox chains	Table cloths
3 Sets of "Bed and furniture"	2 Harrows	Pair of sugar tongs
Folding table	Plow	2 Silver tea spoons
2 Linen wheels	Pair of iron wedges	Hackle
Wooling wheel	Cart	6 Out (?) hogs
Cotton gin	4 Ox chains	Sow and pigs
8 Chairs	2 Axes	Meal bag
Gin case and 10 bottles	3 Weeding hoes	Bridle
Stool	Grubbing hoe	Churn and can
Large stone jug	Negro man called Daniel (15 £)	6 Sheep
Small stone jug	Negro man called Jediah (45 £)	Clevis
Wine decanter	Negro woman called Alse (30 £)	Tray
3 Tumbler glasses	Negro man called Isaac (45 £)	Barrel
"Delf and queens ware plates"	Negro woman called Patt (30 £)	13 Pounds of tallow
Looking glass	Negro girl called Elon (20 £)	2 Small ____
Course earthenware	Negro girl called Ester (15 £)	Two sides of leather - in fat
2 Shovels	Negro boy called Jacob (10 £)	9 ____
Reafr. Hooks (???)	Negro boy called Isaac, Jr. (2 £)	3 Sheep
5 Lbs. Old pewter plates	2 Yokes of cows	Weeding Hoe
23 Lbs. Pewter plates	5 Cows	Man's saddle
Large iron pot	Heifer	Scythe
Iron kettle	Stear	
2 Iron pots	Bull	Total Appraised Value -
2 Iron basins	2 Cows with calf	347 Pounds, 15 Shillings
Frying pan	6 Yearlings	and 4 pence
2 Pot trammels	Calf	
3 Pot hooks	Loom	Appraised Value of Slaves
Roast meat hook	Some farming tools	Almost 212 Pounds
Flesh forks	Man's saddle	
Grid iron (iron griddle?)	Black mare	
Pair still yards (weights & measures)	2 Siftors	

---

279   Spelling as in original in Archives of Delaware, Sussex County Probate, John Evans Sr, 1795.

In 1760 John Sr. and Catherine were both about 43 years old. Daniel was about 22, John Jr. about 20, William about 18, Rebecca about 16, Elizabeth 14, and Mary about 12.

Their Lands

Over the years, John and Catherine acquired significant additional lands in today's Cedar Neck and Ocean View.[280] In 1742, John patented <u>Hazzards Agreement</u> for 100 acres. The farm was adjacent to the tract, <u>Cedar Neck</u>, owned by his father-in-law, Daniel Wharton. It was situated along today's Whites Creek in Ocean View. The tract may have included the site on Whites Creek where I now live. In 1754, it was resurveyed for John Evans to <u>Evans Venture</u>.

- In 1752, John inherited through Catherine from her father, Daniel Wharton, 150 acres of his tracts, <u>Cedar Neck</u> and <u>Hogg Quarter</u>.[281]
- In March 1765, John purchased from Joshua Evans and his wife, Betty, 50 acres of <u>Timberland</u>.
- In January 1765, John purchased from John Onions and his wife, Susanna, 20 acres of <u>Adkins Lot (Atkins Lot)</u> located adjacent to and west of <u>North Petherton</u>.
- In 1766 John inherited from his father, William, all but 100 acres of the balance of <u>North Petherton</u> which William had given to John's brother, Solomon.

With their land holdings, including these tracts received as gifts or by inheritance and lands they patented, John and Catherine ultimately owned much of the northeast quarter of today's Bethany Beach (except for 60 acres he had sold to his brother, Solomon, in 1761) and significant parts of Cedar Neck and Ocean View. John and Catherine were clearly in the upper economic strata of Sussex County farmers. Their land holdings were six to twenty times larger than the average—approximately an irregularly shaped square mile.

Most of their lands were probably productive—either as cleared farmland, timberlands, pasture, or hay marsh. However, their extensive lands along ocean, creek, and bay shores, which constitute much of today's Bethany Beach, probably was considered at that time to be of little value.

---

280 Information on tract locations is based upon both Dryden, op. cit., and the Short map, op. cit.
281 Will of Daniel Wharton, November 4, 1752, Worcester County Wills, Vol. JW2, pages 123-124.

Their House

Houses did not reflect the sometimes large land holdings of this period. Dr. Bernard Herman of the University of Delaware has made extensive studies of colonial buildings in Sussex County and has concluded that most houses were small. A high percentage measured less than 450 square feet.[282] Atop a 15-by-24-foot main building would be a small sleeping loft. Herman reported that homes were typically surrounded by a few outbuildings, such as a "separate kitchen, smoke or meat house and a corn house or a barn." The typical home described by Dr. Herman was packed with "an average of three beds, two blanket chests, six chairs, two tables, two spinning wheels (probably one for wool and one for flax), loom, corner cupboard, and seven inhabitants."[283]

While John and Catherine's farm was far larger in acreage than the typical farm, their house in their early years on North Petherton was probably similar to Dr. Herman's typical home in size and content. However, based upon the list of furnishings in John Sr.'s inventory, their last home on Cedar Neck (present day Cedar Neck), which they inherited from Daniel Wharton in 1752, clearly was a substantial home for the times. While multiple beds were often crammed into smaller homes, the three sets of "bed and furniture" are an indication that the house probably had a second story with two bedrooms instead of a simple loft. The probable, original one-story house with a loft must have been enlarged with a two-story addition. With the new addition, it probably had at least three rooms on the first floor, including a bedroom, parlor, and working room.

The house would have been surrounded by a number of other buildings. One or two, perhaps small one- or two-room houses with a loft, provided quarters for the Evans' nine slaves, which apparently included two families and an elderly single man named Daniel. The well in the yard which was sunk into the high water table provided good-quality fresh water. The house and farm were probably similar to Dick Carter's rendition of a farmstead of the times on page 143.

Catherine had the fully supplied cupboard included in most homes. She also had three spinning wheels, including two flaxing wheels and a "wooling" wheel, a loom, a cotton gin, three tables, "Delf and queens-ware" plates and a large quantity of pewter plates (rather than the commonplace wooden plates), earthenware crockery, a looking glass, and a well-equipped kitchen with a fireplace, as indicated by the

---

282   Hancock, *Delaware Two Hundred Years Ago*, op. cit., pp. 24-25.
283   Ibid. Two quotes.

various hanging hooks and utensils. Since all the children were by now married and probably established in their own homes, furniture needs were presumably reduced.

The True Inventory sets forth a list of farm and household items which help define John and Catherine's house and farm and workday doings in their later years. The sheep shears and wooling and flaxing wheels and hackle to dress flax make it clear that wool and flax were grown and processed on the farm. The listed cotton gin signals that cotton was processed, perhaps from a small patch grown for family use. The loom was apparently used for weaving wool, linsey-woolsey, linen and cotton cloth. The extensive list of kitchen utensils and implements for the preparation of food, including a churn, and the list of livestock give some indication of the kinds of food on the table and how it was prepared. The amount of furniture listed is one measure of the size of their house. The fishing line heralds regular catches and the importance of fish in the family's diet. The number of slaves reflects the significant acreage that was under cultivation, which is further defined by additional information in John's and Catherine's estate documents. The axes and wedges point to tree-felling and clearing and chopping and firewood-splitting—almost daily chores.

Other structures: privies; probably a detached kitchen with fireplace where most meals were cooked, particularly in the summer; a large barn with numerous stalls and an attached equipment shed and pig pen; a corn crib; a wash house for laundry and soap-making; and a smoke house to cure and store meat. This portrait of a late-18th-century farm is all too reminiscent of farms I remember as a boy in Baltimore Hundred in 1946. Other than electric power, telephones, kerosene-fired space heaters, running water and flushing toilets (not in all 1946 farmhouses) houses, steel plows and cultivators behind tractors, and better ways of transporting goods to market, not many changes were apparent in the first half of the twentieth century.

Their Farm

Farm couples like John and Catherine, together with their slaves and any servants, were generally self-sufficient, possessing all the tools and farm implements necessary to grow food and fiber for the family. But they depended on others for some manufactured goods, such as shoes from the cordwainer, metal goods from the blacksmith, major or specialized carpentry work and kitchenware.

The immense labor involved was two-fold: life on the colonial farm was characterized by the field work of clearing, fencing, plowing, planting, cultivating and harvesting, and the almost Herculean everyday house and barn work—maintaining the garden, preserving food and cooking meals, making clothes

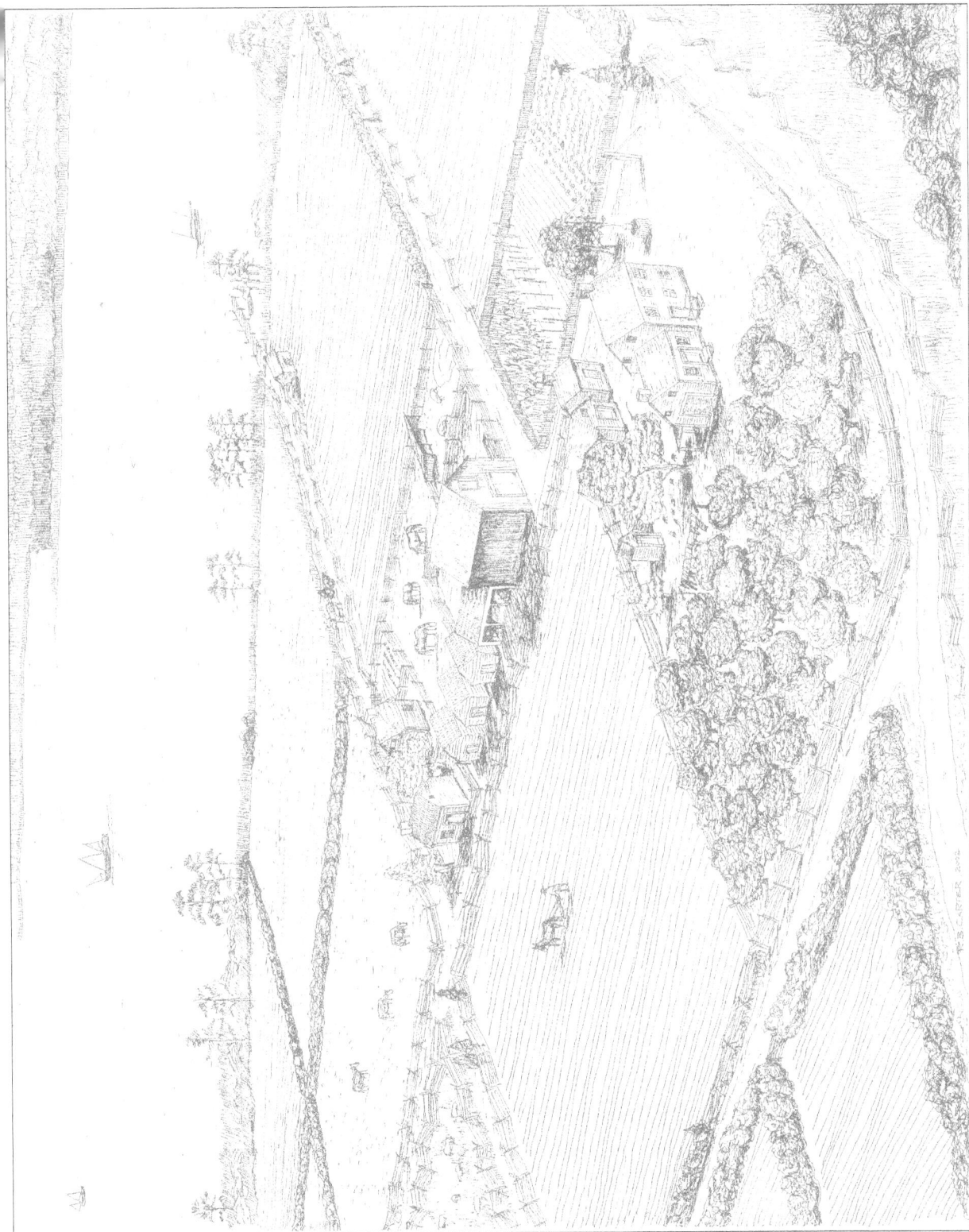

143

(Page Intentionally Left Blank)

(See previous side for Dick Carter's drawing of farm.)

and some of the footwear, housecleaning, animal husbandry, caring for small children, and equipment maintenance and repair. Husband and wife became jacks-of-all-trades. As for the children, the girls had household and kitchen garden chores, and the boys (girls too) were expected to help outside in fields and in the barn. Slaves and laborers, and possibly even indentured servants, made the whole enterprise possible.

Early on, John and Catherine had to depend on the children and limited help from locals for farm labor during planting and harvests. Naturally, farmers helped each other at harvest time and at such tasks as ditching and dyking. Later, as their farms grew and their economic position improved, the services of slaves and hired hands became available.

By the middle of the eighteenth century, with fields cleared and stumps now removed with the aid of teams of oxen, it was possible to plow and harrow with a team of oxen. Wheat farming was now economical and wheat became an important crop. A significant part of the farm was hay marsh, which was likely to be partially dyked to reduce tidal flooding and ditched to increase arable land.

In these times, even the few farmers with huge tracts did not sow over twenty acres of wheat nor tend more than thirty acres of Indian corn. The land was fertile and productive when cleared and plowed. Just as in the present day, two plantings were possible. Winter wheat was sowed by hand in the fall and summer wheat in March, three bushels of seed to the acre. Similarly, other important grains such as rye and barley were planted in the fall for summer harvest. Oats, flax and corn were planted in the spring. Buckwheat was planted after wheat was harvested and was gathered in September. The different crops allowed for a certain amount of crop rotation.

When land was cleared, it was often enclosed with post-and-rail or worm fences to protect crops from foraging domestic and wild animals. Four fenced fields could be rotated, one always serving as pasture—a good farming practice that provided natural fertilizer.[284] By the end of the century, the utility of fertilizer was becoming apparent.

The harvesting and processing of grain crops in colonial times was very labor-intensive. Plowing and cultivating were done with wooden plows and harrows drawn by two or three horses or as many or more oxen. Wheat was cut with a hand sickle,

---

284   Wilson Lloyd Bevan, Editor, *History of Delaware, Past and Present, Vol. I* (New York: Lewis Historical Publishing Co., 1929), p. 272.

cradled and bound into sheaves and hauled to the barn in a cart or wagon. It took a man one day to cut an acre of wheat with a sickle. Threshing the wheat was accomplished by hand or by harnessing a horse to a swivel on a post and walking it in circles as it trod on the unthreshed wheat to knock the kernels off the stalk. The stalks or hay were raked away. The wheat was easily separated from the stalks by tossing the mix into the air, usually above a wooden platform, where a breeze blew away the chaff, leaving the threshed wheat. It was a simple and effective but labor-demanding procedure. Rye, oats and buckwheat had to be thrashed out by hand by pounding on a wood floor with a flail so as not to lose grain. A flail is defined in Webster as a "threshing implement consisting of a wooden handle at the end of which a stouter and shorter stick is so hung [on a chain] as to swing freely."

A part of the threshed grains was set aside for seed for the next planting season, but seed storage was a problem because insects, mice and rats, and other small animals were a constant peril to next year's seeds. The family cats and dogs were obviously important pest controllers.

In the early years on the farm, the grains were ground or pulverized by a mortar and a pestle, often consisting of a hollowed stump and a pestle shaped to match. In later years, mills, powered by waterwheels fed from ponds on dammed streams, such as the ones on Derrickson's Creek or in Bishopville, ground larger quantities of corn and wheat for a fixed fee equal to about one-sixth of the flour or cornmeal produced.

Corn and a lesser quantity of wheat were shipped out of streams along the coast and up the Delaware River to markets. Other exports from Sussex were manufactured goods, among them pine boards, barrel staves and bald cypress shingles. Some were shipped from the Indian River in small locally built boats which sailed to Wilmington. Shipbuilding had started on the Indian River and its tributaries, including Whites Creek in the vicinity of present-day Ocean View, Millville and Cedar Neck. Oh, if only I could look out my den window now and view their sails and nature's sights of the late 1800s on Whites Creek!

Shoes were often made and repaired on the farm using oiled and tanned hides from steers raised on the farm. Thomas Evans, a cordwainer (shoemaker) also sold shoes, and John and Catherine may have been customers for their church shoes. Remember those silver shoe buckles that she left to granddaughter, Sarah Cord Evans?

146

Life Inside and Out

Not only was Catherine a true partner on the farm putting in a full day's work every day, but like most women of her day, she became pregnant every two years. This meant breast-feeding each baby for a year or more. Large families were common in spite of the high child mortality rate, which periodically caused great tragedy and sadness in colonial families. Just about every family lost a little one, and even though John and Catherine had 11 children, it is not unlikely they lost one or more others to disease.

Season after season, Catherine made clothing from raw wool, flax and cotton, cooked and preserved foods, housecleaned and gardened. In addition, during planting and harvesting seasons, the women and children joined the men and their "spare hands" to help get crops seeded and harvested. The growing of flax and cotton and the processes of fiber preparation, spinning and weaving are very time-consuming. (See a separate section on flax and cotton at the end of this chapter.)

Clothing was as homemade as apple pie. It came from cloth loomed at home. The women spun yarn from wool sheared from the family sheep and the flax and cotton which they presumably grew on a small plot. Homespun woolen and linen cloth became serviceable garments in the hands of Catherine and the slaves. Linen was also used for curtains, towels and quilts.[285] One can imagine the wooling wheel, the two flaxing wheels, the loom and the cotton gin whirring away all the time.

Catherine's own work clothes? Probably a simple linen shift and a full skirt above the ankles. She would often wear a long blouse with short or long sleeves, depending on the season. For warmth, she added more petticoats, as skirts were called. The omnipresent apron kept everything clean, and its pockets freed busy hands.

Catherine, probably with the help of one of the slave girls, cooked hot meals three times a day, probably in a large fireplace in an outside kitchen, which removed both confusion and heat from the main house. Fireplace meals were prepared with the aid of hanging pots, hooks, spits and Dutch ovens. In the summer, mutton, beef, poultry, and fish were served, along with homegrown vegetables, fruits, and berries. In the winter the variety of food was reduced and they ate less. Salted and cured meat, especially pork and salted fish, were available. Large quantities of bacon were cured, stored and served throughout the year. As already noted, four salted-down

---

285   Gardell Dano Christensen and Eugenia Burney, *Colonial Histories, Delaware* (Nashville, Tenn.: Thomas Nelson, Inc., 1974), p. 90.

large hogs could feed a family through the winter. By spring, before new garden produce was available, the only things in the larder might be salt meat and corn in the form of hominy, which were supplemented with hunted game. A staple was a stew of boiled meat, corn, beans and greens—eaten with a spoon and mopped up with cornbread. By this time, new-fangled forks were added to the standard collection of eating utensils.

Of course, farm families depended upon their own efforts for fruit, berries, vegetables, flour and meat. Catherine was responsible for planting the gardens, which she, the children and the slaves kept weeded and hoed during the summer. Because it was common for some form of alcoholic beverage to be consumed with most meals, it can be expected that apples were pressed for cider, peaches and perhaps some grain were fermented and distilled for brandy and stronger spirits, and grapes and other berries were put down for wine.

The cows were milked twice a day, and butter was churned for family use and to barter with neighbors. The children collected eggs from under the hens. With help from the men on the farm, the women preserved meat from slaughtered hogs and fresh fish for winter menus. Hams, pickled with salt, brown sugar or molasses, saltpeter and lye, were available through the winter.

"Store-bought" items for the household in later years were not inconsiderable: hard liquor, molasses, sugar, coffee and dishes and pewter ware. They were perhaps from a store up the Indian River near Millsboro which probably got its supplies from Wilmington. Money doled out for these purchases came from sales of corn, wheat, oats, barley, and pork and livestock.

Salt, a necessity, was produced locally either by boiling down saltwater or evaporating it in pans. Saltwater could be easily bailed from "shallow salt ponds which occur naturally" or from potholes deliberately dug behind the sand dunes in areas where there was washover from the sea.[286] Natural evaporation from the ponds and potholes increased the salt content and reduced the amount of wood required to boil down the salt water. Perhaps a cord of wood would be required to boil down 250 to 300 gallons of seawater to produce a bushel of salt. Salt could also be purchased from a nearby salt works then located near Cotton Patch Hills, south of the Indian River Inlet. Moses Dazey Sr. made salt and left to his son, Moses Jr., "a right to make salt . . . in my salt work" which was located near the beach east of Assawoman Bay.

---

286   Paul and Dorothy Pepper, "*An Original Fenwick Island Salt Pot*" (A paper prepared to distribute to visitors to the Fenwick Island Lighthouse), 1986.

Sanitation and personal care were regular tasks. Saturday night was tub night. Keeping hair clean and free of lice was a continuing problem. Most men shaved. Cleaning clothes was a regular chore. Linens and cottons could be washed with lye soap made on the farm, but woolens would shrink and had to be brushed and hung up to air out.

Mosquitoes, black flies, greenheads and other biting insects could be intolerable. Have you ever been on the boardwalk in the summer when mosquitoes were on the attack, or on the beach when there was a land breeze and the flies were biting? In 1790, there were neither the extensive ditching and dyking to drain marshes, insecticides sprayed from planes nor screened porches or windows. Attacks from insects could be intolerable for man and beast. Inside, smouldering cattail smoke helped keep them out of the house, but outside, people could only cover up, making summer heat even more oppressive. Animals took refuge in ponds where they submerged all but their heads.

Slavery

John and Catherine were slaveholders. Having said this, I must add that it is the purpose of this work to research and describe my family and discuss life in Baltimore Hundred, and it is not the purpose to address or dismiss the larger issues regarding slavery. I make no excuses for my ancestors and their neighbors. It is not sufficient, perhaps, simply to say that the institution of slavery was immoral and a tragic and enduring chapter in our Nation's history, which I believe. Not an idyllic model, and not enough, perhaps, but I leave this discussion with this and continue with a review of slavery during the times of John and Catherine.

By 1790, about one-fifth of Sussex County's population of approximately 20,000 was black. Most were slaves, many of whom had been brought into Delaware from Maryland by their masters.[287] Slaves were also sold by merchants in markets as close as the Nanticoke River and in Seaford, Laurel, Milton and Lewistown (Lewes). By the time of the Revolution, births replenished and increased the slave population. The ratio of slaves to free blacks was more than two to one, a figure that was to change rapidly in the next decades.

In the 1780s, important changes were made in Delaware's laws governing slaves. The General Assembly forbade the sale of slaves into the state—and made easier the manumission of slaves. By 1860, fewer than 2,000 slaves remained in

---

287   Ibid., p. 11.

Delaware, most of whom were in Sussex.[288] Much, and probably most, of this reduction was due to changing economics and farming methods rather than social pressures.

Considering the size of John and Catherine's farm, slaveholding issues possibly had real impact. They, their three sons, "Our Daniel," John and William, and three daughters, simply could not cope with their expanding farm without added help. Slaves were not just an economic necessity but valuable assets on such a farm. John and Catherine must have purchased slaves, since there is no record of their inheriting them from their parents who had earlier shifted from the cultivation of tobacco to grain crops with reduced labor needs. They remained slaveholders during their lifetimes, leaving their nine slaves, including at least two children, to their heirs. Their combined value was over 200 pounds while the total value of John's estate, not including his extensive real estate holdings, was just over 347 pounds. A prime Negro man was valued at 45 pounds, and a prime Negro woman was valued at 30 pounds. Slaves were considered a commodity. By comparison, a yoke of oxen was valued at about 10 pounds.

Absent other supporting or contrary information, I have assumed slaves, Daniel, Jid, Ike, Patt, Alse, her child, Elan, and the other Negro children were well treated. Again, the word "well" is relative, and it is understood slaves were property to be bought and sold, exploited, and worked. My conclusion is based on the fact that only a healthy, working slave had value. Moreover, the words of John's will, which provided that slave Daniel could "choose his own master" after Catherine died, seems to be a clear indication that John and Catherine probably had a level of affection for old Daniel. This does not mean Daniel was freed, but it does mean he may have had his choice of sons, Daniel, John or William, or their sisters as a master. However, this is conjecture. In the Inventory of John Sr.'s assets made during the probate of his estate in 1795, Negro man Daniel is appraised at 15 pounds while Jediah and Isaac are appraised at 45 pounds. This is an indication that Daniel was elderly or physically impaired and of reduced economic value. Less than a decade later, neither Catherine nor her sons mentioned slaves in their wills. I have found no record of their destiny, or why or for what reason they were not again mentioned.

While the Mason-Dixon Line became the dividing line between slave states and free, Delaware, the only state in the nation that is east of the Mason-Dixon line rather than north or south of it, retained slavery for many decades. Delaware regiments served with the North during the Civil War, but when slavery was

---

288   Ibid., p. 16.

150

abolished, strict segregation became the norm.[289] It lasted for almost one hundred and fifty years. The Delaware General Assembly, controlled in the post war decades by southern Democrats, declined to ratify the 13th, 14th and 15th Amendments to the United States Constitution until the Republicans took over 30 years later. Schools were segregated in Sussex County in the 1950s when I was in high school and remained predominantly so until 1968. Not a proud record!

Delaware's supposed ambivalence in the Civil War is illustrated by an apocryphal saying of an elderly customer in my Dad's hardware store around 1950. "Delaware has three counties," he said. "The sympathies of New Castle to the north were with the Union. The sympathies of Sussex to the south were with the Confederacy. Kent in the middle made moonshine for whichever side was winning." In summary, in Delaware there was support for the South but not for secession.

Women in the Society

John and Catherine lived at a time when the rights of women were limited. They had few political rights and were barred from voting or filing suit in courts. Married women normally could not own real estate or even inherit land. In this manner, John became the owner of land willed to Catherine by her father, Daniel Wharton. Apparently Daniel Wharton considered John to be an honorable man who would properly manage the inherited lands and distribute them to John and Catherine's children, either during their lifetimes or by will.

If the husband died with a will and wanted to provide land to his wife, he could "lend" it to her as a life estate, which would go to another stated legatee when she died. If a husband either died without a will or did not satisfactorily provide for his wife, she was entitled to a claim for the "widow's share," one third of her husband's estate, including land.

Book Learning

Harold Hancock writes that in 1768 there was not a single grammar school in Sussex.[290] This may be misleading because the term "grammar school" probably referred to a secondary school. The 1795 will of William Hall mentions a schoolhouse on his lands in what is today's Bethany Beach or South Bethany.[291]

---

289   Christensen and Burney, op. cit., p. 98.
290   Hancock, *Delaware Two Hundred Years Ago*, op. cit., p. 92.
291   Will of William Hall, January 21, 1795, Sussex County Wills, Liber E, pp. 208-210.

William provided that his wife, Mary, was to have "...the hole use of all my lands and posessen Tell my Son David Hall comes to the age of twenty one Except the School House and where it Stands that to be for the use of a School . . . [original spelling]." There is apparently no written history of the Hall schoolhouse—when it started, who the teachers and students were, or what happened to it.

Families of the time often collectively paid a teacher a specified sum for a specified term to teach children, usually males, to read and write. A small log or pine-slab cabin would be constructed in no time at all and the children would attend for the specified "term," from several weeks to several months a year. Often, the cabin also served as accommodation for the hired teacher.[292] Perhaps this describes the Hall School which was probably attended by Hall, Evans and Daisey sons and those of other landowners in the Muddy Neck area.

The John Evans commonly known as John, School Master, who died as a relatively young man in 1794, might have been a part-time teacher in the Hall Schoolhouse. He lived in Muddy Neck near William Hall's lands. He witnessed and probably drafted many wills during this time and it is easy to understand why. His handwriting was beautiful and precise. His accomplished penmanship and teaching might explain the ability of a number of residents of the area to sign their names and presumably to read the Bible, the only book listed in most inventories.

Religion

At this time, religion was important in Baltimore Hundred. John Evans Sr. is recorded as being a supporter of the Blackwater Presbyterian Church in 1778 and 1779, having agreed to pay "part of the ministerial labors of Reverend John Rankin, so long as he shall remain our stated minister and a regular member of Lewistown Presbytery."[293] Three other Evanses, another John, Ebenezer, and William, also supported the Blackwater Presbyterian Church.

We can assume John, Catherine and the children hitched up the horse and cart and made the trip of more than three miles to Blackwater every Sunday over the road leading from Cedar Neck to the head of Indian River which went by Blackwater. The inventory of John's estate included only two books—a Bible and a "Child's Bible,"

---

292   Hancock, *Delaware Two Hundred Years Ago*, op. cit., p. 92.
293   Wright, *Vital Records of Kent and Sussex Counties Delaware 1686-1800*, op. cit., p. 154.

so Bible reading, including evening and Sunday readings to the children, probably was a regular part of life in the Evans family.

Other local churches included the Prince George's Chapel in Dagsboro, the Sound Methodist Church at the head of the Assawoman Sound, and the Sounds Baptist Church—also at the head of the Sound. While John Sr. and Catherine and their family apparently supported the Blackwater Presbyterian Church, this clearly was not their only option. The Sounds Baptist Church, formed in 1782, met in members' homes—no house of worship was ever erected.[294]

The Sound Methodist Church was built on a one-acre tract purchased for 20 shillings. The deed, dated April 1784, was granted to the Trustees, including John Sr.'s brother Solomon.[295] Solomon apparently was a leader in the organization of this church. Solomon and his wife twice hosted Francis Asbury, the circuit-riding Wesleyan preacher. Asbury preached "at S. Evans" on July 20, 1779, and "about a hundred people were present."[296] In July 1796, Asbury returned and ". . . lodged with Solomon Evans, whose house I visited sixteen years ago: here are two people above seventy years of age who have lived together forty-eight years."[297]

While today's Bethany Beach area was very isolated at the end of the eighteenth century, it is not surprising that Asbury visited. He traveled over a quarter of a million miles in his five decades of preaching. He was more widely traveled than any other man of his generation and known by more people. His 1779 visit must have inspired Solomon and the other Trustees and supporters to start the Sound Methodist Church. Perhaps John Sr. and Catherine were among the "about a hundred people."

Socializing

Visiting neighbors was the main social event. These events often took place on Sunday evenings. Sunday was also a night for "sparking," as visits to an eligible young lady were called. Hunting, fishing and oystering could be social events as well, but providing food for the table was the main goal of these pursuits. At holiday time, there was much visiting, shooting of guns, and shooting matches.

---

294   Scharf, op. cit., p. 1342.
295   Ibid.
296   *The Journal and Letters of Francis Asbury, Vol. I, 1771 to 1793*, Edited by Elmer T. Clark (Nashville, Tenn.: Abingdon Press, 1958), p. 306.
297   Ibid., *Vol. II*, p. 91.

Politics and the Revolution

Harold Hancock reported that ". . . the typical male Delawarean in the 1780s was of English descent, living with his wife and several children on a small farm of thirty to one hundred acres. He had served in the militia during the Revolution, and he or a neighbor had been involved in combat during the war in New York, New Jersey or the South. Before the Revolution he probably thought of himself as Anglican, even though he seldom attended services. Following the Revolution he turned to Methodism. If he lived in Sussex County during the war, he was probably conservative in his political outlook. When national parties were formed in the 1790s, he became a Federalist."[298]

Not withstanding Hancock's statement, I found no record of John Sr's. serving in the military. He was probably too old as well to serve during the French and Indian War which ended in 1763. Hancock's statement is probably not as relevant to males in remote Baltimore Hundred, which was part of Maryland until 1775, as it is to men in Kent and New Castle Counties. It is likely that John and his sons served in the militia, possibly with some time outside Sussex County. Again, it must be said that there are no surviving records to support this likelihood other than Harold Hancock's statement that most men "joined up." Daniel's extended absence from rent rolls may have meant he was serving elsewhere, but there is no known corroboration.

The Stamp Act was passed by Parliament in London in 1763. Its passage was a direct result of the French and Indian War, known in Europe as the Seven Years War, which drastically increased the British national debt. Parliament thought America should assist in carrying the burden. Thus began the unrest leading to the Declaration of Independence. The colonists claimed that Parliament had no more to do with the colonies than the Assemblies in the colonies had to do with Parliament. And things went downhill fast. Even though the Stamp Act was repealed in 1766, later acts of Parliament incited great resentment at a time when the colonies were much more able to resist. Had Parliament tried to enforce the Stamp Act in 1766, the outcome might have been different. By 1775 the colonies were much more ready for a showdown than they had been in 1766. By retreating in 1766, England may have helped to assure the victory of the American cause in the Revolution.

It is a matter of record that there were significant Loyalist sympathies in the Three Lower Counties. According to a British officer stationed off New Castle, the people "are certainly well-affected in general and brought us large supplies of

---

298   Hancock, *Delaware Two Hundred Years Ago*, op. cit., pp. 10-11.

everything we wanted." The loyalists were incited to action by British Vessels off the coast. Some, like Joshua Hill, Simon Kollock and William Robinson in Sussex County, actually supported British forces. Kollock used counterfeit money to purchase a large quantity of cattle to supply British ships off Lewistown (Lewes). Their hopes were dashed, however, when the large British fleet which arrived off Lewistown in July 1777 sailed for the Chesapeake instead of Philadelphia. Antagonism was understandable in such cases. The Loyalists were threatened and some actually fled home, county, province and even the country.

The likelihood that John Evans supported the Revolution and opposed the Tory Loyalists may mean he and his sons participated in repeated and emotional conflicts between the Loyalists and Whigs even though most of such activities were in the western parts of Sussex and in the vicinity of Lewistown. Maryland militia were sent into Delaware in July 1777 to join the Delaware Militia as authorized by the General Assembly for the purpose of "Tory-catching."[299]

Indians

The Indian inhabitants of the area were gone before John and Catherine established their household. Settlers had continued to push the Indians farther and farther back into the swamps and take their lands. It was a continuing story of deceit, bullying and outright theft of Indian lands. In 1742, the Shawnee Indians from the north proposed to the Nanticokes that they call a meeting of all the Indian River Indians. Indians from all parts of the peninsula met for six days. Queen Weocomocus, ruler of all the Indian River Indians, agreed to join the Shawnees to fight the White people. The White people were well-informed about the meetings and the Indians' intent. The Native leaders were brought to court, but they denied planning an attack. Since none had been made, the Whites did not punish the Indians in order to avoid causing more trouble. On July 24, 1742, another treaty was signed.[300] The Indian River Indians eventually took the bones of their honored dead and paddled up the Chesapeake in their log pirogues. They settled temporarily on the Susquehanna River under the protection of the Iroquois.

For more information on Indians in Delaware, see Volume I of Charles B. Clark's book, *The Eastern Shore of Maryland and Virginia*.[301]

---

299   Hancock, *The Loyalists of Revolutionary Delaware* (Cranberry, N.J.: Associated University Press, 1977), pp. 68-69.
300   Ibid., p. 100.
301   Charles B. Clark, op. cit.

Clothing – From the Ground Up

While the processes of producing wool from sheep and the shearing, cleaning, carding, spinning, and weaving of woolens and the growing and processing of cotton are generally understood, the very prevalent production of linen from flax, common throughout the Middle Colonies, is less understood. The Chapter, "Flax Culture and Spinning," in a delightful 1898 book, *Home Life In Colonial Days*, by Alice Morse Earle,[302] inspired this discussion of flax farming and linen production, step by step.

Like most farmers, John Sr. and Catherine probably allocated a small plot of cleared land for a patch of flax. Their three sheep were a source of raw wool, and they may have grown some cotton to supply the cotton gin in John Sr.'s inventory.

Seeds for the flax patch were broadcast in the spring, and the children weeded the young plants when they were three to four inches tall. Ripe by midsummer, the plants were pulled, roots and all, and spread in the field to dry in the sun. The multi-stage process was colorfully described as including "rippling," "breaking," "swingling," "bundling," "swingling" again and "hackling." The basic process hadn't changed since Biblical times. "Rippling" the stalks of flax involved combing them with a coarse comb that had "great teeth" attached to a plank. The seed-bolls were removed and saved for next year's seeds by drawing the stalks through the comb and collecting the seeds on a sheet. "Bundling" was tying the stalks at the seed end forming them into bundles and placing the bundles into a tent-shaped stack to dry. When dried, the stacks were placed in a pool under weights to rot the leaves and soften fibers. After four or five days under water, the stacks were taken out of the pool and the rotted leaves removed. They were dried again and rebundled. Next came the "breaking" process. The fibers were broken away from the woody material in the stalks by actually bending and breaking the outer layers of the stalks. "Swingling" was the beating that followed, which removed remaining bark from the fibers. Basically, the dried stalks were beaten against a "swingling block" or vertical board with a tool similar to a wooden machete or small diameter rolling pin. An experienced, hard-working man could process forty pounds of flax a day.

Now came additional "bundling" and "swingling," by which time a coarse thread could be spun from the coarse fibers for bagging fabric. "Hackling" the fibers divided them into their finer filaments to produce still finer thread and fine woven

---

302   Alice Morse Earle, *Home Life in Colonial Days* (New York: The Macmillan Company, 1898), Chapter VIII.

fabrics. Up to six hackles of increasing fineness were used to obtain a small quantity of fine flax that could be separated according to fineness before being spun into linen thread.

Spinning on a flaxing wheel was work for the women and older girls. In a full day, two skeins of linen thread could be produced—about a third of a pound. The process continued with multiple washing, rinsing, bleaching, drying and winding, all of which could take a number of weeks. Bleaching in colonial times was done with hot water, ashes, slaked lime or buttermilk. The womenfolk would often haul their flaxing wheel to a neighbor's home for a day of spinning and socializing.

Weaving of the thread into linen cloth was laborious. Only a few yards of cloth could be woven in a day's work. Still more washing and bleaching followed, then, dying and sewing. Clothes had to be produced not only for the family, but also for any indentured servants and slaves.

Cotton was not forgotten. John's gin was no doubt put to use with cotton the family either grew or purchased. Slaves were traditionally a necessary part of the labor-intensive cotton production process. The amount of cotton grown on John and Catherine's farm was small compared to the large farms stretching from Virginia to the Gulf of Mexico.

Assuming that three yards of material per person had to be produced every year to meet their needs and that there were fifteen people on the farm, total annual production would be 45 to 50 yards of cloth per year—a formidable task. If a pound of ginned cotton yielded between two and four yards of cloth, depending on the weave, close to seventy-five pounds of raw cotton yielding about twenty pounds of ginned cotton was necessary to produce the needed fifty yards of cloth. Good rich land could produce 2,000 pounds of seed cotton per acre. The sandy loam near the ocean would probably produce less, say about 1,000 pounds per acre. Using these numbers, perhaps a tenth of an acre would be planted—a patch about fifty by one hundred feet. If some were sold to neighbors or if they produced cotton for grown children and grandchildren as well, their patch might have measured as much as 100 feet square.

Even a cotton patch as small as one-fifth of an acre required many man-days of hard labor to plow, harrow, plant, weed, remove bugs and pick. But producing 70 pounds of raw cotton and 20 pounds of ginned cotton was just the beginning. At the rate of half a pound of spun cotton per person, per day, forty person-days were required to spin the ginned cotton. Another two days were needed to weave two to four yards of cloth from each pound of ginned cotton. Thus, it took another 40 person-days to weave cloth and many more such days to cut and sew clothes from the cloth. In sum, up to a half a person's time a year would have been required to grow and process the cotton from their small patch. Clearly, cotton could not even be grown and processed until slaves or indentured servants were available. The production and processing of wool was similarly labor intensive.

Certainly, even in John and Catherine's time, the production of clothes required a significant part of the homestead labor. Even limited cotton production required much slave labor. This situation explains why cotton production in Baltimore Hundred, always limited, must have declined rapidly at the end of the eighteenth century, by which time British cloth could be purchased in Wilmington.[303]

With the improvements brought about by the Industrial Revolution in coming years, machine-produced cloth of good quality from England and later, New England, became affordable for some folks.

Money

When John was a young boy, tobacco was the generally accepted medium of commercial exchange. While the price of tobacco varied from year to year, the average price at that time was about 1.5 pence per pound. In a 1754 inventory, 150 pounds of tobacco was valued at 12 shillings and 6 pence—a rate of 1.64 pence per pound. At this rate, a thousand pounds of tobacco was worth just over six English pounds. A cow with calf might cost one-and-a-half pounds. A prime Negro man might bring thirty pounds, or five thousand pounds of tobacco, on the slave market. A hundred bushels of wheat might cost around sixteen pounds. In 1769, about two hundred acres of Baltimore Hundred land along rivers or bays could be purchased for twenty pounds.[304]

Transportation

Travel in eighteenth century Sussex County was, of course, land-bound. Horseback was the preferred early mode of transportation before family wagons came into general use. By the end of the century, some carriages were in use. The 1794 inventory of John Evans, School Master, included a carriage. Except for mariners who made their living on the water, travel by Baltimore Hundred residents was mostly local. Longer trips were seldom required.

---

303   Hancock, *Delaware Two Hundred Years Ago*, op. cit., p. 81.
304   One Pound equals 20 shillings, and one shilling equals 12 pence.

There was a stagecoach route from near Berlin to Wilmington by 1802 when James Hempill traveled around the peninsula. His account of his trip[305] was quite detailed. He and a companion traveled from Wilmington to Salisbury, Snow Hill and Berlin, Maryland, and back. He took a stagecoach on the return trip leaving from Trap, a small village near Berlin, at "20 m. past 4 oClock A.M."and stopped in "Dagsborough at 20 m past 8" where they had breakfast and the drivers changed horses and greased the stage. They arrived at Georgetown at 11 and at Dover at "10 min. past 6." They traveled around 80 miles in a 14-hour day—almost six miles an hour, including stops.

Roads often followed old Indian trails and could be crooked, swampy and rutted. In the spring, they were very muddy.[306] Roads of the time included one from the head of the Assawoman Sound to Cedar Neck and one which went by Blackwater Church, today's Clarksville to Frankford road.

Construction of new roads was managed by the Levy Court of Sussex County in Georgetown. Landowners filed a signed petition for a new road with the Levy Court. An interesting November 17, 1801, petition with sixteen signatures sought a road from the "Bridge on the Head of Millers Creek down the Neck until it intersected with Cedar Neck Road between the House and Plantation of Moses Dazzey and the house and Plantation of John Dazzey."[307] This is probably the existing County Road 362 from Millers Creek to the back road from Ocean View and Muddy Neck to Bethany Beach. When approved, adjacent landowners were required to pay a road tax. Some worked out their contribution with labor on the road.[308]

Travel by boat was common. John and Catherine probably had rowboats and possibly a small shallop to go to a store in "Rock Hole," present-day Millsboro, and across the Indian River to Long Neck, where John had land holdings. Shallops and even larger sailing vessels were used to transport grain and other crops and lumber and shingles up the Delaware River.

While both the 1795 Inventory of the Estate of John Evans and Catherine's 1797 will included horses and saddles, there was no mention of wagons, carts,

305   James A. Hemphill, *Account of a Visit to Maryland, 1802*," ed. John A. Monroe, *Delaware History, Vol. III*, (1948-1949), p. 61.
306   Hancock, *Delaware Two Hundred Years Ago*, op. cit., p. 82.
307   Archives of Delaware, R. G. 4805, Road Papers, Baltimore Hundred, Nov. 17, 1801.
308   Hancock, *Delaware Two Hundred Years Ago*, op. cit., p. 86.

carriages, boats or shallops. John was almost eighty when he died, and any such possessions might already have been given to their children.

John and Catherine were generally self-sufficient. It is not likely they traveled very far. The extent of their journeys was probably no more than a day's ride on horseback or by farm wagon, or a day's sail in any direction. Their longest regular trip was probably the family's Sunday wagonride to the Old Blackwater Church.

Will of John Evans Sr., February 15, 1791 Archives of Delaware, Vol. A70, p. 131 (Original spelling)

In the Name of God amen. I John Evans of Sussex County and State of Delaware being weak in body, of sound mind and Memory Blessed by God and calling to mind the uncertainty of Life, and knowing that it is appointed for all men to die, do this fifteenth day of February in the Year of our Lord one Thousand Seven hundred & ninty one make and Publish this my last Will and Testament, in manner and form following that is Say) ----- ----- ----- ----- ----- ----- ----- ----- ----- ----- -----

Item 1st   I give and bequeath unto my Son John Evans, all the land and Plantation where I did formerly live called North Petherton, together with the Twenty acres of land that I bought of John Onions and what land I Received to North Petherton, together with fifty acres of land that I bought of Joshua Evans Except fifteen acres of the aforesaid land on the south side I give to my son William Evans, all the aforesaid land and Premises to be holden by them and their Heirs and assigns for Ever likewise a piece of marsh being on the Beach against Cherry Bush to be Equally divided between my Two sons John and William, to be holden by them and their heirs and assigns for Ever. ----- ----- ----- -- ----- ----- ----- ----- ----- -----

I also Give and bequeath to my said Son William Evans one hundred Acres of land lying in Long Neck, that I swapt with John Hollaway for to him and his heirs and assigns for Ever. I also give and bequeath to my said Son William Evans fifty Pounds in Cash to be paid out of my Estate to him and his Heirs and assigns for Ever ----- ----- ----- ----- ----- ----- ----- ----- ----- ----- ----- ----- --- -- -----

Item   I lend my loving wife Catharine Evans a Negro man Called Daniel and one Negro boy called Jid, and one Negro Girl Called alse [Elsie?] and her Child Called Elan, and one hand Mill, during her Natural life and to return to my Estate allowing Daniel to choose his Master, and after her death the hand Mill I give to my son William and also I lend to my beloved wife a Corner Cuboard during her Natural life, and then to return to my son William. I also Give unto my loving wife one third of all my Stock Cattle and Sheep and hogs and goose and fowls also two feather beds and furniture, and one third part of all my Pewter and one third part of all my pots, and one third of my knives and forks my looking Glass and the delf ware dishes and plates. Likewise two spinning Wheals one Plow and harrow box iron and heaters Three Chairs one loom and _____ and one iron chain and Clevis and Ox Yoke and one third of my hoes and axes ----- ----- ----- ----- ----- ----- ----- ----- -----

Item   I lend to my daughter Rebeckah Mumford Twelve Pounds in Praised Goods such as my Executor can spare to her ----- ----- ----- ----- ----- ----- ----- ---

-- -----

Item   I give to my Son William all my Right Claim and Interest of all the land and marsh that lyes in Cedar Neck that I have by my Catherine whareon I now live for Ever —

I also give to my three children (Viz) Elizabeth Dale Mary Hall and William Evans all the Rest and Residue of all my estate not yet mentioned to be Equally divided between them and their heirs and assigns for Ever ----- ----- ----- ----- ----- -----

Item   I do hereby nominate ordain and appoint my son William Evans my whole and Sole Executor of this my last Will and Testament, and also, I do revoke disannull and make void all Former wills bequeaths made by me in any wise heretofore. Ratifying and Confirming this to be my last Will and Testament In Testamony Whareof I the said John Evans have to this my last Will and Testament set my hand and seal day and Year above written. ----- ----- ----- ----- ----- ----- ----- ----- ----- -----

       Signed Sealed and Declared by the Said John Evans as and for his last
       Will and Testament, in the Presence John Evans Senior-----Seal
       Of us who were Present at the Signing &
       Sealing throughout ----- ----- ----- -----

       Littleton Townsend
       James Wharton
       Samuel Cord

Chapter 13   Letter to Annmarie – Cousins

June 1995

Dear Annmarie,

Well aren't you special! It sounds funny I know, and confusing for sure, but being the daughter of my third-born son and Lauren, you really are your own cousin—third cousin once removed, that is. Another way of saying it is that you are both Alonzo and Lib Evans' great-great-granddaughter and their third great-granddaughter. How I enjoyed introducing you, the infant Annmarie, as both to the family at the 1994 family reunion.

That's special—two ties to the same ancestor. Your mother, Lauren, and your father are second cousins once removed. It is not unusual for cousins to marry cousins, and it has happened numerous other times in our family. Alonzo Evans' mother's maiden name was Harriet Evans, and Harriet and Alonzo's fathers were somewhat distant cousins.

Since you are your own third cousin once removed, it is most appropriate to ask what that means. It is a complicated subject, deserving of explanation. What is a cousin? What is a third cousin? What does "once removed" mean? Are there different types of cousins? Simply said, cousins have common ancestors. True first cousins have common grandparents. Similarly, second cousins have common great-grandparents, and so on. For example, I am both your and Laura's grandfather, so you and Laura are first cousins. Similarly, Annmarie, you are a second cousin of my two sister's grandchildren, Leslie, Shelby and Matthew, and Brooke and Will Dolby, because you all have the same great-grandparents, Great Mom-Mom Hilda and Great Pop-Pop Richard Wood.

The definition of a cousin is still more complicated. Remember, I said cousins have a common ancestor. That common ancestor, however, doesn't have to have the same relationship to all the cousins. If two people have the same ancestor, but they don't have the same relationship to that ancestor, they are still cousins, but cousins once or more times removed. For example, your Dad and Bruce Ray are first cousins because they have the same grandparents, but you are his first cousin once removed because you are one generation further removed from great Mom-Mom Hilda than Bruce Ray.

You are also both my granddaughter and my second cousin once removed. Ask your mom or dad to explain that someday. As I said, it sounds funny, I know, but it really is so!

As of the 1995 Alonzo Evans Family Reunion, he had almost 400 direct descendants. There are a lot of cousins in the family tree, some distant, but still cousins. By now in Alonzo and Lib's family, there are fourth cousins at least, and possibly fourth cousins once removed.

Annmarie, you are a part of another old Delaware and Sussex County family, the Laytons. Your mother, Lauren, is the granddaughter of Uncle Neil and Aunt Maria Evans and Frank and Anna Shockley Layton. Both the Shockleys and Laytons are very old Delaware and Sussex County families. Ask you mom to tell you about these families.

Annmarie, you are a positively delightful and special little girl, and your Pop-Pop loves you very much. Let's go to the beach together, often.

Love,
Pop-Pop

P.S. I don't want to confuse you, but years ago Evanses also married Daiseys and Halls as well as other Evanses, so it gets even more complicated. You are also your eighth cousin, eighth cousin once removed, ninth cousin, and ninth cousin once, twice and three times removed, and probably more. That means you are related to yourself and your sisters at least eight different ways. Is this mind-boggling, or what?

Chapter 14 Daniel (c. 1745-1800) and Sarah Evans (c. 1760-after 1812)

Contemporaneous Happenings

1763 The French and Indian War ends with Treaty of Paris

1776 Declaration of Independence

1781 Cornwallis surrenders at Yorktown, ending the War of American Independence

1783 The Peace of Paris signed, giving the United States west to the Mississippi, north to Canada and south to the Floridas

1786 Mozart composes The Marriage of Figaro

1793 Eli Whitney invents the cotton gin

1796 Napoleon assumes command in Italy and begins meteoric rise in France

1799 Rosetta Stone found in Egypt

Daniel Evans was the son of John Sr. and Catherine Wharton Evans. This conclusion, reviewed in Chapter 7, is based upon a preponderance of circumstantial evidence and the absence of conflicting evidence, but not absolute proof.

Because Daniel and Sarah are discussed so thoroughly in Chapter 7, this chapter instead addresses man's extensive environmental impact from their time to now on the land and waters of Baltimore Hundred. So much has changed since Daniel and Sarah lived near the beach at the head of Assawoman Sound that it is appropriate to reflect on and discuss changes in the place they lived, including environmental factors over the past two centuries.

It may well be that Daniel and Sarah Evans were the first of the Evans generations in Baltimore Hundred to be impacted by severe environmental insults. Specific and continuing actions dating back to the seventeenth century severely and probably irreversibly impacted the environment. As early as the 1630s in Zwaandael (today's Lewes), there was opposition by the West India Company to land clearing by the first settlers causing a scarcity of profitable fur-bearing animals.

Would that we could visit Daniel and Sarah's eighteenth century farm in today's South Bethany area to observe all its wildlife and game, its wetlands and clear rivers, streams and bays, and its virgin forests essentially untouched since the glacial age. The waters were oyster-filtered, and bottom grasses swayed in the clear water with the winds and tides. They were rich in fish and shellfish.

Even now, in the twenty-first century, mandatory environmental impact statements do not, and perhaps cannot, provide a full understanding of the possible effects of significant engineering, farming, construction and development. It was not until the last third of the twentieth century that a real, national environmental consciousness developed, and the necessity to understand the economic, social and environmental impacts of our actions became apparent. Even with all this understanding, it is not always possible today to make the right decisions. The technology is not always available or affordable. The political and social will falters at times. In Daniel and Sarah's time, the knowledge and significance of environmental impacts certainly were not understood.

Theirs was a time of different priorities than ours. Daniel and Sarah's top concerns were providing food and shelter for their family, fighting disease and providing for the future. Their understanding of environmental impacts was based solely on their perceptions from their own experience.

Daniel and Sarah and their neighbors worked hard clearing new fields from virgin forests when the soil became exhausted so they could continue to raise crops and feed their family. They dyked and ditched marshes to make harvesting hay easier, cleared and built roads through the woods, and built docks and moorings for the small boats necessary for travel and shipping. This type of activity continued at the Head of the Sound, as it was known, with little change through at least four succeeding generations.

Water transport and shipping were an important part of Baltimore Hundred's history and economy. The numerous inlets up and down the ocean coast gave access for ocean transport and provided the benefits of significant tidal flow. These inlets were somewhat mobile and their location changed often with severe hurricanes and northeasters. The Indian River Inlet, for example, is shown as a very wide inlet with shoals on a circa 1690 map of the area recreated in 1986 from the "most Authentic and Original Surveys from the Ancient Records of the Colonial Provinces of Maryland, Virginia and Delaware."[309] There was a direct, full but meandering inlet to Rehoboth Bay with changing shoals and sandbars, and tides flowed into and out of Rehoboth Bay. This flow was significantly enhanced by today's stabilized and relocated Indian River Inlet and Massey's Ditch.

---

309   John L. Amrhein Jr., Map, The Ancient Seacoast of Maryland, Including Part of Delaware and Virginia, op. cit.

Daniel's children and their neighbors who lived on Assawoman Bay or contiguous creeks were impacted by the damage to the Bay caused by the Fenwick Ditch, which was dug on the landward side around 1800 to connect the Assawoman Bay with Assateague Sound (Sinepuxent Bay) to the south.[310] Through the action of the tide, the ditch became a deep channel, irreversibly changing water circulation patterns and causing far-reaching and negative impacts on the Bay, reducing its utility as a harbor and the supply of fish and shellfish.

Fenwick Island, a narrow strip of land fringing the ocean, was cut by three inlets two centuries ago. "The northernmost was called the Little Assawoman Inlet and the southernmost was called Green River. Midway between these was Sinepuxent Inlet."[311] Two of the three, the Little Assawoman Inlet and the Sinepuxent Inlet, filled with shoals and disappeared almost two centuries ago. The Green River Inlet, presumably near the site of today's Ocean City Inlet, was also filled in, but it was reestablished during a twentieth century hurricane.

The unexpected impacts of the Fenwick Ditch on the Little Assawoman Inlet resulted in a petition to the Delaware House of Representatives at their session in February 1800, stating "the aforesaid inlet was stopped by the tide taking its course through the aforesaid ditch from one Bay to the other, which caused the oysters and cockles to die and the fishing greatly decreased." The petition was "to have the aforesaid ditch stopped by a wharf [sic] . . . by which the above privaledges [sic] [the harbor and fish and shellfish] will be restored . . ."[312] Great quantities of fish, oysters and cockles (as clams were known then) had been found in Assawoman Bay, but now, as stated in the petition, they and the harbor were destroyed. Shipping from Little Assawoman Bay, which had passed through the inlet, was essentially eliminated.

Also disappearing decades ago was a mapped inlet crossing from the Salt Pond to the ocean across John Evans' North Petherton tract, which included the site of today's ocean-side developments at the north end of Bethany Beach. This inlet, which probably came and went with storms, existed as late as the early 1900s. Its demise could have been sealed by the reduction in the volume of storm waters flowing through the inlet to the ocean. This reduced volume was decreased further

---

310   John A. Munroe, *Federalist Delaware (1775-1815)*, (New Brunswick, N.J.: Rutgers University Press, 1954), pp. 118-119.

311   James, op cit., p. 437.

312   Archives of Delaware, Legislative Papers 1799-1802, Misc. Petitions, Microfilm Roll 018, p. 253.

by the newly dug Assawoman Loop Canal, which acted as a pressure release valve. The existence of the inlet is confirmed by early twentieth century deeds in which Route 26 was known variably as "the road from Ocean View to the Salt Pond Inlet" and "the road to Hall's Beach."

Just as the digging of the Fenwick Ditch was well-intentioned, and the deleterious impacts were unexpected, the Assawoman Canal from Whites Creek to Assawoman Sound, approved by Congress and then dug in 1891, probably changed water circulation in Assawoman Sound, thereby causing other hard-to-quantify damage to the ecosystem.

The cutting of timber for buildings, wood products and firewood, and the clearing of land for farming had another severe impact on Baltimore Hundred and the river and bay systems. Productive tributaries of the Indian River, which were used for water transport, were no longer protected from silt-loaded runoff from cleared forests that filled in channels, changed river and bay beaches from sand to mud, and killed bottom grasses.

Imagine Daisey Landing far up Whites Creek from the Indian River being a commercial landing for sailing vessels and small steamboats. Until early in the twentieth century, produce was shipped from Daisey Landing and other similar landings in the inland bays to Philadelphia and Wilmington.[313] The trip to Wilmington took almost 24 hours in good conditions, but travel depended on the tides, winds and changing channels in inlets. It was not unusual to have boat travel from the Indian River Inlet delayed for days because of unfavorable winds and tides. The river has become much too shallow to support anything similar today.

Maintaining the viability of Whites Creek and other similar tributaries of the Indian River for recreational small-boat traffic now requires the dredging of channels. Dredging has its own predictable and absolute result: increased shoreline erosion. And that justifies bulkheading which reduces access of fish, shellfish and wildlife to important nursery areas. Since Whites Creek was dredged in 1999/2000, a small island across from my home has all but disappeared and shoreline erosion, previously measured in inches per year, has accelerated to yards per year in some spots. Today, the non-thinkers, ignoramuses and scofflaws who fail to heed no-wake zones further exacerbate shoreline erosion and damage the inland bays and the very fish and shellfish resources they want to enjoy.

---

313   Shipping from Indian River is discussed further in Chapter 23.

Marsh hay was a valuable crop for coastal residents in Colonial times. Large quantities of coarse hay could be harvested from marshes when dykes were raised to prevent flooding from high tides and storms.[314] Nurseries for fish and shellfish were damaged with impacts not recognized for decades, if not centuries. The impact of constructing dykes was compounded by the digging of ditches 70 years ago to drain marshlands as a curb on mosquitoes, and by the digging of large inland ditches by "ditch companies" as early as 1865 for the purpose of draining lowlands. The consequence of these actions was still more silting in Indian River and Whites Creek from the drainage ditches and erosion of marshes from the mosquito ditches. The productivity of nurseries for fish, shellfish and wildlife has surely been reduced.

Before 1796, Rehoboth Bay had so many oysters that a man could harvest thirty bushels a day. Alas, early over-harvesting soon decimated the oyster population, leading to a petition to the 1796 General Assembly to control the harvest.[315] A chain of circumstances: over-harvesting, point source and surface runoff sources of nutrients and other pollution, and reduced tidal flow through the restricted entrances to Rehoboth Bay from the Indian River and Lewes and Rehoboth Canal impacts, likely have combined to prevent successful reintroduction of environmentally beneficial filter-feeding oysters to Rehoboth Bay. Let's hope current science-based initiatives to reintroduce oysters to this once-productive Bay proceed and are successful.

Daniel and others who lived on the internal rivers and bays witnessed environmental damage from well-meaning projects two hundred years ago. We continue today—in the name of economic progress—to inflict damage. Poor farming practices introduce nutrients and pesticides into the waters. The combination of explosive population growth, which requires more land clearing and increased nutrient pollution into the waters, could be devastating to these "home" waters and others like them—and probably will be. Some authorities predict that it will be decades before we can rectify the deleterious surface and subsurface impacts of nutrient loads and restore the marine and shore—or littoral—environment. The difference between Daniel's time, over two hundred years ago, and now is that today we have a better understanding of the science and can muster the resources to do better.

---

314   Hancock, *Delaware Two Hundred Years Ago*, op. cit., p. 135.

315   Delaware Public Archives, Legislative Papers, Miscellaneous Petitions 1796, Micro-film Roll 016, p. 084. Such petitions resulted in legislation throughout the years to protect oysters, including an Act of the Legislature in 1841 to protect oysters that may hereafter be planted in the waters of Indian River and Rehoboth Bay.

The combined impacts are huge. The cutting of the Fenwick Ditch caused the closing of one, and possibly two, ocean inlets to Assawoman Sound. The Lewes and Rehoboth Canal has had less-visible impacts. Timbering caused soil erosion that silted in the streams. Poor farming practices exhausted soils and increased silt loads. Overoystering ruined the industry in Rehoboth Bay. Dyking impaired the function of natural marshes as nurseries for fish and shellfish and wildlife. Ditching for land drainage and mosquito control increased silting and detrimental nutrient loads. By today's standards, all these dynamics, some of which have persisted for more than two centuries, add up to an unquestionable environmental disaster. While we still have an absolutely wonderful place to live, we must remember our obligations. Will ours and future generations work together to pursue protection or slowly backslide?

The Will of Daniel Evans – September 1, 1798 Sussex County Wills, Liber F, p. 17

IN THE NAME OF GOD AMEN I Daniel Evans of Sussex County and in the Delaware State being very sick and week in body but of perfect sound mind and memory thanks be to almity god first and calling to mind the mortality of my body and considering allmen are born to Die Do make and ordain this my Last will and testement in the manner and form as followeth. First of all I Recommend my soul unto the Hand of God who give it me hoping in the general Resurrection at the last day will Reais it up together with its body and fashon like unto the glorious body of Christ and unto my body to be buried in a desent forme at the Discretion of my Executors and as touching my world Estate which it hath pleasd God to bless me with, I give and bestow in the manner and forme as followeth.

Item. I give and bequeath to my son Daniel Evans the one half of my land called Partnership the said Half to be Laid of a line Drawn East and West across the said Land part of a old Paten issued in maryland Right and part of a resurvea Dividing equally for quantity of acres I mean that Daniel should Have the north side of the Divisionall line and if Daniel should die without Hare that Zadock Evans should injoy his part, I give Daniel Evans one yoke of oxen non by the young stirs also the cros cut saw to him his Heirs or asign.

Item I give and bequath to my son Zadock Evans all the Remainder of my Land and Plantation where I now Live him his Hears or asigns but if Zadock dies without heare that Daniel shall enjoy His part, also my wearing Close and working tools and the young hors to Zadock Evans. I desire that my wife Sarah Evans may have a peaceble Home as long as she lives a wider.

Item I lend my beloved wife Sarah Evans the third part of all my clair Estate so long as she lives after her Dath that the same may be divided among my children.

Item I give Martha Taylor one Bed to be Delivered after her mothers Death a bed and trunnel Badstad and that no more of my Estate. I give Roday Barns one cow cold pride.

Item Sarah one bead and finuteer and no more of my estate.

Item I give and bequeath to my Daughter Elizabeh Evans one Rad Cow and Calf and all Hir increes tell she taks her away also I give her one Bed and fornuteer also a large puter Dish one Chist one Table one _____ and one hog to be Hurn forever, and further I do hereby Constitute and apoint my beloved wife Sara Evans to be my Whole and Sole Executer of this my Last Will and testament and I do hereby Revoak, Disannul and Denie all and every Other Will, testament, ligusy or Executor made or given before this Acknowledge This to be my last will and Testament ___as

Wittness my hand and seal this 1 day of September 1798   Daniel Evans (Signed)

Witness present, testo

Thomas Evans
Job Freeman
Comfort X Evans (her mark)

PART IV

ESTABLISHING DAISEY AND GREEN FAMILY ROOTS

Chapter 15   The Daisey Family[316]

My Mom-Mom Sarah Eleanor "Nellie" Daisey Evans was the daughter of Thomas Frank and Anna "Annie" Fernetta Green Daisey. I met Great Pop-Pop Daisey around 1941 when I visited his house and farm in Bayard, Delaware. It was located on the northwest corner of the intersection of the Camp Barnes Road and the Ocean View-Bayard Road. I remember him only as an old, slight, soft spoken man with a full mustache, who took me across the dirt road to see the barn. I remember little more than the house with a front porch and the barn; I wish I remembered more (see photo on next page). The house was occupied until being torn down in 2016.

<u>Great Pop-Pop Thomas Frank Daisey (1868-1943) and Great Mom-Mom Anna "Annie" Fernetta Green Daisey (1868-1935)</u>

Thomas Frank was known as Frank, and he signed his name, "Frank Daisey," as he did on a receipt made out to him by H. H. Hickman. Frank was born May 10, 1868, and he died on March 29, 1943, at the age of 74 years, 10 months and 19 days. Frank and Annie were both eighteen when they were married on June 11, 1886.[317]

Frank and Annie now rest in the Mariner's Bethel Methodist Cemetery next to Frank's father, "**Samuel H. Dasey**" (on his tombstone), and his mother, Sarah Hudson, who remarried after Henry's death. The surprising name, "Samuel H. Dasey," and not the always understood Henry Dazey confounded research for years and left an unsolved mystery now resolved in this Second Edition on pages 178-179.

Great Mom-Mom Annie was born April 23, 1868, to David Martin Green and Fernetta Anna Green, who lived in the Omar area near Dagsboro before moving to Bayard. She died April 2, 1935.

Frank and Annie and their growing family lived in Muddy Neck "way back in a field," according to Uncle Vaughn Daisey, "not far from the Jeffersons." They started their family of twelve here before they bought the Bayard Farm in 1906.

---

316   Much of the information in this chapter is from extensive but unorganized notes prepared by my Great Uncle Maurice Daisey and given to me by his wife, Frances, after his death. I am deeply indebted to Frances for this wonderful gift and to Uncle Maurice, a special person, for his extensive research on the Daisey family. Parts of the extensive materials on the Green family in Chapter 17 were provided by Joseph H. Green Jr. of Georgetown, Delaware. This was supplemented by materials on the Green and Sockrider families from my mother's first cousin, Phyllis Hudson Meyer, the granddaughter of Frank and Annie Daisey.
317   Public Archives of Delaware, Marriages, Vol. 75, p. 119.

Mom-Mom Nellie spent her early years on the farm in Muddy Neck. Their land went from the Muddy Neck Road near today's Jefferson's Bridge all the way back to the shore at the head of the Assawoman Sound (Bay).

The farm in Bayard was home for a large family which shared both hard work and the riches of a wonderful family life with unbounded love. Mom says visiting her Pop-Pop and Mom-Mom Daisey was always a pleasure. Mom and Aunt Daisey have emphasized how Frank and Annie were deeply respected and loved by their children and grandchildren. Even so, theirs was a time of just getting by—a national situation at the time. As with many families at that time in Baltimore Hundred, resources were clearly limited, but they weren't poor for their times. While the perceived poverty in Sussex County was a source of jest in New Castle and Wilmington, there was a certain quality of life in a large family on a small farm which transcended the apparent poverty of subsistence farming.

My Great-Grandparents, Frank and Annie Green Daisey,
at the Bayard Farm In 1933

The family home in Bayard had a kitchen in the back with a kerosene stove used for cooking in the summer. The adjacent multipurpose room in the middle of the first floor served as a family room, dining room, and sitting room. It had a pot-bellied woodstove, also used for cooking in the winter. The parlor in the front of the house was reserved for Sunday company only. The second floor had three obviously crowded bedrooms. The yard around the house and outbuildings was bare—devoid of grass. A regular children's chore was sweeping the yard with a brush broom made by Frank, an expert at making cornstalk fiber brooms which he sold for spare cash. The barn across the dirt road housed the cows, horse, two mules, hogs, the wagon known as a "derby" (or "durban," short for Dearborn) and a surrey. At the time, there was a pond across the road where the children and friends ice-skated in the winter.

Frank raised strawberries, and his children and grandchildren picked berries every spring for three cents a quart. On a good day in the middle of the picking season, Mom, Daisey, Aunt Frances Daisey and Uncle Maurice Daisey could each earn a dollar. Strawberry farming started in earnest after the Civil War, and in 1900 more strawberries were grown in Sussex than any other county in the nation. In 1918, 250,000 crates were shipped. Local berries were taken by wagon to the railroad in Selbyville for purchase by agents and shipment to Wilmington and Philadelphia. Strawberries were auctioned at Selbyville and Millsboro for shipment north. Large-scale strawberry production ended from plant disease and the World War II labor shortage.

With the coming of the railroad and enlightened farming, Sussex County eventually started to bloom. The railroad branched from Harrington to Milford in 1859. It was later extended to Georgetown and Rehoboth and in about 1874 to Millsboro, Dagsboro, Frankford and Selbyville, connecting to the Maryland line that continues to Pocomoke. Peaches became an abundant crop, and the railroad, sailing vessels and barges were taxed to their full capacity transporting them.

Frank Daisey was a mild-mannered man. "He never raised his voice," according to Aunt Daisey. He was a lot like his youngest son, Uncle Maurice, whom I liked and respected so much. Frank, however, once got aggravated at Mom and Daisey because they sat on strawberries while they were picking them for market. He simply said, "Children, that's my living."

Mom tells about how Frank used to go on overnight surf-fishing trips to catch fish to salt down in barrels for the dinner table. The ocean beach is a beautiful place and surf-fishing is a great pleasure. For Frank, however, it was also a way to help feed his family. Surf-fishing was simpler then. The mule and farm wagon provided access to the beach. Instead of the long surf rods of today, Frank probably used a sling of the type used by Mr. Harry Daisey of Roxana. He was an old man in 1946 and a great friend of mine as a boy of ten who had just moved to Roxana from Long Island. Mr. Harry had what looked like a normal surf rig with a sinker and two hooks, but instead of a rod, he had an about six-feet-long sling of heavy twine attached to the sinker on one end and to a hand-carved wood "toggle" on the other. The toggle was about three inches long with a hole in the center similar to the handle on a lawn mower starting cord. He held the toggle in his hand and rapidly twirled the sinker over his head to the proper velocity and then let go of the toggle to fling the sinker and baited hooks far into the surf. It was simple and effective. He had to be very careful when retrieving the line—with or without fish. To prevent tangles for the next cast he laid the line back and forth on the sand as he backed up the beach. He had to be even more careful when he released the toggle while casting to make sure his hand did not get caught up in fast-moving line. Severe cuts were a real hazard.

Church was important to Frank and Annie who were early members of the 1871 Mount Zion Church—next to the Old Mount Zion Cemetery on Bayard Road. The original building was moved to Ocean View and still stood at the north end of the Ocean View Church of Christ until the building was replaced in 2010. They went every Sunday in the surrey which was used for visiting and church and probably not much else. It had front and back seats and a roof.

While Frank was a farmer in Delaware, his son, Uncle Vaughn, reported that at one time his father was a streetcar operator in Philadelphia. It sounds plausible, because so many young men of Baltimore Hundred went to the city for work. However, I now doubt this, realizing Uncle Vaughn may have been referring to his brothers, Royal and David, whom I know from census records had been streetcar operators in Philadelphia.

Annie wore long dresses to the ankles, with long sleeves. She had white hair worn in a bun. Annie was always busy and seldom smiled, but everyone knew by her demeanor that the smiles were there but just didn't show. With twelve children of her own, including Olive, who died as a teenager of scarlet fever, and at least two grandchildren that she and Frank raised, she just didn't have time to express herself.

Annie was a great cake baker. Uncle Lorne told of her delicious and pretty coconut cakes. Aunt Daisey told a funny story about her making a beautiful cake and using Raleigh's Liniment instead of vanilla (the bottles looked the same and sat together on the same kitchen shelf). Aunt Frances tasted the cake and said it tasted like liniment. Annie checked and sure enough, the cake was medicated. Times were tough and money was tight, however, so Annie said, "I have too much in it to throw it away." They gritted their teeth and ate it. Annie also baked apple pies using apples that had been dried on the roof.

Uncle Lorne also told a story which demonstrates Frank and Annie's love for their family. He remembers the couple standing in the yard with tears in their eyes as Linwood and Nellie and their family prepared to return to Brooklyn after a summer vacation.

Aunt Daisey Furman was pregnant in early 1935 with Barbara, who was to be Annie's first great-grandchild. Annie wanted very much to see her first great-grandchild. Unfortunately, travel for babies at that time was restricted for six weeks, and Daisey and Barbara did not make it to Delaware until three weeks after Annie died of "hardening of the arteries." Daisey remembers all of Frank and Annie's children standing in the parlor of the Bayard home with tears in their eyes when Daisey and Barbara visited.

Great-Great-Grandparents Samuel Henry Dasey/Dazey/Daisey (1824-1887) and Sarah Daisey (1831-1914) - Second Edition includes updated research on Henry

Frank's father, Samuel Henry (known generally as Henry), was a mystery before this Second Edition until Barbara Slavin of Ocean View recently and timely found information on "**Samuel Henry Dasey**" on his tombstone located next to Frank's mother, Sarah, in the Mariner's Bethel Cemetery. He was born August 4, 1824, as a **Dazey**, and he died November 10, 1887, as a **Dasey**. Henry and family are recorded in the 1880 U.S. Census under Samuel H. **Dasey** and in the 1870 Census under Samuel H. **Daisey**. He is recorded as a farmer in each. **Dazey, Dasey** or **Daisey**? In the 1830 Census, all in the extended family had the surname Dazey. By 1890, most were known as Daisey. Henry's last name, Dasey, seems to be an artifact of the extended family name change from Dazey to Daisey.

Henry was the son of Prettyman M. and Leah Evans Dazey and was born August 5, 1824. Henry married Sarah H. Quillen, who was born July 11, 1831, and was the daughter of Peter and Lucy Quillen. The 1850 U. S. Census lists a Sarah Daisey, age 18, as part of Peter Quillen's household, but no Henry. Where was Henry? Probably at sea; we know Henry was a sailor, at least for most of 1847 and likely before and thereafter.

There are no known records of other contemporary Henrys other than the land transactions and a notation on his nephew's gravestone discussed below, the only other information found and included in the First Edition about Henry are entries in Capt. John W. James' ledger of the Schooner *Henry Brown*[318] which record that Henry Dazey "Shipped on board of Sch. Henry Brown at $16.00 [per month],

---

318   Ledger of the Schooner *Henry Brown*, by Capt. John W. James, April 1846 - May 1848. One of four ledgers prepared by Capt. James covering parts of the period from 1846 through 1871. One of the ledgers records household expenses for the James family and three record expenses for the Schooner *Henry Brown*. These ledgers were given to Gerald W. Wilgus of Bethany Beach by Capt. James' grandson, and they remain in Gerald's possession. I am most appreciative of Gerald's making this wonderful resource available for review.

February the 17 – 1847," and was paid off on December 27, 1847. Henry signed the receipt entry for his pay in the ledger. Capt. James, Eby Evans, and John S. Evans, other locals, also signed on February 17, 1847, confirming that this local Henry Dazey is our Henry.

An 1884 grave marker in the "Daisey" Cemetery on the south side of the Muddy Neck Road is engraved with the words "**Sister to Henry Daisey**." This marker is toppled, heavy and can't be read (2017). It appears to be for Henry's eighteen years old nephew, Royal Furman, the son of Henry's sister, Abigail M. Daisey Furman. Apparently his survivors intended to identify young Royal and his mother as a Daisey and her relationship to her brother Henry. Abigail M. Daisey and Lemuel Furman are buried in the Furman Cemetery on Windmill Road in Millville.

Henry and Sarah had four children, William Jacob, Ebenezer (who moved to Philadelphia), Thomas Frank and Lucy. Henry was not eligible for Civil War service because of a previously broken leg, according to 1863 eligibility records.

The 1868 Beers Map of Baltimore Hundred[319] shows a "Mrs. H. Daisey" living in the Bayard area. This probably is a further indication that Henry was at sea most of the time. Uncle Vaughn, Frank and Annie's son, remembered that when he was a boy, his grandmother, Henry's wife, lived in Ocean View, probably on the Bayard Road near the Mariner's Bethel Church. Uncle Vaughn remembered nothing about his grandfather who had "died before he was born."

Sarah Daisey of Millville married again in 1892 at age 61 to William H. Hudson who was 51. Sarah died June 9, 1914. She and William Hudson rest in the Mariner's Bethel Cemetery in Ocean View next to Samuel Henry Dasey, our Henry, and near her son, Great Pop-Pop Frank, and Great Mom-Mom Annie.

Henry's brother, Thomas Daisey, had a son, Ike, who petitioned the Sussex County Orphans Court in 1877[320] to sell a part of Thomas' lands to pay debts. The Court papers identify certain of the lands as being adjacent to lands of Henry and William Daisey.

In 1850, Henry and his brother Thomas paid $700 for 156 acres, part of Hall's Lott and David's Discovery in Muddy Neck.[321] In 1869, Henry paid Henry

---

319   Map of Baltimore Hundred, Atlas of the State of Delaware by D. G. Beers, Philadelphia, 1868.
320   Sussex County Orphans Court, Petition for the Sale of Lands of Thomas Daisey to Pay Debts, p. 319, 1877.
321   Sussex County Deeds, Book 57, page 143.

Tunnell $200 for 35 acres in Muddy Neck, just west of the tract <u>Littleworth</u>.

Third Great-Grandparents Prettyman Marvel Dazey (1798-1868) and Leah Evans Dazey (1790-1885)

Prettyman M. Dazey was born in Baltimore Hundred to Moses Dazey Jr, and Sarah "Sary" Prettyman Dazey on November 28, 1798, according to the old Dazey family Bible.[322] The date of birth is recorded in the records of the Blackwater Church as December 5, 1797,[323] possibly his baptism date. He is listed in the 1860 U. S. Census as being 63 years old. Sarah, the daughter of Thomas Prettyman Jr. and Elizabeth Inloes Prettyman, was first married to a David Marvel on January 5, 1789. The will of David Marvel's father, Thomas David Marvel, was accepted for probate in September 1796.[324] Sarah remarried to Moses Daisey Jr. after Marvel's death. Thomas Jr. was the son of Thomas Prettyman Sr., who died in 1688,[325] and Comfort Leatherbury. Thomas Jr. died in 1719, on Tower Hill in Lewes & Rehoboth Hundred.[326] Elizabeth Inloes Prettyman was the daughter of Thomas and Mary Inloes. Mary Inloes was possibly the daughter of a John Hill, who died in 1726.

Prettyman and Leah Evans, who were married on April 6, 1820,[327] had six children: Thomas (born December 9, 1820), William Jacob (born July 3, 1822), Samuel Henry (born August 4, 1824), Betsy M. (born March 10, 1827), and Abigail M. (born January 5, 1830).[328] Henry was included in the May 5, 1848, will of Moses Jr. (admitted to probate May 7, 1849) which listed three grandsons, Thomas, Wm. Jacob and Henry (known by now by his middle name), and two granddaughters, Betsy M. Holt and Abigail M. Furman.[329] Administration of the estate of Prettyman

---

322   Ibid.
323   F. Edward Wright, op. cit., p. 157.
324   Will of David Marvel, January 4, 1796, Sussex County Wills, Liber E, Folios 69-70.
325   Rev. Edgar Cannon Prettyman, *The Prettyman Family in America*, Private Printing, 1968. (Copy in Delaware Technical and Community Library in Georgetown).
326   From information on Internet posted on Roots Web by Eva J. Ruben on 1/5/2000.
327   Marriage of Prettyman Daisey and Leah Evans, Sussex County Marriage Bond, Vol. 41, 1820, p. 203.
328   Daisey Family Bible Printed by Joseph Crukshank, Market Street, Philadelphia, (1782). (The front half of which is now in the possession of Gordon E. Wood Sr. of Ocean View, DE. Disputes over possession of family Bibles were often settled by cutting the Bible in half and transcribing written information in the back half to a page in the front half, as was done in this case).
329   Will of Moses Dazey Jr., May 5, 1848, Public Archives of Delaware, Sussex County Probate, Vol A-68,

M. Daisey, who died intestate, was initiated in 1868. Henry received $63.20 from his father's estate.

Leah, who was known as Lear, was born February 20, 1790, to Jacob Evans and Comfort Johnson Evans, Jacob's second wife. Leah lived to the age of 75 years, 10 months, and 5 days. Her father, Jacob Evans, the son of Solomon and Agnes West Evans, was born August 8, 1751. He died June 21, 1832, in Ocean View. Solomon was the son of William and Catherine White Evans, who were Our Daniel Evans' grandparents—another example of intermarriage within the large families of Baltimore Hundred. This means my Pop-Pop Linwood Evans and Mom-Mom Nellie were sixth cousins!! Agnes was the daughter of Thomas West.

Comfort Johnson Evans was the daughter of Peter and Rachel Johnson. She was born December 19, 1755, and died in Ocean View in 1831. Peter's will is dated March 5, 1778. For some reason there is no record of probate.

Fourth Great-Grandparents Moses Dazey, Jr. (1768-1849) and Sarah Prettyman Marvel Dazey (1768-1849)

Moses Jr. was born September 19, 1768, to Moses Sr. and Mary Dazey.[330] As noted above, he married Sarah Prettyman Marvel, a widow, in 1797. Moses Jr. was married a second time at age 60 to Rhoda Collins on December 13, 1828. His will, signed with his mark "X" on May 5, 1848, was admitted to probate on May 17, 1849. Shortly before his death, Moses Jr. and Rhoda had moved to Illinois. There is a notation in Volume 54 of Sussex County land records that Moses Jr. and Rhoda were in Koscusko County, Illinois, in 1848. Moses Jr. left his lands to his three grandsons, William Jacob, Thomas and Henry, with their father Prettyman as trustee until they became of age, so at least one grandson was underage in 1848. At age 24, Samuel Henry was known as Henry.

Fifth Great-Grandparents Moses Dazey Sr. (c. 1730-1796) and Mary Jacobs Dazey

Moses Sr. was born about 1730 to Thomas Dazey Sr. and his wife Jemima. His January 12, 1796, will was admitted to probate March 12, 1796.[331] Moses Sr. and his wife, Mary, had sons, Moses Jr., Abraham, Jessee and Jacob, and three daughters, Mary Hudson, Sarah Sipple and Leah Schearam. Moses patented

---

330   Daisey Family Bible, op. cit.
331   Will of Moses Dazey Sr., Sussex County Wills, Liber E. pp. 78-79.

<u>Addition,</u> a 50-acre tract in 1747 which was resurveyed to become <u>Conclusion</u> in 1760.[332] It was in or near today's South Bethany.

Sixth Great-Grandfather Thomas Dazey Sr

According to Uncle Maurice's notes, Thomas was the son of Jonathan Dazey of Worcester County, Maryland, and was born about 1707. This may not be correct. Thomas patented the tract <u>Littleworth</u> on the ocean south of South Bethany in 1728. Thomas Dazey was on the Baltimore Hundred Tax Assessment lists in 1723-1739. His November 13, 1777, will was admitted to probate on December 22, 1777.[333] Named heirs were wife, Jemima, sons, John and Moses, and daughters, Assenath, Martha, Anne, Elizabeth Dazey, Sarah Hodgson, Mary Powders and Rachel Latchem. A Thomas Dazey Jr. was first recorded in the records of Prince George's Chapel in 1754. Thomas Dazey Sr. and Moses Dazey are also listed in these records.[334] It was his son, John, who left 60 acres of <u>Partnership</u> in what is now Bethany Beach or South Bethany to Our Daniel Evans to settle a debt. This John was known as John Dazey Jr.—the "Jr." possibly recognizes a grandfather as the "Sr." It should be noted that the terms "Sr." and "Jr." do not necessarily denote kinship. They were often used in these times as an aid to distinguish a person from another person in that hundred with an identical name.[335] I believe this Thomas Sr. was the same person as the Thomas Jr. who was in Bogerternorton Hundred in 1738.

Unverified Seventh Great-Grandfather Jonathan Dazey

According to notes compiled by my uncle, Maurice Daisey, Jonathan Dazey died in 1734 and his will names three sons: Thomas, Mark and John. I have not been able to find such a will in Virginia, Maryland or Delaware, and I am very suspicious of this entry. There was no Jonathan listed in Somerset County Tax Lists between 1730 and 1740. Jonathan's birthplace and parents are unknown. Uncle Maurice's abilities are well respected, but he may have been mistaken. Hopefully, someone will have greater research success.

---

332   Dryden, op. cit., pp. 9, 125.
333   Will of Thomas Dazey Sr., Sussex County Wills, Liber C, pp. 129-132.
334   Betty Blackwell, Descendants of Thomas Dazey Jr., graciously provided to Gordon Wood in July 2000.
335   Delaware - 1782 Tax Assessment and Census Lists, (Wilmington: Delaware Genealogical Society, 1994), p. 15.

Earlier Dazeys?

No earlier Dazeys were found in either America or England. The name Jonathan is very English, however, and it is possible the unverified Jonathan had English roots. It was suggested to me that the surname in England might have been an old Norman name like Doucey. According to Uncle Maurice's notes, Jonathan simply appeared in Baltimore Hundred with no Doucey or Dazey preceding him in Delaware, Maryland or Virginia. It is reasonable now to believe Dazey was a new spelling of a name such as Dawsye, Dawsey or Dayse, each of which appeared in early Accomack County records.

A Ralph **Dasey** and a John Smith were transported to Maryland in 1660 by a Richard Preston, and in 1668, Preston assigned to Ralph **Dasey** his right to one hundred acres of land for transporting Dasey and Smith. The Surveyor General was warranted to survey the one hundred acres to Ralph Dasey in July 1668, with a return date of April 14, 1669.[336] It would seem that Dasey was an indentured servant and that he received this land upon completing service as an indentured servant for Preston. Added research is required to determine the location of Dasey's new land. A Richard Preston and seven children immigrated to Maryland in 1650,[337] probably to the Western Shore.

Since most of the early inhabitants of Baltimore Hundred came from Accomack County, Virginia, via Somerset and Worcester County, Maryland, I am further inclined to believe the Dazeys came from Accomack County, where Court Order Abstracts, Vol. 3, 1671-1673,[338] lists a James **Dawsye** who was transported to Accomack County from England by a Deverox Browne who received Dawsye's head rights of 50 acres of land on May 7, 1671/1672. A Thomas **Dayse** was reported in Volume 7, 1682-1690,[339] as being the runaway servant in November 1683 of a Teague Anderson. Dayse was captured by a Captain Robert Hill twenty miles from his master's house. Also included in this volume is a Thomas **Daisey** and a second person, presumably his wife, in the list of 1691 tithables in Accomack County.[340] The two references to a Thomas Dayse/Daisey probably refer to the same person. Possibly he was young and unmarried in 1683 and freed from his servant duties sometime thereafter and married by 1691. I found no other references to a Daisey or Dayse in Accomack County records after these two entries.

---

336   Maryland Hall of Records, Patents, Liber. 5, p. 535.
337   Skordas, op. cit., p. 371.
338   McKey, op. cit. Vol. 3, p. 50.
339   Ibid, Vol. 7, p. 41.
340   Ibid, p. 339.

Was either the early Thomas **Dayse** or Thomas **Daisey**, or both, an ancestor of Thomas Sr.? With no supporting evidence, it is reasonable to believe they were the same person. The absence of any early records of a Dazey in either England or America, the possible appearance of Jonathan Dazey in Baltimore Hundred in the early 1700s without evidence of his past, and the absence of subsequent references to a Dayse/Daisey in Accomack County lend some support for this view.

An Ensign John **Dawsey** of Dorchester County received 600 pounds of tobacco pursuant to a 1678 Act for Payment and Assessing the Public Charge of the Provence.[341] A Thomas (a servant) and a William **Dawsey** were transported to Maryland in 1680 and 1659, respectively.[342] The will of a William Dawsey in Dorchester County in 1730 named a John Dawsy (sic) as next of kin.[343] Further, a John and a William Dawsey sold land in Dorchester County before 1731. The timing of the will of the unverified Jonathan Dazey from Uncle Maurice Daisey's notes, the land sale in Dorchester County, and the listing in the Tax Lists of Somerset County could refer to the same person. This possibility is doubtful, however, because of the general lack of cross-peninsula migration. We may never know absent more thorough research or the serendipitous surfacing of new information in an unlikely place.

The phonetic and varied spelling of proper names by recording officials at a time when many were unable to write their names suggests a possible kinship between those listed as Dawsey, Dawsy, Dayse, Daisey and Dazey. It is irresistible to try tracing the names back to Accomack County, but research efforts have drawn a blank. They likely left the county, tending to support the premise that Jonathan was from Accomack County. It is certainly consistent with the movement from Accomack County through Worcester County to Baltimore Hundred of contemporaries like Walter Evans, Walter Powell and many others.

The General Armory of England, Scotland, Ireland and Wales[344] lists Daisie or Deisie as being from Scotland and Daisie, Deasie and Daises as also being from Scotland, each with their own coat of arms. The coat of arms for one was "three daiseys stalked and leaved vertical." In the absence of similar listings for Wales, England or Ireland, this probably means Daisey/Dazey is a Scottish name and the Dazey ancestors originally came from Scotland. The following is a chart of the Descendants of Thomas Dazey Sr.

---

341   Archives of Maryland, Vol. VIII, pp. 92-94.
342   Skordas, op. cit., p. 127.
343   Will of William Dawsey, August 11, 1730, Dorchester County Wills.
344   Sir Bernard Burke, *The General Armory of England, Scotland, Ireland and Wales, Reprint 1996*, (Bowie, MD, Heritage Books).

Descendants of Thomas Dazey Sr.

```
1  Thomas Dazey Sr.  1700 - 1777
..  +Jemima
........  2 John Dazey Sr.  1742 - 1811
............  +Sally
..................  3 John Jr.  1758 -
..................  3 Thomas Jr.  1760 - 1811
........................  +Sally
..............................  4 Rhodes.
..............................  4 Thomas
......................................  5 Aaron
......................................  5 Amos
......................................  5 John
......................................  5 Joseph
......................................  5 Nathaniel
......................................  5 Elizabeth
......................................  5 Job Aaron
..............................  4 Jonathan
..............................  4 Rhoda
..............................  4 Suphia
..................  3 Joseph  1762 -
..................  3 George  1766 -
..................  3 Comfort.  1768 -
..................  3 Zipporah  1770 -
..................  3 Fannie Aydelotte.  1772 -
........  2 Moses Dazey Sr.  1744 - 1796
............  +Mary
..................  3 Moses Dazey, Jr.  1768 - 1848
........................  +Sarah Prettyman  1770 - 1830
..............................  4 Prettyman Marvel Dazey  1798 - 1876
..............................  +Leah Evans  1790 - 1865
......................................  5 Thomas Dazey  1820 -
..........................................  +Eliza Ann
......................................  5 William Jacob Dazey  1822 -
......................................  5 Samuel Henry Dasey 1824-1887
......................................  +Sarah A. Quillen  1831 - 1914
..............................................  6 Thomas Frank Daisey  1868 - 1943
..................................................  +Anna Fernetta Green  1868 - 1935
......................................................  7 Ebe Royal Daisey  1887 - 1945
......................................................  7 Nellie  1889 - 1967
............................................................  +John Linwood. Evans, Sr.  1889 - 1966
......................................................  7 David Henry Daisey  1891 - 1967
......................................................  7 William Martin Daisey  1893 - 1951
......................................................  7 Nellie Daisey 1889-1967
......................................................  7 Lora Birch Daisey  1898 - 1979
......................................................  7 Axie  1901 - 1979
............................................................  +Rollin Hudson
......................................................  7 Bertha Ann Daisey  1905 - 1971
......................................................  7 George Vaughn Daisey  1905 - 2000
......................................................  7 Olive Daisey  1908 - 1919
......................................................  7 Maurice Daisey  1910 - 1991
......................................................  7 Frances Elnora Daisey  1912 - 1994
..............................................  6 William Jacob Daisey
..............................................  6 Ebenezer Daisey
......................................................  7 Harry Daisey
..............................................5 Betsy M. Dazey 1827 -
..............................................  +Holt
..............................................5 Abigail M. Dazey 1830 -
..............................................  +Furman
```

DAZEY TO DAISEY AND DASEY

Why did the Dazeys change their name to Daisey over 50 years?

There are no known explainations of this curiosity, and I have no real idea how to research this question. An answer would be interesting.

Chapter 16   Letter to Sam and Sydney – Your Grandma

May 2001

Dear Sam and Sydney,

Just as your Grandma Pat is so special to me, so also are you two special to her, her very own grandchildren. While we together have twelve grandchildren, you two are all hers. Words can't describe how she revels in seeing you or receiving pictures—Sam, your ready smile, the picture of health. And Sydney—a beautiful infant. She is lucky to have a grandson and granddaughter such as you two, and you are lucky to have a Grandma such as her.

I wanted you to have my letter about My Pat, your Grandma. Shortly after we started dating, more years ago than I care to remember, I met her dad, Eli, on a day sail on the Chesapeake Bay. It was a nice day, but I had the feeling I was being sized up as to whether I was worthy of Pat. She seemed to think so, and that was all that really mattered, but I wanted to let him know my feelings for her---how I felt. The following letter states my thoughts about your Grandma and my intentions. I read this letter to our family and friends at our wedding reception on October 4, 1997.

I hope you enjoy reading about your Grandma. This letter was written also to congratulate Eli on a special night for him at the Elks Lodge. Eli was very ill and his Lodge was honoring him. Ask Pat to tell you about the Elks and how much they meant to Eli.

Love to you both,

Pop-Pop

Letter from Gordon Wood Sr. to Eli Klingensmith about his daughter Pat

June 6, 1985

Dear Eli –

Honors from friends and fellow Elks don't come to everyone. Public honors say even more. I hope it is a marvelous evening and that you can enjoy every moment.

You and I are lucky guys. You have a daughter, Pat, who is a most wonderful person. I have a special lady in my life whom I love very much, Pat.

I know she is special to you too, but I wanted to describe her for you – some things you may not know.

Pat is energy – sometimes almost too much. Every moment for her is one to be cherished and used. At the end of most days she is spent. Those amazing batteries, however, recharge by 5:15 am. I operate at a slower pace. I guess that makes us good for each other.

Pat is beauty – in so many ways. I think she is pretty. Look at her eyes. They are beautiful – always – but particularly when she is excited about something – and that is most of the time. Look at that smile – engaging isn't it? Finally, there is that special beauty that comes from being special to so many people – and she is.

Pat is a friend – a good friend – to so many people. Have you ever known anyone you would rather have as a friend? She gives, helps, shares, comforts, consoles, encourages. One who has Pat as a friend has a treasure.

Pat is a daughter. She loves you and Dee. She thinks about and worries about you a lot. She must have provided many memories – almost all good.

Pat is a neighbor – to all around her. She is sharing and caring and always willing to lend a hand, stop and talk, meet and greet, or simply being known as being there if needed and always willing.

Pat is smart. I'll bet you don't know how smart. She is good at what she does – very good! The combination of her ability, knowledge of the area, and so many friends, plus that energy, makes her a very good lobbyist. Eli, she is good!

Pat is a real woman. She can be businesslike, but she is very feminine. Her home is important to her. It's behind schedule but maybe she can blame me for that. You know she is a good cook. Her intuition is uncanny. She is an affectionate woman and I love it. And, yes, Eli, she is sexy too.

I guess all of the above means something. You are lucky to have her as a daughter. I am lucky to have her in such a special way. I love her very much!

At the right time and in the right place we plan on marriage. We will. When? Not sure – probably in a year-and-a-half or so. We'll see – there is no rush. The point is we love each other and it will come. I wanted you to know that.

Be honored by your friends. Enjoy!!!

Gordon

NOTE: People who know, laugh whenever I read this letter to them. Pat and I were married not in a year-and-a-half, but thirteen years later.

Chapter 17   The Green Family

Mom-Mom Nellie Evans' mother was Anna "Annie" Fernetta Daisey. Her maiden name was Green, a family name in Worcester County, Maryland, and Sussex County, Delaware, since at least the early eighteenth century.

Second Great-Grandparents David Martin Green (1827- c. 1910) and Fernetta Anna Sockrider Green (1836-1891)

Annie's father, David Martin Green, was the son of Rev. Jesse Green and Nancy Knowles Prettyman Green of Dagsboro Hundred.[345] David was recorded in the 1860 U. S. Census as being 33 years old, and his Dagsboro Hundred household included his mother, Nancy Green (58), brothers Joseph (23) and "Jessee" (18), and sisters Angeline, N. Emaline (9) and Sarah (5). His father had died in 1860, and David was the head of the household, living at his parents' home. He is listed in the 1870 U. S. Census as a cooper (barrel maker). My cousin, Phyllis Meyer, reports he was also a farmer and school master. On January 12, 1882, he was appointed a Justice of the Peace,[346] a position he held for sixteen years. He presided over the first meeting of the Ocean View Town Council in October 1889. Squire Green, as he was known, "held hearings" in his home in Bayard, according to a cousin. As told by Steve Dougherty, "It is a legend that he would periodically get up early in the morning, walk the back roads to Georgetown, the County Seat, file his papers, conduct his other business in the courthouse or around town, and then walk back, arriving home late at night—quite a feat for a man already 56 years old when first appointed." He was reappointed as a notary public later in 1882. His engraved seal on an 1884 certificate appointing John W. James as one of the Public Overseers of roads in Baltimore Hundred notes that his term as a notary expires on November 27, 1889.

Annie's mother, Fernetta Anna Green ("Fernetty"), was born in 1836. She died on March 10, 1891, of pneumonia. David and Fernetty now rest in unknown plots in the Mount Zion Cemetery in Bayard.

---

345   Parts of this information were generously supplied to the writer by my first cousin once removed, Phyllis Hudson Meyer, the daughter of Achsah "Axie" Daisey Hudson and grand-daughter of Frank and Annie Daisey. Parts were in notes by Aunt Frances, Frank and Annie's youngest daughter. I learned recently that Steve Dougherty of Millsboro had worked with them and was their source of some original research. Steve was also helpful to me and generous with materials from his extensive Green, Sockrider and Hart research files. I appreciate his most valuable and cheerful help—a nice fourth cousin.

346   Scharf, *Vol II.*, op. cit., p. 1213. He actually was in this role on December 30, 1881, two weeks earlier, having received and attested to, as Justice of the Peace, a sworn account statement of the estate of A. J. McCabe.

David and Fernetta Anna Sockrider Green, My Great-Great-Grandparents

Fernetty was the daughter of Christopher (1796-1846) and Nancy Hart Sockrider who were married December 20, 1824. Christopher was married first to Elizabeth "Betsy" Wolfe on April 23, 1818.[347] According to notes from Aunt Frances and materials provided by Steve Dougherty, Christopher Sockrider was born in Germany, possibly near the German-Holland border, but I have been unable to find any record of his emigration or any information as to how or when he came to America. There were Sockriders in the Philadelphia area, so it is possible Christopher came from that area.

Christopher's first wife, Elizabeth Wolfe, was born in 1797 and died after 1820. Christopher and Elizabeth had two children, Jacob, who died as an infant in 1819, and Sarah Ann, who was born August 11, 1820. Christopher married again to Nancy Hart on December 20, 1824. Christopher was in Dagsboro Hundred as early as 1828 where he was assessed $1.34 in taxes. Christopher Sockrider is first

---

347   Letter, Beulah Sockrider to Louise Garcia, October 23, 2000, providing detailed information on Sockrider family tree emanating from Christopher Sockrider and his wives, Elizabeth Wolfe and Nancy Hart. Louise Garcia's providing a copy of this letter is most appreciated.

recorded in the 1840 U. S. Census in Indian River Hundred in Sussex County along with a female, presumably his second wife, Nancy. Both were reported as being between the ages of 30 and 40.[348] Christopher and Nancy are also recorded as having four slaves. Christopher was taxed the same $1.34 in 1844 in Indian River Hundred.

Nancy Hart was born in Sussex County[349] and was from the line of a Zachariah Hart, a shipbuilder, who emigrated from Ireland, according to brief notes prepared by my Aunt Frances Daisey and given to me by Uncle Lorne Evans, who looked after her affairs. Materials with the Beulah Sockrider letter (see footnote 347) note that Nancy's grandfather, the Zachariah Hart who emigrated from Ireland, was born in 1733 and died in 1786, and that he was a master mechanic and ship builder. He married Mary Burton, a descendent of the William Burton, who had considerable land holdings in Long Neck. According to files obtained from Steve Dougherty, this William Burton was a direct descendent of a William Burton of Accomack County who was the progenitor of the Burton families in Sussex County. Nancy's father was Zachariah Hart Jr., who was born in 1759 and died in 1809. Zachariah Jr.'s wife and Nancy Hart's mother was Nancy Johnson whom more research may show to be the daughter of Major and Abigail Johnson. Zachariah Jr. was a blacksmith. Nancy Hart Sockrider is recorded in the 1850 Census as being 46, but she is not recorded in the 1860 Census. She presumably died before that date.

Third Great Grandparents Reverend Jesse Green (c. 1804-Feb. 25, 1860) and Nancy K. Prettyman Green (1803-1866)

Jesse was born in 1803 or 1804 to Ezekiel and Polly Green of Broadkiln Hundred. After his father died, his mother Polly moved the family to Dagsboro Hundred. Jesse became a Baptist minister who served at the Old School Baptist Church near Laurel.[350] Apparently, he had a Doctor of Divinity Degree and also served as minister at the Broad Creek Baptist Church in Sycamore, Delaware. Jesse also was a farmer in Dagsboro Hundred from 1822 until his death in 1860. By 1852, he had 300 acres of land.

Three Jesse Greens are listed in the 1830 U.S. Census, including one in Dagsboro Hundred and Gen. Jesse Green and his son, Jesse Jr. While some believe Rev. Jesse's father was the well-known Major General Jesse Green who lived in

---

348   The normally accurate 1840, 1850, and 1860 indexes of the Delaware Census record Sockrider as "Lockrider," making the Census search for Christopher Sockrider most difficult.
349   1850 U. S. Census.
350   Scharf, Vol. II., op. cit., p. 1243.

Concord, Delaware, a town near Seaford, this is not correct. The general's son, Jesse Jr., married Eliza Ann Harris pursuant to a marriage bond dated July 22, 1829.[351] Further, Betsy Green, the General's wife, made a bequest in her July 21, 1849, will to her three grandchildren: Angeline H., Ann Eliza and Elvira, "the children of Jesse Green." Rev. Jesse and Nancy had eight children: James, David Martin, George, Joseph, Jesse, Angeline, N. Emaline and Sarah E.[352] Rev. Jesse is not the son of the general.

The Grantee Index in the deed room in Georgetown records a "Jesse **(of E)**," who purchased two adjoining tracts in Dagsboro Hundred, one of eighty acres and one of twenty acres, from Sheriff Purnell Johnson at a Sheriff's sale in 1831. The deed for the purchase of these lands, which adjoined lands of Simon Wilson and John Ingram, also includes the "(of E)" notation.[353]

The "Jesse (of E)" notation in the Grantee Index as well as the indexed deed indicates that this Jesse Green was the son of someone whose first name started with "E." The only E. Greens found in contemporary census and property records are named Ezekiel. The attempt to sort out the various contemporary Ezekiel Greens is discussed in a section below, "The Ezekiel Greens."

Nancy Knowles Prettyman Green was the daughter of Captain Zachariah Prettyman of Dagsboro Hundred, who died July 3, 1804,[354] when Nancy was about one year old, and Asseneth Knowles, the daughter of Richard Knowles (1715-1791). Zachariah was the son of George Prettyman and Levina Jones. Levina was the daughter of Ebenezer Jones and Hannah Kenney.[355]

Zachariah purchased a part of Kollocks Choice in 1795, located "a little south of Sheep's Paw Branch." This tract appears to be the same tract discussed below which contains the site plot where Jesse and Nancy are buried—or nearby.

---

351   Archive of Delaware, Marriage Bond, Jesse Green Jr. to Eliza Ann Harris, July 22, 1829.

352   1850 and 1860 U. S. Census.

353   Sussex County Deed Book 43, p. 12.

354   Sussex County Deed Book 92, p. 441.

355   Much of the information on Zachariah Prettyman and Nancy Knowles and their ancestors was provided by D. Mitchell Jones of 3025 Kline Road, Jacksonville, FL 32246. His website includes in-depth information on these families. I am indebted to him for sharing an extensive work product.

This small plot, which appears to contain only three graves, is located not far from Ingram's Pond, just northwest of Millsboro at the intersection of Godwin School Road and Country Lane, not far from the intersection of County Road 410 and Delaware Route 20. Their tombstones record that Jesse died February 25, 1860, and Nancy died in 1866 at age 63 years, 7 months and 23 days. The plot is overgrown with briers and brush, and their headstones which had fallen to the ground were reset in concrete by Joseph H. Green of Georgetown.

In 1868, Nancy's heirs of Dagsboro Hundred petitioned the Sussex County Orphans Court to sell the land left sixty years earlier by her father, Capt. Zachariah Green. The combination of the death of two siblings and an agreement with a brother finally allowed the estate to be settled by Nancy's heirs after sixty years. Her heirs included her and Jesse's six sons, one of their three daughters, Angeline, and daughters-in-law, including David's wife, "Frenetta" (Frenetta Sockrider). The land was finally sold on April 15, 1880.[356] The land that Jesse purchased at the Sheriff's sale in 1831 may have been distributed to his heirs after his death in 1860. Nancy retained the land she inherited from her father. This was not researched further.

The Ezekiel Greens

The number of Ezekiel Greens in Sussex and Worcester Counties have been sorted out by studying estate, land, church, tax, and census records.

The first Ezekiel Green appears on Somerset County tax lists for Nanticoke Hundred for the years 1730 through 1735 and 1738 through 1740.[357] Another Ezekiel Green and a David Green, who appear in the same household on the tax lists for Baltimore Hundred for the years 1736 through 1740, probably are brothers but possibly father and son. There are no Ezekiel Greens recorded on Somerset Rent Rolls in 1723 or before.[358]

The Ezekiel and David Green in Baltimore Hundred are listed in the tax lists for 1739 and 1740, either with or near the listing of a Richard Jefferson. This may be worthy of note because in 1773, many years later, a Richard Jefferson purchased a sixty-acre tract of land, Little Neck, at the head of the Indian River, from an Elizabeth Reynolds. This was the tract that her father, Ezekiel Green "of Worcester County," had purchased from a Gabriel West in 1754 and willed to her in 1768.[359]

---

356   Sussex County Deed Book 92, page 339.
357   Russo, op. cit.
358   Calvert Papers 1663-1723, Somerset Rent Rolls.
359   Dryden, op. cit., p. 366.

This tract was patented in 1714 by Lazarus Kenney, who assigned it to Stephen Kenney.[360] This land is on or near Kennys Branch, which must have been named after a Kenney landowner. This probably indicates that the Ezekiel Green in Baltimore Hundred (still in Worcester County at that time) is the Ezekiel Green who had tracts at the head of the Indian River and was a taxable in both counties. A Mary and Ezekiel Green (presumably Ezekiel Jr.) also witnessed Richard Jefferson's January 2, 1780, will. Presumably, they were neighbors.

Richard Jefferson was the Administrator of the estate of Edward Wheatley in 1726, and he made a payment to Ezekiel Green, who was a creditor.[361]

In 1739, an Ezekiel Green, "late of the County of Worcester" but now in Sussex County,[362] received three, or possibly four, Pennsylvania Warrants from General Thomas Penn for 200 acres each. One was on the north side of the main branch of the Indian River, one was near the north side of his dwelling plantation, and one adjoined the north side of his dwelling plantation.[363] Another possible warrant was on the north side of the main branch of the Indian River in Indian River Hundred. The "late of County of Worcester" reference indicates this Ezekiel Green was in Sussex County in 1739, probably on the Indian River. If the Jefferson connection discussed in the previous paragraph is correct, Ezekiel had taxable land in Baltimore Hundred and then in Worcester County, but he had now moved to the head of the Indian River.

In 1758, Ezekiel received a Pennsylvania Warrant for another 200-acre tract on both sides of Kennys Branch of the Indian River, south of his dwelling lands.

On September 11, 1758, David Green, "late of the County of Sussex on Delaware," sold a 300-acre tract to Major Warren on the east side of a branch of Beaver Dam Branch out of Indian River,[364] the same 300 acres that David Green purchased from Josiah Rotten on August 7, 1750.[365] The two most interesting clues in the 1758 Indenture were (1) David's appointment of Ezekiel Green Jr. to have his

---

360   Ibid, p. 264.
361   Prerogative Court of Maryland, Probate, Liber 7, Folio 418.
362   Worcester was created out of Somerset County in 1742 by the General Assembly of Maryland. Apparently, this process took time because the 1739 statement that Ezekiel Green was "late of Worcester County" anticipated the General Assembly action.
363   Sussex County Deed Book, 1776 Warrants C, pp. 291 & 293.
364   Ibid, Book 9, p. 190.
365   Ibid, Book 8, p. 268.

power of attorney to execute the transaction, and (2) the fact that David no longer resided in Sussex County. Presumably he was in Worcester County which then included part of the southern tier of Sussex County. The close relationship of trust indicated by the power of attorney possibly means that David and Ezekiel were brothers, probably the same brothers who were together in Baltimore Hundred in 1736-1740.

On May 1, 1764, an Ezekiel Green of both Worcester County and Southern Sussex in Delaware sold 200 acres of land near Millsboro, on the south side of Peter Kennys Branch, to a Daniel Steel.[366] Apparently Ezekiel sold one of the four tracts for which he received warrants, three in 1739 and one in 1758.

An Ezekiel Green of Worcester County died in 1769. His December 4, 1758, will was accepted for probate over ten years later on August 18, 1769,[367] and the inventory of his assets was filed Sept 21, 1769, and approved on March 8, 1770.[368] An Ezekiel Green was the executor. Heirs included children, "Elleanor Runnels" (Reynolds), **Ezekiel, David** and Mary. This clearly defines Ezekiel Sr. as having sons, Ezekiel and David, and a daughter, Elleanor Reynolds. His estate included tracts, Green's Chance and Oak Hall.

Ezekiel's will left four tracts of land to his children. To Daughter Eleanor Runnels he left 60 acres of Little Neck, the land she subsequently sold to Richard Jefferson. To son David, he left 200 acres of the plantation where he (David) formerly lived in Sussex County called Green's Chance. To son Ezekiel Jr. he left the remainder of Greens Chance (presumably 200 acres) and the plantation "where I now live" called Oak Hall. To Ezekiel Jr. he also left a warrant for 200 acres "when surveyed." This has to be the tract discussed above for which he received a warrant in 1758, just before he wrote his will.

We know also that an Ezekiel, Son of David Green, is recorded by the Anglican Saint George's Church at Indian River as being born October 4, 1747.[369] Baby Ezekiel Green possibly is the grandson of the Ezekiel Sr. of Baltimore Hundred/ Worcester County. These same church records record the birth of a Susannah on September 16, 1768, to May and Ezekiel Green. Susannah might be the daughter of the Ezekiel born in 1747. No other records were found of this Ezekiel

---

366   Ibid, Book 10, p. 73.
367   Calendar Maryland of Wills, op. cit. Vol. 10, p.103.
368   Maryland Prerogative Court Inventories, 1769-70, Liber. 104, p. 22.
369   F. Edward Wright, op. cit., p. 93.

and May Green. The father, David, may be the David Green on tax and census records in 1782, 1785, and 1800 who is discussed below.

An Ezekiel Green and Mary Green, presumably Ezekiel Sr./Jr., witnessed Richard Jefferson's 1780 will.[370] Thus Richard Jefferson's widow and at least three of his sons were in Dagsboro Hundred in 1782. Ezekiel and Mary Green were either neighbors or friends.

On November 18, 1794, an Ezekiel Green sold a 60-acre tract on the east side of Kennys Branch in Indian River Hundred to a John Wilson, which was "granted to Ezekiel Green, father of the aforesaid Ezekiel Green."[371] This is a clear indication that this is Ezekiel Jr. and that his father was Ezekiel Green Sr. who had obtained land warrants in 1739 and 1758.

On February 9, 1799, Ezekiel Sr. granted to Ezekiel Jr. lands in Broadkill Hundred including houses, outhouses, barns, stables, woods and waters.[372]

On Nov. 7, 1802, an Ezekiel Green gave a 68-acre tract, Two Necks, to his son David Green. This tract was on the main branch of the Indian River "northeast of my dwelling plantation where I now live."[373] The deed refers to "my old Pattent Land" by "Kennie Branch" that I got of Richard Jefferson. This Ezekiel probably had at least two sons, David and Jesse, and this David became of age in 1802. This would be consistent with the Ezekiel in Indian River Hundred who had one male, age 10 to 16, in 1800.

Scharf reports an Ezekiel Green in Broadkill Hundred and an Ezekiel and a David Green in Indian River Hundred as taxables in 1785. Similarly, the 1800 U.S. Census of Sussex County records an Ezekiel Green in Broadkill Hundred and two David Greens, one each in Broadkill and Dagsboro Hundreds:

Ezekiel Green in Broadkill - 1M 26-45, 1M over 45, 1F under 10, 1F 26-45
David Green in Broadkill - 1M 26 -44, 1M over 45, 1F under 10, 1F 26-44
David Green in Dagsboro - 1M under 10, 1M 26-45, 1 F under 10, 1F 25-45

---

370   Will of Richard Jefferson, Sussex County Wills, Liber C, Folios 237-240.
371   Sussex County Deed Book 15, p. 375.
372   Sussex County Deed Book 21, p. 589.
373   Ibid, Book 23, page 110.

The Delaware - 1782 Tax Assessment and Census Lists[374] includes no Ezekiel Greens and one David Green in Indian River Hundred.

In 1804 an Ezekiel Sr., Ezekiel Green Jr. and Mary Green sold a tract of land to Paynter Frame which was a part of an old patent, Green's Chance, partly in the forks of a branch, the southwest prong of which is Kenney's Branch in Broadkill Hundred.[375]

There are two common threads in the above land and tax records, Kennys Branch and the Richard Jefferson references. Together, they demonstrate that the Ezekiel Sr. (c. 1700-1769) who received the payment from Richard Jefferson, the executor of the Wheatley estate, the Ezekiel of Baltimore Hundred in 1740, and the Ezekiel who received the Broadkill Hundred land warrants in 1739 and 1759 are one and the same. The common threads and Ezekiel Sr.'s will of 1759/1768 tie Ezekiel Sr. to Ezekiel Jr. and his brother David. The common threads along with the 1804 land sale by Ezekiel Sr., Ezekiel Jr. and his wife Mary indicate that after Ezekiel Sr.'s death, Ezekiel Jr. was known as Ezekiel Sr. For the purposes of this narrative, the second Ezekiel is designated as Ezekiel Jr./Sr. This is further substantiated by the 1799 grant of a tract of land from Ezekiel Sr. (Jr./Sr.) to Ezekiel Jr.

This information, together with the fact that there is no other known Ezekiel Green in Sussex County in about 1804 when Rev. Jesse Green was born, leads to the conclusion that Rev. Jesse Green, who was born in 1804, is the son of Ezekiel Green Jr., and his wife, Polly, in turn, the grandson of Ezekiel Green Jr./Sr., and the great grandson of the Ezekiel Green Sr. who received warrants for the 200-acre tracts in Broadkill Hundred in 1739. This conclusion is buttressed by the fact that Rev. Jesse's wife, Elizabeth Knowles Prettyman, was raised in this same area near Millsboro.

The two remaining mysteries are: (1) What happened to the Ezekiel Green who was born in 1747, and (2) Who is Ezekiel Sr.'s father? The first may remain a mystery, and the second requires more research.

Perhaps Ezekiel Sr. was the son of the Edward Green, the chief ranger in Somerset (1692 commission), who was responsible for taking up and utilizing all "drift whales or other fish" and "all other drifts, wastes or wrecks whatsoever as shall at any time . . . come or be cast on shore on the seaboard side of the this Province." He was also responsible for collecting all wild horses and mares running at large and

---

374   Nelson, op. cit.
375   Sussex County Wills, Book 23, page 400.

"to turn horses and mares upon Assateague Island."[376] This quote regarding Assateague Island horses and mares raises questions regarding the source of the famous Chincoteague ponies.

Or, perhaps Edward was the son of William Greene of Pocomoke and Elizabeth Manlove who married in 1666.[377] These Somerset County Greens possibly are descended from the Greens of Accomack County. Obviously, the relationship to Edward and William is pure speculation, unsupported by research. No Somerset wills from this period were found which might provide more information.

A descendants chart of Ezekiel Green Sr. is on the following page:

---

376   Torrance, op. cit., p. 362.
377   Ibid., p. 452.

Descendants of Ezekiel Green Sr.

1 Ezekiel Green Sr.
.... 2 Ezekiel Green Jr./Sr.
.... 3 Ezekiel Green Jr.
.... 4 Rev. Jesse Green Jr. 1804 - 1860
.... +Nancy Knowles Prettyman - 1866
.... 5 James Green
.... 5 George Green
.... 5 Joseph Green
.... 5 Jesse Green
.... 5 Angeline Green
.... 5 N. Emaline Green
.... 5 Sarah E.
.... 5 David Martin Green 1827 - 1910
.... +Fernetta Anna Sockrider 1836 - 1881
.... 6 Anna Fernetta Green 1868 - 1935
.... +Thomas Frank Daisey 1868 - 1943
.... 7 Ebe Royal Daisey 1887 - 1945
.... 7 Nellie Daisey 1889-1967
.... +John Linwood. Evans, Sr. 1889 - 1966
.... 7 David Henry Daisey 1891 - 1967
.... 7 William Martin Daisey 1893 - 1951
.... 7 Archie Frank Daisey 1896 - 1969
.... 7 Lora Birch Daisey 1898 - 1979
.... 7 Axie 1901 - 1979
.... +Rollin Hudson
.... 7 Bertha Ann Daisey 1905 - 1971
.... 7 George Vaughn Daisey 1905 - 2000
.... 7 Olive Daisey 1908 - 1919
.... 7 Maurice Daisey 1910 - 1991
.... 7 Frances Elnora Daisey 1912 - 1994
.... 6 Martin Green
.... +Hetty Green
.... 7 Ella Green Betts
.... 7 Axle Green Truitt
.... 7 Clara Green Vickers

Chapter 18

Letter to Elizabeth—Determination

Summer 1999

Dear Elizabeth,

What a beautiful, perky and precious little girl with a wonderful Evans and Hall family name. What lovely brown eyes! You are so loved and cared for by your parents and you're very dear to me. Your mother and father named you after my mother, Hilda Elizabeth Wood, and her grandmother, Elizabeth Breasure Hall Evans, two of the special ladies to whom this book is dedicated.

How you enjoy the beach. How I have enjoyed watching a two-year-old on the beach, the busiest person there—in a magical world all your own.

It's way too early to talk about goals in life, and it is meaningless at this time because there will be many opportunities ahead for one so bright, so determined. I have never seen a little one with so much determination to do your very own thing, a special asset. Elizabeth, never lose that determination and use it to full advantage.

Wherever opportunities lead, one thing is always required to supplement that determination, learning! There are two types of learning, book learning and that thing called common sense which some are born with and all others can acquire. Both are needed. Common sense generally comes from observing as you grow—what works and what doesn't.

The combination of common sense and book learning with the proper level of determination and work makes one ready to seize those many opportunities that come along and capable of reaching for and achieving any and all goals.

So Elizabeth, my advice to you is to listen, watch, and learn and excel in school. If you do these things and maintain that wonderful determination, you will be able to do and be anything you want. You can do it all, and I look forward to being a spectator.

Love,

Pop-Pop

PART V

NINETEENTH CENTURY BALTIMORE HUNDRED

Chapter 19   Zadoc (1782-1852) and Nancy _____ Evans (c. 1782-1850)

```
┌─────────────────────────────────────────────────────────────┐
│                  Contemporaneous Happenings                   │
│                                                               │
│  1803  Jefferson purchased the Louisiana Territory from France│
│  1804  Napoleon crowned Emperor of France                     │
│  1807  Fulton's Claremont navigates the Hudson River          │
│  1812  War of 1812 Declared with England                      │
│  1823  President Monroe publishes his Monroe Doctrine         │
│  1824  Beethoven's Symphony No. 9 performed in Vienna before  │
│         the totally deaf composer                             │
│  1828  Andrew Jackson elected President of the United States  │
│  1830  Open debate on slavery begins with Hayne/Webster debates│
│  1840  Physicist James Joule formulates First Law of Thermodynamics on │
│         conservation of energy                                │
│  1850  I. M. Singer invents sewing machine                    │
└─────────────────────────────────────────────────────────────┘
```

Zadock or Zadoc? His will is signed "Zadoc." His father's will includes a bequest for his son, "Zadock." Other references seem to use one or the other interchangeably. Assuming he knew how to spell his own name, we will use "Zadoc."

Zadoc and Nancy lived and raised their family during an exciting time in American history. Growth in American influence, technology and the arts was unprecedented. For Zadoc and Nancy, however, the events in young America and, indeed, the world had minimal impact. Theirs was a life with little change from that of their parents. Farming methods were little changed, and only by unremitting labor was it possible to survive on the family farm.

Zadoc and Nancy had at least the eight children listed in Zadoc's will: sons John M., Clemeth, Henry, Jacob and William T., and daughters Rhoda (apparently not married), Elizabeth Lynch and Nancy Bennett.

Unfortunately, Nancy's maiden name could not be determined for sure. A possibly good clue to her maiden name is that Zadoc and Nancy purchased Sandy Ridge, from a John and Rhoda Lynch on February 9, 1829, for $162.50.[378] Perhaps Zadoc and Nancy purchased Sandy Ridge from Nancy's parents and named their first daughter

---

378   Sussex County Deeds, Book 40, p. 70.

Rhoda after Nancy's mother, but we do not know. Neither property nor probate records helped confirm or eliminate this possibility.

Another possible clue is Zadoc and Nancy's purchase of 67 acres of a tract, Small Timber, at a sheriff's sale in 1837 that they then sold in 1845. This tract adjoined lands of James and John D. Lynch, but as in the case with Sandy Ridge, nothing was found to confirm or eliminate Nancy's relationship to a John Lynch.

The approximately 50 acres they purchased for $162.50 ($3.25 an acre!) did not include a graveyard on Sandy Ridge which was "accepted" (excepted) in the deed. If Nancy is the daughter of John and Rhoda Lynch, perhaps Zadoc and Nancy now rest in this traceless graveyard. Another possibility is the Old Sound Church burial yard at Johnson's Corner, only a little over a mile southeast of Sandy Ridge. Perhaps Zadoc and Nancy and their family worshiped and now rest there. There are no records or indications to support such a surmise other than proximity.

A major event in America's history, the War of 1812, occurred when Zadoc and Nancy's children were young. Although the War of 1812 had minimal impact on Baltimore Hundred, eligible men served in the Militia and some were detached for service with the U.S. Army. Zadoc, then 31, was no exception. He was called to active duty for eight days at "Lewes Town" with the Sixth Company of the Tenth Regiment because Lewes was threatened by British fleets. On June 5, 1813, he received three dollars pay for this service.[379] His brother, Daniel, also served in Lewes at the same time. Daniel appealed for pay for June 8, 1813, service at "Lewes Town."[380] Neighbors Enoch Evans, Lemuel Wharton and Aaron Dazey were similarly called for duty in "Lewes Town." In 1814, Zadoc's brother, Daniel, was detached from the Militia for service with the Eighth U.S. Infantry Regiment.

Zadoc provided for his wife Nancy in his February 5, 1848, will which was admitted to probate on December 16, 1852. Zadoc (72) and daughter, Rhoda (46) are listed in the 1850 U. S. Census. Nancy, however, is not mentioned in either the probate records or the 1850 U. S. Census. Presumably, Nancy died after Zadoc wrote his 1848 will and before the U. S. Census was taken in July 1850. No records of Nancy's death were found.

---

379   Archives of Delaware, Military, Vol. I, p. 433.
380   Ibid, Vol. II, p. 517.

Zadoc left two tracts of land to his sons. The first bequest was "My home place that I now <u>reside on</u> . . ." to his son, William T., ". . . after the death of his mother . . ."[381] He also left one half of his plantation, <u>Sandy Ridge</u>, to his son, "Clemeth," and one half to his grandson, Zadoc Aydelotte Evans, the minor son of John M. Evans. The location of the "home place"could not be determined in either property records or the probate records of his son, William T. The location of the "place that I [Zadoc] now reside on." is not known. Similarly, it was not possible to find records of other lands purchased by Zadoc or Nancy or inherited by Zadoc. The only viable presumption is that Nancy at some time had possibly inherited another tract, but no supporting documentation was found.

The bequest to Zadoc's grandson, Zadoc A., started an interesting and time-consuming saga in the courts worth the telling. Zadoc A. was still a minor at the time of probate, and Clemeth, who signed his name "Clemeth," notwithstanding its being spelled "Clement" in some records, necessarily brought a petition for partition of <u>Sandy Ridge</u> before the Sussex County Court of Chancery on September 22, 1853. The Court subpoenaed Zadoc A. to appear before the Court on October 14, 1853, to show cause, if any, why the partition should not be made. Apparently, Zadoc A. had no reason to attempt to stop the partition, and the Court appointed five Commissioners on March 18, 1854, to partition the land pursuant to the Court's order and to allot equal parts to Clemeth and Zadoc A. After review, the Commissioners reported to the Court on August 12, 1854, that partition would operate to the disadvantage of the two owners and recommended a sale of the land at their appraised value of $12 per acre. The court met on March 17, 1855, and agreed with the Commissioners' recommendation, ordering a public auction of the land at the storehouse of Jacob Wilgus in Centerville (now Roxana) before the next session of the Court (March of 1856). The Commissioners duly advertised a sale at the storehouse on June 2, 1855. On the appointed day, Rhoda, Zadoc's unmarried daughter, who was about 49,[382] surprisingly—and sadly to contemplate—appeared at Jacob Wilgus' storehouse and, claiming she was infirm and crippled, announced she was claiming her rights to the land for her maintenance per Zadoc's will (Item 2 of will). The befuddled Commissioners, saying they supposed her dead and "believing that the said lands would sell to great disadvantage and sacrifice, adjourned the sale of said lands *sine die*," to await further orders from the Court. The Commissioners reported the situation to the Court on September 25, 1855. Rhoda's petition to the court was

---

381   Will of Zadoc Evans, op. cit.
382   1850 U. S. Census.

either denied or the heirs otherwise made an agreement with her, because on March 12, 1856, the Court again ordered the sale. A sale was finally held at the storehouse on May 24, 1856, and the land was purchased by Robert B. Houston for $530. Rhoda petitioned the Court on September 16, 1856, for maintenance needs from time to time. Apparently this was to no avail, because, on September 17, 1856, the Court ordered that the net proceeds of $430.06, after costs, be paid one-half each to Clemeth and Zadoc A. Somehow, I like to think that at least her brother, Clemeth, provided for Rhoda.

The interesting saga of this land continued. John W. Evans, Zadoc's son and Zadoc A.'s father, was sued for waste of the land's forests by Robert B. Houston, the buyer of Sandy Ridge. Apparently John W. was a tenant on the land and he harvested timber in excess of the amount considered acceptable for maintenance of the farm. The survey of Sandy Ridge for the Commissioners, which is included with the court papers, notes that about 60 percent was arable and 40 percent was wooded, including all of the land on the west side of the county road. John W. was ordered by the Court to stop.

Houston sold Sandy Ridge to Nathaniel W. Evans shortly thereafter. It is readily apparent from study of the names of adjacent landowners on the 1868 Beers Map of Baltimore Hundred[383] that this tract is located on the road from Roxana to Johnson's Corner, almost a mile north of the corner. According to Clemeth's petition to the Court, Sandy Ridge adjoined lands of Capt. Nathaniel Tunnell, Jacob Barnes, and Nathaniel Evans. The report of the Commissioners to the Court included a detailed map of the metes and bounds of Sandy Ridge, including the "County Road" which passed through the western side of the tract. A comparison of the metes and bounds of the plot with plots along the Roxana to Johnson's Corner road on the 1996 Sussex County Tax Map was conclusive. Current plot boundaries, notwithstanding substantial breakup of the lands of the original Sandy Ridge patent, were essentially identical, making it relatively easy to locate Zadoc's Sandy Ridge. The sum of the acreage of the current plots also was equal to the 53 acres of the original Sandy Ridge land patent.

The northern end of Sandy Ridge is on Delaware Route 20, approximately 800 feet south of the intersection of Route 20 and County Road 383. The southern end is about 1,200 feet down Route 20. Most of the site is on the east side of Route 20, and about one-fourth is across the road. A substantial number of homes and lots, as well as a restaurant, are currently located on the lands which once made up Sandy Ridge.

---

383   Beers Map of Baltimore Hundred, op. cit.

Looking east from Route 20, one can see the "Sandy Ridge" which gave Zadoc's land its name.

Perhaps other researchers will be able to confirm Lynch to be Nancy's maiden name and the location of Nancy and Zadoc's "home place" mentioned in his will.

Zadoc Evans Last Will and Testament – February 5, 1848 Sussex County Wills, Liber K, Folio 43. Admitted to Probate December 20, 1852

IN THE NAME OF GOD AMEN, I Zadoc Evans of Sussex County State of Delaware being now of sound mind and good memory do this Fifth day of February in the year of our Lord one thousand eight hundred and forty eight 1848 Make Constitute and confirm this my last will and testament as follows to wit:

Item first. I give & bequeath to my wife during her Natural life the following named articles & at her death if any thing remains to go as hereinafter directed. One cow, choice, one bed of furniture, choice, chairs, cubard, furneture, sufficient of the pots & cookery and to have whatever is reasonable of my other household & kitchen furniture also corn fodder for her own private use also my wife Nancy is to have her home & maintainance of the home place that I now reside on during here natural life then to go as herein after directed which at her death I give whatever of the personal property is left to my three daughters namely Rhoda, Elizabeth D. Linch, & Nancy Bennett equally ------.

Item 2. I give & bequeath to my grandson, son of John M. Evans the one equal half part the tract none by the name of Sandy Ridge to my Grandson Zadoc Aydelotte Evans except Rhoda should need them for her to have a maintenance of the said whole of Sandy Ridge to him his heirs & assigns forever -----.

Item 3. I give and bequeath to my son Clemeth Evans the other half of Sandy Ridge except as before excepted to him his heirs & Assigns forever.

Item 4. I give & bequeath to my Son William T. my home place that I now reside on after the death of his mother to him his heirs & assigns forever also to Wm. T. one cart.

Item 5. I give to my daughter Rhoda one Cow One bed & furniture part of the Chairs & pot metal to her heirs & assigns forever -----.

Item 6. I give to my Son William T. One pair of broune stears if they are in my Estate.

Item 7. I give and bequeath to my five sons equally all the lumber in the barn . . . such as plows, harrows and whatever may be commonly in the barn.

Item 8. I give to my three daughters equally all the balance of my moveable property not before named forever.

Item 9. I give and bequeath to my Son William T. twenty bushels of Corn if there is enough to supply the demand before given.

Item 10. I give to my five sons namely John, Clemeth, Henry, Jacob, William T. all the balance of money, note or bonds after my lawful debts, burying Charge administering expenses are paid to them their heirs & assigns forever, and now this above written date I do Ratify this to be my last will & Testament which I hereby Sine & Seal The first written date.

Signed, Sealed & Delivered as my last
Will & Testament in presence of us

Wm. S. Hall   Zadoc Evans (SEAL)
Isaiah Ellis
Henry J. Hall

Chapter 20   Letter to Neal – Travel

Dear Neal,   September 1999

As I write this you are only six months old, but already you have an engaging disposition and ready smile. It was delightful today to have you in my lap and see such a little guy laugh, giggle and cackle at your Daddy's antics. Never have I seen such fun and emotion out of such a little one. You are a lot like him, and if you continue to have your father's wonderful disposition, ready smile, and engaging laugh you will be truly fortunate. A willing smile and sunny disposition wins friends and overcomes adversaries. Be sunny!

As the last of four sons, your Daddy was the "little guy," but he had many advantages. While always fun to be around and a delight, he learned many growing-up lessons years earlier than most. He took in everything. As a first child, you won't have that advantage, but working to emulate your Daddy (Mommy, too) would be a good place to start.

Your Daddy and I had many opportunities to share wonderful experiences together. We lived together for a number of years after he finished at the University of Virginia. He always did his share and more- willingly. We also had opportunities to travel together. Seeing new places, natural wonders, major cities, new cultures, great art and music, and beautiful buildings is one of life's greatest and most worthwhile pleasures. Going to Hawaii, meeting in Istanbul and traveling to Russia, a weekend of games at Fenway Park in Boston, a weekend of games at Tiger Stadium in Detroit with his brothers, two great camping tours of the West and one to Prince Edward Island with his brothers, and other excursions together—how fortunate we were.

Neal, seek and take advantage of opportunities to travel and see and know America and the rest of the world—with your parents and on your own. Travel in high school and college whenever you can. Semesters overseas will bring lifetime memories, greater understanding of others and great pleasure. Diligent study in school is important, but travel puts it all into perspective. Travel when you can, and prepare for it by reading extensively about the places you will see and the people you will meet. You will enjoy it and reap many and unexpected rewards. The memories and pleasures of travel enrich and last a lifetime.

You should be proud of your family.   Love,

Pop-Pop

Chapter 21 — Clemeth (1809-1868) and Elizabeth Hopkins Evans (1812-1873)

Contemporaneous Happenings

1851 Harriet Beecher Stowe's *Uncle Tom's Cabin* contributes
      to movement against slavery in the North
1854 Thoreau publishes his tract, *Walden or Life in the Woods*
1859 Charles Darwin publishes his *On the Origin of the Species*
1860 Abraham Lincoln elected President of the United States
1861 Civil War begins at Fort Sumter
1863 Emancipation Proclamation takes effect
1865 Civil War ends at Appomattox
1867 Alaska ceded to United States by Czar Alexander

Clemeth or Clement? His father spelled his name "Clemeth" in his will, and he signed his own will as "Clemeth." We will use their spelling even though it is spelled Clement in many records. Grandson Alonzo called him Clemma.

Clemeth was born April 16, 1808, and Elizabeth Hopkins was born December 12, 1812. They were married September 19, 1832, pursuant to a marriage bond dated September 9, 1832.[384] Clemeth died November 22, 1868, and Elizabeth died October 30, 1873.

Clemeth and Elizabeth had nine children according to the Godwin family Bible.[385] Their oldest child, John A. Evans, was born December 24, 1833, and their other eight recorded children, Hettie M., Rhoda, William T., Mary A. C., Sarah T., Margaret C., Harriet M. and George C. W., were born about every three years thereafter. George C. W., the last, was born in 1855.

According to my Uncle Louis Evans, Clemeth is buried in Roxana, but he did not know where. Is it in the Evans-Lynch Cemetery which is on the road from the Roxana Methodist Church to Route 17? I visited this cemetery, but the combination of summer heat, vicious briars, and biting insects precluded further investigation.

---

384   Delaware Public Archives, Marriage Records and Delaware Public Archives Bible Record Collection, Godwin Family Bible, Folder #336.5. John A and Harriet's daughter, Hettie M., married into the Godwin family.
385   Ibid.

There were a number of overturned markers bearing the family name "Lynch" and at least one Evans. This is worthy of more investigation.

After the Civil War and the emancipation of remaining slaves, life for the typical Baltimore Hundred family did not change much up to the turn of the century. Farming methods did not change significantly. Cereal grains, the main crop, were still seeded and harvested by hand. Road improvements and the coming of the railroad to Frankford and Selbyville in 1874[386] provided a new market for wood and farm products shipped north, but expanded commerce had minimal impact on families on small farms. Peaches became an important Delaware crop, but with little impact in Baltimore Hundred. Another effect of the railroad was the ease with which local men and boys could now travel to Philadelphia to work in the harbor on tugboats, river boats and steamships—a significant future occupation for Baltimore Hundred's sons as discussed in Chapters 24 and 26.

The lack of change and economic improvement for Baltimore Hundred's farming families, including the Halls, Daiseys and Evanses, is confirmed by a review of Sussex County Assessments. Assessment for taxes on livestock, land, and, in one case, a slave owned by David Hall, listed in 1856 and 1860, changed little during the four-year assessment-to-assessment period. Assessments of livestock and land for a number of Hall, Evans and Daisey Ancestors follow:

Sussex County Tax Assessments for 1856 through 1896

1856

Capt. William R. Hall	One yoke of oxen, one cow and yearling, two sheep, two shoats
David Hall	One negro man, 18 years, one yoke of oxen, one horse, two dry cows, two young cattle, one sow, 360 acres of land
John A. Evans	One horse, one cow and calf, no land
Clemeth Evans	One horse, two yoke of oxen, one yoke of yearlings, two cows and calves, one heifer, six sheep, one sow and pigs, three hogs, 122 acres of land

1860

| Prettyman Daisey | One horse, two yoke of oxen, two cows and calves, four yearlings, seven sheep, one sow and three shoats, 100 acres of land. |

---

386   Julian D. Winslow, *Sussex Awakens to the Toot* (Wilmington, DE: Julian D. Winslow, 1999).

Clemeth Evans	Two horses, one yoke of oxen, one cow and calf, two yearlings, twelve sheep, one cow and pigs.
John A. Evans	One horse, two cows and one calf, one sow and pigs, no land.
David Hall	240 Acres of land

1864

Prettyman Daisey	Some animals, 100 acres of land.
Clemeth Evans	One horse, one pair of oxen, one cow, four young cattle, one sow and shoats, six sheep.
John A. Evans	Two 101 acre plots of land.
Capt. William R. Hall	One horse, one pair of oxen, three cows, three yearlings, four shoats, no land. Note: at this time Capt. Hall was keeper of the Fenwick Island Lighthouse.
John C. Hall	Two cows, three yearlings, three sheep, 100 acres of land.
David Hall	240 Acres of land

1868

John A. Evans	One yoke of oxen, one cow and a heifer, four sheep and two plots of land totaling 102 acres
John C. Hall	Three cows and three yearlings, 240 acres of land
David Hall	240 Acres of land

1872

| John A. Evans | One horse, one yoke of oxen, one cow, two yearlings |
| John C. Hall | Four sheep, one sow, 100 acres of land |

1877-1880

| John A. Evans | One pair of mules, two cows, 33 acres of land |
| John C. Hall | One horse, one yoke of oxen, one cow, two yearlings, four sheep, one sow, 100 acres of land. |

1884-1888

| John A. Evans | One pair of mules, two cows, 33 acres of land. |

1888-1892

| John A. Evans | One horse, two cows, a calf, a sow, 50 acres of land |
| John C. Hall | 110 acres of land |

1892-1896

| John A. Evans | Three cows, one horse, one colt, 59 acres of land |
| John C. Hall | One horse, one mule, two cows and a calf, two heifers, one sow |

During these years, Clemeth and John A. Evans and John C. Hall were farmers. In his later years John A. was a "house carpenter." As noted earlier, John C. was also a mariner; he sailed to Wilmington and Philadelphia carrying produce.

The above assessments are typical for most family farmers of these times. A typical farm, which changed little over the last half of the nineteenth century, was assessed for one or two yoke of oxen, a horse, two or three cows, some sheep, and one or two sows and pigs. The average farm was 100 acres, of which only a small part could be plowed and cultivated with one or two yoke of oxen. The horse was for riding and pulling a cart or carriage. The sheep provided wool and meat. Cows provided dairy products and steers, meat. Clemeth's inventory included a carriage, "dearborn" wagon, and two oxcarts.

Clemeth owned land valued at $500 in 1850. He eventually owned three farms, including one where their son William lived. This indicates Clemeth and Elizabeth were in the upper economic tier of post-Civil War farm families. This is consistent with Clemeth's inventory, which provides a good assessment of their house and farm. The five sets of "bed and furniture" probably indicate there were at least three bedrooms and possibly more. The spinning wheel, cupboard, desk, large number of chairs, "set tee," three looking glasses, multiple tables and stands, rocking chair, bureau, and two "lots of carpet" indicate theirs was a comfortable home for the times. The "clock," something not included in most inventories, was a further indication of relative affluence.

Clemeth wrote his will on November 16, 1868, six days before he died on November 22.[387] He left to his "beloved wife, the Farm where I now live known as the 'Basin land' . . ." As best determined, this tract is located on Delaware Route 54, south of Roxana, near Derrickson's Creek and not far from Johnson's Corner.

Clemeth is recorded in the 1860 U. S. Census as being in Hall's Store (Ocean View). Apparently, the Basin Land (72-plus acres) was either closer to Ocean View than Roxana, or the Census-taker for Hall's Store was also responsible for this area.

---

387   Will of Clemeth Evans, at end of chapter.

Clemeth and Elizabeth's other farms, the <u>Bennett Tract</u> and <u>Phylis's Point</u>, were near the Selbyville Ditch, west of Roxana and about two-thirds of the way from Selbyville to Frankford. Their son, John A., subsequently bought the <u>Bennett Tract</u> from Elijah Bennett in 1868.

Clemeth and Elizabeth continued in the mode of most families in Baltimore Hundred, hardworking farmers, but apparently were somewhat better off than the average family.

<u>Captain John W. James of Hall's Store and His Four Ledger Books</u>

Captain John W. James was a contemporary of Clemeth. Captain James kept ledgers of both his household expenses and the many expenses of his ship, the *Henry Brown.*

The household ledgers tell much about expenses and income for a farm family, including expenses for hired hands. Captain James' family, as recorded in the 1870 U. S. Census, consisted of Capt. John, his wife, Ann, and their children Hiram, Robert and Henry. Of particular interest are the hired hands and household help with local names, including the following, which might be of help to other researchers (spelled as in the ledger with today's spelling added). The wages for some of these hands are given to provide a wage baseline for the times and to show the difference between wages for white and black help:

Some of the James Family Hired Hands:

Mitchel Messeck and William Rickoards [Messick and Rickards]	14 Weeks starting January 2, 1866, at $13.00 per month
Hired hand William Watson and a horse	Worked for about 10 days in May-June 1865
Capt. Thomas Dasey (his wife)	
Isaac Taler [Taylor] (black man)	Rented house and worked for 50¢ per day
William Watson	$13.00 per month
Joshua Swain	
James Collins	
John Hickman	
Hiram Littleon [Littleton]	
Isaac Hall (black man)	$10 per month
Elizabeth Burton (a seamstress black girl)	$5.00 per month

Sary [Sarah] Long	
John Hall and Wife [Probably John C. Hall]	He had left job as Assistant Keeper of the Fenwick Island Lighthouse
John Outten	
Charles Hall and Sons, Charles, Levin, Joshua and Robert	
Silas Burbage	$9.50 per month
James C. Short and his wife	
Levin Anderson	
William Lerner	
Emeline Hopkins (Misses)	
John Rust	
Luke Burton	
Philip Horton	
Philip Furmon [Furman]	

Feed for farm livestock, consisting of corn fodder and corn, house and farm supplies, clothing and food were purchased from other farmers, neighbors and merchants, including these (spelled as in ledger with today's spelling if known):

James H. Dorekson [Derrickson]	Lemuel Vigars [Vickers]
Charles Cord (colored man)	Izary [Israel] L. Hitchson [Hitchens]
William Watson	David Evans
Jacob Hocker	Eligha [Elijah] Howard
Mitchell Messeck [Messick]	Richard Hickman
Joseph Sadler	Isaac Hall ("black man")
Joseph Cobs [Cobb]	George Hall
Isral [Israel] Townsend	Isaac Hall
Edward Evans	John Hickman
Elisha Vigars [Vickers]	Mary E. Furman
Peter Quillen	Milby Gray
David Dasey [Daisey]	Elizabeth Burton (dress and materials)
Luis Burton	Ann Williams
Captain Henry Hutson [Hudson]	Milby Williams

The following carefully recorded purchases reflect local grocery and clothing prices just after the Civil War in the late 1860s:

Potatoes	$1.00 per barrel	Lard	20¢ per pound
Sweet potatoes	$1.00 per bushel	Tobacco	86¢ per pound
"Meat"	25¢ per pound	Chewing tobacco	5¢ per piece
Meal [corn?]	$1.50 per bushel	Pair of shoes	$1.70 and $3.25
Molasses	60¢ per gallon	Shirting [cloth]	15¢ per yard
Chicken	25¢ each	Bonnet [hat]	25¢
Eggs	15¢ per dozen	Turnips	30¢ per bushel
Flour	5¢ per pound	Corn	$1.20 per bush
Buckwheat	$2.50 per bushel	Oats	$2.00 per barrel
Phosphate	25¢ per pound	Stack of fodder	$4.50
Salt	19¢ per peck	Cole [coal] oil	7¢ per pint
Taller [tallow]	12¢		

Food purchases consisted mostly of cornmeal, flour, sweet and white potatoes, molasses (no sugar), and meat (beef). Equally instructive are items not purchased such as pork, poultry, eggs, and vegetables, all of which must have been produced on the James farm. They must have raised chickens for eggs and the pot. Hogs provided fresh and smoked meat, bacon, sausage, scrapple, and lard. Soap was made from rendered fat. Cows provided milk, butter and buttermilk. Most beans, greens, tomatoes, onions, peppers, cabbage and herbs must have come from the family garden. Theirs was a simple but hearty diet. The big treat must have been fresh beef and chickens for Sunday dinner. Smoked meat and salted fish were winter standbys.

Cloth was purchased and, as demonstrated by the absence of clothes purchases in the ledger, most clothing was sewn at home by hired maids and seamstresses and probably Mrs. James herself. Shoes were purchased from the local cordwainer.

Captain James' ledger tells us a lot about life in and near Hall's Store (Ocean View) around the time of the Civil War. While James and his family lived in the upper level of local families, it can be expected that the contemporary William R. Hall, Clemeth Evans, Jesse Green and Prettyman Dazey families had similar table-fare, though, as smaller landholders, they probably ate less meat and more fish, cornbread and beans.

Captain James' ship ledger[388] contains expense records for the Schooner *Henry Brown* of Hackensack, New Jersey, during the 1850s. Included are names of crewmen, their wages, and when they signed on and left. Also included in this ledger, for some reason, are three pages of the ship's log for a trip from New York to Norfolk.

While it is not the purpose of this book to review ocean-going schooners in any detail, as compared to our Indian River Schooners, we do know, as discussed in Chapter 23, that there were a number of ship captains from the Ocean View and Millville areas. It is appropriate to discuss briefly Captain James' Schooner *Henry Brown*, which regularly carried almost 100 cords of wood from the Middle-Atlantic area to New York Harbor and was probably typical of schooners ranging in size from 80 to well over 100 tons which regularly plied East Coast waters. These ships were significantly larger than the Indian River Schooners discussed in Chapter 23.

The *Henry Brown* was built in 1838 in Hackensack, New Jersey, by John Lozier and John Anderson of Hackensack. She was 80 feet long, 24 feet, 6 inches wide, with a draft of 7 feet, 8 inches. She was a 130-ton, two-masted schooner with a square stern and a billet head. Her master was Captain John W. James of Hall's Store (Ocean View, Del.). Her prime cargo was pine wood although she also carried coal and corn. She generally had a master and three crewmen, some of whom, like Captain James, were from Baltimore Hundred with easily-recognizable local names. Especially gratifying was the finding of my Great-Great-Grandfather, **Henry Dazey/Dasey**, among Captain James' crew in 1847, confirming that he had gone to sea. Some of these crewmen (below) recorded in the ledger for 1846 - 1847 with local surnames, <u>may</u> have been from Baltimore Hundred:

From the ledger for 1851 to 1854 (Local surnames only):

Eli Daesy [Daisey]	June 1, 1848	Peter Cord	April 23, 1846
James Carey	July 25, 1848	John C. Burton	April 20, 1846
Thomas Hickman	July 27, 1848	John Vickars	Sept. 1, 1848
Eley Evans	July 28, 1848	Thomas Puzey	April 20, 1846
John Vickars	April 20, 1846	William T. West	June 11, 1846
George Williams	Sept. 1, 1848	John S. Evans	Feb. 17, 1847
William Steele	Sept. 21, 1848	**Henry Dazey**	Feb. 17, 1847
F. Edward White	Oct. 5, 1848	Eley Evans	Feb. 17, 1847
Philip H. James	Oct. 28, 1848	John S. Bennet	Dec. 4, 1847
Luke G. Barnett	Nov. 29, 1848	Peter Cord	Dec. 3, 1847
Charles Burton	April 20, 1846		

---

388   Ledger of the Schooner Henry Brown, op. cit.

John Burton	Aug. 16, 1851	William Green	Jan. 27, 1853
Benjamin Chamberlin	Aug. 16, 1851	Joseph Pusy (Pusey)	July 18, 1853
John D. Furman	Sept 16, 1851	Elisha Rickards	Dec. 3, 1853
Philip H. James	Oct. 21, 1851	Ezekiel W. Evans	July 31, 1854
Thomas C. Godwin	Nov. 6, 1851	George Bennett	July 2, 1852
James H. Law	April 19, 1852	William Evans	Aug. 23, 1852
Peary Hutson	May 13, 1852	Charles Williams	Nov. 5, 1852
John Burton	June 3, 1852	James Mumford	Oct. 15, 1852
Samuel Hutson	June 3, 1852	Richard Williams	Jan. 27, 1853
George Tingle	June 11, 1852		

Hopefully, the listing of these names will help other family history researchers.

Last Will and Testament of Clemeth Evans –

November 16th 1868
Sussex County Wills, Liber M,
pp. 484-485. Admitted to
Probate December 1, 1868

In the Name of God Amen, I Clemeth Evans of Baltimore Hundred Sussex County State of Delaware, being of sound mind and memory and considering the uncertainty of this life, do therefore make ordain publish and declare this to be my last will and testament: That is to say, First after all my lawful debts are paid and discharged the residue of my estate real and personal, I give bequeath and dispose of as follows to wit:

To my beloved wife, the Farm where I now live known as the Basin land also ten acres of the Bennett tract where my son William now lives commencing at a peach-oak close to the Winding Blades and then square across to Elijah Lynch's land; and at her death to my son George the afore said farm with the ten acres.

To my son John the Bennett farm except the afore said ten acres by paying my daughters Sarah and Mary Ann each five hundred dollars.

To My son William the farm known as Phylis's Point adjoining land of James A. Carey and James Jacobs. At my wife's death, my son George is to pay my Daughters Margaret and Hetty each five hundred dollars if he is living if not they are to have a five hundred dollar share in the farm. To my beloved wife I give and bequeath the residue of my property. Likewise I make constitute and appoint my wife to be the executrix of this my last will and testament, revoking all previous wills made by me.

Signed

Witness

Clemeth Evans

James D. West

     his

James B. X Hudson

     mark

Joshua M. Bishop

Chapter 22   Letter to Allison — God's Great Out of Doors

September 1999

My dearest little Allison,

After having had four sons of my own, I am delighted now to have six granddaughters. How lucky I am to have one who already shows signs of being independent – a trait which will serve you well. Be independent, but always know you can get help from your parents and family when wanted.

I am writing this in my den in the fall of 1999 while marveling at the beauty outside my window—the marsh is flooded by Dennis, a meandering hurricane turned into a tropical storm which has plagued the coastal states for over a week. How wonderful it is to be able to enjoy such scenery every day.

God's out of doors has many wonders. Just this morning a beautiful, huge bald eagle was perched in a large pine tree across the creek. How majestic! It is most gratifying, knowing these eagles were an endangered species not that many years ago. I don't remember ever seeing one while growing up here. I was excited enough to watch him for almost half an hour and then I called Pat to tell her. A beautiful bird, and they are all beautiful, is most worthy of "bird watching" time.

As I write this, a crested cormorant is perched on a piling, two bluebirds are catching flying insects under the pine tree, and around the dock, a flotilla of young mallards are dabbling in the flooded marsh, a kingfisher just plunged into the creek from a piling—don't know if he caught a minnow, and myriads of gulls and terns are wheeling around the dark stormy sky. These are all in addition to the pair of graceful and majestic great egrets in the marsh and the great blue heron who passes like a large airplane. What sights! The variety and beauty of birds know no bounds—if you keep your eyes open.

I have always thought a salt marsh is the most beautiful place in the world, and now I get to spend many hours each week just watching the marsh. The last two evenings, the sunset has been spectacular—every color in the rainbow and all shades. Just last week, while watching the marsh from my shower, I saw an amazing sight. Two otters were playing in the creek. I spent a wonderful half-hour watching. Always keep your eyes tuned to what is going on around you; the marvels of nature continually amaze.

You never know when or where you will see something special. Surely, God does not subtract from our allotted time that which we spend observing the out of doors. Allison, I can't tell you how much pleasure, relaxation and even solace it has given to me. Observe and love the out of doors; it's there for the looking—and fun too!

Love,

Pop-Pop

Chapter 23 — John A. (1833-1889) and Harriet Jefferson Evans (1837-1875) and Angeline T. Daisey Evans (2d wife, 1855-1910)

Contemporaneous Happenings

Contemporaneous Happenings

1861 Civil War begins at Fort Sumter
1865 Civil War ends at Appomattox
1870 Fifteenth Amendment to the Constitution adopted - guaranteeing voting rights
1892 Sierra Club organized to protect America's environment
1893 Columbian Exposition in Chicago displays advances of technology
1897 Joseph John Thompson of England demonstrates the atom is divisible
1898 Explosion sinking the *Battleship Maine* in Havana provokes Spanish-American War

John A. Evans was born December 24, 1833. Harriet Jefferson Evans was born November 18, 1837. John A. and Harriet married on January 3, 1855, when he was 21 and she was 17.

They were both an Evans. Harriet was John A.'s third cousin if I am correct in my belief that Daniel is the son of John Sr. As discussed in Section Q of Chapter 7, she was the daughter of Stephen Riley Evans, the granddaughter of Enoch Evans who also married an Evans second cousin, and the great-granddaughter of John Jr., Daniel's brother. Harriet's mother was Sarah Elizabeth Jefferson.

John A. died May 6, 1899, at age 65. Harriet died on February 22, 1875, at age 37, the mother of seven surviving children. They now rest in the St. Georges Cemetery.

Like many another young widower or widow with a family, John A. remarried four months later. The bride was Angeline T. Daisey, aged about 20. The marriage, it would seem, was an expedient solution to the problem of caring for children. Whether love was the primary motivation or not, the marriage lasted until John A.'s death 24 years later. They had six children between 1876 and 1887, two and possibly three of whom died as young children.

The 1880 U. S. Census records John A. as being 46 years old and Angie as 25. Included in their household were John A. and Elizabeth's children—Stephen, 21,

Louisa, 19, Josephine, 16, and Alonzo, 12 ("Laborer"). Thirty years later, the 1910 Census of Angie's household lists four of John A. and Angie's surviving children.

The 1890 U. S. Census, the first which reported on ability to read and write, records John A. as not being able to read or write, even though he signed his will.

A man named John A. Evans served in the Union Army as a corporal in Company D of the Sixth Regiment, Delaware Volunteer Infantry, which was composed of men who were mainly from the southern part of the state. It was organized pursuant to a call by President Lincoln on August 4, 1862, for three hundred thousand "nine months men."[389] A search of census and other records found only one other John A. Evans who was too young to have served in the Union Army.

Other surnames on Company D's roster include Lynch, West, Williams, Bennett, Bunting, Derickson, Evans, Hickman, Hudson, Megee, Murray, Rickards and Wilgus. Clearly, this company was recruited from residents of Baltimore Hundred and the surrounding area. The 28 year-old John A., married and the father of three very small children, was enlisted and mustered into service as a corporal on November 19, 1862, in Centerville (today's Roxana) by Lieutenant Morgan.

On June 27, 1863, the more than nine hundred men of the Sixth Regiment were called into service and ordered to Havre de Grace, Maryland, for garrison duty on the important Susquehanna River supply route. The Sixth Regiment was subsequently ordered to Fort Delaware for a brief tour guarding Confederate prisoners. Fort Delaware is on Pea Patch Island in the Delaware River south of Wilmington. It was a dreaded prison for Confederate soldiers who endured terrible conditions and disease and died by the thousands. Guard duty may have been almost as bad as being a prisoner. In July 1863, following the Confederate defeat at Gettysburg, almost 9,000 additional prisoners were added to the 3,673 already there at the beginning of the month.[390]

Just a couple of months later, on August 23, 1863, nine months after their original enlistment, all the regiment's companies were transported to their homes in Kent and Sussex County and the unit was mustered out of service.

---

389   Scharf, Vol. I, op. cit., pp. 370-371, and Appendix p. xxvii. All of the materials on the Sixth Regiment were adapted from Scharf's excellent history.
390   Dale Fetzer and Bruce Mowday, *Unlikely Allies* (Mechanicsburg, Pa.: Stackpole Books, 2000), p. 152.

The Fourth Delaware Regiment was on the island a year later when 219 prisoners escaped. Accused of Southern sympathies, the Fourth was soon transferred.[391] The Ninth Delaware Regiment, recruited specifically for guard duty at the Fort, took over in the fall of 1864 and remained until the war's end.

The men of Company D of the Sixth Regiment were honorable volunteers and presumably their service was honorable and willing, although abbreviated. With all the great battles and campaigns in the two years after 1863, it is puzzling that the Sixth was mustered out of service when it was. These "nine-months-men" only served their nine months, and never saw real combat. Only one private in the regiment is listed as "killed," and eleven were listed as "died of disease."

John A. Evans's army travels may have been the only time in his life he ventured more than a hundred miles from home—more than any Evans ancestor since Walter. John A. resumed life on the farm when his enlistment was completed.

The economic viability of slavery, a cause of the Civil War, had diminished in this area before the war. By 1850, the U. S. Census reported almost 50 percent more free "colored" males than slaves in Baltimore Hundred—237 to 162. Even with slavery having become a declining part of Baltimore Hundred life, John A. returned from service to a world in which slavery was as dead in spirit as it would soon be in legal fact. While the Emancipation Proclamation of January 1, 1863, did not apply to Delaware and other border states, the 13th Amendment in 1865 made it official: there was no more slavery.

There is no argument against Lincoln's freeing the slaves, and it was obviously the right, proper and just thing to do. The right choice was made; the implementation was a failure. Unfortunately, freeing the slaves had continuing impacts, some extending to this day. Untrained and uneducated and generally without land, the former slaves were ill-equipped to get ahead. The last third of the nineteenth century was a time of little economic development. Delaware's free and newly freed Blacks had been allowed to accomplish little in the way of economic progress even after decades of freedom. By Delaware law, Blacks were not political or social equals. Jim Crow laws passed in Delaware in 1875 reduced prospects further. Segregated schools were separate but not equal. Schools were still segregated and not equal in the 1950s when I graduated from a high school a mile from where I lived. Local Black students, on the other hand, had to be bused to the segregated Black high school in Georgetown. The results were predictable. Small

---

391   W. Emerson Wilson, Fort Delaware (Newark, Delaware: Institute of Delaware History and Culture, University of Delaware, 1957).

disadvantaged Black communities developed in Selbyville, Frankford, Clarksville and elsewhere in the area, generally with a local church being the center of social and economic activity. Vestiges of these disadvantages continue to this day.

On August 8, 1865, John A. paid $1,150 for 101 acres along the county road that leads from the Sound Church to the ditch William Williams deeded to James A. Brashur Jr. This tract was part of <u>Cow Quarter</u>, a 500-acre patent taken out by Thomas Fenwick on March 12, 1685, located on Derrickson's Neck, on the south side of Derrickson's Creek, upstream from the Little Assawoman Bay.[392] John A's son, Alonzo, who was born in 1868, stated that he was raised in the Williamsville area, probably in a home on this tract.

In 1868, John A. inherited the Bennett Farm from his father, Clemeth. As noted in Chapter 21 on Clemeth, this farm was north of Roxana. On January 17, 1871, John A. bought more than 33 acres in Roxana on the north side of the Roxana School Road, adjoining lands of Jacob Evans, Eli Daisey and Joshua Evans.

John A. later purchased a 59-acre tract on the southeast corner of the intersection of routes 26 and 17 where the Hocker's Supermarket is now located. He owned this tract when he died in 1899. Aunt Mary confirmed that this was John A's home. In March 1911, John A.'s surviving children sold the 13-acre part of this tract that their mother, Angeline, had received as her share of her husband's estate to their brother, Calvin A. Evans. It was described in the deed as being "on south side of the Blackwater Church to Millville road." Calvin A. Evans later sold this plot to William P. Quillen (Sussex County Deed Book 217, p. 331). Quillen, in turn, sold it in 1922, to James H. Williams.

John A. and Angeline's house on this tract, known as the Williams House, is one of the oldest in Sussex County. The original house, a post and beam house, was in 2014 the small western wing on a major, two-story addition. The original house was located back in the field about two hundred feet south of Route 26. It was moved to its present location about 1926. The construction is fascinating and worthy of study. Electa Evans who died in 2005, previously lived on a lot which was on this tract. (Note: This house was torn down in 2014.)

John A.'s farm was typical of farms in Sussex County. He planted corn, raised vegetables and had a variety of fruit trees. They raised hogs and salted away pork, raised chickens for eggs and an occasional hen for dinners, kept milk cows for <u>fresh milk and</u> churned butter. Farming methods remained generally unchanged,

392   See Short Map, op. cit.

except for the increased understanding and use of manure to fertilize fields. The farm produce including corn not only served family needs, but was also sold to people in the small towns. These communities grew around mills and manufacturing plants which turned out wood products mostly.

John A's generation was the first to benefit economically from the coming of the railroad to Frankford and Selbyville. Work commenced in 1874 on the Frankford and Breakwater (Lewes) Railroad extension from the north, and the first engine came to Millsboro on June 23, 1874. The extension to Delaware's southern border with Maryland at Selbyville soon followed. A new avenue of commerce was available to the region. Production of grain and other products, including strawberries, increased. Agents bought produce at the farm and arranged for hauling it in carts and wagons to the stations in Selbyville and Frankford and shipping it to Wilmington and Philadelphia.

Not only were the stations at Frankford and Selbyville focal points for Baltimore Hundred economic development, they offered transportation to the ports of Wilmington, Philadelphia and New York where local young men increasingly sought employment on tugboats and merchant vessels.

Schooners on the Indian River

Shipping from the Indian River through the Indian River Inlet to points north on the Delaware River and Bay was another boost to the economy in the late nineteenth and early twentieth centuries. Sloops and small schooners from 10 tons to just over 40 tons and ranging in length from 30 feet to nearly 60 feet sailed from such places as Daisey and Pennewell's Landings in Ocean View, Whites Creek in Millville, Blackwater Creek and Millsboro. The smaller sloops had one mast with a gaff rig. The schooners had two masts.

These small ships plying the Indian River and tributaries generally carried lumber to northern ports such as New Castle, Wilmington, Philadelphia and Millville, N.J. The schooner, *William Ellison*, Captained by Edward Lathbury, carried grain from the granary at Sandy Landing to Philadelphia and Atlantic City. They also carried fruit, tomatoes, and possibly other crops. The schooners returned with flour, lime, coal oil, materials for clothing, and manufactured goods, generally of significantly greater value than the lumber sent north. The combination of competition from the railroad and new roads and silting of the river and landings eventually brought an end to the schooner shipping.

The Annual Reports of the Life-Saving Service[393] and Daily Logs of the Indian River Life-Saving Station are excellent sources of information on shipping from the Indian River and Bay area.[394] They record life-saving actions by the Station Keeper and surfmen to rescue ships and crews in distress. Most incidents involved schooners that ran aground on sandbars or in the surf while entering or leaving the Indian River Inlet, a meandering and treacherous natural inlet then located about a mile north of the present inlet. The incident records include the date, the ships and Master's names, number of crew, description of the incident and actions taken, weather, ship size (tonnage),[395] the value of ship and cargo, port of embarkation and destination.

The following excerpts from Station logs from 1882 through the end of the century provide an understanding of shipping from and to the Indian River and tributaries. All the schooners in these incidents were refloated off sandbars, shoals, and shorelines, and no crewmen were lost:

- October 6, 1882 - Schooner *Dan*, of 28 tons, "Chamberlain," Master and three crewmen. Becalmed outside Indian River Inlet and carried ashore by current and grounded. Cargo of oak lumber from Indian River to Port Penn, N.J. Ship value $1,000 and cargo value $400.[396]

- October 6, 1882 - Schooner *Chief*, Melson, Master and two crewmen. Becalmed like *Dan*, above, and grounded. Cargo of pine lumber from Indian River to Millville, N.J. Ship value $700 and cargo value $325.

- October 23, 1883 - Schooner *Dan* [2nd time], "Champlain," Master and three crewmen. Grounded. Cargo of pine wood from Frankford, Del. to Philadelphia. Ship value $1,400 and cargo value $160.

- October 8, 1884 - Schooner *Sea Foam*, of 13 tons, Tunnel, Master and one crewman. Ran on bar south of Inlet. Cargo of pine lumber from Ocean View to Philadelphia. Ship value $1,200 and cargo value $150.

- June 22, 1887 - Schooner *Addie* of 17 tons, "Aydelett," Master, and one crewman. Ran aground. Cargo of lumber from Indian River to Millville, N. J. Ship value $1,000 and cargo value $150.

---

393   Annual Reports, U. S. Life Savings Service, U. S. Government Printing Office.

394   Indian River Life-Saving Station Logs, National Archives and Record Center, 900 Market Street, Philadelphia, Pa. (E-mail - archives@philarch.nara.gov.).

395   Ship tonnage is a measure of volume. One gross ton is equal to 100 cubic feet. Net tons in sailing ships is gross tons less that volume in units of 100 cubic feet devoted to crew space.

396   The ship size and ship and cargo values were estimates by the Station Keeper. Values for the same ship could vary from incident to incident by as much as a factor of two.

- October 19, 1889 - Schooner *Starlight* of 10 tons, Steel, Master, and one crewman. Grounded on bar. Cargo of bricks from Morris River, N.J. to Indian River. Ship value $500 and cargo value $40.
- May 6, 1890 - Schooner *White Cloud* of 9 tons, Justice, Master, and one crewmen. Cargo of lumber from Indian River Inlet to Millville, N.J. Ship value $500 and cargo value $150.
- July 1, 1890 - Schooner *J. W. Somers* of 18 tons, Burton, Master, and one crewman. Cargo of lumber from Indian River to Red Bank, N.J. Ship value $1,000 and cargo value $100.
- September 22, 1890 - Schooner *Northern Lights* of 19 tons, Lynch, Master, and one crewmen. Cargo of lumber from Indian River to Millville, N.J. Ship Value $800 and cargo value $250.
- November 25, 1891 - Schooner *Northern Lights* [2nd time], Lynch, Master, and one crewman. Cargo of lumber from Indian River to Bridgeport, N.J. Ship value $1,000 and cargo value $200.
- December 1, 1891 - Schooner *Adella Maud* of (15.6) tons, "Chamberlin," Master and two crewmen. Cargo of lumber from Indian River to Millville, N.J. Value of ship $1,200 and value of cargo $350.
- April 12, 1892 - Schooner *Northern Lights* [3rd time], Lathbury, Master and one crewman. Cargo of lime from Bridgeton, N.J., to Millville, Del. Ship value $800 and cargo value $100.
- June 25, 1892 - Schooner *William Ellison* of 16 tons, Lathbury, Master, and one crewmen. Cargo of lumber from Indian River to Bridgeton, N.J. Ship value $800 and cargo value $100.
- May 8, 1893 - Schooner *Addie* [2nd time] of 17 tons, "Aydelot," Master, and one crewman. Cargo of flour from Wilmington to Blackwater. Value of cargo $100.
- November 27, 1893 - Schooner *Emily Belle* of 25 tons, "Jestis," Master and one crewman. Cargo of flour and coal oil from Wilmington, Del., to Millville, Del. Value of ship $1,000 and value of cargo $1,000.
- October 31, 1896 - Schooner *Emily Belle* [2nd time] of 26 tons, Justice, Master. Cargo of flour from Wilmington to Millville. Value of ship $1,000 and value of cargo $1,000.
- December 14, 1896 - Schooner *Addie* [3rd time] of 17 tons, "Sympler," Master and one crewman. Cargo of flour and coal from Wilmington to Blackwater, Del. Value of ship $600 and value of cargo $400.
- August 24, 1898 - Schooner *Emily Belle* [3rd time] of 26 tons, "Jestice," Master, and one crewmen. Cargo of lumber from Indian River to Philadelphia.
- October 24, 1898 - Schooner *Emily Belle* [4th time] of 26 tons, Justice, Master, and one crewman. Cargo of lumber from Indian River to

Philadelphia. Value of cargo $200.

- December 1, 1898 - Schooner *J. W. Somers* of 19 tons, Lathbury, Master, and one crewman. Cargo of lumber from Blackwater, Del., to Millville, N.J. Value of ship $600 and value of cargo $200.
- May 22, 1899 - Schooner *Addie* of 16 tons [4th time], Lathbury, Master, and one crewman. Cargo of lumber from Indian River to Millville, N.J. Ship Value $500 and cargo value $200.

At least four of the above schooners were built locally: *Starlight* (1885) and *Adella Maud*[397] (1883) in the shipyard at the mouth of Blackwater Creek, *Dan* (1867) in St. Martins, Md., and *William Ellison* (1887) in Rehoboth. Other locally built schooners included the *Belle* (1872) in Millsboro, the *Ethel Dukes* (1888) in Millville, Del., the *J. T. Long* in Frankford (1864), and the *Comadator* (1860), the *J. C. Townsend* (1871), the *J. W. Houston* (1847), and the *Onward* (1866), all built in "Indian River, Delaware."[398] The Sloop *Fawn* was built in 1900 in Ocean View. The table on the next page includes length, beam, draft and tonnage for these locally built ships, as recorded in the Annual Lists of Merchant Vessels of the United States.

Most of the two-masted schooners had a very shallow draft and were about three times as long as they were wide, with a full midsection and a sharp bow. The registration records of the *J. C. Townsend* indicate she had one deck, two masts, a square stern, and a "scroll" head while the *J. W. Houston*, on the other hand, had a round stern. As recorded in the Indian River Life Saving Station reports, they were manned by a master and one to three crewmen, depending on their size. They were schooner-rigged because the smaller sails on the two-masted schooners were easier to handle than the large mainsail on single-masted sloops.

---

397   Ribs and the stern of the *Adella Maud*'s hull may be seen at low tide, north of the Vines Creek Bridge on Route 26. Mr. Franklin Timmons of Piney Neck remembers his father telling him the hull was the *Adella Maud*. Her last owners were George H. Townsend of Millville (½) and Eben Townsend of Dagsboro (½) whose grandson, C. P. Townsend, also confirmed her name. She sailed from 1883 when she was built at Blackwater Creek by Joshua C. Townsend of Frankford (3/4 share), her first Master (named her after his daughter), and Jacob Wilgus of Roxana (1/4 share). She was chartered through 1914. Other Masters included Edward J. Daisey in 1907, George H. Justice in 1905, Charles H. Chamberlain in 1903 (1/3 owner), Edward T. Lathbury of the *William Ellison* in 1889, Isaac M. Steel in 1888, Edward H. Lynch in 1884, and Mark H. Roach of Lewes in 1901 (owner and Master). She was probably abandoned on the marsh in 1914 or 1915 and burned to the waterline. She rests near the timbers of a dock where ships were loaded, probably with lumber from a close-by mill. A competent survey of the remains of the *Adella Maud* would tell us much about the construction of these old schooners.
398   U. S. Department of the Treasury, *Nineteenth Annual List of Merchant Vessels of the United States for the Year Ending June 30, 1887* (Washington, D. C.: U.S. Government Printing Office), 1888.

While I found only one picture of any of these schooners that plied the Indian River, the *Liberty*, in the Newport News Maritime Museum (page 234), I am confident they were very similar to the line drawings of a schooner and the cross section of a centerboard on page 233, which are based on the Chesapeake Bay Centerboard Schooner. Boatbuilders traveled between the Chesapeake Bay and Delaware Bay shores of Delmarva, so the Chesapeake Bay Centerboard Schooner probably also typified the schooners plying the Indian River.

Some of the Schooners Built on the Indian River and Bay

Schooner	Tons (Net)	Length (ft.)	Beam (ft.)	Draft (ft.)
Starlight	10	35	13	4.0
Adella Maud	15.63	50	17	3.2
Dan	36	64.3	20.4	3.5
Belle	19.24	48.5	18	3.3
Ethel Dukes	12.42	41.2	14.6	2.8
Comadator	21.90	54.0	17	3.0
J. C. Townsend	34.10	58.5	20.7	4.5
J. W. Houston	43.82	65.2	21.9	5.3
Onward	38.65	53	19.0	6.0
John T. Long	38	54.4	20.0	4.2
Liberty	29.06	57	19	4.0
William Ellison	15	39.5	15.0	4.0
Fawn (Sloop)	7	39	14.5	4.0

Much like the Chesapeake Bay Centerboard Schooner, they had one deck and a straight keel. Most had a square stern, and a billet bow (straight large timber attached to the keel) with a long bowsprit and possibly a long cutwater. The mainmast was offset slightly from the keel to accommodate the centerboard well, which was adjacent to the keel (page 233). The limited crew probably meant most Indian River schooners had no topsails, resulting in shorter masts, and possibly most only a single jib. The *Liberty*, however, had a topsail.

In 1880 it cost about $55 per ton (100 cubic feet of cargo space) to build one of these schooners.[399] This is roughly equal to $22 per foot. The typical 50-foot schooner could cost about $1,100 to build. This is consistent with the values of the ships in the Indian River Life-Saving Station incident reports.

A number of the schooners and Masters in the Life-Saving Station Reports were involved in multiple reported incidents—four each for Schooners *Addie* and *Emily Belle*, four for Master Lathbury, and five for Master Justice. At first, I concluded that these schooners or Masters must have been accident-prone. On reflection, however, considering the small number of incidents over almost twenty years and the schooner's design, it is apparent these small schooners were expertly handled by experienced Masters. They regularly confronted changing wind, visibility, tide, current and surf conditions, as well as changing shoals in and around the inlet. The wonder really is that there were so few recorded incidents involving the Indian River Life-Saving Station during this period and none with loss of life involving schooners sailing from or to the Indian River.

Most of the rescues involved carrying the ship's anchor seaward in surfboats and heaving a grounded schooner off a shoal at the next high tide. Some also required the removal of part of the cargo to help float the schooner off a sandbar, shore, or shoal. A very small number required pumping and leak repair.

Most Masters had local names such as Aydelotte, Lynch, Tunnel, Justice, Burton and Lathbury, even though the schooners may have been home-ported elsewhere.[400] There were others, I am sure, including my great-great-grandfather, Captain John Cornealius Hall, who was master of a schooner. A number of contemporary "Captains" are buried in the Bethel Methodist Cemetery in Ocean View, some of whom must have also sailed Indian River schooners.

As I write this, I often look out my window at Daisey Landing in Ocean View, and it is difficult to imagine ships of such size loading and unloading years ago here in Whites Creek. They must have been beautiful to behold. By 1915, only three or four of these ships were still in service. Regrettably, these schooners are gone now.

---

399   Paul C. Morris, *American Sailing Coasters of the North Atlantic* (Chardon, Ohio, Block and Osborne Publishing Co, 1973), p. 67.
400   The full names of some of these Masters may be found at the end of Chapter 21 in the list of local crewmen on the Schooner *Henry Brown*.

A Typical Centerboard Schooner on the Indian River[401]

Artist's Rendition

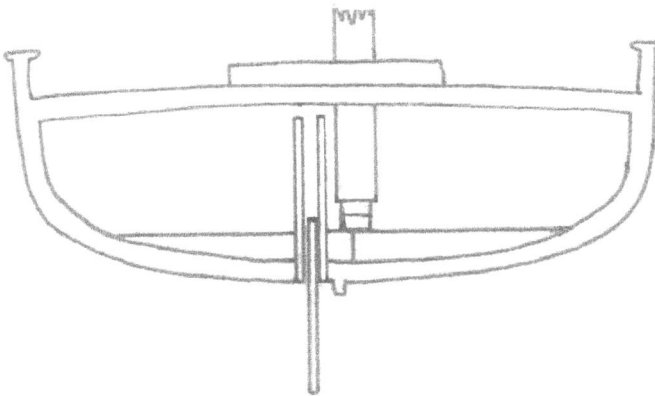

Centerboard Keel Cross Section

---

401   Drawn by Carol Lindeman, a friend and artist from Takoma Park, Maryland.

Indian River Schooner - The *Liberty*, c. 1890

Built 1857. Owners: Reuben West (Master), 1/4; Benjamin Gray, 1/4; Lemuel Derickson, 1/8; Kendal Rickards, 1/8; Nathaniel Tunnel, 1/8; Elijah Lynch, 1/8.

Courtesy of The Mariners' Museum
Newport News, Virginia

PART VI

THE TWENTIETH CENTURY

Chapter 24

Alonzo (1868-1955) and Elizabeth Breasure Hall Evans (1870-1909) and 2d wife Emma West Evans (Ma Em') (1873-1947)

Contemporaneous Happenings

1901 Marconi sends transatlantic wireless message

1905 Albert Einstein propounds the theory of relativity

1908 Henry Ford develops the Model T automobile

1914 Archduke Ferdinand assassinated, setting off World War I

1918 World War I ends. Influenza epidemic claims 500,000 lives in United States

1920 The Nineteenth Amendment granting suffrage to women is ratified

My maternal Great-Grandfather Alonzo was born January 24, 1868, the son of John A. and Harriet Jefferson Evans. Elizabeth was born January 31, 1870, the daughter of John Cornealius and Sarah Jane Breasure Hall. Elizabeth died April 1, 1909, at age 39, the mother of twelve children, eleven surviving. Alonzo died October 27, 1955.

My Great-Grandmother,
Elizabeth Breasure Hall Evans

As reported above, Alonzo's mother, Harriet, died February 22, 1875, when Alonzo, one of seven surviving children, was seven years old. His father married Angeline T. (Angie, Anza) Daisey only four months later on June 17, 1875. They left six children of their own, two or three of whom died in childhood. Alonzo had nine surviving brothers and half-brothers.

Elizabeth's mother, Sara Jane Breasure Hall, died June 17, 1883, just before her forty-first birthday, when Elizabeth was thirteen. Her father, John Cornelius Hall, remarried to Henrietta J. Johnson four years later in 1887, the same year Alonzo and Elizabeth were married. John C. and Henrietta were married twenty-three years when she died in 1910.

At age 12, Alonzo was listed in the 1880 Census as part of John A. and Angie's family. He was recorded as a laborer. Clearly he was working to help support the family and not in school. John A. was a house carpenter, so Alonzo may have worked for his father.

Alonzo grew up in a home near Williamsville with John A. and Harriet and then with John A. and Angie. Elizabeth grew up in today's Bethany Beach in the prosperous home of John C. and Sarah Jane Hall, who owned much of today's Bethany Beach.

Consistent with the times, Alonzo and Elizabeth married young. She was 17, and he was 19 when they married in 1887. The newlyweds moved into a small house on the east side of Kent Avenue in Bethany Beach (later known as the Captain Taylor House which was subsequently moved twice). Twelve children followed, one about every two years. Linwood, Uncle Bill, Aunts Gertie and Linda, and possibly Aunt Edith, were born in the Capt. Taylor house which is still on Kent Avenue in 2017. By 1900, the growing family moved up Kent Avenue into a new, much larger house where the other children were born. This house, next page, is still occupied, over a hundred years later. They owned their new house without a mortgage, according to the 1900 U. S. Census.

By the time of the 1910 U. S. Census, there were 15 neighboring households in Bethany Beach with fifty-six inhabitants. Family names included: Evans, Drexler, Knox (J. C. Hall lived then with Harry and Lindy Knox), Bunting, Addy, Henderson, Ayres, Lacey, Collins, Remagen, Cullen, Wilson, and Daisey.[402]

---

402   Thirteenth U. S. Census, 1910, Baltimore Hundred, Sussex County, Delaware.

Elizabeth, who bore twelve children (one was stillborn), was with child nine of her twenty-two years of marriage. The physical burden took its toll. Elizabeth died of blood poisoning in 1909, three weeks after the birth of her twelfth child. The blood poisoning was caused by an infection related to childbirth, now known as septicemia, which is routinely treated with antibiotics.[403] It was a tragedy.

According to Uncle France, she instilled in her children the need to "help everyone." Aunt Mary, Alonzo and Elizabeth's daughter, told me her mother was known as "Lib," adding, "her children adored her and everyone liked her." In her later years she was also known as "Lizzie." A deed of sale of land from Alonzo H. Evans and Lizzie B. Evans to John Addy of Pittsburgh surprisingly named Elizabeth as "Lizzie."

The Evans Family Homestead on Kent Avenue in Bethany Beach, circa 1908

Like many young men of the times in Baltimore Hundred, Alonzo wound up going to Philadelphia, where he went to work on the "tow boats." He went in about 1888, when he would have been about 20. The 1900 U. S. Census lists Alonzo's occupation as "Captain, tow boat."[404] Hence, he was known as Captain "Lonzo" the rest of his life. Captain Alonzo worked on towboats almost 20 years from about 1888 to November 1907, when he left Philadelphia and returned to Bethany Beach to be closer to his family. As we will see, towboats were in the blood of Alonzo's six sons.

---

403   Medical information provided by Dr. William Colliton Jr., a great neighbor in the Beach House in Bethany Beach.

404   Twelfth U. S. Census, 1900, Baltimore Hundred, Sussex County, Delaware.

We know from both the 1900 U. S. Census and transcripts of taped interviews with Uncle France and Aunt Mary included in Appendices A and B that Alonzo was Captain of a towboat in Philadelphia. On the other hand, Alonzo's second wife, Ma Em', as she was known, a lady with a great sense of humor, jokingly related to Marge Knox (Steve's wife) that "He was never Captain of anything bigger than a chamber pot." Life with Ma Em' must have been lively.

As many as one in fifteen Baltimore Hundred young men worked on the towboats as captain, fireman, cook, mate, or engineer. Alonzo's brother-in-law and neighbor, David Hall, is listed as a fireman in the 1900 Census. In contrast, far fewer from neighboring Dagsboro Hundred worked on the boats. There were more mills and stores in Dagsboro Hundred and fewer young men needed to leave home to get jobs. In the early days of Baltimore Hundred, sailboats were a major means of transportation, and sailing and boat-building were vital. In some ways, towboats were the continuation of a sea-faring tradition.

With most other men working as either a farmer (owner), farm laborer, laborer, fisherman or sawyer in a lumber mill, it is easy to understand why young men were drawn to the harbor. There were a few merchants, one teacher, and a preacher listed in the 1900 Census in Baltimore Hundred. Unless one's father was a farmer with significant land holdings and there were few brothers, prospects were poor; the harbor beckoned. Baltimore Hundred in 1900 was a pleasant place to live, but the word "poor" described many families. Many young men simply packed their bags and moved to the city for good. Most farms were small, as had been the case for a century. They provided family food which had to be carefully managed. While life was hard, most families did not see themselves as being poor. They were content with their lot.

Like their father before them, Alonzo and Lib's older children spent little time in school. Linwood at age twelve is listed in the 1900 Census as a "farm laborer." Linwood probably did not attend school past the third grade, according to family recollections. It was a difficult time for the children. Neither he nor his brother, Bill, nor his sisters, all between the ages of six and ten, were reported as attending school for any part of 1900. Contradistintively, all were reported as being able to read and write. Perhaps the reporting of school attendance was sloppy. Louis, the youngest son, attended school at least through the sixth grade. Delena, the youngest sister whose birth led to complications fatal to her mother, did attend school. Even though she was adopted by the Daiseys, Alonzo paid for her to attend business school in Philadelphia.

Tender in age, heartsick over the loss of a wonderful mother, and missing their father stationed at the Indian River Life-Saving Station and away from home six days a week, the children must have suffered greatly. The combination of the now-motherless children's age, Alonzo's regular absences from home, and the knowledge from Aunt Mary's comments that Lib was such a wonderful mother and person all compounded the tragedy for Alonzo and the children. The small children had to move in with other families to make it possible for Alonzo to continue working at the Life-Saving Station. The table on the next page lists Elizabeth and Alonzo's children, their age when she died, the age when the older children married, and the family with whom the younger children went to live.

Captain Alonzo's Family

Front Row: *Louis, Captain Alonzo, Mother Em*
Second Row: *Bill, Lon, Edith, Delena*
Third Row: *Neal, France, Gertie, Lindy*
Fourth Row: *Linwood, Mary*

    Readers are referred to the Letter to Caroline (Chapter 3) which elaborates on Lib and the small children.

    Alonzo must have had a continuing good relationship with his stepmother, Angie, because the one-and-a-half-year-old Louis went to live with his step-grandmother. Angie had been a widow for ten years and her four surviving children were now adults. According to Aunt Dot, "he had a nice home."

ELIZABETH AND ALONZO'S FAMILY

Children in 1909	Age When Elizabeth Died*	Age When Married	Lived With**
John Linwood	20	23	
Sarah Gertrude	18	19***	Kent Ave. with Alonzo
Linda Myrtle	16½	16½***	" " " "
William David	14½	25	
Olive	(stillborn****)		
Edith Elizabeth	11		Clay & Edith Evans, John and Elsie Mitchell, and David and Katie Hall
Alonzo Harrison II	9		Clay & Edith Evans, Ike and Mary Bennett***** and then John and Elsie Mitchell
De Witt France	8		Five different homes including Wilmer Vanzant and Uncle David Hall
Stephen Cornealius	5½		Uncle Steve and Ella Evans and then Alonzo and Emma
Mary Elizabeth	4		Jim and Elsie Megee and then Alonzo and Emma
Louis Baxter	1½		All over, including step-grandmother Angeline Evans who provided a nice home, according to Aunt Dot, and then Alonzo and Emma
Delena Louise	3 weeks		Her Sister Linda and then Eber and Mamie Daisey (adopted)

* Elizabeth died April 3, 1909.
** After Elizabeth died and Alonzo was alone and stationed at Indian River Life-Saving Station—as related in my interview of Aunt Mary and by a taped interview of Aunt Mary and Uncle France by Bill Ingram.
*** Apparently, Alonzo asked his daughters Linda ("Lindy") and Sarah Gertrude (Gertie) to take care of Delena Louise when Lib died. Lindy did for awhile, but both married significantly older men shortly thereafter. Eber and Mamie Daisey agreed to take Delena provided they could adopt her. Delena did not know she had brothers and sisters until she was old enough to go to school, where she learned of her birth parents from schoolmates.
**** Aunt Dorothy Evans provided the information on Olive. We do not know the date of her birth, but according to Aunt Dot it was around 1895, after Uncle Bill and before Aunt Edith was born. The Twelfth U. S. Census in 1900 lists Elizabeth at that time as being the mother of seven children with six living, confirming Aunt Dorothy's information.
***** The 1910 U. S. Census lists "Alonzo Evans" as being part of the household of Ike and Mary Bennett, the parents of Sidney Bennett, the Postmaster in Bethany Beach for many years.

All of the other children weren't so lucky. Life was difficult for some of the little children in new homes with new families. Uncle Lon and Aunt Edith were grossly mistreated by Alonzo's cousin, Clay Evans. Lon had to sleep on a bed of corn shucks in an outbuilding, and he ate leftovers, biscuits and milk. He lived with scars from a horsewhip administered by Clay Evans. Edith was afraid of the dark, so she was punished by being locked in a dark closet.

Neighbors advised Alonzo that his children were being mistreated, but Clay was always in the first row at church and Alonzo didn't believe it. Eventually, he realized the problem and found new homes for Lon and Edith. In the interim, Lon lived with Ike and Mary Bennett, the parents of Sid Bennett.

As mentioned earlier, Alonzo joined the U. S. Life-Saving Service[405] and he is first listed in the November 2, 1907, Log Book of the Indian River Life-Saving Station.[406] He was 37 years old and the father of ten children at home. The position at the Indian River Station had opened up because a number of surfmen were transferred to the newly opened Bethany Beach Life-Saving Station. Alonzo was selected through a competitive process from among a number of other candidates. The 1910 U. S. Census lists Alonzo as a "surfman" at the Indian River Life-Saving Station.

Station staff worked six days a week and had an annual leave of one or two weeks. Their main duties were patrolling the beach, standing watch in the observation cupola looking for ships and manning the lifesaving boats rowed through the surf to ships in distress. They made round-the-clock patrols along the beach—two and a half miles north to exchange a token with a surfman from Dewey Beach and a mile or so south to record a stop on the recorder they carried around their neck at the key-box at the Indian River Inlet.

November 19, 1909, as recorded in the log, was a typical day at the station. Alonzo was on "station & day watch" from 4:00 A.M. to sunrise, 4:00 P.M. to sunset and 7:00 P.M. to 8:00 P.M.[407] He was on beach patrol "to the N" (north) from sunset to 7:00 P.M. It was a clear, cold day with temperatures ranging from 31 to 42 degrees. Just imagine a two-to-four-hour shift on patrol, with a lonely trek along the surf, on stormy winter nights—half of it into the wind.

---

405   The U. S. Life-Saving Service was launched in 1878 by an Act of Congress as an agency of the Treasury Department.
406   Log Book of the Indian River Life-Saving Station, op. cit.
407   Ibid., November 19, 1909.

To perfect their rescue abilities, they spent many hours training with the surfboats and such beach apparatus as the Breeches buoy used for rescues in the surf. Signal training with lights and semaphore flags was regularly scheduled. Resuscitation training was conducted every Friday.

The routine of training, maintenance, patrols, and camaraderie at the Station was only occasionally interrupted by the drama of life-threatening rescues at sea— usually in adverse weather or surf conditions. Sailing vessels entering or leaving the Indian River Inlet encountered changing weather, wind, visibility and shoal conditions. The wonder is that there were not more vessels in distress.

The Station logs are a font of information on rugged everyday life along with derring-do. They could be the basis for a fascinating series of articles. Each vessel sighting is a recorded event. For a typical April week in 1909, an average of about seven schooners, four steamers, one sloop and two barges in tow made an appearance. Most vessels passed without incident. As noted in the previous chapter, assistance rendered to schooners in distress was reported for the period from 1880 to the turn of the century.[408] These are of special interest.

To repeat, it is thrilling to imagine ocean going schooners sailing through the Inlet to and from landings in such local places as Ocean View, Millville, Frankford, Blackwater Creek near today's Clarksville, and other landings on the Indian River and Bay. The fact is that schooners loaded and unloaded at Daisey Landing where I live in Ocean View. There they went, 20- to 30-ton schooners sailing up Whites Creek to load lumber and farm produce and unload manufactured goods, flour, coal oil, bricks and lime. It wasn't just a stirring sight–this shipping was an important part of the local economy of the time.

Getting back and forth from home to the Station was quite a trip for Alonzo. In the earlier years, Uncle Bill—teenager Bill—would hitch a team of horses to a wagon and go up the marsh to the Indian River Inlet where he would drop off or meet Alonzo, who rowed a small boat across the Inlet. Imagine the hazards of such a crossing. Later, Alonzo and Paul Lekites from the station traveled back and forth from home to the Station in Alonzo's boat, the *Mary Helen*, crossing the Indian River and Bay and Rehoboth Bay from Pennewell's Landing at the head of today's Assawoman Canal in Ocean View. Bad weather transits must have been harrowing.

Alonzo became part of the U. S. Coast Guard in 1915, when the Life-Saving Service was incorporated with the Revenue Cutter Service into the new U. S. Coast

408   Log Books of the Indian River Life-Saving Station, op. cit.

Guard by an Act of Congress on January 28 of that year. He had over twenty-five years of combined service from 1907 until, as reported in the Station Log, he retired from the Indian River Coast Guard Station on February 1, 1932, as a Boatswains Mate, First Class, and second-in-command at the Station. He had been on sick leave from the previous May 27 when, according to the log, he visited a doctor for unknown reasons. The final entry in the log was brief and to the point: "At mid-night A. H. Evans (103-369) BM1C (L) was retired from active Service 'Auth.' Department Letter 14 January 1932 – James S. Baker, Officer in Charge." And so ended a long career at the Indian River Station. Captain Alonzo received his monthly Coast Guard retirement check from 1932 until his death over 23 years later in 1955.

Alonzo married the widowed Emma West in 1911, about two years after Lib died. After having spent two years with relatives, Neal (Stephen Cornealius), Mary and Louis, the three youngest children, returned to live with Alonzo and Emma in a house in Ocean View, now the Seaman's Antique Prints, Inc. The children called her Ma Em' and it bears repeating that the children loved her. As Uncle Louis said, "I didn't know my mother, but I couldn't have had a better mother than Ma Em'." He was four years old when he first met his new mother. They later moved to a house behind today's Lord Baltimore School in Ocean View, which was of the same design as the Robinson House across from the Food Lion store in Millville (house moved to 32 Cedar Lane for construction of another supermarket). In about 1921, Alonzo and Ma Em' built their new house in Bethany Beach, on the north side of Route 26, right at the end of Kent Avenue, where they lived the rest of their lives.

A couple of funny stories I remember reflect on Alonzo's demanding duty, which required that he be away from home at the Coast Guard Station for two-week stretches. One was about Alonzo's wanting to be alone with Ma Em' for awhile during leave at home. But there were always children around—intruding on Alonzo's intentions. The word was that Alonzo would send them out to "pick pussley weeds," apparently an annual herb. The children were said to have picked many a pussley weed over the years.

The two-week stretches were shortened by the convenience of surfboat training. It is said Alonzo would have the crew row from the Indian River Station to Bethany Beach, where Alonzo made daytime visits to Ma Em'. One knows the surfmen knew what was going on. There must have been much conversation while the men waited on the beach and interesting comments when he returned. Training was important, but that was a long row just for Alonzo to visit Ma Em'! But he was in charge, right? That's how it goes.

Captain Alonzo and Ma Em'

It is appropriate here to relate a couple of Ma Em' stories. As noted earlier, she had a great sense of humor. She was a target of practical jokes by grandchildren and neighbors. Once, she visited the city and left some of her laundry on the line. She returned to find her bloomers flying on the flagpole in the front yard. She enjoyed the joke. Another story from Milton Cooper, a Bethany Beach institution, tells of the children tick-tacking her house. Now, tick-tacking is a two-step process. First, a nail with a kerosene-wetted string attached near the head is inserted under a shingle on the side of the house. Then, the string is pulled taut, and young fingers move along the string to create a vibration of the string. The result is a house-shaking racket inside. It sounds like the shingles are being torn off. Ma Em' would always come to the front door and feign anger to chase the youngsters away—their desired result. Ma Em' was always known for her good humor.

She and Alonzo lived a good life together for many years. Life with Alonzo had its travails, however. Alonzo's tightness with a dollar was legendary—he was downright stingy. It is said that Ma Em' was always on an impossible budget. She went to the store for a pound of onions with a dime in her pocket—Alonzo wanted to know what happened to the change. Apparently, she once visited relatives in New York with almost no money in her pocketbook. Her stepsons revered Ma Em' and the budget problem was rectified.

After Alonzo retired from the Coast Guard, he and Ma Em' lived on his retirement check and income from buying and selling property, including lots and larger parcels from his large land holdings along the north side of Route 26. Sussex County Deed Books include six purchases of land and 20 sales over the years. I am not aware of his having a regular job after he retired—he really retired.

According to Aunt Marie, the first family reunion was in 1939 on Alonzo's birthday (January 24), when a dinner was held at the Lord Baltimore School, served by the Ladies Aid Society from the Methodist Church. These reunions are now a family tradition, held almost every summer. Aunt Dorothy Evans, the dutiful keeper of family records, reported at the 2001 Reunion that Alonzo and Elizabeth had almost 400 direct descendants. At the 2016 Reunion, daughter Betty Jane reported 497 "blood relatives."

I remember my great-grandfather quite well. He had a gruff voice, and a number of his sons took after him. In his later years, he reveled in visits with his children. Their continued demonstration of close family ties was a source of pride.

Alonzo was always proud of his family. One memory from his funeral in 1955 is especially vivid. In his sermon, Pastor Wildey of Mariner's Bethel Methodist Church shared that Alonzo was always ready to talk about his children and their doings. How his pride showed. All of his sons and some of his sons-in-law worked "on the boats." His sons made it their careers, and Alonzo was proud of their career choices. It is profoundly satisfying to feel proud of your sons: I know the feeling.

At this point, it is appropriate to include a wonderful recent letter from my first cousin once-removed, Alonzo H. Evans III, reflecting his wonder at how the family stuck together and some of his memories of his Pop-Pop Alonzo:

246

Gordon:

You know, Gordon, these Evans children are a remarkable group of people. It's incredible they remained so close throughout the years. When you consider the differences in their ages (some twenty years between the oldest and the youngest), coupled with the loss of their mother early in life and being farmed out, they are a unique and extraordinary group of individuals. Now, I know blood is thicker than water, but these circumstances could have resulted in an estrangement between them. Not so, for these brothers and sisters! They became closer and more loyal to one another than many other families experiencing similar trials. One might argue that it was a genetic link that sustained these tight bonds. For whatever reason, they never let go and were admired by anyone who knew them.

Growing up, I looked forward to hearing the stories they told on one another. No matter who the center of their pranks was about, and there were many I didn't hear, they all enjoyed hearing it one more time! Both Mom-Mom and Pop-Pop reveled in hearing their stories each time they gathered in their presence. I particularly loved to watch Pop-Pop's face as he listened, because it caused his eyes to twinkle like a little boy thinking about a mischievous incident. His chuckle was always accompanied by his tummy rolling. Mom-Mom, on the other hand, would always assume the part of agitator just to get them to tell on one another. She was a master at it! Once they started with their storytelling, it went on for hours. Throughout these sessions Pop-Pop sat back in his chaise lounge puffing on his pipe, rarely uttering a word. In today's jargon, they were a hoot!

Gordon, I want you to know how much I appreciate your efforts to assemble such a vast amount of material and documenting it for others to enjoy. I hope the information enclosed will be of value in writing on the lighter side about the family members. I look forward to seeing your initial draft whenever it's finished. Good luck and persevere!

Lon

Correspondence from Lon also included stories of a number of "episodes" involving one or more of Alonzo's six sons. The "episodes" richly deserve to be told and are included in Appendix C, "Boys Will Be Boys." Recognize that these stories only scratch the surface, but they provide insight into the boys' determination to help each other, their good character, and their propensity to be "characters." We should all be grateful to Lon, a wonderful storyteller.

Chapter 25   Letter to Christopher—A Pop-Pop's Views

April 2001

Dear Christopher,

As I write this, you have not arrived yet, and you could turn out to be the last of my grandchildren to arrive. This being a real possibility, it is the right time to leave some words of wisdom to one to whom I plan on giving a full measure of my love—and to your cousins, too.

There are so many responsibilities, privileges and pleasures of being a Dad and a Pop-Pop. The responsibilities come with the job. The pleasures, big and little, are a privilege. They come daily and are reveled in, especially the antics of the little ones and the unabashed pride in their accomplishments. There are other privileges of the assignment, and I intend to take full advantage. One is the accompanying respect. One also likes to think it was earned in some measure. A corollary of privilege is the giving of advice. I take that responsibility to heart. So here goes.

My four sons will find this to be familiar. So the words are repeated and offered with the full level of confidence they work.

- *The harder I worked, the luckier I got—a good lesson.*

- *The family has been privileged in the combination of guidance, schooling, abilities, and acquired talents. This means there are responsibilities to contribute the combination of talents, and abilities, and tools gained from schooling and guidance received to the benefit of others not so fortunate. Charity of self and substance is a must that pays dividends in ways you can't ever anticipate.*

- *Family is more important than anything else. Spending as many vacations together as we do just proves it over and over again. Brothers and their families spending time together and enjoying it, at the beach, cherished holiday gatherings, Redskins games, or wherever and whatever—it just doesn't get any better than having a family.*

- *Time with grandparents and great-grandparents is a privilege not available to all—one to be exercised as often as possible. Self-serving, perhaps, but true.*

- *The physical self is important. Maintain your health, participate in physical activity* when you can. It is good for you. So is competition. It's good for you to learn to win and lose with grace. Winning isn't everything, but, like everything else worthwhile, it requires hard work; it is more fun, too.

- Participate in government. It is said we get the type of government we deserve.

- Follow leaders you respect and admire and be critical in your determination and judgment of each.

- Maintain your spiritual health. God loves you. His plan for you isn't always obvious. Seek it.

- All work and no play is no fun. Play often, hard and fair, but earn the right to play by being responsible and getting work done well and on time.

- Know the bounty of the talents of man. A beautiful painting, pleasing or exciting music, good museums, a great play, a symphony or a concert, a good book, a poem—they all contribute to the pleasure of life, development of potential and the serenity of the soul.

- There is a difference between right and wrong. Knowing the difference in each situation is sometimes difficult, but possible to determine with study. One can never go wrong in any situation by working to determine what is the right thing to do and then doing it.

- Some things just don't work the way they should, but there usually is a way to figure how to make them work. The one way which is almost always wrong is to force it. This applies in both mechanical and people situations. Don't force it!

- Reasonable punctuality is a fair expectation of everyone we deal with—family, friends or associates. They deserve our attention in terms of being fair to them.

- If you are as lucky as I, you will have a family, wife and children of your own. You have to earn their respect. Love them, support them in every way, and be there when needed. It is hard work sometimes, but the rewards know no end.

- Don't forget the Golden Rule.

These seemed to work for me and I commend them to you and your cousins.

Love, Pop-Pop

Chapter 26 John Linwood (1889-1966) and Sarah "Nellie" Daisey Evans (1889-1967)

Linwood and Nellie Daisey Evans - My Grandparents

My Pop-Pop (grandfather), John Linwood Evans Sr., known to everyone by his middle name, Linwood, was born on April 25, 1889, in the then family home,

250

the Taylor House on Kent Avenue in Bethany Beach, across the street from the house pictured on page 238. He was the first of Alonzo and Elizabeth Breasure Hall Evans' twelve children (one died in childbirth).

My Mom-Mom (grandmother), Sarah Eleanor "Nellie" Daisey, was born on August 17, 1889, on the Daisey family farm in today's Muddy Neck on the road from the "Head of the Sound" (present day Assawoman Bay) to Ocean View and near the present-day Jefferson Bridge over the Assawoman Canal. She was the second of Frank and Annie Green Daisey's twelve children.

Linwood's early life was that of a child with many chores and later as that of a farm laborer at age twelve, as reported in the 1900 U. S. Census. While still a boy, he worked at available jobs to help support Alonzo and Elizabeth's large and growing family. Like his father and so many young men in the area, Linwood left home at age seventeen and went to Philadelphia and then New York Harbor to get work. He was a fireman on a tug. He was 21 when his mother died whereupon he came home to run the family farm while his father was away. According to Uncle France, "That didn't work out." Linwood never was and never would be a farmer, and he returned to the tugboats. Alonzo hired a blind man and his wife to work the farm, but that "didn't work out either," so, as discussed in Chapter 24 on Alonzo, the young children went to live with other families.

I often wondered how he got his middle name, Linwood. The 1900 U. S. Census lists a Linwood Holt from Baltimore Hundred as a towboat captain. Perhaps he and Alonzo worked and traveled together and were good friends.

Linwood and Nellie grew up less than two miles apart, separated by the Assawoman Creek which later was dredged, dug and straightened to became the south end of the Assawoman Canal. As the oldest of eleven surviving children, Linwood had the responsibilities of an older brother and he probably only went to the old, one-room school in Bethany Beach through the third grade. Nellie, on the other hand, is reported in the 1900 U.S. Census, when she was eleven years old, as attending school for seven months during the preceding year. She is reported to have completed the eighth grade and possibly more in the Hall School on the road to Bayard. One-half of this two-room school building exists as a house.

Nellie was an outstanding student. One of her teachers, Mr. Thomas Hickman Sr., who taught in this old school, the new Lord Baltimore School, and others for over 50 years, said she was one of the best students he ever had. She wanted to be a teacher, and she taught for a couple of years at the same Hall School she attended. Actually, she was a teacher all her life, teaching her eight children the paths of integrity, love, responsibility, caring and worship in an exemplary fashion. In the words of her children, "There may have been others as fine as she, but there were none finer." Her children adored her.

Nellie, being bright and industrious, also went to New York City as a young woman and worked in a department store and then in a shirt factory. She was a hard worker and most capable. It wasn't long before she was supervisor of all the women in the factory. The 1910 U. S. Census reports Nellie as being a "Forelady, clothing house." She made $6.50 a week and with that she paid all expenses and always saved a little. Being frugal was necessary. As generous and loving as she was with her future family of eight children, her frugality served her well for the rest of her life.

As it happened, Linwood and Nellie were both boarders at Mrs. Free's Boarding House in downtown Brooklyn. So were a number of others from Baltimore Hundred, including Linwood's brother, Uncle Bill. Mrs. Free's establishment was sought out by folks from Baltimore Hundred; it must have seemed like a home away from home.

More happenstance: Linwood and Nellie were acquaintances back home in Delaware, but they did not know each other well, having gone to different elementary schools. Getting to know each other better at Mrs. Free's, they soon started dating. It obviously was a good match, lasting their lifetimes. They were married on November 6, 1912, in New York. They spent the evening after their wedding at the old Hippodrome Theater in Manhattan, known for vaudeville extravaganzas. Returning to their hotel they listened to returns of the election of Woodrow Wilson as President. According to Linwood, their first child, Daisey, was born nine months, nine days and nine hours later.

One after the other, Linwood's brothers connected with their future wives through church, family introductions and possibly blatant matchmaking. Four of Linwood's brothers, Bill, Lon, Neal and Louis, all met their future wives in a chain-reaction of sorts started by Nellie. Aunt Maria chronicled this story in a wonderful letter to my son, Chip, a little while before his marriage to her beloved and only granddaughter, Lauren. This book would be incomplete without it. It follows and is fascinating!

AUNT MARIA'S LETTER TO CHIP
SUNDAY AFTERNOON, OCTOBER 15, 1989

Chip had asked questions about the family and Aunt Maria followed up on their discussions with this letter. The letter reflects her love of family and faith in God. The notations in brackets are the only edits.

Dear Chip,

Well this is my special rambling paper. Feel honored because not everybody gets it. I am going to try to continue our conversation of last night. As you remember, your great-great-grandfather and great-great-grandmother had eleven children, six boys and five girls. The girls all married local boys and did not leave, with the boys it was different. There was Linwood – your grandmother's father, Bill, Lonzo (Alonzo H. Evans II), France, Neal and Louis who is the only one that survives.

Linwood married a local girl and after some time, had two little girls, Daisey [nine months later] and Hilda. Their father went to New York to work on a tug and then he moved his family up to the city. Your great-grandmother [Great Mom-Mom Nellie] went to a Baptist Church with her girls and there befriended their Sunday School teacher. Next was Bill. At that time, there was a train which came to Rehoboth, yes right down the main highway were railroad tracks and you could go on it to New York, on the weekend for 2 cents a mile. So Bill went to see Linwood and Nellie decided she would invite Mildred, the girls' Sunday School teacher, (things obviously progressed fast) and Bill got a job on the boat and they married. Then came Lonzo, and Mildred invited her best friend Sophie (Peterson, whom he married). Well, Lonzo bought 4 tickets to a New York stage show, Indian Love Call and invited Neal, and Sophie invited me. As of that time, she was our babysitter when my mother and father went out for the evening. Dot [Maria's sister Aunt Dot] and I certainly could take care of ourselves, but Mother felt better with someone else in the house. Then Neal and I dated and one day he said, "I have a brother, Louis, who is lonesome, and I wonder if he could come with us and go with Dorothy, who was only 13. So then we double-dated.

On August 19, 1925, Neal and I were married and when we came home from our honeymoon, Louis was all packed away in the guest room of our apartment, which was in the same house as that of our Mother and Father. On January 18, 1930, Dorothy and Louis were married. At least on one Saturday we would congregate in one of the homes. Brothers on one side of the room running tugboats up and down New York Harbor. We women could never separate them, so we called ourselves the Outlaws instead of In-Laws. So you see, it all started with two little girls going to Sunday School. That is why Louis is sometimes very quiet. He misses them [his brothers] very much.

More and more you will see that with your Dad. Like when he wants the four of you to play golf with him, or he wants to be alone with one. Enjoy it, honey, as time slips away so quickly. Also never be too busy to forget to be in the Lord's house.

I wrote to Lauren the other week and told her now that the summer was over, I wanted her to find time to go to His house.

If you have children, some time in the future, walk down the aisle; I want our Heavenly Father to look down from His Throne and nod His Head in approval, not wonder who you are. I know He is with me always, that is why I do not feel alone, living by myself. [Uncle Neal died in an automobile accident over thirty years earlier.] I remember when I first moved into this house. I came home after midnight from playing bridge and the key froze in the lock and all I could do was shut the door, and at that time, it was the only house on 42 acres of land, but I prayed and asked Him to watch the door and I would do the sleeping and take care of the lock in the morning. You know what, Chip, He did.

Well, darling, I have to get ready for church. Hope you can understand this note.

Take care and may our Heavenly Father Bless you and always keep you in His loving care.

Love you,
Lauren's Grandma

I lift up the fallen,
I strengthen the weak,
I help the distressed,
I show mercy, bestow kindness and offer a friendly hand.
I am the Church.

****

Linwood and Nellie lived in a rented flat in Jersey City. Nellie always wanted a family, but as she said, "I never had time to look forward to having a child; they all came too soon." Their first child was Daisy Emma, whose first name was her mother's maiden name and her middle name was after Alonzo's second wife, Emma West, a clear indication of the esteem in which she was held by her stepchildren.

Their second daughter, Hilda Elizabeth, my mother, was born December 19, 1914. Mom's middle name was after her grandmother, Linwood's mother, Elizabeth, who died in 1909.

Linwood continued to work on tugboats in the engine room, first as a fireman (shovel coal, keep things clean and learn the ropes) and as an oiler. Diligently, and with the help of Nellie on the required math, he pursued and obtained his engineer's license, no small achievement.

Nellie and the two small children spent much of the time in the apartment, because hours on the tugs were long and Linwood was gone on two-week or longer shifts on the tug. It must have been a lonesome time. Memories of Delaware and the families at home were an ever-present, continuing attraction. They must have been the focus of many conversations.

The family moved to Brooklyn in 1915, shortly after Hilda was born. Little did they know this would begin a shuttle between Brooklyn and Bethany Beach that went on the rest of their lives. Linwood always worked in the harbor when they lived in Brooklyn. The family continued to grow with Linwood Jr., born in 1918, and Irene Myrtle in 1921. She was named after Nellie's cousin, Myrtle Daisey Barclay, and possibly Aunt Lindy (Linda), Linwood's sister, whose middle name was Myrtle.

In 1920, Nellie became very ill and was hospitalized in Brooklyn with appendicitis, which developed into peritonitis. An infected ovary was removed. Before the age of antibiotics, survival was a question in such cases, and Linwood was told her chances were less than one in a hundred. God watched over her. The standard of care must have been excellent. She survived. The removal of the ovary contributed to a funny family story discussed below.

During her hospital stay, the two older girls went to Delaware. The six-year-old Daisy stayed with Alonzo and Ma Em', who by 1919 lived in a house behind the Lord Baltimore School in Ocean View. Mom stayed with Frank and Annie in Bayard. Aunt Daisy tells of a trip during this visit in a ten-person ferry from Pennewell's Landing on Whites Creek in Ocean View to the Rehoboth Bay shore in back of the Indian River Life-Saving Station for a long weekend where Alonzo was stationed. She and Ma Em' had to trudge across the sand to the oceanfront Station to visit Alonzo—a long walk. The Ocean Highway didn't come until 1934.

The family made other excursions to Delaware for vacation visits a couple of those summers when they first lived in Brooklyn. What a trip! The family of at least five traveled by train from New York to Wilmington where they transferred to the line which went down the seaboard side of the peninsula through Dover, Harrington, Georgetown, Millsboro, Dagsboro and Frankford. Nellie's father, Frank Daisey, met the train in Frankford with his old, horse-drawn buckboard. Pop-Pop Frank and the visitors with baggage climbed on and headed on the ten-mile wagon ride to the family farm in Bayard. How Frank and Annie loved to have the family visit. The family went from urban Brooklyn to the farm in very rural Bayard to be with beloved grandparents, where treats for the visitors included picnics and swimming in Assawoman Bay at the nearby Mulberry Landing at today's Assawoman Wildlife Refuge. There were also good visits with Alonzo and Ma Em', then in Ocean View. Memories to last a lifetime.

Vacation trips usually coincided with the annual August Homecoming festival in Ocean View. So many families and young folks had moved to Philadelphia, New York and other places to find work that there was an annual reunion picnic at the park in Ocean View to celebrate the "homecoming" of those who had moved away and who made great efforts to come home to attend. I remember going once in 1941, I believe, and it was memorable. A picnic supper of fried chicken and everything that goes with it, patriotic speeches, welcoming speeches, and much meeting and greeting. My most vivid memories are of long speeches and a woman's singing, which tortured the ears of a five-year-old. Homecoming was held for years before ending in the '40s. A few years ago an attempt was made to revive the tradition, but too much had changed, and its original purpose had lost some relevance. Too bad!

Delaware and home were ever-present attractions, and Linwood and Nellie and the four small children, including the infant, Irene, moved back to Bethany Beach in 1921. They bought a small farm and home originally built and lived in by Linwood's maternal grandfather, John Cornelius Hall. The house stood where the Saint Ann education building now stands on Route 26. There were two other identical homes built by John Cornealius Hall on the other side of what was then a dirt road, one across from Grotto Pizza and one near the eastern end of Bethany West, where he lived with his son and daughter-in-law, David and Katie Hall. His extensive land holdings included both sides of today's Route 26, from the beach to a point west of Bethany West. The beach was known around the end of the nineteenth century as Hall's Beach.

Mom joined Mary Evans' second-grade class in the old, large, wooden Lord Baltimore School, which was built in the '20s when the small schools were consolidated. It was where today's gymnasium building is. Having myself moved from Long Island to Delaware after the fifth grade, I can understand the change must have been great for a seven-year-old.

Linwood became a farmer, but as Mom says, "he wasn't a farmer." They planted strawberries and cantaloupe melons to sell and a kitchen garden and had some chickens for eggs and the stew pot, a cow, pigs and hogs, one for slaughter each year, and little income. The cleared land behind the house was generally wet and of little use before it was ditched and drained. Nellie's father regularly harvested the hay which grew on the land that otherwise had little use. It was a difficult time and Linwood soon gave up farming, and for seven years he was an engineer on the trawler fleet operating out of Lewes. The actual boat Linwood worked on, the *McKeever Brothers*, which was built in Connecticut in 1911, was until recently a restaurant on Route 13 in Seaford. Linwood was home more now. The boat made port in Lewes and he was up and down the coast following the schools of bunker (menhaden), but he was still away much of the time during the warm-weather fishing season. Family finances continued to be tight.

In about 1926, Daisy, who was twelve, and Linnie, who was about seven, set out to make some money selling melons at the beach. With Nellie's permission, they filled the old Chevrolet with melons up to the windows and Daisy, who had learned to drive, and Linnie headed to the beach. Profiting a nickel on each, they had sold about half of their supply to vacationers when they stopped at the home of State Sen. Drexler of Pennsylvania–a house still standing on Atlantic Avenue after being moved at least twice because of beach erosion. Mr. Drexler asked how many they had left, and he was escorted out to the drive to see for himself—dozens. Being the gentlemen he was, he bought them all! Well this was great, and the successful marketeers returned to Nellie to ask for the opportunity to double their money. In her kindly way, she let them know that Sen. Drexler was being nice to the children and wouldn't want more. He was later quoted as saying if those children worked that hard to make some money, he couldn't do anything but help.

Mom and Daisey also worked picking strawberries for three cents a quart basket to earn money for their Fourth of July dresses. Everyone contributed to meet family needs, and the children understood the rewards of hard work.

After the first two years, Mom and Aunt Daisy transferred from Lord Baltimore School to the old one-room school on Kent Avenue in Bethany Beach, just across and down the street from the new South Coastal Library where her mother's old teacher, Mr. Hickman, still taught. Mom was there for the second and third grades before transferring back to Lord Baltimore School, which she attended through the eighth grade.

Imagine attending a one-room school just a few hundred yards from the ocean. Recess must have been fun in the spring and fall. Mom tells the story of

257

boys' locking Mr. Hickman in the school during one such recess when everyone went down to the beach. When the children returned, Mr. Hickman required all of them to go outside and get their own switch. If the switches weren't sturdy enough they had to get another. Each child was switched on the legs. It seems like a fair discipline for such mischief. The students liked and respected Mr. Hickman, so I suspect the punishment fit the crime. Older boys in an earlier class had locked Mr. Hickman in the privy and set a fire under it. He wasn't harmed, beyond an insult to his composure, and I don't know the punishment, but it probably exceeded a good switching. Uncles Neal and Louis Evans were involved in that caper.

The family continued to grow: Lorne was born in the family home in Bethany Beach in 1922, Royal in 1926 and Ralph in 1927. Lorne was named after Lorne Barklay, Myrtle's husband, who was a senior executive in the Boy Scouts of America for a number of years. Royal was named after Nellie's brother. The family purchased an almost new seven-passenger Huppmobile in about 1921 and needed every seat. In a couple of years, they bought a 1922 Ford and then a 1924 Chevrolet.

Because Nellie had an ovary removed in 1920, the doctors had told Linwood and Nellie that subsequent children would all be the same sex—the medical understanding then being that one ovary supplied male eggs and the other provided female eggs. Linwood Jr. was a boy, so Irene was expected to be a boy also. Surprise! She was a girl–thereafter described imaginatively as developing "from a leftover egg." Lorne, Royal and Ralph were all boys, confirming the theory–so they thought. When Nellie again became pregnant in 1933, a boy was expected and either Ronald or Donald was to be his name. In fact, Linwood called from the hospital to tell the other children they had another brother. Not so. It was a girl, who was named Eleanor! Medical and biological science sure have progressed significantly since then.

Linwood continued working on the trawler, a cramped, uncomfortable, damp, smelly place, but crews developed a camaraderie, and the engineer was near the top of the ship's hierarchy. And the pay was decent for the times. The bunker schools were abundant, the boats were busy, and Lewes became at one time the top-tonnage fishing port in the United States. Though Linwood was gone most of the summer, he always brought big boxes of cookies with him on trips home. Unfortunately, the bunker boats tied up in the winter, and winter jobs in Baltimore Hundred were almost nonexistent. Linwood had little to do beyond tending the garden and the cow, horse, hogs, chickens, and the mule.

Progress and change came to Bethany Beach in the form of a two-lane, concrete road to the beach from Ocean View, which passed in front of the house.

258

Lorne remembers the roadgrading, which was accomplished by men with a mule pulling a two-handled scoop. The Christian Church Conference Grounds were developed and the roots of a real beach resort grew with a newly constructed boardwalk and numerous new homes. The Evans, Hall and Bunting family teenagers made up most of the crowd of a dozen or so on the beach on a nice summer day. Walter and William Evans would have been startled to see what had developed since Walter arrived in what is today's South Bethany in 1702 and William purchased most of what is today's Bethany Beach in 1719.

Lorne and Irene were great playmates, and when Irene started school, he missed her very much when she left each morning on the old school bus. It had steps and an entrance in the back. One morning, Lorne, waiting until Irene was aboard and the door was closed, attempted to climb the steps and hitch a ride to school. Slipping when the bus started and afraid to let go, he was dragged on his knees almost two hundred feet along the rough-surfaced new road. Thanks to neighbor Eber Daisey's calls, the driver stopped. Lorne's knees were severely injured, but not permanently.

In 1928, a boom year before the Great Depression, Linwood again sought a job in the harbor in New York. After a wait, a call came and Nellie hurried out to the field where he was working with the mule and announced, "You have the job in New York!" Leaving the mule in the field for the children to put away, Linwood packed up and caught the first train from Frankford to a tugboat in New York harbor. The family followed soon thereafter—back to Brooklyn, where they lived in a second story flat at Sixth Avenue and 57th street.

The year 1929 saw the stock market crash and the beginning of the Depression. Linwood was saddled with a number of years of uncertain work schedules and extended periods out of work. The Depression impacted the family greatly. It was catch-as-catch-can—a couple of days here and a few days there. It was a difficult time. Dependable work didn't return until just before World War II. The small family savings account was lost when the Lincoln Savings Bank went under like so many banks during the depression. To help make ends meet, Linwood sold part of his small farm back to his father for one dollar and other considerations–probably forgiveness of loans necessary to support his large family. When he was back on his feet, Linwood wanted to buy it back, but Alonzo would not sell it.

Among the tugboats Linwood worked on were the Bouker N° 6 and the Bouker N° 7. Fellow crew on these tugs included Uncles Bill and Lon and his nephew, Steve Knox, and neighbor, Paul Hitchens. Linwood was Chief Engineer and his brothers were assistants. Uncle Bill also served later as a Chief Engineer.

Chief Engineer Bill Evans on the Bouker N° 7

Mom, who had completed the eighth grade at Lord Baltimore School before the move, was now a teenager and freshman at the large, all-girls Bay Ridge High School—another culture shock. Family finances were obviously very tight and the older children worked to help. Mom worked behind the candy counter in the Abraham and Strauss five-and-ten-cent store. Brooklyn, however, was a fascinating and colorful place for all the children with its ethnic neighborhoods, many immigrants, trolley cars and subways, movies, Coney Island, and stickball and roller-skating in the streets. There were good schools and lots of neighborhood friends.

Linwood worked hard to provide for his family. Uncle Lorne tells of seeing his father sitting in his rocker in the basement simply worrying about prospects and how best to care for his family. He remembers seeing his father resole the boys' shoes with tread from worn-out tires. Having lived in times of plenty, it is hard for more recent generations of our family to imagine his occasional despair over meeting his family's minimum needs. Aunt Axie Hudson in Williamsville, Delaware, had crates of eggs trucked to Brooklyn, which the children sold in the neighborhood to regular customers, helping the family budget. The term "egg money" had real meaning in the always busy Evans household.

Nellie contributed her skill as a seamstress, honed to perfection in the shirt factory. She said making a dress and petticoat for each of the four girls was a day's work for her. She cut and sewed all day and did the trim in the evening. She would make a beautiful child's coat from a used man's coat. One of Mom's cousins, Louise Wharton, said that she could magically sew a coat out of a small scrap—an exaggeration which was a credit to Nellie. With all the little ones she must have been sewing all the time.

The family always had a focus, notwithstanding the tight budget, simple "countrycooking" meals for the large family (featuring a lot of beans—especially navy beans which Linwood loved—and sowbelly) and the succession of homemade and hand-me-down clothes. They attended church together. I remember going regularly to Lefferts Park Baptist Church in Bay Ridge with Eleanor, Royal and Ralph. Nellie would have it no other way.

Just as Alonzo, his father, had been very strict with his children, so also was Linwood, who followed his father's example. Too strict! He was gone on the boats a lot, and Uncle Lorne as a little guy was once asked how he liked having his father home. His reply was a classic. "He's too drottin' bossy." Meaning he was a disciplinarian and, often, according to Aunt Daisy, "blew a gasket." In today's terms, "tough love." But none of the children ever long doubted his deep love for them, and he was respected and loved by each. Years later, Linwood relented and expressed regret for being too stern. Nellie, on the other hand, never raised her voice—except for the time Linwood unintentionally plowed up her row of beautiful dahlias at their home in Bethany Beach.

Life in Brooklyn included a series of moves in essentially the same Bay Ridge neighborhood. In 1928 they moved to 1069 73rd Street, in 1930 to 1029 73rd Street and in 1932 to 1029 70th Street where they rented, and then came to own, and where the family resided until 1945. Uncle Bill and Aunt Mildred lived up the street at 1053 70th Street, and Mom and Dad and I lived in an upstairs apartment at 1043 70th Street.

Eleanor, the unexpected surprise, was born in 1934. Her arrival delayed my parents' wedding; Mom's help was needed with the five and soon to be six children at home. During the war years, I remember going downstairs to the Gadeberg residence, where Mr. Gadeberg listened to the evening news of the war. I remember also the earlier radio announcement about Pearl Harbor, but a child's understanding was limited. The gravity hit home when we learned that Buddy Hickey, who lived upstairs from Mom-Mom and Pop-Pop, was lost in a B-17 over Europe.

Linwood and Nellie's home was always full of visitors. Brothers of each from Delaware who worked in the harbor were regular overnight visitors or short-term tenants. Steve Knox, a nephew, was always in and out. Others from Delaware, including Paul Hitchens, visited regularly. In 1918, during the influenza epidemic, Linwood's brothers, Lon, France and Bill, were taken ill, Lon very seriously—his life endangered. Nellie cared for them all. The story is told that Lon was so very ill that Nellie determined he needed an emetic to rid him of stomach distress. The almost delirious Lon was offered "a cool drink" which he gulped down. The result was predictable and violent, but it worked. He improved rapidly thereafter. Nellie just knew! It is no wonder Nellie, who was so willing to share and help, was so loved by all.

Holiday times, including Nellie's Thanksgiving and Christmas dinners were a wonderful time and fully attended. Thanksgiving dinner was in the basement because of the huge crowd. I remember cranking the two ice cream freezers in the backyard, one vanilla and one pineapple. Everyone took turns, and it was great fun. See the Letter to Caroline (Chapter 3) for more on family gatherings.

Notwithstanding the economic conditions in New York, the family would not forgo regular visits to Delaware. While they rented out all but two rooms and the attic of the Bethany Beach home, Nellie and the children spent some time each summer at the beach in the unrented two rooms and the attic. It was crowded but fun. The 1924 Chevrolet, which had replaced the Model T, was packed with bags tied on everywhere. The children were more or less in each other's laps for the over-12-hour trip through all the cities and towns in creation.

One summer, they brought a turkey back to fatten for Thanksgiving. It soon became a cherished pet who was walked around the neighborhood on a leash. Over strong protest, the executioner prevailed. But the dinner's main course was shunned by all; the children simply could not eat their pet.

Every story about these summers brings back fond remembrances of a close family, time at the beach, many visitors and good fun. Summers at the beach were usually only for the well-to-do, but Linwood and Nellie's family, through good and

Linwood and Nellie's Home in Brooklyn at 1029 70th Street[409] (picture 2010)

bad economic years, spent part of their summers in Bethany Beach. A multitude of relatives visited regularly, and lifelong friendships developed with other "locals."

They were blessed with the important things in life. Few families, wealthy or not, were as fortunate.

Linwood worked on tugboats in New York for years. I found in my grandfather's Bible a copy of a McAllister Lighterage Line, Inc., Manning Table Data Sheet dated April 29, 1943; he was Chief Engineer "In charge of the engine room." He had one assistant engineer. The report of previous employment for the past five years noted that he had worked for Morris & Cummings Dredging Co. as Assistant Engineer from 1938 to 1939 (and probably before) and from 1939 to 1943 for McAllister. His rate of pay was $220 per month.

---

409   Taken long after the family had moved to Delaware.

One early incident on a tugboat was related by Uncle France in a 1973 taped interview with his son-in-law, Bill Ingram. Linwood's tug was out on a cold winter night with a tow. Ice floes and whitecaps covered the turbulent harbor. A deck hand fell overboard. Without hesitation, Linwood dived into the ice-filled water and reached the sailor. Both were safely hauled aboard, cold and wet but alive. A life was saved by a hero. Mom remembered this when I related it to her.

Linwood and Nellie remained in Brooklyn until the end of World War II in 1945 when they again moved to the family home in Bethany Beach with children Royal and Eleanor. Ralph stayed in Brooklyn with Uncle Bill and Aunt Mildred to finish high school. Linwood worked in the harbor as a chief engineer during these years on 70th Street. Three of their sons had gone off to war, and the three blue stars on the flag in the parlor window flew proudly. Linnie (Linwood Jr.) served in New Guinea, where there was considerable action. Lorne served in training squadrons and airplane maintenance units all over the country, and Royal was discharged after a training accident which severely injured his arm. Ralph served in the Navy after World War II.

Life in Bethany Beach was quiet and productive after the war. The seeds didn't fall far. Seven of the eight children eventually lived nearby, five having moved their families back to Delaware from New York.

Children and grandchildren were always stopping in, a testament to the closeness of their family. I have so many pleasant memories of my Mom-Mom and Pop-Pop during family get-togethers. Some are funny.

Pop-Pop had false teeth, and his grandchildren delighted in seeing him pop his teeth in and out. Nellie, on the other hand, would never do such a thing.

Linwood would engage in liars' contests with his brothers and coworkers. Linwood won a contest with his tale of a man who was so strong he could grab himself by the chest and hold himself up at arm's length.

It is Linwood, full of mischief himself, who would recall Lon's story about how he once used his new tractor to pile snow high around sister Delina's front and back doors trapping her and Al in their house until Linwood relented and removed the snow.

Then there is the time Mom-Mom had to get medicine for Linwood. Pop-Pop had a heart condition and his doctor recommended a "snort" of whiskey every day. Nellie had to go to Holt's Dispensary in Clarksville. She entered with trepidation and the fear that one of the ladies from church would see her. She persevered, however, and brought home the "medicine." Mom-Mom was a good sport. I remember her really belting a pitched softball at a family fish fry at Sandy Landing.

Linwood and Nellie died in 1966 and 1967, respectively. They rest today in the Bethel Cemetery in Ocean View with six of their children, four grandchildren, and three sons-in-law, as well as their parents and at least two grandparents (as of 2017). They are visited often; they gave so much to all of us. They were loved by their family and friends.

Linwood's and Nellie's Family at Ralph and Sylvia's Wedding (March 1950)
Front Row: *Nellie (Mom-Mom), Ralph, Sylvia, Linwood (Pop-Pop)*
Middle Row: *Hilda Wood (Mom), Marilyn Evans, Irene Hocker, Daisey Furman,*
                Eleanor (Breasure), Bessie Evans, Grace Evans
Back Row: *Wilbert Hocker, Chester Furman, Dick Wood (Dad), Lorne Evans,*
                Linnie Evans, Royal Evans

Chapter 27

Letter to Chip (Richard Kenneth Wood III) – Your Great-Grandfather, Richard Kenneth Wood

July 1998

Dear Chip,

Your's is a wonderful name, Richard Kenneth Wood III! I thought enough of my father to name my first son after him. According to Mom, my Dad "almost popped his shirt buttons" when I told him we had named your Dad after him. I am not sure if I was more proud to give it to your Dad, or proud that he and your mother gave it to you. I know Dad is prouder still that it is your name now.

Richard has been a prominent name in the family for many generations. My grandfather, Leslie Joseph Wood, who came from Prince Edward Island, (P.E.I.) Canada, had a favorite cousin, Richard Wood, and a brother, Richard Thomas Wood. Further, Leslie's father, Richard Wood of Travelers Rest, P.E.I., Canada, was the son, grandson and, I believe, great-grandson of Richard Woods, including the Richard Wood who emigrated to P.E.I. from Colchester, England, in the eighteenth century. It is an honored and enduring name.

I like my name, Gordon, and we gave it to your Uncle Chip, but Mom asked me recently if I ever wished my name were Richard. I never really thought about it a lot, but it would have been an honor. It is also a name with a nice sound; it's a handsome name. Your Great Pop-Pop got a speeding ticket once, and when the cop saw his license, he noted, "That's too nice a name to give you a ticket." But, he did anyhow!

What was my Dad, Richard Kenneth Wood 1, like, and what made him that way? I hope these materials will help you know your Great Pop-Pop, a great guy.

Love,

Your Pop-Pop

Richard Kenneth Wood I
(January 19, 1910 - January 3, 1986)

Your Great Pop-Pop was a good guy, from the beginning to the end. Even when he was sadly stricken with a stroke, his basic friendliness and sense of humor were apparent. His love for Mom and the rest of us was clear and strong. Probably, his love for Mom and her devoted love to him defined him and her best. His children, grandchildren, family and friends were important to him. It showed, in a strong but not effusive way—a special way. Chip, you would have been special to him—and he would have been special to you.

Your Great-Grandfather, My Dad
Richard Kenneth Wood I, About 18 Years Old

My dad was generally quiet and thoughtful, a good guy. At his funeral, one of his closest friends said it best in a quiet conversation, "He was one of the good ones." He was! Dad was a caring guy, sensitive, and emotional too, regarding things that mattered. But he didn't always outwardly show his feelings. I always knew Dad loved me—us. It showed in so many ways. I always knew Dad was proud of his children; it showed, but he didn't really come out and say it. It was a great day when Mom commented—explicitly—how proud of us he was. I never forgot it; it meant a lot. So much so, I suppose, that I deliberately never hesitated to tell your father and his brothers that I loved them and was proud of them. [My sons knew that the thing I liked best in the world was for them to give me even more good reasons to be even more proud of them.] It's important.

Dad was a good baseball player and a fast runner. I remember a town softball game in Long Island when he beat out an infield hit and a neighbor said, "Man look at that guy run." That was my Dad, and was I proud! At 38, he was the first baseman on the Bethany Beach Beachcombers in the Sussex/Worcester Softball League.

I remember going to Boston with my dad and your dad when he was about four. Dad and Gram-Pop embraced; I was impressed. After that, Dad's and my greetings always included an embrace, and I never hesitate now to embrace your Dad and his brothers. Real men do that; they show emotion.

His is a fascinating story, one he never really talked about. Unlike yours, Chip, and mine, his was not a particularly happy childhood, but he never said so. He told many stories about things he did as a "kid," and they were all happy stories. For his own reasons, he never talked about the other side of his childhood or indicated that he felt deprived, and I never inquired—that is until shortly before he died, when we talked for hours. He was very ill, perhaps not always aware of his surroundings—I felt I might be intruding. He didn't seem to mind, so I asked many questions and he answered each. The conversation jumped around, but what a fascinating series of recollections. I wish I had inquired earlier.

One story he told was about the time his father, Leslie, was gone and he, a thirteen-year-old, "practiced" driving the car up and down the lane to the house. As you might expect, he proceeded to wipe out a hundred feet of pasture fence. As I remember his telling it, his only punishment was to repair the fence. He always seemed to be proud of that escapade. Maybe that's why he never asked what really happened to the transmission in the '37 Ford pickup I drove.

He loved horses and never tired of talking about old John W., his father's horse, a truly great horse, a workhorse and a racehorse. I remember seeing John W. on a visit to Gram-Pop in Lexington in 1944. He lived to the ripe old age of 28—old for a horse. John W. was a Morgan, or mostly so, as beautiful a horse as one would ever see—white blaze on his face and four white feet against his chestnut coat.

John W. hauled teamster wagons around the Boston Market, he hauled Dad around on the morning milk wagon route he memorized, and he ran in harness races on weekends at the fairgrounds. Dad said John W. always stopped without a prompt at each milk customer's house. I also remember Dad saying he had a mile time on a half-mile track of just over 2:13. I don't know if this was an exaggeration. In any event, John W. was a great horse and a source of pride. He won the Boston Work Horse Relief Association's First Prize on May 30, 1919. Dad was only nine. I have the beautiful "First Prize" medal. Another year's edition of the same medal was on display at the Smithsonian Institution in

Washington, DC. Ask me to show you John W.'s medal. I always enjoyed the stories about John W., and Dad enjoyed telling them—Gram-Pop too.

John W. Hitched to L. J. Wood's Wagon
Boston Work Horse Relief Association, First Prize, May 30, 1919

John W. was probably a reason why Dad had such a love for harness horses. He loved to go to a friend's farms to work out horses in the early morning. He also enjoyed handicapping and making wagers at the harness track.

Pop-Pop was born in 1910 in Cambridge, Massachusetts, to my Gram-Pop, Leslie Joseph Wood, the son of Richard and Barbara Waite Wood, and my Grammy, Sarah "Sadie" Ramsey Johnston Wood. She was a widow when she married Leslie.

I really do not know much about many other details of his sometimes difficult childhood. Gram-Pop and Grammy separated and divorced. Dad and his brother Roy, who was two years older than Dad, grew up with Gram-Pop. Aunt Mabel never got over a level of lifelong bitterness toward Gram-Pop. I suppose she had her reasons, although Aunt Hazel always said Gram-Pop was good to her. I never really inquired.

Dad adored his two older brothers, Linton and Arnold, and his sisters, Mabel and Hazel, who lived with Grammy or were on their own. He talked often about how they all looked out for him and how Arnold took him fishing on weekends. His love and respect for them endured. I suppose he owed his brothers for his lifelong love of fishing. How I enjoyed fishing with him!

Apparently Dad did not like school. Gram-Pop used to drop him off at school, and he would often make it back home before his father. One cold morning, being especially determined, Gram-Pop escorted the young truant to class, ceremoniously hung his overcoat on a peg on the wall, and announced he planned to stay at school all day to keep an eye on him. The ploy worked. The hanging coat was a sentinel, reminding the boy of his Pop's presence. Gram-Pop meanwhile drove home in his shirt sleeves on a cold morning. Being a parent can be tough duty. It's tough to outwit a determined kid.

Dad loved dogs but wasn't real big on cats. I remember his coming into the kitchen with a puppy hidden behind his back who betrayed his presence with a whine. I think he was more pleased than the ten-year-old recipient, me. He thought a boy needed a dog. Perhaps, he didn't have one as a boy; I never heard him say. As I said before, he was like that.

Why wasn't he big on cats? Perhaps it was because of the old tomcat on the farm in Lexington. He told the story often of how the cat went across the pasture every morning to meet the neighbor's tomcat. Every morning the same story—a beaten-up tomcat returning to lick his wounds. Dumb cat! Perseverance is admirable. On the other hand, a definition of stupidity is to do the same thing over and over, expecting a different result. This cat never learned, and maybe that's why Dad never favored cats. But, that didn't stop my sisters, your Aunts Lois and Susan, from having a kitten.

Dad's brother, Roy Newton Wood, Les and Sadie's first son, was two years older than Dad. They were quite different people. Dad left home; Roy didn't. Dad, tired of the push and pull over custody by his parents who both loved him, got himself out of a difficult situation by running away. Roy didn't. Dad had many adventures or travails; Roy didn't have the adventures because he stayed home, alone with his dad. Dad liked a beer but didn't drink much; Roy did for a number of years. Dad was bighearted and generous; and Roy was, too!

I liked Uncle Roy; he was full of fun. I wish we had lived closer. He was the kind of guy who would have been a great fishing buddy. You'll know what that means someday—a real friend, unconditional, no questions asked, simply fun to be around.

Roy always called Dad "Joe." As a kid, he was known as Joe after Smoky Joe Wood, the Red Sox pitching great. The picture of Dad in Hawaii in his uniform was on the back of a postcard. It was signed, "Regards, Joe." Later, for some reason Dad called every stranger "Joe." "Hey, Joe, how do we get to Shibe Park?" "Joe, where is the drugstore?" "Hey, Joe, can I get a push?" I guess I thought it was odd then—but not now. That's the way he was—he knew every stranger and got along with most.

Dad's mother, my Grammy, was New England through and through. To me, she was somewhat stiff and very proper. But, I knew I was the apple of her eye. She lost one husband and divorced another and lived alone for many years. She would not remarry because that was "against God's teachings." Is it? I don't think so. When one partner either wants out or makes a life together untenable, is a lifetime of punishment warranted? There is always enough blame to go around, but, no, I don't think it is wrong.

Les remarried a few years later when Dad was about 13, I believe. Agnes, Les' second wife, apparently was a nice lady, and she planned on helping Dad go to college, but his father's remarriage was another big change, and the combination of a new mother and conflict over custody must have been too much. At the age of fifteen, Dad ran away from home. Thus began a fascinating saga.

Some in the family in Massachusetts did not know where he was for a few years. It was your Great-Mom-Mom Hilda who convinced him to let his dad know where he was. I wish I knew more of the details. Real life is better than fiction.

At the age of 16, on a Gulf odyssey, he had traveled to Galveston, Texas, where he apparently worked as a painter for a while before going on to Tampico, Mexico, on a freighter. I do not know the real details, but in Tampico, he said he was told, "We don't want you anymore," and there he was in Tampico without a job. Next came another freighter. He talked about Cuba and Morro Castle in Havana.

Instead of this broad outline, a story with more detail, people-to-people highlights and the good and bad would be a fascinating read. In retrospect, I am sure he would have described his travels had I inquired, but, true to his nature, he would have emphasized the good parts. On the other hand, while he had itchy feet and loved to travel, many of his adventures may have seemed to him a kind of uneasy day-to-day existence as compared to the security and relative luxury he and Mom provided for their children. He probably yearned to get settled, find the special benefits of family and enjoy the kind of home life most teenagers and young adults experience. Throughout his adventures, or travails, somebody got it right when, in later years, the Army described his character as "excellent" on his discharge papers.

The supreme adventure—or alternatively, horrible experience—was being present during a mutiny on a freighter in the Gulf. His recollection seemed so vivid as he sat in his big hospital chair in the nursing home, unseeing and probably in discomfort.

It must have been around 1927. Exactly what or who precipitated the action isn't clear, but apparently the crew wound up taking over all or a part of a freighter. Such ventures are doomed to fail, and this was no different. The crew, Dad included, were brought ashore in New Orleans, some or all in shackles. At the end of the gangway, he heard, "Hey kid, how old are you?" Always quick and alert, he blurted out, "Fifteen," a shading of the truth by two years. The retort, "Get the hell out of here," must have been a relief. There he was in New Orleans, no job, no ship, and every incentive to "get the hell out of here." He did!

*My Grandparents, Leslie and Sarah "Sadie" Ramsay Wood
of Somerville, Massachusetts*

Grampop Leslie rests in the Westview Cemetery in Bedford, MA. Grammy's ashes rest in Niche G-3 in Bigelow Chapel in Mt. Auburn Cemetery in Cambridge, MA.

Where would he go from New Orleans? Anything would look good after shackles.

*My Great-Grandparents, Richard and Barbara Waite Wood
of Travelers Rest, Prince Edward Island, Canada*

Another freighter, enlist in the Army or a hitch to California? Dad talked about going through the Panama Canal twice, at least once on an Army transport. He also spent time in California. Perhaps he sailed on another freighter.

He joined the Army in Boston on August 27, 1927. Actually, he did it twice. To do this the first time, being underage at seventeen, he had to have a parent's signature. He talked his mother, my Grammy, into signing for him. She thought "it would be good for him." His father was not aware of this, because, as I understood it, he still didn't know where Dad was. After a short time at the Brooklyn Army Base, he was assigned to a cavalry unit in the Second Battalion of the 35th Infantry Regiment, the "Cacti Regiment," a cavalry unit in Hawaii. I know from his stories that he loved Hawaii. He grew up on a horse farm, so an assignment training artillery mules was a natural.

Now, at Schofield Barracks, he was an aide to a colonel who was a "good fellow." He told the story many times of his daily horseback ride with the colonel, picking mangos along the trail. Looking back on that time from his hospital chair years later, he said he "had it good."

We have a wonderful picture of Dad in uniform with a dog—on a horse. You should have a copy. (I could not get a good enough copy to include in this book). While in the nursing home, I asked him the name of the horse. He replied, "Gray Dog." This was perplexing so I asked him for the name of the dog, "Gray Dog." No, Dad, the dog? "Gray Dog!" Okay, what was the name of the horse? "Gray Dog!!" The dog? "Gray Dog!!!" They were both named Gray Dog? "Yes!!!!" I'll never forget that conversation. Bless him, I thought he was confused, and he thought I was dense. Why couldn't Gray Dog be the name of a horse <u>and</u> a dog? Gray Dog the horse and Gray Dog the dog.

Dad's hitch, his first, was one year, eleven months and twenty-seven days, according to his enlistment record. While stationed at the Presidio in San Francisco, he was a guard at Alcatraz, a military prison at the time. He was discharged as a private in Headquarters Company of the 35th Infantry. The discharge record shows his character was "excellent." I don't doubt that. For the "sum of $120," he reported, he had bought himself out of the Army—you could do that then. The discharge paper shows he paid $15.07!! He got out of the Army at Fort McDowell in San Francisco and took a troop ship back through the Canal and on to New York. He said the troop ship was the "*Sostransco*" (I am not sure about the spelling).

The story is a little less clear here. Back in New York, he got a job handling freight, but he still had itchy feet and ended up in California again. He worked on a farm in Petaluma, California, a place known for its White Leghorn chickens. I am not sure what else he did between getting out of the Army in August 1929 and June 12, 1931, when he again enlisted in the Army, this time for three years. He served the full three years stationed at Fort Hamilton, Brooklyn, New York, where for awhile his main assignment was training polo ponies. A swift kick from one broke his leg. His unit was a part of the famous Big Red One, the First Infantry Division. I have his First Division and unit lapel insignias and treasure them—they will be yours some day.

Real happiness came when, as an Army private at Fort Hamilton, Brooklyn, New York, he met Mom at a dance. He was 23; mom was 17. He had been a lot of places and had seen and experienced a normal lifetime's worth. Until meeting Mom, he probably had no real direction or plans.

Mom was part of a huge family: as already recounted, Pop-Pop Linwood and Mom-Mom Nellie had eight children. They possessed a strong moral compass, love, church, purpose and direction. Courting at their house in Brooklyn had to be difficult, however, with Mom's four younger brothers, including one who asked for a nickel to leave them alone in the parlor. Not only that, but Pop-Pop Linwood really checked up on Dad. His First Sergeant told Dad that a stranger was inquiring about him. At about that time he said, "There he is now." It was Pop-Pop Linwood, who wanted to make sure he was the right type of person for his daughter. He was. Dad was always polite and respectful. In fact, Pop-Pop Linwood used to tease him over it. Dad always stood up when an elder walked into a room, so Pop-Pop would walk in and out of the parlor deliberately making Dad jump up and down.

For Dad, I suppose it was a most happy time, the beginning of direction, purpose, settling down and accomplishment. The happiest part of his life started when he met Mom. He and Mom married on August 1, 1934, two months after Dad completed his enlistment. Now he was part of a family imparting love, meaning and purpose. Things weren't always easy for Mom and Dad—getting married during the Depression and with less formal education than they both deserved. As a youth, Dad had missed the stability that most of us experience from our families. But theirs became a good story.

Earlier in 1931, he had applied to and was accepted into the New York City Police Academy. At that time, Mom says, he had the highest entrance exam score ever. He never bragged about anything he did, even a little bit; he never mentioned it. The competition was tough in those Depression years, even though most young men had not gone to college. Being a police officer would have been a demanding, tough, somewhat risky job that would keep him away from his family. Before they were married, Mom-Mom talked him out of continuing. I like to think he would have made a great police commissioner had he continued. He had the ability and personality.

Your Great-Pop-Pop and namesake (my Dad) was a very intelligent man—an excellent mind that hummed even though formal schooling was cut short. He read all the time. He had few peers in history and geography and was a good businessman. He read the *Saturday Evening Post*, *Colliers*, and *LIFE* every week. He read newspapers and good books–all the time. He introduced me to the Horatio Hornblower Series of books by C. S. Forester, as wonderful for teenagers as adults.

When Eleanor, Mom's new baby sister, became an unexpected new arrival in 1934, she delayed my parents' wedding; Mom's help was needed with the five, and soon to be six, children at home. After they were married, Dad went to work on the boats and became a full-fledged member of the Evans family. He got a job on a Barwick tugboat in New York that made a regular run to and from New London, Connecticut, where he and Mom lived for three months. The newlywed wife (Mom-Mom to my future grandchildren) who was used to being part of a large family, was alone all week. She tells of hearing the tug's whistle when it returned and passed under the bridge and of running down to the river to wave and welcome him back. The "Be Sunny" plaque in our back hall was "swiped" from their New London apartment. Pop-Pop Linwood got that tugboat job for Dad. "See what he's made of," he said. An honest day's work and more, for an honest day's pay is what he gave, always. Then he got a job in New York Harbor on a tug with either Uncle Neal or Louis. That's really getting your feet wet and being a part of the Evans family. He always did anything needed to better his family's situation.

I was born November 29, 1935. According to Mom, he was very proud. "Everyone in the hospital knew he had a new son."

I barely remember living in the Ciminella's upstairs apartment on 67th street in Brooklyn about 1938 or 1939, and in an apartment on Fort Hamilton Parkway, briefly, before moving to 1043 70th Street in Brooklyn, a few houses up from Linwood and Nellie, my Mom-Mom and Pop-Pop, and a few down from Uncle Bill and Aunt Mildred. We lived there until February 1942, when we moved to 637 Wellington Road (the number has changed) in West Hempstead, Long Island, where we lived in a nice new home.

Your Great-Pop-Pop worked hard and was gone a lot when I was a small child in Brooklyn and Long Island. My first memory is of his working on a moving van which he owned with a friend. His Uncle Will had a moving company in Somerville, Massachusetts, and Dad and Mom saw this as a way to get ahead. Financial problems and a lack of honesty by others cost him the truck and the business.

One of my earliest memories is of going to Florida in Dad's moving van with Mom and Dad; I was about three (Dad was trying to start a moving company). "Miami" became the source of a cute story. If you say, "Miami," then a three-year old would say, "Yourami." This went on for a long time, and I continued to call it "Yourami." Another early memory was my introduction to beer. Dad worked long hours, but there were those Saturday walks with a stop for a beer. I got a juice glass full and all the pretzels I could eat. They remain a favorite.

The Tugboat
Isabel A. McAllister

After the moving business he became a deckhand on a tugboat with my Pop-Pop. I believe it was the *Isabel A. Mcallister.* He took me, a four-year-old, on an overnight trip on the tug in New York Harbor. Again, it is an early memory, but one thing stands out. It was a stormy night and I was frightened. I had to go to the bathroom and the only way to get to the head was to go out on deck. I was told not to, and I ended up wetting the bed. I remember him helping rather than chastising.

During the war years, I remember going downstairs to the Gadeberg residence where Mr. Gadeberg listened to the evening news of the war. I remember also the earlier radio announcements about Pearl Harbor, but my child's understanding was limited. As noted earlier, the gravity hit home when we learned that Buddy Hickey, who lived upstairs from my Mom-Mom and Pop-Pop, was lost in a B-17 over Europe.

Thereafter, in order, Dad served as a barge master on an Anaconda copper barge, crewman on an ammunition boat during the war, carpenter in the Brooklyn Navy Yard, and trainman on the Pennsylvania Railroad. He changed jobs often–either for advancement or higher pay. The trainman job was great for me, an eight-year-old on Long Island. I got to go to work with him at least twice. Once we went on a day trip to Bay Head, New Jersey. I have vivid memories of going out onto the beach with him to look for shells. On the way home, we rode in the cab of the engine. What a trip for a kid! Another time, we went to Washington DC, with my Grammy. Perhaps, best of all, because comic books were currency for me and my friends, he always brought home comics which had been left on the train. I had many, many more comics than all my close friends combined. I was always able to trade for any comic I wanted because I had so many, all traceable to his thoughtfulness.

Although Dad was not home much, I remember often walking the mile with him to Schillings Hardware Store in Franklin Square on Long Island. I liked to go with him. I remember his spending a long time on each trip simply looking around the store. I didn't realize he was dreaming of, thinking about and planning to open his own hardware store some day.

In June 1946, we moved from a modern home on Long Island to Roxana, Delaware. Roxana was an experience for all of us, living in the only house available during the housing shortage after the war. It had no running water, indoor plumbing or central heat. I attended the three-room school in Roxana. Dad worked as a carpenter at the chicken plant in Georgetown while preparing to open the hardware store in Millville.

Dad and Uncle Wilbert—ask me about him, another good guy—built the building and opened the hardware store in 1947. From the time they opened the store, Dad was a happy man, restless perhaps, with itchy feet and ready to travel at the drop of a hat, but happy. Over fifty years later, long after Dad and Wilbert sold the store, it became the Miller's Creek gift shop just west of their house in Millville.

I really enjoyed working in the store with Dad and Wilbert, waiting on customers and even stocking shelves—but I did not enjoy cleaning shelves. The store was a fun place, the source of the straight scoop on everything going on in town. For me, the best thing was listening in on Dad's conversations with friends and customers.

Dad was at home with anyone and everyone, and he could hold his own in conversations with anyone. There were no strangers in this typical, have-everything hardware store, and everyone was welcomed. Fishing buddies included William Randolph Hearst Jr., and George Dixon, a syndicated columnist for the Scripps-Howard papers. I remember distinguished judges and generals in the store, including one man who had been a prosecutor at the Nuremburg War Crimes Trials after World War II.

Dad had a heart for the needy. I remember one Christmas Eve going with him to distribute unsold toys to children less fortunate than our family.

When he decided to sell the store, all the ladies in town were disappointed. I bet he helped fix every lamp in the area at one time or another. Another lady despaired of ever again being able to get help deciphering her husband's sketchy instructions so she could bring home what her husband sent her for. She often didn't know exactly what he needed, but Dad always seemed to.

He enjoyed his nine grandchildren so much, and they loved and respected him, too. He enjoyed their visits. He felt the same way I do now when I get visits from you, your sisters and cousins. A lot of commotion, but everyone had a good time. It was funny though. He was always concerned that one of the little ones would get hurt, and it made him nervous. After awhile, I would notice him outside walking along the ditch in the back of the house—the one named "Crab Creek" by your uncle Rob when he was three. That was his way of getting away for awhile when the commotion got to him.

He was always ready to go to a ball game—baseball or football. Best of all was when some of his grandchildren were along. The absolute best were two World Series games in Baltimore in 1971—the Orioles against the Pirates. Uncle Bruce, your cousins Bruce Ray and Leslie, Pop-Pop and I had one great day together. Two days later, Dad and I went to game seven with your Dad and Uncle Rob. What a great series–Brooks Robinson, Frank Robinson and Roberto Clemente were stars. He and I always enjoyed being together at the last Redskins game of the year in Washington, with the usual half-time visit from Santa Claus. They were special days for both of us—memories to last forever.

Yes, he was a good guy who knew everyone in the area, a good father, grandfather and husband. His children liked him for the simple reason that he was likable, loved him because he dispensed love, and respected him because he earned it. What described him best? He loved Mom very much and was proud of his family. If he had good reason to be proud, it was because of the example set by him and your Great-Mom-Mom. He rests now with Mom in the Ocean View Mariner's Bethel Methodist Cemetery. I think he'd enjoy your visit there. And, that's a good place to leave his story.

Chapter 28   Letter to Sarah (Added in the Second Edition)

August 7, 2007

Well, aren't you someone exciting—my lucky 13th grandchild. Your sisters think you are wonderful. You are. I have enjoyed getting to know you and your ready smile this summer. Your first birthday party with Grandma Claire, Grandpa Brice, Ms. Pat and me was so much fun—you are such a sweetie—but we missed your parents and sisters who were in Hawaii.

You are so very lucky to have such special sisters, Annmarie, Elizabeth and Allison. You will have many friends in your lifetime, but no friendships will be as true, sharing and supportive as those with your sisters. Having such sisters as friends truly makes you lucky.

I was so touched after you were born to learn you were named Sarah Evans Wood. Sarah is such a beautiful Old Testament name. Sarah was a revered woman of God, the wife of the Patriarch Abraham and the mother of Jacob and Isaac. Her beautiful name was given to a number of newborns in our family over many generations and family lines. Both of my grandmothers were named Sarah—your great-great grandmothers. Sarah "Nellie" Daisey Evans, my mother's mother, was a very wonderful grandmother who was so loved and respected by everyone who knew her. My other grandmother, Sarah Ramsey Johnston, my father's mother, lived in Boston. I didn't see her often enough, but I knew she loved me and had me in her thoughts.

Grandpa Brice also had a grandmother named Sarah Evans Shockley. That means you are named after at least three of your great-great grandmothers. Not many people can say that!

You, your daddy and I share the same middle name, Evans, and last name, Wood. I can't think of anyone with whom I would rather share those names.

Another Sarah, Sarah Breasure Hall, was both your 3rd and 4th great-grandmothers. She was Grandma Claire's great-grandmother and my great-great-grandmother. Grandma Claire can explain this to you someday. It means you are your own cousin and your sister's cousins—complicated!

A number of other family Sarahs came before you. A 4th great- grandmother, Sarah Quillen Daisey of Ocean View, was the wife of Henry Daisey. A 6th great- grandmother, Sarah Prettyman Marvel Dazey, lived near Bethany Beach around 1800. A 7th great -grandmother, Sarah Evans, the wife of Daniel Evans, lived in Bethany Beach well before 1800. In addition, there are aunts and cousins named Sarah. Your daddy's Aunt Sally Young is a Sarah. It has been a popular name for thousands of years—because it is so beautiful and revered.

Someday your parents will read to you about some of these special women from your copy of <u>Letters to the Little Ones</u>, my story about our Delaware family.

Sarah Evans Wood is a special name—it means so much to me and others who have memories of other Sarahs who came before you. I know the earlier Sarahs are honored to share their name with you and that you will honor them by being a credit to their name.

Love,

Pop-Pop

Chapter 29   Letter to All My Grandchildren

May 2001

My Dear Little Ones,

As one adds years, family roles evolve and become very different from the earlier active one of fathering growing children and mentoring teenagers and young adults. Now, Medicare-eligible, with Pat such a special part of my life, it has changed to being a proud observer—while trying to set a good example for adult children and my grandchildren.

How grand it is to see your children become accomplished adults, setting good examples and guiding their little ones. In some regards, this is the best role of all, and I am getting used to it and enjoying it immensely. Your parents have given me good reason to revel in them and you—all thirteen of you. (Was twelve in 2001). I am gratified and pleased with what I observe.

I like to think that this new role was earned. It isn't always passive. There are the calls starting with, "Dad, what do you think of . . ., or I am interested in your views on . . ." I suppose this means one's views and guidance are still valued.

I have enjoyed working on this book, my attempt to give you an understanding of your Delaware roots. It is a story of good people and a wonderful place. Read it and be joyous that those who love you in turn were loved and cared for and given guidance and so on, all the way up the line. What each set of parents gave is based upon the totality of their parents' experiences, the roots of which go back to the seventeenth century.

The stories are based upon extensive research and interviews, but I am certain there are inaccuracies in the developed genealogies and histories. It would be pleasing to know that one or more of you had sufficient interest to review them with a critical eye and an intent to revise and extend them as appropriate.

Your Pop-Pop was blessed with four wonderful sons, Pat, and, together, thirteen wonderful grandchildren. How fortunate! You are all great. Thank you for being so special to us.

To help you know and understand your Pop-Pop I have included a brief outline autobiography.

I love you all so much, Pop-Pop.

Chapter 30   The Little Ones' Pop-Pop, Gordon Evans Wood Sr.

Five phenomena best characterize your Pop-Pop. First is the upbringing, guidance and example provided by my parents, which started me off on the right track. For this I am eternally grateful. I understand what I received. Second, are my four sons, Richard, Rob, Chip and David. They are major influences in my life and its many paths and a limitless source of pride and pleasure. And now, grandchildren are like icing on the cake. Third, is the opportunity I have had to work capably in both the legal and engineering worlds. Fourth is the opportunity I have had to see our beautiful country and much of the world. Last and so special is the happiness brought to my life by Pat.

My Parents
Richard Kenneth and Hilda Elizabeth Evans Wood

My sons and my love and affection for them are in my thoughts always, every day. They and their children are an omnipresent source of pride. "Your Old Man loves you, kid," came easily and constantly. They have helped make whatever it is I am today. What is there left to say?

Being able to work as both an engineer and a lawyer is a source of pride, but it is more than that. I have been able to do and see so much and had so much fun doing it. Few have had a career that was more fun than mine. Who else has had the chance to study engineering, management and law; manage the design and development of a solid propellant rocket on the Minuteman intercontinental ballistic missile; design and manage many small rockets used on most of the early space probes and tests for the manned trip to the moon; write an early paper on reducing pollution from the combustion of coal; make major contributions to the Clean Water Act in 1972 and 1977 as a counsel on a U. S. House of Representatives committee; manage a major corporation's government relations

Pop-Pop and Ms. Pat

program; manage the programs of an industry association; and help manage a major, cutting-edge government environmental research and development program?

Seeing a large part of the world through both business travel and travels with my special wife, Pat, has been a source of education, cultural enhancement, broader understanding and wonderful pleasures. Tigers in India; gorillas, lions, cheetahs, leopards, elephants and migrations in Africa; Darwin's clues to evolution in the Galapagos Islands; the wonders of Australia, China and Southeast Asia; Komodo dragons in Indonesia; our cultural heritage in Europe; the art and architecture of Russia with Pat and David; the wonders of Turkey on trips with Pat, David and then Richard; and many other wonderful and special places too numerous to mention. How great it is to have shared and to continue to share so much with Pat.

Here is a summary of major happenings in my life:

- Born, November 29, 1935, in the Shore Road Hospital in Brooklyn, New York, where most of Mom's family lived while the men worked in New York Harbor.

- Moved to West Hempstead, Long Island, in 1941—a nice suburb. Attended Johns Street Elementary School which was outstanding.

- Moved to Roxana, Delaware, in June 1946. Attended Tilghman Johnson's great sixth grade in the three-room Roxana School and learned even more about life following him around on his farm which was across the highway from our house.

- Moved to Ocean View in the spring of 1947 and then to Millville in 1950. Completed Junior and Senior High School at the Lord Baltimore School.

- Attended the University of Delaware, 1953-1957, studied Chemical Engineering, receiving the Bachelor of Chemical Engineering degree in 1957. Played lacrosse—starting goalie in 1957—received varsity letter.

- Commissioned a Second Lieutenant, U. S. Army Reserves, after ROTC summer camp in 1957.

- Married Susan Kimmel of Ohio on December 16, 1957. Four wonderful sons and sources of enduring pride followed; Richard Kenneth II in 1960, Robert Kimmel (Rob) in 1962, Gordon Evans Jr. (Chip) in 1964 and David Neal (Dave) in 1967. Sadly, Sue and I drifted apart over the years and separated and divorced.

- Worked for Amoco Chemicals in Chicago (1957-59), served as Second Lieutenant in the U. S. Army Signal Corps (six months in 1958 and six years in inactive reserve, Honorable Discharge). Worked for Thompson-Ramo-Wooldridge in Cleveland (1959-1960). Studied rocket engineering and fluid mechanics at Illinois Institute of Technology and Case Institute of Technology (1957-1960).

- Joined Atlantic Research Corporation in Alexandria, Virginia, for ten years of work on solid propellant rockets (1960-1970).

- Studied Engineering Administration at George Washington University at night for three years, 1962-1965, receiving the Master of Engineering Administration degree in 1965.

- Studied Law at George Washington University at night for three-and-a-half years, 1967-1971, receiving the Juris Doctor, With Honors, degree in 1971. Member of Virginia State Bar.

- Worked briefly for the National Coal Policy Conference in 1971 on coal-related environmental issues.

- Joined Committee on Public Works of the U. S. House of Representatives in 1971 for over eight years. Was lead Minority Staff Member on the 1972 and 1977 Amendments to the Clean Water Act.

- Served as an Organizing Director of the new First National Bank of Georgetown, which opened for business in April 1979. Continued to serve as Director of the renamed Delaware National Bank.

- Joined Olin Corporation for ten years. Appointed Vice President, Government Relations (1978-1988).

- Joined Synthetic Organic Chemicals Manufacturing Association as Senior Vice President for four years (1988-1992).

- Joined Office of Chief Counsel, U. S. Army Corps of Engineers. Appointed Deputy Director and Counsel, Department of Defense Strategic Environmental Research and Development Program. Retired in 1997.

- Married Patricia Ann Hill on October 4, 1997, at the Old Blackwater Presbyterian Church.

- Lived happily ever after in our new home on the Point at Daisey Landing on Whites Creek in Ocean View.

- Served productively for two terms as Mayor of Ocean View.

Life is full. Life is good. I've done a million things and have a million left to do. Visits with children and grandchildren are eagerly anticipated and always enjoyed! We have taken advantage of the opportunity to spend time with our families and go to the symphony, opera and theater in Washington. Redskin games are a pleasure—especially going with my sons and grandchildren. Bird watching and fishing contribute to the quality of life in Delaware. Pat and I have created and taken advantage of regular opportunities to see the world—what a pleasure! Life with Pat is a joy!

My greatest pleasure has been having reasons to be even more proud of my four sons, brothers who enjoy each other—and now the grandchildren.

And that's your Pop-Pop, a very lucky man, for which I am grateful.

Epilogue

From Walter and Mary Evans, Thomas and Jemima Dazey, Ezekiel Green and his wife (unknown maiden name), and William and Margaret Hall, through Linwood and Nellie Daisey Evans, they ventured, worked hard, survived, even prospered, and set good examples. Collectively, they left their invaluable legacy—the importance of family and the treasure of family ties.

There was more to this story than just the generations past. The unique, frozen in time, geographical isolation of Baltimore Hundred until the middle of the twentieth century and the forest, land and water resources molded the culture and heritage of our generations past into a positive expression of both Baltimore Hundred's isolation and resources.[410]

We leave the stories of the generations here, content in the knowledge that we are not orphans of unknown generations past and, hopefully, are anchored by a better understanding of our Delaware family's origins and history.

Who will remember them when we who do are but a memory?

If you seek out their monuments, say hello to a cousin!

I hope this chronicle helps!

---

410   Generously paraphrased from Tom Horton's *An Island Out of Time, A Memoir of Smith Island in the Chesapeake*, (New York: W. W. Norton & Co., 1996), p. 309.

Interview of Uncle De Witt France Evans
by Bill Ingram in 1973

This Appendix presents the transcription of the tape of a 1973 interview of De Witt France Evans, son of Captain Alonzo and Elizabeth Breasure Hall Evans, by his son-in-law, Bill Ingram. The tape was made available by the generosity of Uncle France's daughter, Gloria Ingram, and her husband, Bill. Bill did a truly wonderful job of bringing out the story of boyhood events after the early and tragic death of France's mother in 1909. She left eleven children and the widower Alonzo in Bethany Beach in 1909. France recalls childhood events involving his brothers and sisters, a lonely and often grim life in numerous foster homes and adventures—at times life-threatening and heroic—on tugboats in Philadelphia and New York. Good times, bad times—flush times and Depression times, trying to live on $100 a month. The tape is a truly priceless chronicle of one of Baltimore Hundred's sons.

This transcription reflects free-wheeling thoughts and unvarnished language in the tape as faithfully as possible. Phrases have been reordered solely to enhance continuity of events and materials on specific subjects. Parenthetical words and phrases are used to clarify meaning, present a more easily understood flow or syntax and logically juxtapose detail on names, places and events. "B" is Bill Ingram, and "F" is France Evans.

* * * * * * * * *

"My Mother Died in 1909 – I was Eight"

B   A lot of people wondered about being a foster child.

F   People said we wouldn't amount to anything [when our mother died and we had to live in foster homes]. But with a little help, we did amount to something!

F   When the rest of us was able to help, we could help one another and say nothing of it. She was dying of blood poisoning after Delena was born. She died; it was the biggest funeral down here at that time that the lower State of Delaware ever had— everyone knew her. Big family. There was one hundred horse and carriages—there was no automobiles. We drove up to the road and the church was filled with enough people outside to fill it again.

While my two oldest sisters, Gertie and Lindy, was going to try to help, Pop wanted to keep us together, and he was only home one day a week. He was at the Life-Saving Station at Indian River. Two colored families lived and worked on the farm.

B   Your oldest brother, Linwood, where did he go to live when his mother died?

F   He had been working away on the tugboats. Out of Philly; he was a fireman. He came home and now he was the boss, Linwood. But that didn't work out, and Pop hired a man and

287

his wife to come to live there to keep us together and grow up together. The man was blind and Pop paid them $45 a month and their keep. That didn't work out; we boys would have to lead the man around for his exercise and we'd lead the man into a ditch of water and that wouldn't work out.

A Boy's Foster Home Odyssey

Age 8	-	Mother died
Age 8	-	Lived on family farm
Age 9-11½	-	Lived with Jake Pusey
Age 11½-12	-	Lived with Capt. Jim Bennett
Age 12-almost 14	-	Lived with Wilmer Vanzant
Age 14-16	-	Lived with Uncle Dave Hall
Age 16	-	Left for Philadelphia

F   So, we went to live with other people. My first place—I lasted three days—was with Lorrie Henderson and his wife, who had the Post Office in Bethany Beach. From there I went to Jake Pusey's place in Cedar Neck, where Jake's store is today [G & E].

B   Why did you only last three days in the first place?

F   They didn't want me.

B   Then you went to the Puseys.

F   Went to the Puseys. I was eight years old the eleventh of April and Mom died the first of April. I lived there until I was eleven or eleven-and-a-half-years old, I just don't remember [exactly]. From there I went to Captain Jim Bennett's in Ocean View. I was there for six or eight months. From there I went to Wilmer Vanzant's in Cedar Neck. There I got a pretty good whipping from my father for things that I wasn't deserving of, but . . .

B   Why did he whip you?

F   Well, the main reason was that my mother and father was in what was known as the Christian Church. I would go out to the Ocean View Methodist Church with them [the Vanzants] of a Sunday night. Their daughter and I in a durban wagon. [The Christian Church was nearby.]

B   What is a durban wagon?

F   A flat-bottomed wagon drawn by a horse that had one seat across the top [short for Dearborn], and Wilmer and his wife would sit there, and we would sit in the foot—the flat part. So I would hitch the horse at the Methodist Church and they went in church and when they went in I went over to the Christian Church. I would be back by the time they got out. On the way back this one night, when we got over the canal bridge in Cedar Neck, Wilmer's wife Angie said, "Ask him where he was tonight." I told them I was in church. "We didn't see you in church." "Well, I was to the church my mother brought me up in." I jumped out of the durban and he jumped out. I run—it was on a sandy road—I fell, and he fell too, and got a mouth full of sand. They went and met my father and told him that and a lot of other one-sided things. And I got whipped. I faulted my Pop, my father, for a long time. But since I had grown to be a man, I understood he had problems.

B   You got whipped another time when you were eating something you weren't supposed to eat, didn't you?

F   This was at Jake Pusey's. They had a big apple orchard, maybe 50 apple trees. Bushels. There was no sale for them. Apples just laying on the ground. I would pick an apple up to eat it and she [Lucy Pusey] would raise Cain because I hadn't asked for it. Anyway, I got this whipping from my father. Some time after that, they got an automobile, and my Uncle Will Evans and Mr. Frank Moore hired them to take a motor to Salisbury to be repaired. They came down that night—planning for a 4 a.m. departure. Helen [Vanzant, who later on married Boyer Hocker] and I were studying our lessons. But, at three o'clock, they got me out of bed and told me the car was broke down and to get on the horse's back and tell my Uncle Steve, Alonzo's brother. And then I told him what Pop had done to me. He was very upset. He met my father on the Cedar Neck Canal Bridge and told him if he didn't take me away from there he would give my father a licking like he gave me, only worse. My father came down and got me. Angie said, "After we feed him all winter and we could get some work from him, you take him away from us." That's when I went to Captain Jim Bennett's. From there I went to Uncle Dave Hall's, which was my mother's brother. And my Grandfather Hall was there. They were very good to me—best home I ever had after the time of my mother's death.

F   [As repeated on tape by Bill Ingram] The time France had diphtheria [while living at the Puseys]. Dr. Hocker was called down to Lucy Pusey's place, but he only had one shot of anti-toxin, and he gave France the one shot. Of course France needed a lot more than one shot, throat all swelled up. Dr. Hocker had these four bay horses on a wagon. He would drive anywhere in the county to treat people who were sick. So he raced back and got two more shots of anti-toxin. The foam was flecked on those bay horses when he got back. [The doctor] said to feed France chicken soup when he started recovering. But they never gave France any chicken. One day when Lucy went out to the outhouse, France said, he took a sweet potato from the cupboard and almost choked on it. They had to hold him upside down and shake him.

F   I was almost fourteen when I left [the Vanzants].

B   So you were there almost two years. And before that with Capt. Jim Bennett?

F   About six or eight months.

B   How did that work out?

F   Not good. He was an old steamboat captain and grumpy. She was good to me, and then there wasn't enough for me to do there and they decided they didn't want me any longer.

B   And then the last?

F   At Uncle Dave's—I was treated equal there. I worked on the farm and I got four dollars a month and I had to buy my own clothes. My brother Bill, he was away working and he came down and took me to Selbyville and bought me shoes and a suit of clothes—very good to me.

I bought a bike and I had no money and I picked strawberries to pay for it. I bought it at Bill Hickman's store—cost me $20. It was a Redbird. When I got it home—it was a rainy muddy night—no stone roads in those times—I cleaned the bike off and put it in Aunt Katie's parlor chamber room, the nicest room in the house. She didn't like that, but there wasn't nothing said about it, and I was up at 4 o'clock in the morning riding my bike. I picked more strawberries that day than any day I ever picked, before or since. I picked 204 quarts at a cent-and-a-half a quart that first day. Berry picking is the way I paid for my bicycle.

B   Didn't you say once that you made a lot of money picking strawberries another time and that you took Lon over to Ocean City?

F   [It was] while I was living at Uncle Dave's, I had 17 dollars and we went to Ocean City by boat from the Canal Bridge with Everett Hickman. Cost 60 cents a round trip. I think it was with Woodburn James or Dave Hudson and my brother Lon. I can't remember which. They didn't have much money, about a dollar apiece. We went to Ocean City, which was only four blocks long at that time. We went up on the boardwalk, and there was a fellow selling hot dogs. He had a little song—"A loaf of bread and a pound of meat and all the mustard you can eat—for five cents." I spent the whole seventeen dollars because my brother and the other fellows didn't have much. When I came back, I didn't have much money for Bethany Beach. I rented my bike out for 35 cents to get money for fireworks.

I have another part to tell you. There used to be what was known down there on Bethany Beach [as] a drug store. A man by the name of Steve Evans used to run it. We called him "Conch Steve." He had a big nose and we called him "Conch." Some of the bigger boys than I, I guess, was testing me. They wanted me to drink grape juice with cigarette ashes in it. Me being a fellow who would just do what they dared me to do . . . I got drunk and sick. I laid out on the lawn at Uncle Dave's and they never knew about it.

We worked with Uncle Dave and he was fun to work with—full of fun. [One day we were working in the field and] the mules pricked up their ears. They had more sense than we did. Uncle Dave heard a noise and asked, "What do you suppose that noise is?" I answered that it must be Mr. Addy's new steamboat coming up the canal. Then we unhooked the mules and took our baths and went up to Ocean View at Hod Derrickson's Corner then—now Parson's Corner [Southeast corner of Central Avenue and Route 26]. Everybody was out there talking about this airship. The next day, we went to church and there was more talk about the airship than there was about the preaching of the sermon. People came out of the church and a man by the name of Clint Quillen, an elder of the church, he came out on the church stoop and he said, " I'll bet you, by God, that airship can beat a wild goose flying."

A Young Man Goes off to Philadelphia

B   What about delivering the ice to Senator Drexler?

F   I told my brothers I was going away and I would give them the bike and they were going to keep me posted about my father. First, I went to Selbyville. I had to get a load of ice for the Red Men's Hall and the festival with a pair of mules and a hauling wagon, and I had to deliver 200 pounds of ice to Senator Drexler at the beach. I passed my father's on the way with the ice. My father was home and he hollered to me to stop. I didn't stop and he hollered again. I didn't stop. When he hollered the third time, I figured I better stop. He came out and he said, "I hear you are going away." I said. "I am going up on the excursion, but I am coming back." He said, "That's not the way I heard it." So I said that was what I wanted to do, and he said that if that's what you want to do you can go. In the meantime I delivered the ice to Mr. Drexler, and I told him my plan. He was a wonderful man and he said, "I know what you have had to live with, and if you ever need any help . . ." and he gave me two dollars.

B   How much other money did you have"

F   Eight dollars.

B   Where did the excursion go? From where to where?

F   It was a train from Frankford to Philadelphia. Anyhow, I got back to Uncle Dave's and took my bath in the washtub. I packed my grip, an old pasteboard thing, and I had a rope tied around it to hold it together. In the meantime, my father drove up in the yard. Pop said, "You lied to me, you have no intentions of coming back, you go upstairs and unpack your grip." He didn't follow me so I went up and sat on the bed, and he left. The next morning, I was laying out on the front lawn waiting for a man by the name of Al Evans, who had an old Buick car with gas lights on it. No relation. He had three or four other people, and when we passed my father's house I was in the foot of the car in case my father was out to the road to see if I was in there. When I got on the train, my Uncle Steve and his son was there. The lady who met me [in Philadelphia] was my sister Edith's mother-in-law, Mrs. Carey. I had never seen her before, but we had markers on.

My brother-in-law, who was my sister's husband, Walter Carey, got me a job in the Baldwin Locomotive Works. The government had taken over a lot of it, making ammunition for England and France—before this country went into the First World War. We boarded in South Philly with my sister, Gertie Phillips. [Apparently "We" referred to France and brother Lon.]

I had to buy a pair of long trousers to pull over my shorts. Walter's father, Mr. Carey, took me down to Dock Street in Philadelphia, and I bought a pair of long trousers. The color of them was green, and so was I, and I went to work. My first job was sixteen dollars a week, working night work. We got paid in all gold and silver. My first pay was a $20 gold piece.

Working there, different fellows would put me up to do things. I was stamping shells with a steel stencil, and two French inspectors would O.K. so many fourteen-inch shells. I would have to stencil them. So, one of the fellows said, "You want to have some fun in there tonight with those Frenchmen, reach up and pull one of their goatees and go 'baa'." That finished that job. So then they put me on a drill press drilling a center in the shells for the lathe. Each few machines had Italian laborers, and they put me up to do a little trick on one of the laborers and another fellow. We had electric chain hoists and he was eating his lunch at midnight sitting on a shell, and he fell asleep. We hooked a hook in his strap, and I pushed the button and hoisted him up. He pulled a stiletto out and was going to throw it at us, but the two guards picked him up and locked him up. And that finished that job.

B   Wait a minute, you had another incident where you had to fight somebody on that job.

F   Oh, they put me up to box another fellow who was used to boxing and I wasn't. He would knock me down, and as fast as I got up, he knocked me down again, so we called that off.

We worked night work; we shifted. They had an explosion there of a morning. We were just getting to bed at my sister's when the place blew up—in Eddystone. Two girls blown up. They had trucks and ambulances all over the place hauling [people] away. They had a seven-foot fence around the place and you got searched for matches when you went in. If you had matches, you had to leave them with the guard. A colored fellow was running out, so frightened, and they thought perhaps he was the guilty one in the explosion—and they shot him.

My father was at Frankford Station to take the train to get us, but they got word down here [Bethany Beach] that we was safe. After that, we went out to West Philadelphia to a place we knew a lot of people and boarded with a Mrs. Elizabeth Evans out there. She run a boarding house. She had several older fellows there, and we were only kids, and they would use our clothes and everything else. It was a sad mistake.

So then I went decking on a tug called the *Dennard Tucker* out of Philadelphia. Everybody knew my father because he used to be captain of tugboats up in Philadelphia. This tug, she tended the submarine net at Fort Delaware. They had three tugs there. Every night at sundown we had to close this big steel net so submarines couldn't come up the Delaware River. I stayed there and the seat of my pants kind of got holes in them, I wore it so much. I had money coming to me and I didn't have the nerve to go in and ask the owners of the tugboat for my money. Mr. Tucker came out and seen me on the sidewalk and wanted to know what I was doing there, and I told him. He gave me money and I went down to South

Street in Philadelphia and I bought one of the best suits I ever had, a blue pin-stripe, for twelve dollars. From there we drifted. Lon went decking on a tug and he got pneumonia and was out at St. Agnes Hospital in South Philadelphia. He finally got better and went on a oil tanker as storekeeper–$55 a month, I think was his salary. He went to Beaumont, Texas. We both wound up in New York, and I had this same suit on and I was growing so fast it was about three inches too short, the pant legs, and people was laughing at me over there, my brother's people.

Six Evans Boys on the Tugboats in New York Harbor – Helping Each Other

F   On December 17, 1917, we had three barges bound for Norfolk. A man by the name of Capt. Bill Cutcher was captain. We'd been in the shop and washed the boiler and had to get going—orders from the office to get them barges and get going for Norfolk. One barge was half-loaded—an all-steel barge. A fellow by the name of Harold Hitchens was first mate. We went out, picked up the barges and started to Norfolk. We got out to Scotland Lightship in New York and the wind was east-northeast breezing up and a circle around the moon. The mate called the Captain and said we better go back; it is going to be a heavy storm and we shouldn't be going. Captain "Cutch" had been home to Philadelphia and he got orders to go and he was going to go. Told him [the mate] to head it southeast by south. That day we had a ninety-mile gale. We lost the first head barge, the steel barge, and three men—sunk. We had two women aboard, the Chief Engineer's wife, Ward Bennett's, and Carl Rickards's wife. He [Carl] was sick and puked all over me. I was tied down in front of the steering engine down below, keeping the bilges free to the pump.

B   How did the men die? Did they drown? Were they swept overboard?

F   No, the men got into the dory and it capsized. The most pitiful sound I ever heard. We could hear them holler as they filled with water. The other barge men had put their valuables on this barge because she was the new senior barge, but the seas had washed the wooden hatches in and she filled up with water. Well, as I said, we had two women aboard. I gave my berth up to Carl Rickards's wife and a lot of water got into her room and she was a hollering and a crying, but her husband was so sick he couldn't do anything. We had a German sailor on board, quite a sailor. I can remember him like it happened yesterday. He had a half-pint bottle of whiskey. He took a big drink out of it and he made a heaving line fast to himself and made it fast to the stern bit and went around to close the door where Mrs. Rickards was. He came back and a sea hit the boat and washed him overboard, and we fished him back in on the line, which saved him. He changed his clothes and sat on top of the boiler until he dried. The Chief wouldn't let him use the steam steering gear because he was afraid they would try to turn the boat and then we would have swamped. There were several other tugs. The tug *Eugenia Moran* went down ahead of us with eleven men on her. The tow she had went on the beach.

Anyhow, [our tug] had a cook on her who came from Wisconsin. He was a wonderful cook. He cooked a lot of turnips. You could not sit to the table to eat [in the storm]. You had to sit on the floor and brace yourself and eat out of a pot. So anyway, he ate a lot of turnips and he wrote a note and pinned it to his inside shirt. He said, "Turnips will help float you, and when I float on the beach, people will recognize me from the note where I came from."

We hung on to the sunken barge overnight and the wind calmed and come to northwest, and we tried to get joined with the other two barges and all of our hawsers practically was washed overboard. We finally got the other two barges into the Delaware Breakwater. We were reported lost and Mr. Card had called all up and down the beach, the life-saving stations. They say he spent 50 dollars making telephone calls. I can't prove that, but that's what he said. But anyway, we got to the Delaware Breakwater and those two women got off; they both lived in Delaware. The office in New York said to "get them off."

Then we had to take these two other barges, which was damaged, to Philadelphia. So we started out and the wind had come around to northeast with a heavy sea running and it started to snow a little. Anyhow, we headed up the Delaware Bay in the rough sea out there. The Chief and I was walking back from having our supper and we could only see one red and green light, so we whistled up the speaking tube to the pilot house and says we could see only one green and red—which meant one barge had broken adrift. It was gone out into the ocean. We went out to pick her up —we finally got her. In the meantime getting her, she bounced up on the rail of the tug on a sea and almost turned her—the tug—over. Then she got the hawser tied up in the propeller of the tug, and it looked like we was gone again, but the Chief, Mr. Bennett, worked the throttles back and forth until he threw the hawser out. We finally got them up to Philadelphia with a lot of ice and things and we all went up town and had a good time. We were reported lost and I finally got word to my father at the lifesaving station.

I got this job. I oiled for my brother Bill a long time on the *Anson N. Bang.* That is [the time] we had the bad epidemic of influenza—so many people died. In my brother's home, Linwood's home, Nellie's brothers was there sick and Lon was there sick and he had the pneumonia, and we thought he was going to die, but he got better. [See Chapter 26 – Nellie nursed Lon back to health with tough love]. I bought a pint bottle of Old Crow whiskey and drank it all and was drunk and went to sleep and I never got the influenza. I think the whiskey the doctor recommended kept it away. [After] I left oiling for my brother Bill, I went on the tug *Nottingham*, oiling there. There was three oilers. The Chief Engineer, his name was Sam Sigafoot, nice man. We run to Portland, Maine, and Boston, towing coal barges. At one time we got in a storm off of Nantucket Shoals and lost a barge. We saved the men but [one], when we was getting him aboard the tug from the lifeboat, somebody threw an oar and knocked all of his teeth out. Anyway we went into Provincetown 'til the storm was over. We come back eventually to Port Johnson, Bayonne, with the tow.

One of the oilers wanted to get married, and he said $80, our pay, was not enough money to get married. I had heard my brother Lon had got his engineer's license, and I didn't think he should beat me too much, so I wanted to get my license, and I was only 18 years old. The other oiler and I, we made a deal that we would endorse our checks and roll for high dice and see who got the dice. I got 'em first and rolled a seven and picked his check up and my check and quit the *Nottingham*. I went over to New York and I got a room in the South Ferry

Hotel and I bought an Engineer's Blue Book and studied. I went up and took the examination for my engineer's license. I had to get letters signed from men I had worked under. I wasn't supposed to get a license until I was 21, but I done a little storying and got my license. I then was pretty short of money, and I got an engineers job, but I had to join the association —MEBA 33, the Marine Engineers Association. It cost 50 dollars, and I didn't have the 50 dollars, and I got ahold of my brother Bill—some way, I don't just remember how. He told me he had left money up at Linwood's for Nellie to put in the bank—to go up and get whatever I needed. I got the money and I got the job. I was making then $55 per month, and was going to save a lot of money, and I never did.

B   Linwood spent most of his time on the boats. A chief engineer. What do you recall about Uncle Linwood?

F   Big family. Four daughters and four sons. He bought my grandfather's place [Cornealius Hall's house in Bethany Beach] where Saint Ann Education Building is now. He owned a place on 70th street in Brooklyn. So did my brother Bill.

B   Did Linwood ever get hurt?

F   One winter night, a man fell overboard. There was floating ice in the water. He dived into the water and hit his head. He saved the man. It never bothered him too much.

B   Didn't you tell me a story about how Bill once lifted a big barrel?

F   As I said, I oiled for my brother Bill on the tug, the *Anson N. Bang.* We used to have to get the engine oil on the boat in 55-gallon drums. The tide was down this time, and the boat was very low in the water and it was quite a struggle. We were at Morrisey Dry Dock at 23rd Street in Brooklyn. So brother Bill was a very husky man, strong, weighed about 270. And he would watch us there and he finally come out and said, "I'll show you how to do it." He picked up the drum himself, 55 gallons, and put it in the boat.

B   How much would you say that drum weighed?

F   Near 400 pounds.

B   He hustled it in all by himself? It was taking two of you and you were having trouble?

F   Three of us. We was doing it for . . . heh, heh! We knew we would get him out there. [Joke on Bill.] He was a good man, Bill!

B   Linwood was a chief engineer?

F   So was Bill. Lon was a chief engineer. I was a chief engineer. Two brothers were captains, Neal and Louis.

B   Why did Neal get out of the boat business?

F   He never cared for it. My brother-in- law, Walter Carey, had the gas business down here, some of it. He bought it and went in the gas business here. Neal was killed in an automobile accident. He was a passenger. Fellow went to sleep at the wheel. We are getting a way ahead [of our story].

F   We got down to Norfolk, VA, [on this trip] and I was engineer. The Chief Engineer of the *Bart Hampstead*, the name of the tug, he lived in North Carolina and he wanted to go home. We had trouble with the engine and I went to work on her and got her into shape. A fellow that I know very well, eventually married my step-sister, Ward Bennett [he was in the big storm with me], come over and begged me to leave that job and go with him—which was a very sad mistake—on the tug *Augustine*. We had a strike and we got three firemen out of a saw mill to take the boat to New York. They couldn't fire coal and one of them went crazy down in the fireroom. We had to take her to New York ourselves. We got there, we had to tie her up. Then Mr. Card of McHale Towing Line took her over and started towing mud to sea in New York. I took a vacation and when I got back, Ward Bennett had got fired, and he didn't know where I was. The new boss didn't know where I was [either], and had to put a new crew on her. And I was out of a job.

I went to work on the *William H. Taylor*, towing mud for Morse and Cummings. When they dredged mud in New York Harbor, they had to tow it to sea and dump it. My brother Bill had left Morse Dry Dock and he was going on as chief of the *Bouker Number 6*. [Now], I went chief of the E. P. Morse, Morse Dry Dock, and we towed mud and one thing or another. I had my brother Lon on there with me as engineer and I had Neal and Louis as deck hands, [plus] Elliot Evans, Roddy Murray, all from down in Delaware, and Elmer Justice and Albert Justice, all on the same boat. We all done our work, but I got told by different owners that I was too good to my family. But they done their work and we never had no trouble, so I always liked to be helpful. I always remembered my mother telling me to be helpful to people. I never felt too bad about being able to help somebody. Well, that continued on and the boat tied up, and they kept me on for several months and kept on paying me my salary. I said this can't go on [because] there was no work for her.

I had an old Apperson car—I used to drive that down there and I was washing her one day down on the pier in the dry dock. One of the Port Captains there—they called them Port Captains, they had several little work boats that took men out to the boats at anchor to work on them—he called over on the megaphone. He says, "Mr. Halleck wants to see you." He was the general manager, and I figured this job was finished. I had a young daughter, my first daughter was Doris Evans; she was about a year old then. So I figured the job was over, and I put my overalls and things in a bag and went over there to see Mr. Halleck. He said, "I am too busy to see you this afternoon, can you come in the morning and have breakfast with me?" So I knew I wasn't going to be laid off, and I went in there and they had an oil-burning system that a man had developed there for steamships and tugboat boilers and power plants and one thing or other. So I went in there in the morning, I think then I was 22 years old, and he says to me at breakfast, "How would you like to go [as] demonstrating engineer for this fuel-oil burning department?" So I told him, Mr. Halleck, I don't have much education, but as far as operating this burner, I can operate it as well as any man that ever lived, I think, because my brother Bill and I was the first men who ever used it. I said, "I don't know if I am the right man for the job or not, I've not got much education." Well, he said, "Well, we think you are."

The job in them days paid me $85 dollars a week, and when I went out of New York City limits, paid me $10 a day expense money. It was considered a very, very good job, and I was quite proud of it, but I had something in the back of my mind I had to tell him before I took the job. I told him, "This is going to sound peculiar to you, but I've got to tell you because I don't want you to think I was pulling a fast one after I am on the job. I have been told by doctors that I have got to have my tonsils out because I get tonsillitis twice a year and I have had my tonsils cut three times in 24 hours—that's how bad it got. They told me if I didn't take care of it, I would eventually get rheumatism of the heart or something like that [rheumatic fever]. I told him that job would give me 12 days sick pay a year and two weeks vacation, and I will have to have it done after I take this job. He says to me, "There's not that many men, I don't think, would come that clean with it. When it comes time, go ahead and have it done."

I took my vacation and took my first wife, Ray, her name was Carpenter before we married, and my daughter, Doris, and we come down to visit my people in Delaware on a vacation. Then I was going back and have my tonsils out. I did that and went down to Dr. Pagluggi who was the doctor when my daughter was born and then became a specialist in eye, ear, nose and throat. He says to me, "Do you think you can stand me taking your tonsils out without taking any anesthetic?" So I said, "Did you ever do it?" "I never found anybody who had the nerve to let me try," he said. I said, "Go ahead." He done it, and I laid down 20 minutes and got my wife and we drove home, and I wasn't supposed to ride.

B   And he didn't take them out with snippers. He pulled them out. With wires around them or what?

F   He got a wire around them and then one wouldn't come and he had to put a finer wire around them—it bled like a bugger. One come out in three pieces. A wire loop. Anyway, I wasn't supposed to ride, but my little daughter was, heh, heh, was getting into everything, and once in a while I would let a whoop of me at her.

Anyway I went back to Morse Dry Dock in five days. Mr. Halleck seen me and said, "You look terrible, go back home." I stayed home then another three days and went back to work. Eventually things got so slow I installed the oil burners in the Mount Sinai Hospital, six steam double boilers. I had charge of it. [Other jobs we did were at] the Dauphin Silk Hosiery at 34th Street in New York, the steamer *Belle Island*, the tug *Pan Am*, oh, several jobs. Everything seemed to be going pretty good. I had to make several trips on the *Belle Island* to satisfy them, myself. I think where we went was to Rocco Point down in Connecticut, where she run an excursion. From there I was walking around in the yard, there was no work to be done.

I finally got called up in the office. Mr. Jack Wiseman was head of the fuel-oil burning department, and, of course, Mr. Halleck had put me in there before he was made in charge of the oil-burning department. So he sent for me to come up to his office. I went up to his office and he says, "I feel bad about having to do this, but things are so bad now we are going to have to give you two weeks' pay and that will be the finish of the job." Well, I had turned down several good engineers' jobs while I was there with different oil-burning jobs people wanted me to take, but I didn't want to take the job away from men that I knew very well and was engineers. So I refused to take the jobs, but each time I was offered a job I talked to Mr. Halleck and told him I was offered an engineer's job on one of the boats [where we had done an oil-burning job] and they was having trouble with it. He said, "You've got a good job here, you stay here." So I stayed there. Mr. Wiseman was going to lay me off, so I finally says to Mr. Wiseman, "I don't want to make you to feel bad or anything, but, you know, Mr. Halleck was the man who hired me, and I turned down some pretty good jobs, and I think I'd like to talk to Mr. Halleck. I don't want to go over your head, so I am telling you." "That's alright with me," he says. And I went in to see Mr. Halleck. He said you can stay around the yard here; we will pay you a dollar an hour, which cut down considerable from what I was getting. He said to just walk around here, "You don't have to do anything and maybe things will change. If you don't want to do that, we will pay you until you get a steady job." I felt kind of excited and I went down there for three weeks and collected my pay, and I said this is not a man, and I don't want to live like this.

In the meantime, my brother, Bill, who was always looking out for one of us boys that was younger than him if we got out of work, he was always watching out to see if he could find or hear tell of a job. So, I lived in New Jersey then, and I had to come over to New York looking for a job. It got rough; I was pretty low on money. My wife went to work in a candy factory once. People thought I was more or less a bum. I took a job as engineer on the tug, *Container*, and got fired every week because I didn't pay the superintendent a little hush money, or a little whatever you call it, to hold your job. I got sent back three times, and I said this is no good and I would go up to see the boss and he didn't know anything about it, and back I would go to Bridgeport.

In the meantime, brother Bill heard about it. I was walking along the Battery Park and his boat was there. He said, "I hear they're looking for an engineer on the tug *Harry Connors*." Their office at that time was Shumate and Connors up in 17 Battery Place on the tenth floor. So, I went up to see Mr. Connors. He was a well-dressed person and a very likeable person. When I first met him, I knew right away I could like the man. But he said to me, "I have already hired two men for the job." So I says, "Why do you have to hire two men if it's a one-man job?" I kind of had him puzzled, and he says to me, "Where can I call you up?" So, I said, "Well if you got two men hired, you don't need a third one." So I said, "If there is anything to it, I will be over here all day and I'll stop up at your office before I go back home at about three o'clock in the afternoon." But his point was that he wanted to know where I worked before. I told him the different places and who for. His point was that he wanted to contact them to see the type of a person I was.

I went up in his office at three o'clock that afternoon, and I can't forget this. He put his arm around me and he said, "You're just the man I want." And I went to work there as engineer on the tug *Harry Connors*, which was a terrible job. They put a boiler in her that didn't suit. You couldn't steam her and you couldn't—it was just terrible. I had a lot of trouble with her. She come near sinking a couple of times in the night when she was tied up—from bum work that was done up to their own shipyard in Kingston. I found the trouble and I lifted the boat over and fixed her— turned the boat over and fixed it ourselves in New Town Creek.

Eventually, Shumate and Connors dissolved partnership and there was a big law case. Mr. Connors got very sick and I got laid off. And I took all the equipment to Kingston, Roundou Creek. Took it there and tied up. And that was the finish of that job. I got a job from Mr. Brinkman, Port Engineer for Moran Towing Line, on the *Joe Moran*—towing garbage twenty-five miles to sea.

I come home on a Sunday and my wife told me, we had no telephone, they had just called down to my father's place. She said that Mr. Connors [Senior] had called up to my father's place two or three times and wants you to call him. So I called him up and he wanted me to come in and see him. I told him I was working and I couldn't come in to see him and he told me over the telephone he wanted me to come back with him. It was a day boat; you only worked daytime—a single-crew boat. I said I can't make money there that I am making here, and he said, "I'll pay you just as much here as you are making there if you come back here." So I quit and went there. I got the boat ready to go, the tug *Arthur Connors*, which was named after him, and I was engineer on her.

And then, it wasn't too soon after that the Depression hit. While Mr. Connors had got it all settled in court and he owned several barges and one tug boat, the man had spent (almost) all of his money, and the Depression hit and there was no work for anything. He bought two or three other diesel tugs and [then] his money was gone. He had all the equipment and no work for it. So we were tied up at Pier 10 at the foot of Montague Street in Brooklyn, The Red D Line. We had the tug *Fidelity*, and the tug *Dynamic*, and the tug *Gramercy*, all diesel boats, all practically new. And we had Norwegian engineers, non-citizens of this country. And so they called me up in Depression days and told me they had to cut my wages and that I didn't need to come down and maybe look at the boat once or a couple of times a week and they would give me 100 dollars a month. Well, I couldn't live on a 100 dollars a month.

I said to my wife that night when I got home, and the two kids, that I thought I was going to have to quit. I wasn't going to let foreigners take the bread and butter away from me. I don't [want to] deprive them of making a living, but that was not fair. So anyway, I took my grip and I made up my mind that I had to go over to the office and tell him how I felt. So I went over there, and I kinda pitied Mr. Connors because he was a nice man—he was nice to me anyhow. He was sitting at a big roll-topped desk—finally, after talking to his sons. Two girls worked there, Miss Beech and Miss Grunwald, and I said to the two girls, "I hope you girls will leave early because I've got a few things to say here today and I use the English kinda careless." They had all had their wages cut and they said they wanted to hear somebody tell him off. I said, "I told you so, so if you hear somebody cussing . . ."

So I went in to see his son, Harry, and Joe Herman. I remember when Joe Herman started for 35 dollars a week there. He was getting up in the company. I told them how I felt. These fellers [on the boats] are nice fellers; they told you, you have got to overhaul the engines, which I don't believe because they are new engines and they've not run much. They are Norwegians, just as good as I am, but their families live over in Norway; they live on the boat. I have taken them up the street a many a time to buy clothes for sixty cents apiece on Myrtle Avenue. They'd send dresses over to their kids in Norway. They live on the boat. They buy a little chuck and eat a few potatoes. I have a family to raise here and I was born in this country and I have a license in this country. I'd quit the God Damn job and I need one pretty bad. Well, Harry [the son] says, "let me speak to pappa." I said, no, your father hired me at Shumate and Connors. I was going to speak to his father myself.

I went in and the old man turned his chair around, and I said, "I have a few things to tell you and it will take me about five minutes." I told him all that I had told Harry about being born here and spending all my money here. While I was telling him off, Mrs. Connors walked in. She used to come down from Pelham sometimes and ride home with him. I could hear her [talk about a ride home] when she walked in.

We looked out of the window on the seventeenth floor of 21 West Street and there was a B&O Railroad tug going by. Of course it was getting dark then at that time of the year where they had the electric lights on. He said to me, "You mean you could go on that boat and run her." I said, "If I couldn't—in two hours—then I should take my licenses and throw them away."

The next morning they called me and put me in charge—of everything. I got a raise in my salary, not too much, but I got enough to live with. I was put in charge. They started to overhaul that engine and I put a stop to it. The engineer on the *Dynamic*, which was the new boat, was Morris Jacobson. Not too long ago he died in Norway. He was a nice man; brought his family here and lived like the rest of us due to my stand [on his behalf]. The other fellow, Ole Byeholtz, the same thing. I hired and fired that guy three times. He brought his family here and owns a home here and he is about ready to die now, from what I hear. Anyway they [the fellows] called me and I came back and Morris Jacobson said, "Well, they can't do that to me," and I quit.

In the meantime, they got a job for one of the tugs to take one of their lighters up the Harlem River. No engineer [was] there and they sent a fellow by the name of Joe Gar over to captain her, and he [phoned and left word] there was no engineer to run the boat. I [called up and said] I'll go over with you. I'll run the boat. They wanted to know where Morris was, and I said I don't know—he said he quit. So I said to Mr. Connors that I'll run the engine. He said, "You mean to tell me you can run that engine." I said that if I don't run her, don't send anyone else to run her because she will never run again.

We got the second job in Hoboken, New Jersey, to take a coal boat to Bass Beach. Morris had found out the boat had gone without him and he was scared to death and was waiting on the dock. He worked for us for 20 years after that.

Then I became the Port Engineer and Port Captain when things got better and we had 72 pieces of floating equipment and our own shop to repair the boats. I was in charge of it from 1933 to 1963, thirty years.

Land Owned by My Father, Alonzo Evans

B   Your father once owned a great deal of land in Sussex County—would you describe the land that he owned? The extent of it? Describe that land.

F   My father owned 100 acres [a farm] right down the Selbyville Road [from the corner of routes 17 and 26]. He sold it to Elij' Tyre for seventeen hundred dollars. His father owned all of this land over on that side there, up to the corner where you turn to go to Selbyville–down that road where the greenhouse is. That was my uncle's. That was all my grandfather's one time. And on the other side of the road, too, all the way to the corner. I think he had a molasses mill up there once.

B   Then he owned other land down on the beach. How much did he own on the beach?

F   I guess he must have had 300 acres there.

B   More or less. And that 300 acres included the area where that Army depot is now?

F   That, and where his house is now there was 75 acres there. [North side of Route 26 from Route 1 to west of Saint Ann Church.] And down the road further, the road that turns there, goes that way, was where we lived. That was the farm that was close to a hundred acres [east of Kent Avenue and south of State Route 26]–where the dual highway is now. Pop sold some of that land and Gram-Pop Hall sold some of his land to Mr. France, the man who named me: De Witt Clinton France Evans.

Appendix B   **Interview of Great Aunts Mary Evans Beck, Maria Evans, and Dorothy Evans by George and Betty Jane Keen in 1991**

This appendix includes a fairly literal transcription of excerpts of the tape of an interview of Aunt Mary Beck (Alonzo's daughter) and Aunts Maria Evans and Dorothy Evans (Alonzo's daughters-in-law) by George and Betty Jane Keen (Alonzo's granddaughter). The tape was made available for this transcription through the generosity of George and Betty Jane Keen.

The following excerpt has been reordered somewhat to enhance continuity of events. Editor's notes in brackets detail names, places and events. In the following transcript, "AM" is Aunt Mary Evans Beck, "G" is George Keen, "B" is Betty Jane Keen, "M" is Aunt Maria Evans, and "D" is Aunt Dorothy Evans.

D   [Discussion of the infant, Delena] Mr. and Mrs. Eber Daisey said they would take her [Delena] but only on one condition—that they could adopt her. Pop Evans had his hands tied, he didn't know what to do. He had to work. So, he let them adopt her. She didn't know she had any brothers or sisters until she went to school. They lived in Ocean View then. When she went to school and the children told her she had brothers and sisters, she was tickled to death.

AM   Delina went to business school in Philadelphia. Stayed with Gertie [her sister]. Pop paid for that.

AM   Neal, Louis and me was raised together. I wasn't quite four when my mother died. She died in April and I wasn't four until June. Neal was two years older than me. Louis was 18 months old.

B   When that happened, Aunt Mary, who took all of you?

AM   I went with Uncle Jim and Aunt Elsa McGee. She was Viola Robinson's sister. Neal went with Uncle Steve [Evans]. Lon went to the Clay Evanses. And Louis, oh my Lord, Louis had so many places. He went to many places. He went with Linda [his sister] until Harry came home. Harry didn't want him. Harry said, "Get him out of here." Then he went to Gram Mom Angie's [Angeline] Daisey Evans, second wife of John A. Evans. She was Pop's stepmother. France was with Uncle Dave. He was also with Mr. Vanzant, Wilbert Hocker's grandfather. Lon was with Clay Evans.

B   Where were your sisters?

AM   Lindy and Gertie, they were older. Edith was with Uncle Dave, also.

B   How long before Pop-Pop remarried?

AM   Two years. He married Emma West. She brought two children, Sally and Elva, by her former husband.

B   When he got married, did you all go back home again?

AM   When I was with Uncle Jim and Aunt Elsie. Anyhow, I was hateful.

B   Tell us what it was like when you went back home.

AM   We got an orange and an apple for Christmas.

AM   My father bought a player piano, and my brother Louis and I took piano lessons.

AM   Pop had a boat. Paul Lekites and he had a boat together named the *Mary Helen*. That's how he came back and forth to the Station. Came up to Pennewell's Landing.

AM   They had five days off out of a month. They got a day off every week.

AM   There was a family that had a summer house near the inlet. He warned them that the inlet was ten feet deep. One day the lady fell in and my dad jumped in with his clothes on and saved her.

B   When did he leave the tugs?

AM   Don't ask me.

AM   I remember he would come home and change his shirt and other things, and Mom would get pregnant.

M   Lon's first wife, Sophie - Aunt Mildred was their Sunday School teacher. Bill came up here, cost two cents a mile on the train. He was staying with Linwood and Nellie. Nellie invited Mildred who was Hilda and Daisey's Sunday School teacher. Bill met Mildred. Sophie, who was Marie and Dot's babysitter, was Mildred's best friend. Mildred invited Sophie to meet Lon. It all started real good in the Sunday School room. Maria met Neal through Lon and Sophie and Louis then met Dot.

M   Came down to meet our folks in 1927. You know the first place we came down to? The Toomey place across from Harriet's Beauty Shop. [Actually, Alonzo's house subsequently burned down after Alonzo sold it. It was replaced by the present-day Toomey home on Central Avenue in Millville]. Uncle Hiram Truitt bought that house. Had a pump and an outhouse. Was a two-story building. I met them all at the family house.

AM   I did hear that my mother died—they put a nightgown on my mother. Gram-Pop Hall told me, "Honey, I had you on one knee and May Hearn on the other."

AM   Uncle Dave got me to read his [Cornealius Hall's] will. Gram-Pop Hall was a wonderful person. I was only 13 or 14 when he died in 1924. I was in church when someone came over to me and told me he had passed away. [February 1924, according to Aunt Dot, so Aunt Mary probably was only nine years old.].

AM   We didn't go to that church [Ocean View Christian Church] all the time. We weren't allowed to. We used to go to Bethel. We used to sneak over to the Christian Church. Louis was baptized there when he was 13.

AM   My grandfather, Cornealius Hall, and another man owned all of Bethany Beach. Sold [a lot of] it for fifty cents an acre. We were all supposed to inherit all that land. Uncle Dave and Linwood cheated us out of it. (Ed. Note: "Cheated" is a strong word. Cornealius Hall's will did leave his land to Alonzo's children so there is a story here worth researching.) My father wanted to go to Georgetown and get a lawyer. Uncle Dave's wife had a lot to do with it. That was why Lon and Linda despised her. I didn't despise her. There was other people I liked better.

AM   Gertie was the oldest daughter. She told me once that she was old enough to be my mother. I said, "But, you are not."

AM   Mother Em' died in 1947. Louis, when he heard she had died, he screamed and threw himself right across the table and cried like a baby. That was the only mother he had—she died.

AM   Edith was shot by Brooks Snyder.

AM   Walter Carey had a wonderful mother and father. He was a wonderful man. (Ed. Note: This is the Mr. Carey who helped France when he first went to Philadelphia.)

AM   Uncle Archie was cook on a boat. He was Horace and Clifton Evans' father.

End of interview.

Appendix C – Boys Will Be Boys - Stories From Alonzo Evans III

By way of introduction to these stories, let it be said, without apology, that the boys occasionally enjoyed a drink, with the possible exception of Uncle Bill who, . . . well, read the first episode. Some of the stories reflect a level of revelry and irreverence, but they do nothing to blemish the good character of their subjects.

Bashful Uncle Bill:

In the early to mid-twenties, Uncle Bill (as told by Uncle France) had become attracted to a young lady in Philadelphia, but he was somewhat shy about letting his true feelings be known to her. When his brothers found out, they decided this could not be tolerated for good ole Bill. So, they convinced him to journey to the city of "Brotherly Love" to make his feelings known to the lady in question. They decided they'd accompany him to provide moral support. The "they" in this situation was brothers France, Lon and Neal. As added insurance, it was agreed that a few sips of wine would fortify Bill's resolve to see it through. It was reasoned further that if a few sips would do the trick, just what he needed, just imagine what a few additional sips would accomplish. By the time they arrived at the Philadelphia station, Uncle Bill was announcing to the other passengers he had discovered there were FIVE fingers on each one of his hands. Needless to say, Bill was in no condition to make his feelings known to this young lady. You see, it was the one and only time Bill had tasted any alcoholic beverage. It is suspected that other members of this entourage were counting the fingers on their hands, too! There's little doubt that one or more of the brothers may also have found more than five fingers on at least one of their respective outer limbs.

The Rabbi – All's Well That Ends Well:

In the 1930s, Lon, Neal, France and Louis frequently visited automobile showrooms to eye the latest models of cars. This was a source of entertainment as they had no intention of purchasing a new car since effects of the Great Depression were still being felt. Each visit to a showroom brought on a gesture of salesmanship by the dealer in the form of an alcoholic beverage with the hopes of encouraging a sale. Little did the dealer realize the sole reason for the boys' visits was to benefit from a few free drinks. On one of the junkets the dealer joined the boys in overindulging and became even more generous with drinks. So much so that Uncle Neal became somewhat inebriated and, in this state, vulnerable to a dare by his brothers. Uncle France dared Neal to go pull the beard of a lonely Rabbi coming down the sidewalk. [Ed. Note: France was involved in a similar incident in Philadelphia as related in Appendix A. Apparently the target was the beard and not the Rabbi.] The dare was taken by Neal, but only on the condition that the dealer break out another bottle. The dealer, in the same condition as the boys, assured Neal this would not be a problem. As dared, Neal quickly accosted the bearded Rabbi and gave a sound yank on his beard. Naturally, the Rabbi was infuriated and enlisted the services of one of New York's finest to have Neal arrested. The Rabbi lamented the indignity of Neal's beard yank, and Neal returned to the showroom in quest of his reward for handling the dare. The Rabbi and the officer came into the showroom to accuse Neal of this undignified act. Before the accusations were lodged, the quick-thinking dealer offered the officer and the Rabbi a drink to warm them up after their search for Neal in the cold (it was a sub-zero day). An hour later both the Rabbi and the officer were hugging Neal and thanking him for curing their chills.

The Magistrate:

In the mid-to-late 1930s, the brothers traveled to Delaware from New York to attend a funeral. They decided to join up and go in two cars (Lon's and France's) to save money for all. At that time, the trip took over six hours on the two-lane highways with a ferry in Philadelphia. Certainly, such a long trip could not be endured without the support of some "spirits." One simply could not be expected to make such a trip without such support. Doubtless, as time passed, the trip became more unendurable and spirits were needed all the more. Especially for Louis! Everything was going without incident until Louis, driving France's car, passed Lon. The ensuing race (boys will be boys) culminated with a police chase and subsequent speeding ticket and an appearance before the local magistrate. Lon paid his fine without incident. Unfortunately, this was not the case for Louis and France. It seems Louis felt the fine was unjust and voiced his objection. A contempt citation and added fine resulted. The objections continued and the scenario was repeated several times until Louis' funds were exhausted and France was forced to pay the contempt citations for Louis. Lo and behold, Louis protested the magistrate's ruling once again. The burden on France's pocketbook became unbearable, to the point that France had to tell Louis to "shut up" or they all would go to jail because of him. The trip's cost was never disclosed, but there is no doubt that France retired Louis from driving for the remainder of the trip. Of course, Lon claimed innocence at being the root cause of their court encounter. He also continued to boast to France that France's car just didn't have the pep to beat his car.

The Snowstorm:

Heavy snowfalls along the ocean at Bethany Beach were quite rare, and when one did occur, people did strange and unheard-of acts of mischief. In the late 1960s, a blizzard left some 20 inches of the white stuff. It seems Uncle Linwood (Gordon's Pop Pop), after clearing his drive with his tractor, drove next door to clear sister Delena's drive—a gesture of goodwill. Being somewhat of a tease, however, particularly with Delena, he removed all the snow from her rather long drive and piled it up at both her front and rear entrances. Seeing him cleaning her drive she thought, "How sweet of him," and went about her housecleaning routine. It happened that this was her day to have her hair done, so she got ready to leave and saw the mountain of snow at both her doorways. Calling her brother didn't help. "The tractor is broken," he said, devilishly. Poor Delena was beside herself until Linwood relented and moved the snow. They were close neighbors for the rest of their lives.

The Inlet:

Then there was the time Neal and Louis purchased a boat for summer fishing pleasures. On an early spring weekend, the sun was shining brightly and they decided it wasn't too early to try out the newly acquired toy. So, they told their wives they were just going out for a trial run in the boat to get the feel of how well it handled. Now, both these men were experienced tugboat captains, so to them the trial run should have been a snap. Well, no maiden voyage could be complete without spirits to christen the boat. Off these two captains went. Their initial plan called for running around the Indian River, but after a few commemorative tastes of the spirits, it became equally important to see how well their boat handled in the open sea. Off through the inlet to the ocean. By this time, a cold front had come through and it became chilly, so much so that more spirits were required to weather the cold and increasing wind. Being unprepared for this turn in the weather, they decided to head in. Amid some lurching maneuvers, they lost the propeller shearpin and were powerless. Fortunately for them, the Coast Guard found them and towed them to safety. They were unbowed by the incident, having consumed their supply of spirits to keep warm. Were they embarrassed as experienced captains having to be towed in, or by the cold reception when they returned to their respective homes? Not at all. In their state, everything was fine by them.

The Copperhead:

In 1958, ex-State Sen. Ed Powell related to young Lon how as a boy he was chased by one Lonnie Evans [young Lon's father] brandishing a dead copperhead snake over his head. Lonnie Evans happened to be courting a certain sweet young lady at this time and had discovered one Ed Powell had dated her right under his nose. Master Powell had to be taught a lesson about taking a girl away from Lon Evans, so knowing Ed was deathly afraid of snakes, Lon captured and killed a copperhead snake. When Lon found Ed, he proceeded to chase him, slinging the snake at Ed's ankles, whereupon it wrapped around Ed's legs. He nearly fainted from fright until finally Lon removed the snake from his legs. Lon politely advised Ed this would happen again if Ed tried to date his girl ever again!

Harness the Horse:

Lon and Ed again. One other time Ed Powell beat out Lon by asking another young lady out to a Sunday evening church service. When Lon heard, he waited until Ed and the young lady were in church and proceeded to completely reverse-harness Ed's horse to the buggy outside the church. When services were over, Ed discovered he couldn't take the young lady home by the promised time. The brazen and crafty Lon stepped in and saw her home receiving a cold glass of lemonade as a reward for his gentlemanly deed.

The Radio Competition:

Lon witnessed this one in 1937, or possibly 1938, and tells this story. The boys did try to one-up each other. They did compete!

Uncle Louis and Aunt Dot lived on the top floor of the Doderer's house [Dot and Maria's parents], a brownstone on Linden Street in Ridgewood, New York. Uncle Neal and Aunt Maria and Lon [a widower] lived on the middle floor, and the Doderers lived in the finished, walk-in basement. Here's what happened.

Louis had purchased a new radio-Victrola combination and was taking delivery when Neal and Lon walked in. The radio-store owner accompanied the delivery man to demonstrate this "first of a kind" combination for Louis and Dot. During his demonstration, he mentioned to Neal that the radio Louis was trading in was one fine radio and that he'd give Neal a good deal on the trade-in. Needless to say, Neal, after a brief discussion with Marie, took the deal.

Lon, radioless, observed the transactions. He couldn't be left out with no radio. Yep! He offered the store owner a ridiculous price for Neal's radio and became a partner in the transactions. I remember hearing the store owner say to the truck driver as they departed, "Boy, I wish I had more deliveries like this." After he left, there was music of all types throughout the house. Each of the boys turned up the volume to be sure they got their money's worth.

Who is Under the Table?:

The boys and their wives visited regularly. Occasionally the boys would consume some spirits. Late one evening, Linwood and Nellie walked in. Linwood, the oldest [Gordon's Pop-Pop], saw what was going on and announced that he was the most experienced and said, "I am going to put you all under the table." Remember, Linwood lived with Nellie and there were no non-medicinal spirits in the house. Later, as young Lon remembers it, when he peeked from his bedroom, Linwood was under the table—alone, still wearing his black derby. His younger brothers were still going strong. Mom's comment on this story is that, "Nellie must have been embarrassed." [Ed. Note: I am sure she was, because the only time I ever saw my Pop-Pop drink beyond his daily shot for his heart was the time Dad, Neal, Pop-Pop and one or two others donated blood for Mr. Clint Quillen, a family friend. The nurse suggested a drink would help the body recover. They overdid it!]

The stories are unending. Everyone enjoyed hearing them at family gatherings, especially the tugboat stories.

Index

Repeated references in this Index to places or people such as Baltimore Hundred, the Evanses in each generation for whom chapter-length discussions are included (Walter, William, John Sr., Daniel, Zadock, Clemeth, John A., Alonzo and Linwood and spouses) and full Hall, Daisey/Dazey, and Green ancestors would unnecessarily clutter this Index. For simplification, they are generally indexed by Chapter only, except in the case where important references may be included in other chapters. The general guide in these cases and in indexing in general has been simplification. Readers are referred to the Table of Contents for these lead chapters.

In the case of the many John Evanses, it is almost impossible to develop a comprehensive index. Instead, Chapters 7 and 12 are included, and special attention is given to the seemingly more important items for the other John Evanses.

The Index also does not include all the names in the Evans, Hall, Daisey and Green Descendants Charts or any names other than my own beyond the generation of Linwood and Nellie Evans. These approaches are intended to increase the utility of this Index.

People:

316

Subjects:

www.ingramcontent.com/pod-product-compliance
Lightning Source LLC
Chambersburg PA
CBHW080042280326
41935CB00014B/1761